SOCIAL WORK TREATMENT WITH ABUSED AND NEGLECTED CHILDREN

SOCIAL WORK TREATMENT WITH ABUSED AND NEGLECTED CHILDREN

Edited by

CHRIS M. MOUZAKITIS, Ed.D., M.S.W., LCSW

Assistant Professor
School of Social Work and Community Planning
University of Maryland
Baltimore, Maryland
Training Faculty of the American Humane
Association, Children's Division, Denver, Colorado, and
Consultant to Child Abuse and Neglect
Treatment Programs

and

RAJU VARGHESE, Ed.D., ACSW, M.P.H.

Associate Professor
School of Social Work and Community Planning
Clinical Assistant Professor
Department of Psychiatry, School of Medicine
University of Maryland
Baltimore, Maryland

(With 19 Other Contributors)

CHARLES C THOMAS • PUBLISHER
Springfield • Illinois • U.S.A.

Published and Distributed Throughout the World by
CHARLES C THOMAS • PUBLISHER
2600 South First Street
Springfield, Illinois 62717

© *1985 by* CHARLES C THOMAS • PUBLISHER

ISBN 0-398-05109-7

Library of Congress Catalog Card Number: 85-2660

With THOMAS BOOKS *careful attention is given to all details of manufacturing and
design. It is the Publisher's desire to present books that are satisfactory as to their physical
qualities and artistic possibilities and appropriate for their particular use.* THOMAS
BOOKS *will be true to those laws of quality that assure a good name and good will.*

Printed in the United States of America

G-R-3

Library of Congress Cataloging in Publication Data
Main entry under title:

Social work treatment with abused and neglected children.

   Includes bibliographies.
   1. Child abuse—Addresses, essays, lectures.
2. Abused children—Services for—Addresses, essays,
lectures. 3. Social work with children—Addresses,
essays, lectures. I. Mouzakitis, Chris M. II. Varghese,
Raju. [DNLM: 1. Child Abuse. 2. Social Work, Psychiatric.
WA 320 S6783]
HV715.S63 1985   362.7′1   85-2660
ISBN 0-398-05109-7

**DEDICATED TO ALL
ABUSED AND NEGLECTED CHILDREN**

CONTRIBUTORS

THELMA BAILY, M.S.S.
  *Training Faculty of the American
    Humane Association, Children's
    Division, Denver, Colorado, and Consultant to Social
    and Private Agencies*

WALTER BAILY, D.S.W.
  *Assistant Professor
  University of Maine-Augusta
  Augusta, Maine
  Consultant to Social and Private Agencies
    and Peasefield Associates, Limerick, Maine*

STEPHEN BAVOLEK, Ph.D.
  *Associate Professor
  Department of Special Education
  University of Wisconsin-Eau Claire
  Eau Claire, Wisconsin*

DOUGLAS J. BESHAROV, J.D., L.L.M.
  *Visiting Scholar at the American
    Enterprise Institute and Ex-Director
    of the National Center on Child
    Abuse and Neglect
  Washington, D.C.*

MOJIE A. BURGOYNE, M.S.W.
  *Private Practitioner
  Southwest Psychotherapy Associates
  Magnolia, Texas*

Ann Harris Cohn, Ph.D.
Executive Director
National Committee for the Prevention
of Child Abuse
Chicago, Illinois

Patricia Wilson—Coker, J.D., M.S.W.
Director, Child Welfare Institute
Saint Joseph College
West Hartford, Connecticut

Thomas Cruthirds, D.S.W.
Associate Professor
School of Social Work
University of Tennessee
Knoxville, Tennessee

Elizabeth Elmer, M.S.S.
Director of Research and Training
Parental Stress Center
Pittsburgh, Pennsylvania
Emeritus Associate Professor of Child
Psychiatry
Department of Psychiatry
University of Pittsburgh
Pittsburgh, Pennsylvania

Donald V. Fandetti, Ph.D.
Associate Professor
School of Social Work and Community Planning
University of Maryland
Baltimore, Maryland

Charles Felzen Johnson, M.D.
Professor of Pediatrics
Ohio State University and
Director of the Child Abuse Program
Children's Hospital
Columbus, Ohio

CHARLES E. GENTRY. M.S.W., ACSW
  Executive Director
  Child and Family Services
  Knoxville, Tennessee
  Faculty of the School of Social Work
  University of Tennessee
  Knoxville, Tennessee

WALTER J. JUNEWICZ, ACSW
  Director of Social Services
  Summit County Children Services Board
  Akron, Ohio

JOHN LATIMER. M.S.W.
  Social Worker
  Hotel Dieu Hospital Kingston
  Regional Human Communication Unit
  Kingston, Ontario, Canada

SPYROS MONOPOLIS. M.D.
  Instructor in Child and Adolescent Psychiatry
  Research Fellow
  Department of Psychiatry
  School of Medicine
  University of Maryland
  Baltimore, Maryland

CHRIS M. MOUZAKITIS. Ed.D., M.S.W., LCSW,
  Assistant Professor
  School of Social Work and
    Community Planning
  University of Maryland
  Baltimore, Maryland
  Training Faculty of the American Humane Association,
    Children's Division, Denver, Colorado, and Consultant to Child Abuse
    and Neglect Treatment Programs

RICHARD M. SARLES. M.D.
  Director, Division of Child and Adolescent Psychiatry
  Sheppard and Enoch Pratt Hospital, Baltimore
  Clinical Associate Professor of Psychiatry and Pediatrics
  School of Medicine
  University of Maryland
  Baltimore, Maryland

KRISTINE A. SIEFERT, Ph.D.
Assistant Professor
School of Social Work
University of Michigan
Ann Arbor, Michigan

NORMA L. TOTAH, M.S.W.
Child Welfare Training Coordinator
Human Resource Development Center
Connecticut State Department of Children
and Youth Services
Farmington, Connecticut

RAJU VARGHESE, Ed.D., ACSW, M.P.H.
Associate Professor
School of Social Work and Community Planning
Clinical Assistant Professor
Department of Psychiatry
School of Medicine
University of Maryland
Baltimore, Maryland

SHANKAR A. YELAJA, D.S.W.
Dean
School of Social Work
Wilfrid Laurier University
Waterloo, Ontario, Canada

PREFACE

Maltreatment of children has become one of the most compelling subjects of modern times. Society is finally opening its eyes to recognize the ever-increasing atrocities to which children are continuously subjected and mobilizing its resources to combat the problem. It is no more a subject mentioned at obscure gatherings or places. Society is becoming more willing to talk about the problem and to search for preventive and remedial measures.

The increased public awareness also has resulted in a demand for more information on this tragic infliction that haunts every human society. This book is an attempt to respond to such a need. The book is presented with two objectives in mind: (1) academic and (2) practice. On the academic side, the book attempts to bring together several theoretical formulations that can throw further light on our understanding of the problem. Many disciplined and theoretically relevant papers have appeared in learned journals but seldom are they organized systematically. Most books of readings on the subject also reflect this undisciplined character of the field. We hope we have achieved a somewhat tighter conceptual framework in the readings presented in this book.

On the practice side, many attempts have been made as to how to remedy the problem without a close examination of the conceptual underpinnings and theoretical alternatives. Mental health professionals from different disciplines view the subject from their own particular vantage point and neglect contributions from other areas. In this book we have attempted to view the problem from a multidisciplinary perspective and argued the relevance of such an approach. It is our hope that we have been able to broaden the scope of many social workers who practice in this area.

The papers in this book reflect the thinking and experiences of professionals in such disciplines as social work, psychiatry, psychology, medicine, law and education. The authors are directly or indirectly involved with child abuse and neglect programs as direct providers of services, therapists, trainers, consultants, and researchers.

The structure and content of this book is a result of our realization of the need for a book which will address in a precise and orderly fashion the various etiological and treatment issues of child maltreatment.

The book attempts to inform the reader about the overall problem from a wider perspective with due consideration of sociocultural factors. But most of all it attempts to avoid a *global and fragmented* approach which does not help the reader to capture the dynamics of the child maltreatment and their relevance to treatment interventions. Although the need for multidisciplinary interventions is emphatically recognized throughout this book, the social worker's role is central in the delivery of services. The centrality of the social worker's role is not a capricious choice but rather a reaffirmation of his/her critical position as the only professional who is always involved in such cases, no matter what form the child maltreatment takes. The book recognizes this role and that of the protective service agency in their true mission as they are historically reflected in the evolution of laws and child welfare programs.

The book is presented in five parts. Part I introduces the reader to the problem of child maltreatment and also examines the context within which the problem takes place. Part II provides a conceptual examination of the etiology of child abuse and neglect. The medical, legal, sociopolitical, and ethical issues that underly the problem as well as impact on conceptual formulations and interventions of the problem are presented in Part III. Part IV identifies intervention strategies with certain target populations. Part V presents problems and issues in the organization of child welfare services for abused and neglected children.

C.M.M.
R.V.

CONTENTS

Chapter

PART IV: TREATMENT

PART V: CHILD WELFARE ISSUES, POLICIES AND SERVICES

SOCIAL WORK TREATMENT WITH ABUSED AND NEGLECTED CHILDREN

PART I

Part I of this book presents the problem of child abuse and neglect in its broader context. Specifically, Chapter 1 introduces the reader to the nature, extent, and broad philosophical and sociological explanations of the child maltreatment phenomenon. It attempts to define the various forms of child maltreatment with a recognition of the existing difficulties to operationalize them for identification and treatment purposes. Chapter 2 attempts to broaden the overall perspectives of this problem by examining existing situations in other countries. The suggestion is made in this chapter that a comprehensive understanding of the sociocultural context where child abuse and neglect occurs will lead to effective treatment interventions. Furthermore, it proposes that a contextual understanding will require the consideration of such factors as personal failures of the parents, changes in family structure, economic and sociopolitical structures, and societal and cultural values. This chapter further provides extensive bibliographical references of the child abuse and neglect problem in many countries.

CHAPTER 1

PERSPECTIVES ON CHILD ABUSE AND NEGLECT

Raju Varghese and Chris M. Mouzakitis

A major resource on which every society depends for its existence and future development is its children. It is in the children that each society finds its future leaders, workers, scientists, philosophers, teachers, and parents of another generation yet to come. However, from ancient times, every society has been guilty of one crime against its future resource: the crime of child abuse and neglect (Kempe and Helfer, 1976).

Infanticide, ritual sacrifice of children, abandonment, mutilation, slavery, child labor, brutal disciplining, and child deprivation that have existed in all societies at different periods of time were used to placate a god or goddess, expel evil spirits, purify the soul, attain economic gain, or maintain stability of the race or gender balance. Practices considered by modern society as child victimization were used under the pretext of religious or social motives (Varghese, 1984).

Concern over the maltreatment of children has grown in recent years. Through legislative efforts, education, and active social awareness, society is gradually replacing its "hands-off" attitude toward child maltreatment; yet, it remains one of the least understood and poorly assessed problems of modern times. Although most people are alarmed and horrified when they hear or read about particular cases of child maltreatment, the question remains: Why is only a tip of this iceberg exposed or understood? Several answers could be suggested:

1. Each case of maltreatment differs from others in intensity, frequency, and complexity, thus making it difficult to suggest any generalized theory.
2. Societies still struggle in defining (a) the limitations of parental authority, (b) the minimum expectations of parents, and (c) the parameters of acceptable parental behavior in society.

3. Society (the public) generally is reluctant to get involved in the child-rearing practices of others. Far too many persons who see suspected cases turn away and even deny the existence of abuse and neglect.
4. Many people feel helpless. They feel that no matter what they do, the problem is not going to change, and even if they report cases to established protective services, no adequate services are available.
5. People fear retaliation in spite of the guarantee of the law that they are immune from prosecution for good-faith reporting.
6. The public generally is still ignorant about the diversity and magnitude of the problem.

This chapter examines the nature and dynamics of child maltreatment, its extent in modern society, problems of definition, and the various types of child abuse and neglect. Even though several of these subjects are addressed individually in the later chapters, this chapter provides a general overview of the problem.

CHILD MALTREATMENT: WHOSE PROBLEM?

Child abuse and neglect is a problem for all communities. Children of all ages from all social and economic classes fall victims to this insidious crime. The maltreatment transcends class, gender, race, and ethnic and religious background. It is a problem of industrialized societies as well as developing countries. Abuse and neglect impact on children, siblings, and members of the family. It is a frightening problem for all societies in which individuals are dehumanized and the family structure is challenged and torn apart.

Yet, in many societies the problem is viewed primarily as involving isolated incidents of individual failures (Giovannoni and Billingsley, 1970; Polansky, 1981) or as resulting from unfortunate circumstances. Despite documentary evidence of child victimization over the ages across social classes and ethnic backgrounds, its acceptance as a social problem of great magnitude and a crime against future generations is yet to be recognized by many societies.

Incidence Rate

...ough child maltreatment is widespread, its exact incidence rate is ...own. However, with awareness of the problem increasing, more and ...ses are reported every year. The 1984 report of the American ...Association indicates that there are about one million confirmed cases of child abuse and neglect every year—a 126 percent increase since it issued the first national analysis of reporting statistics in 1976. Since these cases represent only those that have been brought to the attention of the authorities, it is generally accepted that for every case that is reported, there are at least four that are not.

This increase in incidence may not represent an actual rise in child victimization but rather improvements in reporting and in public awareness. Of the substantiated increases, 26 percent represent cases of abuse only, 43 percent neglect only, and the rest both abuse and neglect (American Humane Association, 1984). It also was noted that while boys and girls were equally as likely to be involved, boys were more numerous among young victims, and girls among adolescents (Faller and Russo, 1981.)

The majority of reported cases are from lower socioeconomic classes and minorities. However, it is uncertain whether this reflects the true incidence or a bias against reporting suspected incidents among other socioeconomic classes or majority groups. While blacks and Hispanics constitute only 16 percent of the national population, they represent 27 percent of the reported cases. In the total of confirmed reported cases, 20 to 40 percent of the children have been injured seriously. Although children of all ages are victims, those younger aged children are the most frequent victims. The average age of maltreated children in the U.S. is 7.1. However, a majority of the victims are represented in the category of children aged 5 and under (43%). Children aged 6 to 11 and 12 to 17, respectively, represent 33 percent and 24 percent of the reported cases.

A Perspective

Cruelty against children by their caretakers is not a characteristic of the modern society, only. For many centuries maltreatment was justified by the belief that severe physical punishment was necessary to maintain discipline, avoid the ill wills of certain gods, maintain parental social esteem, expel evil spirits, or to transmit educational and moral ideas. "Spare the rod and spoil the child," a dictum backed by the Bible, was the guiding principle for many in dealing with children.

In the Eastern societies, children were/are whipped or starved to death to ward off evil spirits. Among the Mugin tribe of Australia, a woman who gives birth to twins kills one of the babies because it makes her feel like a dog to have a litter instead of one baby. In the Hawaiian royal family, in which brother/sister marriages were the rule, the problem of defective offspring from inbreeding was solved by relegating such infants to death by exposure, a custom also followed in ancient Greece.

A related practice was followed in certain parts of rural India. Because daughters required dowries, they were considered economic liabilities. So, by commission of cruelty or by omission of adequate care, female infanticide was common. Even today, in some Indian villages male children outnumber females by about 50 percent, a disproportion that is continuously reinforced, in part, by neglecting medical attention and/or proper nutrition for infant girls.

Throughout history there are accounts of the customary extremes to which children were subjected to under the guise of parental authority and/or religious and social sanctioning.

Despite these social, philosphical, and ideological factors, maltreatment of children has been a problem that in varying degrees has attracted the attention of the helping professions as well as judicial and political institutions. Since the 1960s there has been a great deal of research seeking to learn and analyze the social and psychological contexts and parental motives in abusing children, in the hope of halting or preventing the maltreatment.

Actually, not much is known about the etiology of child abuse and neglect. This is not surprising in view of the complexity of the problem. What do exist are a number of approaches to locating the causes, some theoretical speculations, and some preliminary connections established in a few instances.

The expanding demand for more effective ways to help abused and neglected children and their families has led to a formidable and often creative array of services. Nevertheless, a systematic theoretical model emphasizing the psychopathology of the abuser, a sociological model stressing the role of such social factors as environmental stress, lack of social supports, and cultural deprivations, and finally a more interactive model focusing on the interpersonal relations of the child and caretaker that elicit maltreatment behavior (Belsky, 1978) have emerged. Although these diverse lines of thinking reflect the complexity of the issue, a more integrated and cogent framework is needed for clarity in etiological research, program design, and clinical interventions.

DEFINITIONS

A major problem in understanding child abuse and neglect is the lack of a common definition. The absence of such a definition has impacted on professionals' ability to comprehensively study the problem in terms of its incidence, prevalence, etiology, and treatment.

According to their disciplinary biases, social workers, physicians, sociologists, psychologists, and psychiatrists have proposed various causes and definitions of child maltreatment. While some have emphasized the personal failures of the parents, others have focused on societal factors; some define it as a personal problem, others as a social problem. To a certain extent, these divergent views and approaches have generated healthy debates, but they also have contributed to a confused understanding of the problem and fragmentation in assessment, reporting, and treatment approaches.

The Child Abuse Prevention and Treatment Act of 1974 has this definition: "Child abuse and neglect means the physical or mental injury, sexual abuse or exploitation, negligent treatment or maltreatment of a child under the age of eighteen, by a person who is responsible for the child's welfare under circumstances which indicate the child's health or welfare is harmed or threatened thereby." This is the result of a decade of efforts to reach some agreement on the subject. This definition is inclusive and, although difficult to operationalize, at least it delineates the various forms of child maltreatment: physical abuse, sexual abuse, emotional abuse and neglect.

Physical Abuse

Physical abuse was the first form of child maltreatment that attracted the professional's attention. It began with publication of the battered-child syndrome by Kempe and his colleagues (1962). They defined it as "a clinical condition in younger children who have received serious physical abuse generally from a parent or foster parent." As the problem became well known, other disciplines were involved in research and new data emerged. It became obvious that that definition was limited in scope and reflected primarily a medical diagnosis.

Fontana (1973), using the term "maltreatment syndrome of children," broadened the scope to include not only physical injuries but emotional and nutritional abuse and neglect. Gil (1970), in his definition, emphasizes the diverse interactional forces in the children's environment that may reduce their capacity to achieve their physical and psychological potential. Gelles (1975) expands the definition to include the social context in which it occurs on the grounds that child maltreatment is an expression of social pathology rather than pathological conditions. On the other hand, Alvey (1975) emphasizes family pathology as an indispensable consideration in addition to social pathology. He defines child maltreatment as "the physical and emotional abuse and neglect of children which results from acts of commission and omission on the part of parents and other individual caretakers."

The evolution of these definitions is apparent in the inclusion of causative criteria. However, such terms as "commissions or omissions," and "emotional maltreatments," are vague and can be interpreted in a host of ways, depending on the individual's value system. Thus, the problem of operationalizing them becomes insurmountable.

The Draft Model Child Protection Act developed by the National Center on Child Abuse and Neglect offers the following definitions (Mayhall and Eastlack-Norgard, 1983):

a. *Child* means a person under the age of 18.

b. *An abused or neglected child* means a child whose physical or mental health or welfare is harmed or threatened with harm by the acts or omissions for his/her parent(s) or other person(s) responsible for the child's welfare.

c. Harm to child's health or welfare can occur when the parent(s) or other person(s) responsible for his/her welfare:

 i) Inflicts or allows to be inflicted upon the child physical or mental injury, including injuries sustained as a result of excessive corporal punishment.

 ii) Commits or allows to be committed against the child a sexual offense as defined by state law.

 iii) Fails to supply the child with adequate food, clothing, shelter, education (as defined by state law) or health care, though financially are able to do so or offered financial or other reasonable means to do so. For the purposes of this act, *adequate health care* includes any medical or nonmedical health care permitted or authorized under state law.

 iv) Abandons the child, as defined by state law.

 v) Fails to provide the child with adequate care, supervision or guardianship by specific acts or omissions of a similarly serious nature requiring the intervention of the child protective service or a court.

d. *Threatened harm* means a substantial risk of harm.

e. *A person responsible for a child's welfare* includes the child's parent; guardian; foster parent; an employee of public or private residential home, institution, or agency; or other person responsible for the child's welfare.

f. *Physical injury* means death, disfigurement, or the impairment of any organ.

g. *Mental injury* means an injury to the intellectual or psychological capacity of the child as evidenced by an observable and substantial impairment in his ability to function within a normal range of performance and behavior with due regard to his culture.

These definitions constitute one step in the right direction, since they are designed to offer some clarity and consistency. As the various forms of maltreatment are differentiated and operational criteria for each form become more precise, the definitions can help in preventive, interventive, and treatment approaches.

These definitions touch an area of child maltreatment not often mentioned in the literature: institutional abuse and neglect. Considering that more than 400,000 children live in residential institutions and another 400,000 in foster care (Harrell and Orem, 1980), it is indeed a serious problem. Although reports of maltreatment in such locations are increasing, no serious interventions had been undertaken until 1984; these resulted from sexual abuse cases in day care centers in California, New York, Maryland, and other states. Institutional maltreatment of children by staff of a facility usually involves physical, sexual, and emotional abuse, and neglect. These children by and large are voiceless and at the mercy of the adults who operate and work in institutions and child care facilities.

Neglect

Research and attempts to define child maltreatment traditionally have focused on child abuse, and generalizations have been made from that point. Child neglect, as a distinct, identifiable form of maltreatment, usually is dealt peripherally or by implication.

Norman Polansky is one of the few researchers who has focused on the neglected child. In a report by Hally, Polansky and Polansky (1980), the following definition of neglect is offered: "a condition in which a caretaker responsible for the child either deliberately or by extraordinary inattentiveness permits the child to experience available present suffering and/or fails to provide one or more of the ingredients generally deemed essential for developing a person's physical, intellectual and emotional capacities."

This definition, too, is quite broad and it is subject to various interpretations. States generally define neglect as:

Medical, meaning that the child's health needs are not met or are not adequately met.

Educational, meaning that the parents fail to ascertain the child's attendance in school.

Hygienic, meaning that the parents or caretakers leave the child unwashed, uncleaned, and subject to environmental unhygienic conditions.

Supervisory, meaning that the child is left alone, subject to hazards at home and in the neighborhood.

Physical, meaning that the child is not provided appropriate clothing and nutritional care.

Emotional, meaning that the child's psychological needs for proper growth and development are not adequately met.

Abandonment, meaning that the child is deserted and the parent(s) whereabouts are unknown.

Protective service agencies in their procedural manuals tend to be specific by identifying the parents' or caretakers' actions or inactions that constitute neglect. However, the breadth of neglectful behaviors is so diverse that there are variations from state to state. This becomes more apparent in states which have attempted to operationalize emotional neglect.

Emotional Neglect

Emotional abuse and/or neglect is a sensitive area for many professionals because of its intangible nature and difficulty in conceptualization. The literature uses a number of terms, including "mental injury," "emotional deprivation," "psychological neglect," "mental suffering," "emotional maltreatment," "emotional abuse," "emotional neglect," and "protracted impairment of emotional health." These variations create confusion as to what condition is at issue.

Whiting (1976) defines emotionally neglected children as those who are "denied normal experiences that produce feelings of being loved, wanted, secure and worthy or are emotionally disturbed due to continuous friction in the home, marital discord, [or] mentally ill parents." Dean (1979) calls the condition "an act of omission frequently the result of parental ignorance or indifference. As a result the child is not given positive support and stimulation."

Both definitions identify as causative factors the parents' inability, for various reasons, to meet the psychological needs of the child. However, the descriptions do not give any clue as to what constitutes a "normal experience" and "positive support." The value system of both the caretakers and the community must be taken into consideration.

For Mayhall and Eastlack-Norgard (1983) emotional neglect implies indifference at a more unconscious level, whereas emotional abuse means overt rejection and usually conscious and deliberate actions or inactions that may result to harm the child.

Garbarino and Garbarino (1980) define child emotional maltreatment as "child abuse which results in impaired psychological development. Frequently occurs as verbal abuse or excessive demands on a child's performance and results in a negative self-image on the part of the child and disturbed child behavior. May occur with or without physical abuse." Indeed, such a condition can be caused by "excessive demands and verbal abuse," but as research indicates, parental withdrawal can damage the child equally.

The definition from the Draft Model Child Protection Act cited earlier is more explicit and it suggests four criteria to be used for the identification of such cases. These criteria relate to patterned behaviors, evidence, duration, and effect on the child:

   1. "The emotional maltreatment is a parental (or caretaker) pattern of

behavior that has an effect on the child." Such behaviors should be identified by their pervasive nature rather than be single sporadic instances.

2. "The effect of emotional maltreatment can be observed in the child's abnormal performance and behavior." In other words the impact of maltreatment should be evidenced through specific symptoms rather than through speculations as to the possible effect on the child in later years.

3. "The effect of emotional maltreatment is long lasting." The symptoms of such behaviors not only are observable, they also have been exhibited by the child for some time.

4. "The effect of emotional maltreatment constitutes a handicap to the child." The child as a result has been seriously impaired and functioning abilities in terms of learning and relating to others are affected (National Center on Child Abuse and Neglect, 1979).

Although these criteria are useful as guidelines, decisions in determining emotional maltreatment still can be difficult since many symptoms are similar to those observed in emotionally disturbed children (Murphy-Barklay, 1963).

SEXUAL ABUSE

Sexual abuse of children is a relatively new concern in the field of child protection. This is not to say that sexual abuse of children *has not been in place;* on the contrary, it has always been as much present as physical abuse and neglect. It "came out of the closet" as a result of the DeFrancis (1966) research and the extensive publicity the other forms of child maltreatment received.

In its broadest sense, it encompasses a wide range of behaviors, including physical and genital fondling, molestation, exhibitionism, forcible or statutory rape, sexual assault, commercial exploitation of children in pornography, pedophilia, incest, and misuse (Mayhall and Eastlack-Norgard, 1983).

Incest

Incest is the most common type of sexual abuse. It refers to any kind of sexual activity between the child and relatives, either blood or legal, including fathers, mothers, stepparents, grandparents, or siblings.

According to Sgroi (1982), it encompasses "any form of sexual activity between a child and a parent, stepparent, or extended family member or surrogate parent figure (common-law spouse or foster parents)."

Sexual Misuse

Sexual misuse of children is defined as activities that expose them to sexual stimulation inappropriate to their age and role in the family. Examples of sexual misuse range from a child observing sexual activity between adults to child pornography and child prostitution (Mayhall and Eastlack-Norgard, 1983). Sexual misuse by many authors is referred to as sexual exploitation (Zaphiris, 1983; Kempe, 1978).

All states define sexual abuse of children as criminal behavior. They have established a tiered structure of offenses, with graduated penalties for family members or others in positions of authority for not protecting children from abuse (Kocen and Bulkley, 1981).

Various researchers have attempted to define sexual abuse, pointing to such factors as cultural tolerance in some families, individual pathology of the offender, and dysfunctional family systems because of their poor sexual marital relationships, role confusion, and ineffective communication. Kempe (1978) defines sexual abuse as "the involvement of developmentally immature children and adolescents in sexual activities that they do not fully comprehend, to which they are unable to give informed consent, or that violate the social taboos of family roles." DeVine (1980) cites the deliberate attempt of adults to gratify their own needs and desires. DeVine sees sexual abuse as "contacts or interactions between a child and an adult when the child is being used as an object of gratification for adult sexual needs or desires." Zaphiris (1983), in differentiating between sexual abuse and misuse or exploitation, defines the form as instances in which the children become the object of sudden sexual penetration and/or aggressive and sadistic attacks. For Zaphiris, such differentiation is not only important in criminal prosecution of the offender alone as it is in treatment.

Definitions of sexual maltreatment, as with other forms of abuse and neglect, vary, depending on the context, the source, and the purpose. Researchers who have studied this factor in various states generally base their definitions on ambiguous, civil and criminal codes that seek to apprehend, try, and punish the offenders, while civil laws aim toward therapeutic intervention.

This dual form of definition is reflected in the attitudes of many practitioners, who often are not too clear as to the various treatment programs. It can be stated, however, that if the purpose of definitions is to assist researchers and practitioners in understanding this problem and to intervene in the most effective way, the definitions have not, as yet, helped.

SUMMARY

Child abuse and neglect constitute a societal problem that cannot be fully understood or effectively treated in a vacuum. Every case is the result of a multifaceted situation inextricably interrelated with other concerns and issues in society.

Investigations of the etiology of abuse and neglect have generated several models of explanations and subsequent treatment strategies. Their diversity is so wide that arguments range from contentions (a) that maltreatment originates with the children or is inherent in child-rearing practices to (b) that family interaction patterns or societal malices cause the ill treatment.

To some extent, these divergent viewpoints have generated healthy debate, but it also has contributed to fragmentation in understanding and treating the problem. However, social workers and other health professionals working in the field are coming to recognize the complex and multifaceted nature of child maltreatment.

The following chapters are designed to bring together the divergent etiological factors, sociopolitical issues, and treatment techniques under one cover.

REFERENCES

Alvey, K.: On child abuse: Values and analytic approaches. *Journal of Clinical Child Psychology, 4*:36-37, 1975.

American Humane Association: Highlights of official child neglect and abuse reporting, 1982. Denver: AHA, 1984.

Belsky, J.: A theoretical analysis of child abuse remediation strategies. *Journal of Clinical Child Psychology, 7*:113-17, 1978.

Dean, D.: Emotional abuse of children. *Children Today, 9*:18, July-August, 1979.

DeFrancis, V.: *Child Victims of Incest.* Denver: American Humane Association, Children's Division, 1966.

DeVine, R.A.: Sexual abuse of children: An overview of the problem. *Sexual Abuse of Children: Selected Readings.* Washington, D.C.: National Center on Child Abuse and Neglect, Children's Bureau, DHHS Publication OHDS, 78-30161, November 1980.

Faller, K.E., and Ruso, S.: Definition and scope of the problem of child maltreatment. In K.C. Faller (Ed.): *Social Work with Abused and Neglected Children.* New York: Free Press, 1981.

Fontana, V.J.: The diagnosis of the maltreatment syndrome in children. *Pediatrics, 51*(4): 780-82, Part 2, 1973.

Garbarino, J., and Garbarino, A.: *Emotional Maltreatment of Children.* Chicago: National Committee for Prevention of Child Abuse, 1980, p. 18.

Gelles, R.J.: The social construction of child abuse. *American Journal of Orthopsychiatry, 45:* 365, 1975.

Gil, D.G.: *Violence Against Children: Physical Child Abuse in the United States.* Cambridge, MA: Harvard University Press, 1970.

Giovannoni, J.M., and Billingsley, A.: Child neglect among the poor: A study of parental adequacy in families of three ethnic groups. *Child Welfare, 49:* 196–204, 1970.

Hally, C., Polansky, N.F., and Polansky, N.A.: *Child Neglect: Mobilizing Services.* Washington, D.C.: U.S. Department of Health and Human Services, OHDS, Administration for Children, Youth, and Families, Childrens' Bureau, National Center on Child Abuse and Neglect, DHHS Publication No. (OHDS) 80-30257, May 1980, 3.

Harrell, S.A., and Orem, R.C.: Preventing Child Abuse and Neglect. *Journal of Clinical Child Psychology, 4:* vii, April 1980.

Kadushin, A.: *Child Welfare Services.* New York: Macmillan Publishing Co., 1980.

Kempe, H.C.: Sexual abuse: Another hidden pediatric problem. The 1977 C. Andersen Aldrich Lecture. *Pediatrics, 62*(3):382–89, 1978.

Kempe, H.C., and Helfer, R.E.: *Child Abuse and Neglect: The Family and the Community.* Cambridge, MA: Ballinger Publishing Company, 1976.

Kempe, H.C. et al.: The battered child syndrome. *Journal of the American Medical Association, 181:*105–112, 1962.

Kocen, L., and Bulkley, J.: Analysis of criminal child sex offense statutes. In Bulkley, J. (Ed.): *Child Sexual Abuse and the Law.* A report of the American Bar Association, National Legal Resource Center for Child Advocacy and Prevention, July 1981, 1–51.

Mayhall, P.D., and Eastlack-Norgard, K.: *Child Abuse and Neglect.* New York: John Wiley and Sons, 1983, pp. 156–57, 175.

Murphy-Barclay, L.: *Problems in Recognizing Emotional Disturbance in Children.* New York: Child Welfare League of America, Inc., 1963.

Polansky, N.A.: *Damaged Parents: An Anatomy of Child Neglect.* Chicago: University of Chicago Press, 1981.

Sgroi, S.M.: *Handbook of Clinical Intervention in Child Sexual Abuse.* Lexington, MA: Lexington Books, 1982.

Varghese, R.: Psychological maltreatment and adolescent development, in press.

Whiting, L.: Defining emotional neglect. *Children Today,* January/February, 2, 1976.

Zaphiris, A.G.: *Methods and Skills for a Differential Assessment and Treatment in Incest, Sexual Abuse, and Sexual Exploitation of Children.* Denver: American Humane Association, 1983, pp. 5–6.

CHAPTER 2

CHILD ABUSE AND NEGLECT: AN INTERNATIONAL PERSPECTIVE

Chris M. Mouzakitis and Raju Varghese

INTRODUCTION

Child abuse and child neglect are becoming recognized as a world-wide problem that does not have geographical, ethnic, religious, class, or caste boundaries. It has been found to exist in all societies and in all walks of life: among the poor, the rich, the employed, the unemployed, single-parent families, and intact families.

There is evidence of child maltreatment in ancient societies. The Roman patriarch had power of life and death over his wife and children. The African Zulu society was strongly patriarchal as well as polygamous. The father's absolute control over property was bolstered by religious sanctionings. He could and did administer physical and mental torture and mutilation and killing of wife and child (Olmesdahl, 1978). The traditional Hindu (in India) and Islam (in Arabian countries) families mistreated their children from a long misreading and misapplication of religious teachings. Historical evidence indicates that the problem has been with the human race for a very long time, often wrapped under the disguise of parental or caretaker authority.

Only in recent years have efforts been made to define and recognize the problem of child abuse and neglect (Birrell and Birrell, 1968; Garbarino, 1977; Gelles and Straus, 1979; Gill, 1973; Hunner and Elder Walker, 1981; Kempe et al., 1962; Polansky, 1975; Spinetta and Rigler, 1972). Despite this increased attention, they still remain nebulous in definition, evasive in identification, and complex in nature. Social scientists, health professionals, and social reformers are gradually awakening the world to the far-reaching impact child maltreatment can have on future generations.

17

CULTURAL AND CROSS-CULTURAL PERSPECTIVES

Realizing the magnitude of this worldwide problem, the United Nations Declaration of Human Rights in 1945 sets of a clear mandate for children: "The child shall enjoy special protection and shall be given opportunities and facilities by law and other means, to enable him to develop physically, mentally, orally, spiritually, and socially in a healthy and normal manner and in conditions of freedom and dignity. In the enactment of laws for this purpose, the best interests of the child shall be the paramount consideration" (United Nations Chapter, Principle 2, Declaration of the Rights of the Child).

Despite the good intentions of the resolution and its guidelines, maltreatment of children continues to be a worldwide problem. More and more professionals from various disciplines have recognized that this crosses all national frontiers and is one in which they all can learn from each other's experiences to the ultimate benefit of those they serve.

CULTURAL CONTEXT OF CHILD MALTREATMENT

The ill treatment of children takes different forms in different societies. Some types leave visible scars, others leave invisible psychological wounds. Both impair the children's physical development, psychological functioning, social relationships, and productivity.

Abuse and neglect result in economic and social loss for any society. Children so treated experience continuous frustration with themselves and with the adult world, are alienated from society, and feel helpless to avoid these conditions. Despite these general similarities, this problem has diverse etiology and dynamics.

Child abuse and neglect, like any other social phenomenon, does not take place in a vacuum. Even though the problem often is addressed as an act between abusive parents and children under their care, its occurrence often is affected by cultural norms and values, social institutions, environmental situations, economic conditions, and the psychosocial conditions that govern the characteristics and attitudes of the families.

No attempts to diagnose, assess, or treat child abuse and neglect can be effective without a simultaneous consideration of both the interpersonal and sociocultural factors. Regardless of the apparent causal factors, professionals should consider such factors as parents' psychological disturbances, abuse-provoking characteristics, dysfunctional patterns, intrafamilial relationships, stress-promoting social forces, and abuse sanctioning cultural values. All cases of abuse and neglect vary in severity, frequency, and intensity, so it is necessary to consider the context in which they occur.

The perspective of this chapter is governed by the belief that child abuse and neglect can be inherent in the discretion that religious sanctions, legal rules, and collective wisdom confer on parents or caretakers. What can be seen sick or deviant in one country or religion is not necessarily different from what many other cultures accept as normal.

For example, in a rural Indian community it is the responsibility of a child seven or eight years old to take care of younger siblings in the absence of the parents. This would be defined as an act of neglect in Western society. Child abuse and neglect can run the gamut, from a legitimate exercise of authority to an unintentional act of parental ignorance.

An example is a recent incident in Baltimore: a two-year-old child died after drinking orange juice left in the refrigerator by his mother. The child did not know that the juice contained methadone prepared for the mother. In another incident, a seven-month-old infant was admitted to a hospital highly intoxicated. It was found that the child, who had been left under the care of his mother's male friend, was fed beer when the man could not find anything else to stop the baby's continuous crying. In the upper class or upper caste of some societies, the victims often are older children and adolescents.

This chapter examines child abuse and neglect in terms of its frequency, etiologies, efforts to deal with it in various countries, its causes in the context it occurs, and a conceptual framework for understanding its multi-dimensional nature.

THE STATE OF THE ART INTERNATIONALLY

The systematic exploration of the child abuse and neglect problem is rather recent. More than three decades ago Tornudd (1948) studied abused children in Finland and England, but his findings stirred no interest among professionals of other countries. It was not until DeFrancis's (1965) study on the sexual abuse of children and Kempe and his colleagues' (1962) article on the battered-child syndrome that professionals from various disciplines began to study the problem.

The creation of the National Center on Child Abuse and Neglect in the United States with federal and state support initiated numerous research projects that had a profound impact on the understanding of the problem, its etiology, prevention, and treatment. The United States succeeded in bringing the problem of child abuse and neglect into national and international prominence. Although concern about the maltreated child was reflected in the legislation of other countries (Meda, Tauber, and Vitro, 1977) and the United States, its etiology and treatment were not understood.

U.S., Canada, Australia, and Mexico

In the United States, as a result of increased public awareness and a more comprehensive reporting system, the reported cases of child abuse reached a high of 929,310 in 1982 (American Humane Association, 1984). It is estimated that for every known case there are ten abused children who are not known to agencies. This suggests that two million to three million children are at risk in the United States (Holder, 1983). Research and articles, monographs, and books on the etiology, treatment, and prevention have no parallel in any other country in the world.

In terms of possible causes, some attribute the situation primarily to psychopathological factors (Birrell and Birrell, 1968; D'Ambrosio, 1970; Fontana, 1971; Schloesser, 1977; Spinetta and Rigler, 1972; Steele, 1968) or environmental and sociocultural factors (Dubanoski, 1981; Eisenberg, 1981; Gil, 1973).

American authors and researchers have done little analysis of the importance of sociocultural and cross-cultural factors in viewing child abuse and neglect in a particular racial or ethnic community and societies at large. Dubanoski (1981), in his investigation of the patterns and possible determinants of child maltreatment in European-Americans and Hawaiian-Americans, found that stress and personal factors played an important role in each culture. Important correlates for Hawaiian-Americans were family discourse, new baby, continuous child care, loss of control, and lack of tolerance. For European-Americans important factors were found to be stresses of recent interpersonal relations, social isolation, family discourse, alcohol and drug dependence, and mental health. Among Navahos, White and Cornely (1981) found that abused and neglected children came from larger families that were socially incomplete, with parents who had a higher unemployment rate and who were supported by public funds.

In Australia, characteristics of child abuse and neglect are similar in terms of occurrence and etiology with those in England, the United States, and Canada (Mancioux and Deschamps, 1975). Research in Australia focuses on innovative approaches to treatment, such as the use of treatment groups. In Australia and Canada expansion of reporting, investigation, and treatment of child abuse parallels the United States.

In Mexico, the situation is not known since no statistics are available. However a study by Diaz-Conty (1975) of female inmates at the Mexico City jail accused of murder and physical assault shows a possible association of abuse and neglect and criminal behavior. The study found that these inmates had been deprived emotionally and abused physically at an early age by parents and significant others. This corroborates the Stampoulis report (1983) in Greece and that of Ishihara and Ikegawa (1974) in Japan.

Europe

In Britain, according to figures from the National Society for the Prevention of Cruelty to Children for England, Wales and Northern Ireland, the number of new cases annually is 16,000 (Bedford, 1983), an increase of more than 10,000 since 1977, when the estimated rate was 3,500 to 4,500 (Lupton, 1977). Extensive media publicity and increased public professional awareness have made child abuse a major issue with tremendous demands on time and energy on child protection agencies (Bedford, 1983).

Buchanan and Oliver (1977) report that abuse retards children's intellectual growth. Cooke's (1982) findings on treatment are similar to those reported in the United States, with emphasis on specific techniques. In Scotland, the child abuse rate is similar to that in England and Wales as reported by Dunning and Templeton (1982). Studies in Scotland have gone beyond explorations of etiologies to assessing of working skills such as the use of supervision and consultation in treatment.

In West Germany, since no statistics were found, it can only be speculated that the occurrence of child abuse and neglect is similar to neighboring countries. Engfer and Schneewind (1982), in a study in West Germany on the causes and consequences of harsh parental punishment, found that it produces a negative impact on the child's development. They suggest that harshly disciplined children develop conduct disorders as well as personality problems characterized by excessive anxiety and helplessness.

In Belgium, Lavaud, Villey and Cloup (1982) report improvement in the reporting system along with changes in the law regarding confidentiality. According to these changes the lay public can report cases of child abuse and neglect to the medical rather than to the judicial authorities. Also, professionals who are subject to the duty of confidentiality, if they do report such cases to the authorities, are protected from being prosecuted. The serious efforts in Belgium to identify and deal with child abuse and neglect are reflected in the four projects which aim to receive referrals and offer treatment, under the auspices of NWK (National Werk Voor Kinderwelzijn)—the national organization for mother and child care—and four universities (Antwerp, Louvain, Brussels, and Liege). On the basis of these projects the estimated occurrence of child maltreatment is about 1,300 children (Clara, et al., 1982). Considering the size of Belgium and that the four projects were serving the entire country, the reported child maltreatment is an indicator of its frequency. Treatment approaches in Belgium focus on treating basic etiology and offering protection to children.

In France, as in many other European countries, the extent of child maltreatment is not known. There is, however, an increased public and professional awareness that has prompted legislative changes on reporting and confidentiality issues (Clara et al., 1982). Lavaud and her colleagues study (1982) at L'Hospital des Enfants Malades in Paris suggests that abuse is related to the parents' problems, such as mental disorders, alcoholism, drug addiction, limited income, and poor living conditions.

In the Scandinavian countries, although neglect of children is not a common practice, abuse is reported frequently. In a 1981 opinion study in Finland and Sweden (Peltoniemi, 1983) to assess the incidence and attitudes toward various forms of family violence, Peltoniemi reports that perhaps there may be 50,000 cases of abuse in Finland, and in Sweden by two-thirds less. Since the estimates are based on the attitudes of the respondents, the figure cited for Finland may be too high. However, Finland is the only Scandinavian country that has not abolished physical punishment (Peltoniemi, 1983).

The Swedish Department of Social Welfare indicates that physical abuse of children is rare in that country. Recently, many children were removed from their homes to institutional and foster care not because of abuse but for reasons such as family dysfunctioning (Larsson and Ekenstein, 1983). Studies of battering children in Finland and in Sweden (Korpilahti, 1981) attribute the etiology to such factors as parents' heavy use of alcohol and their legal right to physically punish their children.

In the Netherlands, the child abuse rate is estimated to be low (Peterson, 1977; Pieterse, 1975). Petersson attributes that to socioeconomic factors such as the high standard of living and to extensive and early use of social and health services for children and young parents. Petersson says the causes are such factors as social misery, use of alcohol and narcotics, and mental retardation.

In Denmark, neglect and abuse of children is rare (Vesterdal, 1977). In 1976 no more than 120 cases of abuse were reported. As Vesterdal indicates, Denmark is one of the most socially conscious countries in the world, since the state through its Social Security System makes services readily available to all citizens.

Tauber and his colleagues, Meda and Vitro (1977), estimate 3,000 to 4,000 cases of abuse (including neglect) in Italy. Although the general public's awareness of the child abuse problem is low, professionals seem to have become more informed of it in Italy. The creation in 1979 of the Italian Association for the Prevention of Child Abuse is the best indication of it (Gaddini, 1981). Its purpose is to inform and educate the public and professionals and to undertake research. It should be noted, however, that the Italian penal and civil code provides guidelines for protection of abused and neglected children, reporting of such cases to authorities, and severe punishment for the offenders.

Knowledge of child abuse and neglect in Greece is limited. However, the reported cases are on the increase (Agathonos, 1983; Nakou, Maroulis, and

Doxiadis, 1978). Research findings indicate that the changing traditional structure of the Greek family, increased urbanization, migration to other countries, and the value system of rearing children (such as corporal punishment) are the basic causes for child maltreatment. Agathonos (1983), who studied institutional child abuse in Greece, found that a great number of children in institutions are abused and neglected there because of staff shortages and unqualified and untrained personnel.

Cases of children who have been abandoned or physically and sexually abused are reported in the Greek press. Stampoulis (1983), who examined the backgrounds of young women in a reformatory, reported that many of them were sexually abused by relatives and/or physically and emotionally abused and abandoned at an early age. A study of Tsiantis, Kokkeevi, and Agathonos-Marouli (1981) reports causal findings similar to analyses in England and the United States. For example, in severe cases of abuse with multiproblem families, most parents were found to have personality problems, mental illness, long histories of emotional deprivation, and poverty. The creation of a child abuse and neglect research team by the Institute of Child Health in Athens (Agathonos, 1983) is a promising step toward an overall assessment of the child abuse and neglect problem in Greece.

Asia

In Japan, in spite of high industrialization and urbanization and the changing role of women in a tradition-oriented society, the occurrence of child abuse is reported low. A survey by the Japan Social Welfare Association in 1979 found that of 3,200 children who had been placed in institutions, half had been abused physically and sexually—in 462 cases by psychotic parents (Ikeda, 1982). Ikeda estimates there are no more than 2,000 cases a year. His survey replicates similar etiological characteristics reported in the West, such as psychopathology of parents and environmental factors.

Ikeda's findings are similar to those in a 1974 study by Ishihara and Ikegawa, who attributed the physical and sexual abuse to such factors as limited finances, alcoholism, and parental desertion and/or criminal behavior. These findings go along with those by Smith, Hanson, and Nobel (1984) in England, who studied the backgrounds of 123 battered children under five years of age. The treatment approach in Japan is similar to that in Europe and the United States.

In India, with a population of more than 600 million—of whom 114 million are children below the age of 14 (Bhattacharyya, 1979)—and with its complex sociocultural and economic milieu, it is simply impossible to measure the extent of child maltreatment. Public awareness of the problem is minimal. The professional community seems to have an increased awareness but most of the time can do nothing because there are no resources or facilities.

The work of Bhattacharyya (1980), Mehta and his colleagues (1980), and Shah (1976) in the study of child maltreatment is pioneering in the vast continent of India. Bhattacharyya (1981), in a study of small groups of battered infants in Calcutta, Bombay, Madras, and Poona, concludes that the causes of abuse are not any different from those in the developed countries: poor marital relationships, desertion of wife, unwanted child, mental illness, and environmental factors such as poverty. However, his statement that "the magnitude of the problem must be much less in comparison to that in the developed countries" should be questioned since reporting is in an embrionic state in India.

The Mehta and his colleagues' (1980) study of rape victims in Bombay indicates that the problem of sexual abuse is wider than originally thought. They indicated broken homes, lack of parental control, and poverty among causes.

Shah (1976) reports that more than 100,000 children under the age of fourteen were beggars. Many were purposely deformed by their parents and many had been kidnapped from them. Such practices are abusive and neglectful and court action would be in order.

However, as Shah indicates, under the prevailing social economic and cultural realities in India, such action is inappropriate. Strictly speaking, if abuse is defined as a deliberate act of commission, the problem of child maltreatment in India is not so much abuse as it is neglect. It is impossible to measure the extent of child neglect since thousands of children are malnourished, 28 percent of all born do not complete their fifth year, and youngsters are forced to beggary and labor at an early age (Bhattacharyya, 1979).

Bhattacharyya vividly summarizes the etiologies of neglect: "The deprivation occurs in a sociocultural milieu which is the product of extreme poverty, precarious unhygienic living, food shortage, large families, ignorance and an incompatible blending of primitive and modern methods and customs of child feeding and rearing. The family is under constant stress, relations and norms suffer, feelings become irrational and blunt."

In Sri Lanka (DeSilva, 1981) and in Malaysia (Nathan and Hwang Woon, 1983), although the extent of child abuse and neglect is not known, it has many or the same etiological characteristics as India. DeSilva says the abuse does not involve violence in the home but, instead, the practice of placing young children as domestics in others' homes, where they are maltreated and exploited, and the practice of exploiting malformed and diseased children as beggars.

Africa

In those African nations where there is increased urbanization and native populations who want to better their living conditions, child maltreatment is on the increase (Loening, 1981). The abused children in many African nations are those placed by their parents with a tutor or surrogate parents in cities in anticipation of training, education, and better living conditions. Such children frequently are exploited, overworked, underfed, malnourished, and physically abused for minor infractions. Parents lose contact with them because they are placed far away. Children who run away from their tutors tend to join local delinquent groups that introduce them to crime (Tevoedjre, 1981).

In many African nations where tribal living is predominant, child-rearing practice appears to include blatant acts of abuse and cruelty. Severe punishment of children is a standard practice among the Chagga tribe of Tanzania, where, depending on the offense, the children may be locked in a hut for several days without food and tied in an uncomfortable position at night (Raum, 1970). The Ik tribe in the mountains between Uganda, Sudan, and Kenya do not share food with their offspring, who are not allowed to sleep inside their parents' shelters although the youngsters still are minors (Turnbull, 1972). Korbin (1979) reports that a woman from Nigeria while living in London slashed the faces of her two male children with a razor blade and rubbed charcoal into the lacerations. She came from the Yaruba tribe in Nigeria where scarification was practiced.

In South Africa, the occurrence of child abuse among whites is not known. One study by Jacobson and Straker (1982) on the impact of physical abuse indicates that the victims are less interactive socially.

CONTEXT OF CHILD ABUSE AND NEGLECT

This review of the literature on abused and neglected children is not exhaustive of what has been written about the problem in the various countries. However, it is a representative picture of the extent of the problem and the efforts to identify, manage, and treat it. Considering that two decades ago the problem was barely mentioned, the progress since then is heartening. This progress can be identified in the following areas.

Increased Knowledge

The maltreated child has become not only a frequent subject of writings and research in the professional literature of the United States and other countries but also has received extensive coverage in the news media. Articles and books of various forms of child maltreatment appear almost daily in most Western countries. This has increased the knowledge and awareness of the problem in both the lay and professional communities, which in turn has prompted helping actions at various levels. Many countries have revamped old child protection laws and/or enacted new ones for the detection, treatment, and prevention of child maltreatment. Although these efforts are apparent in many Western countries, in Third World countries they still are in an embryonic state.

Incidence and Occurrence

It is impossible to define the extent and occurrence of this problem in all countries, including the United States. Although a reporting system exists and statistics are reported annually, their validity can be questioned since definitional criteria are vague. The lack of standardized reporting systems and operational definitions does not permit even speculation as to how extensive the problem is in other countries.

Trends in Research and Programs

Many of the programs, research, and treatment in other countries are patterned after the American models, based on clinical observations of the most severe types of physical abuse and early infant deprivation. This tends to put abuse and neglect in a psychopathological context, to the exclusion or minimization of societal variables that may have contributed to the conditions. Except for some recent systematic efforts in research and treatment in the United States and some fragmented attempts in other countries, the sexually abused child is still generally a peripheral issue. In other countries, the sensitivity of the subject and its taboo nature may be a contributing factor for many individual researchers and countries to explore this area. The common expression that child neglect is neglected seems relevant in many countries with the exception of Norway, Sweden, Denmark and Belgium, where neglect is reported low as a result of early preventive interventions.

This review has also indicated that attempts to understand the child abuse and neglect problem is along single causal dimensions such as biological, psychopathological, economic, social, etc. This fragmented isolated approach tends to ignore the interdependence of such variables in child maltreatment cases.

It is the authors' view that this problem will be understood if it is examined within its total context. Variables within a particular sociocultural structure should have a different significance in terms of causation. What is abusive or nonabusive in one country has significance in characterizing certain appropriate or inappropriate behaviors toward a child.

For example, physical punishment in Scandinavian countries is considered abusive and the law prohibits it, but in other countries such parental behaviors are acceptable and are sanctioned by law and social custom as rightful. In the words of Leon Eisenberg (1981), cultures differ markedly from one another:

1. In modal patterns of child rearing.
2. In the extent to which they recognize childhood to be a developmental stage meriting special consideration.
3. In the condition they consider necessary for healthy development.
4. In the "rights" they accord to children, if such rights are indeed recognized at all.

SCHEMA FOR MALTREATMENT ANALYSIS

The authors offer the following schema to analyze causes of child maltreatment:

- Personal failures
- Change in family structure
- Economic and sociopolitical factors
- Societal and cultural values.

Personal Failures

It has been confirmed through extensive research in the United States and in other countries that the parents' abusive behavior and failure to provide appropriate care can be attributed to mental disorders. Such disorders range from neurosis to psychosis (Kaufman, 1975; Pollock, 1968; Simpson, 1967). Personality defects manifested in aggression and poor impulse control also have been identified as causative factors (Spinetta and Rigler, 1980; Steele and Pollock, 1968; Wasserman, 1967). Parents' cruelty and indifference toward their own offspring also have been traced to the abusive experiences and general neglect they experienced as children.

The contributing factors are endless, ranging from tension (Nomura, 1966) to inability to face stresses of daily living, to feelings of inadequacy in attempting to fulfill the parental role. The lack of child-rearing knowledge as manifested in unrealistic expectations, role reversals, and poor techniques are cited by Steele and Pollock (1968) and Melnick and Hurley (1969).

The question is whether these findings have applicability in other non-Western societies. Of course, no matter where they are, mentally disordered parents, especially those suffering from psychosis and/or schizophrenia, are unable to meet their role responsibilities. On the other hand, parents with personality defects (aggression, poor impulse control) or deprived childhood experiences might or might not be thought abusive and/or neglectful in other cultures.

What is parental aggression and poor impulse control in India and some African nations is entirely different from what it is in the West. Similarly, what constitutes deprived childhood experiences is defined differently in many countries. The same problem of definition arises in reference to poor child-rearing methods. What is poor child-rearing practice in Finland and in Sweden is the norm in Africa and Latin countries.

For example, in the Scandinavian countries it is abusive to hit a child, but in India it is a culturally accepted norm.

It seems to the authors that the factors mentioned as causative for parents' maltreating behavior in any country cannot be generalized to other countries. Generalization risks oversimplification of the issue, which properly should be viewed within the context of the particular society in which it occurs.

It is very clear from the review of the literature that the efforts by researchers, especially in Third World countries, to define maltreatment are patterned in terms that are relevant in the United States and European cultures. Their research, as a rule, is limited to the most severe cases found in hospitals and institutions. However, if these definitions were applied on a wider scale outside of these institutions, they could reveal a bleak picture of maltreated children and abusive and uncaring parents. Understanding of child maltreatment and its etiological dynamics from a wider perspective in Third World countries requires definitions reflecting their sociocultural elements.

Change in Family Structure

The family as the primary institution in all societies is in a process of change. In the West, changes are apparent in terms of its composition, function, and the roles performed by its members. In other countries, although many of its traditional functions are still preserved, the family also is going through changes. The factors that have impacted on the family—industrialization, urbanization, mobility, migratory labor—are well known. The consequences of all these is the nuclear family, separated from its extended group, changing of roles and responsibilities of spouses and parents, and higher divorce rates.

One function of the family, no matter what its composition, is procreation. Children are raised, at least in part, in families. Most commonly, child abuse and neglect occurs within the family context (Mayhall and Eastlack-Norgard, 1983). Raising children in a nuclear family and/or single-parent family can become an overwhelming task, especially if the family lacks supports from natural systems. Alienation and isolation of the families have been found by many researchers to be contributing factors to child maltreatment, since parents lack supports to cope with the child's demands.

Parents traditionally have family shared responsibilities for the material welfare and the daily care and raising of the children, and these responsibilities and roles were well delineated. When roles are not clear, they can create tension in the marital relationship and affect the parents' communications with the children and their care. If this is the case, many families turn to discontent, anger, hostility, and violence to resolve conflicts. In the process, parents tend to try to make the children the scapegoats. Family violence and child abuse and neglect could then be the result of role diffusion and shirking of responsibilities as well as isolation and alienation.

Understanding of these factors partly explains why children are abused and neglected in industrialized countries of the West and not as much in Third World contries, where, in spite of certain changes, families' roles are well defined and extended supports are available. Generalizing on the basis of Western patterns of family life and experiences does not help in understanding child abuse and neglect in non-Western cultures.

Economic and Sociopolitical Factors

Neglect of children has been defined generally as an act of omission; that is, the primary caretakers do not provide and care for the youngsters' needs. One explanation for parents' inability to do so is their limited financial resources and, in some cases, complete poverty. Poverty and its concomitant effects has been identified as a major reason why parents become neglectors in the United States and many Western European countries. In Third World countries, neglect of children because of poverty, lack of hygiene, malnourishment, and related diseases has reached epidemic proportions.

Majmudar of the Institute of Mental Health in Almebadad, India reports that "every month 100,000 children die from malnutrition" (Besharov, 1981). In other words, 1.2 million children die from malnutrition every year in Third World countries. Would their parents be characterized as neglectors if the Western definitions were used? Most likely they would if the fact that the parents themselves lack the means for their own survival is ignored. Neglect in Third World countries is not the parents' failure to provide care and protection for their children but rather the social system's failure to meet the needs of its citizens—adults and children alike.

The low rate of neglect and abuse in the Scandinavian countries and in the Netherlands is the result primarily of a social system that provides effective services to parents and children. A caring social system does not necessarily eliminate the parents' poor financial condition but at least it guarantees that such conditions will not have an adverse effect on the children's growth and normal development.

Cultural and Social Values

The overall culture of societies and the value systems they have developed through the centuries are fundamental considerations in the understanding of child maltreatment. Child-rearing practices, appropriate discipline, rituals of maturation, expected roles, and status in the family are intricately interwoven in the societal fabric as a result of customs, mores, traditions, and religious beliefs. Practices that in the eyes of an outsider could be inhumane, ignorant, and brutal are for many societies the culturally accepted norm. For example, in some social, racial, or ethnic groups or societies, scarification (Korbin, 1979), circumcision, genital mutilation of females, and unusual forms of discipline are practices that are regarded as enhancing a child's identity in the social group and integration into the community. If circumcision is considered abusive for certain African people (Tevoedjre, 1981), why is it not abusive when practiced in the West? The fact that the latter use more sophisticated methods does not make it less abusive, since it mutilates the body. In Africa such practices can be attributed to ignorance and superstition, but they cannot be characterized as abusive or neglectful there since they serve a societal function and have its sanction.

Judging customs and beliefs of people of a particular culture on their behavior toward children on the basis of Western standards and values is simply ignoring the range of variation of such behaviors. For example, in many cultures an extremely hot bath for a child is said to inculcate culturally valued traits; severe beatings aim to impress on the child the necessity of adherence to cultural rules; harsh initiation rites that include genital operations, deprivation of food and sleep, and induced bleeding and vomiting (Korbin, 1981) and various forms of homosexual practices (Langness, 1981). By Western values and standards, such practices are abusive and neglectful.

SUMMARY

In summary, understanding child abuse and neglect across cultural boundaries requires definitions that should reflect the cultural norms of a particular society, e.g. such cultural variability as child-rearing practices, the family's structure and its characteristic functions, the parents' pathological and idiosyncratic characteristics as they are viewed by a particular society and the prevailing societal conditions such as poverty, inadequate housing, poor health care, and unemployment. Such considerations place the problem of child maltreatment in its true context where it occurs. The impact of such an approach will have a bearing on programs designed to ameliorate and treat effectively child maltreatment.

Child abuse and neglect is a universal phenomenon and has been present since the dawn of human existence. Its frequency in different societies can only be speculated on because of the lack of definitions that reflect sociocultural variations, the limited awareness of the problem among professionals and lay people, and the absence in most countries of a reporting system. This chapter has suggested that the problem of child maltreatment in its various forms will be better understood and effectively treated in different countries if it is viewed in its total societal context where it occurs.

REFERENCES

Agathonos, H.: Institutional child abuse in Greece: Some preliminary findings. *Child Abuse and Neglect, 7*:71-74, 1983.

American Humane Association: *Highlights of Official Child Neglect and Abuse Reporting 1982*. Denver: The AHA Child Protection Division, 1984.

Bedford, A.: Aspects of child abuse in Britain. In Eberling, N.B., and Hill, D.A. (Eds.): *Child Abuse and Neglect*. Boston: John Wright Publishers, 1983, pp. 293-317.

Besharov, D.J.: The third international congress of child abuse and neglect: Congress highlights. *Child Abuse and Neglect, 5*:211-15, 1981.

Bhattacharyya, A.K.: Child abuse in India and nutritionally battered child. In Kempe, H. et al. (Eds.): *The Abused Child in the Family and in the Community*, Vol. 1. Oxford, England: Pergamon Press, 1979, pp. 607-14.

Bhattacharyya, A.K.: Nutritional deprivation and related emotional aspects in Calcutta children. *Child Abuse and Neglect, 5*(4):467-74, 1981.

Birrell, R.G., and Birrell, J.H.W.: The maltreatment syndrome in children: A hospital survey. *Medical Journal of Australia, 55*:1023-1029, 1968.

Buchanan, A., and Oliver, J.E.: Abuse and neglect as a cause of mental retardation. *British Journal of Psychiatry, 131*:458-67, 1977.

Clara, R. et al.: Vertrouwen Sartscentrum-Antwerpen (Confidential Doctor Center of Antwerp). *Child Abuse and Neglect, 6*:233-37, 1982.

Cooke, P.: A family service unit's approach to working with child abuse. *Child Abuse and Neglect, 6*:433-41, 1982.

D'Ambrosio, A.: *No Language but a Cry*. Garden City, NY: Doubleday, 1970.

DeFrancis, V.: *Protecting the Child Victim of Sex Crimes*. Denver: American Humane Association, Children's Division, Publication 28, 1965.

DeSilva, W.: Some cultural and economic factors leading to neglect, abuse, and violence in respect of children within the family in Sri Lanka. *Child Abuse and Neglect 5*(4):391-405, 1981.

Diaz-Conty, R.: The feeling of injustice as a cause of homicidal passion. *Revista de Psicologia*, Universidad de Monterey, 4(1):41-49, November 1975.

Dubanoski, R.A.: Child maltreatment in European and Hawaiian-Americans. *Child Abuse and Neglect, 5*:457, 1981.

Dunning, N.M., and Templeton, J.D.: Consultation and supervision in cases of non-accidental injury to children. *Child Abuse and Neglect, 6*:403-12, 1982.

Eisenberg, L.: Crosscultural and historical perspectives on child abuse and neglect. *Child Abuse and Neglect, 5*:209, 1981.

Engfer, A., and Schneewind, K.A.: Causes and consequences of harsh parental punishment. *Child Abuse and Neglect*, 6:129-39, 1982.

Fontana, V.: *The Maltreated Child*. Springfield, IL: Charles C Thomas, Publisher, 1971.

Gaddini, R.: Report from the Italian Association for the Prevention of Child Abuse (AIPAI). *Child Abuse and Neglect*, 5:503, 1981.

Garbarino, J.: The price of privacy in the social dynamics of child abuse. *Child Welfare*, 56(9):565-75, 1977.

Garbarino, J., and Sherman, D.: High risk neighborhoods and high risk families: The human ecology of child maltreatment. *Child Development*, 51:188-98, 1980.

Gelles, R.J., and Straus, M.A.: Violence in the American family. *Journal of Social Issues*, 35(2), 1979.

Gil, D.: *Violence Against Children*. Cambridge, MA: Harvard University Press, 1973.

Holder, W.: Statement before the Senate Subcommittee on Family and Human Services. April 11, 1983.

Hunner, R.J., and Elder Walker, Y.: *Exploring the Relationship Between Child Abuse and Delinquency*. Montclair, CA: Allenheld and Osmun, 1981.

Ikeda, Y.: A short introduction to child abuse in Japan. *Child Abuse and Neglect*, 6(4):487-90, 1982.

Ishihara, T., and Ikegawa, S.: Family structure associated with offense in brothers and sisters. *Japanese Journal of Criminal Psychology*, 10(2):41-52, 1974.

Jacobson, R.S., and Straker, G.: Peer group interaction of physically abused children. *Child Abuse and Neglect*, 6:321-27. 1982.

Kaufman, I.: The physically abused child. In *Child Abuse Intervention and Treatment*. Acton, MA: Publishing Sciences Group, Inc., 1975.

Kempe, C.H.: The battered child syndrome. *Journal of the American Medical Association*, 181:105-112, 1962.

Korbin, J.E.: A cross-cultural perspective on the role of the community in child abuse and neglect. *Child Abuse and Neglect*, 3(1):9-18, 1979.

Korpilahti, M.: *Born Misshandel: Finland Och Suerige* (child battering in Finland and Sweden). Helsinki: Research Institute of Legal Policy, Publication 50, 1981.

Langness, L.L.: Child abuse and cultural values: The case of New Guinea. In Korbin, J. (Ed.): *Child Abuse and Neglect: Cross-Cultural Perspectives*. Berkeley, CA: University of California Press, 1981, pp. 13-30.

Larsson, G., and Ekenstein, G.: Institutional care of infants in Sweden: Criteria for admissions in 1970, 1975, and 1980. In *Child Abuse and Neglect*, 7(1):11-16, 1983.

Lavaud, J., Villey, B., and Cloup, M.: Serious cases of battered children: Experience of a multiservice pediatric intensive care department. *Child Abuse and Neglect*, 6:231-32, 1982.

Loening, W.E.K.: Child abuse among the Zulus: A people in cultural transition. *Child Abuse and Neglect*, 5:3-7, 1981.

Lupton, G.C.M.: Prevention recognition, management and treatment of cases of non-accidental injury to children. *Child Abuse and Neglect*, 1:203-209, 1977.

Mahmood, T.: Child abuse in Arabia, India and the West: Comparative legal aspects. In Eckelaar, J.M., and Katz, S.N. (Eds.): *Family Violence*. Toronto: Butterworths, 1978.

Mancioux, M., and Deschamps, J.P.: The battered child. *Vie Medicale An Canada Francouse*, 4(3):244-49, 1975.

Mayhall, P., and Eastlack-Norgard, K.: *Child Abuse and Neglect*. New York: John Wiley and Sons, 1983, pp. 22, 70-107.

Mehta, M.N., Lakeshwar, M.R., Bhatt, S.S., Athavale, V.B., and Kulkarni, B.S.: Rape in children. In Kempe, H. et al. (Eds.): *The Abused Child*, Vol. 2. New York: Pergamon Press, 1980.

Melnick, B., and Hurley, J.R.: Distinctive personality attributes of child abusing mothers. *Journal of Consulting and Clinical Psycology*, 746-49, 1969.

Nakou, S., Maroulis, H., and Doxiadis, S.: The syndrome of child abuse in Greece. Paper presented at the Fourth Panhellenic Medical Congress, Athens, April 1978.

Nathan, L., and Tai Hwang, W.: Child abuse in an urban center in Malaysia. *Child Abuse and Neglect*, 5:241-48, 1981.

Nomura, F.M.: The battered child syndrome: A review. *Hawaii Medical Journal*, 25:387-94, 1966.

Olmesdahl, M.C.J.: Parental power and child abuse: An historical and cross-cultural study. In Eckelaar, J.M., and Katz, S.N. (Eds.): *Family Violence*. Toronto: Butterworths, 1978.

Peltoniemi, T.: Child abuse and physical punishment of children in Finland. *Child Abuse and Neglect*, 7:33-36, 1983.

Pieterse, J.J.: The confidential doctor in the Netherlands. *Child Abuse and Neglect*, 1:187-92, 1975.

Petersson, O.P.: Child abuse and neglect as a public health problem. *Child Abuse and Neglect*, 1:199-201, 1977.

Polansky, N.: *Profile of Neglect*. U.S. Department of Health, Education, and Welfare, Social and Rehabilitation Service, Community Services Administration, 1975.

Pollock, C.: Early case finding as a means of prevention of child abuse. In Helfer, R., and Kempe, C. (Eds.): *The Battered Child*. Chicago: University of Chicago Press, 1968, p. 149.

Raum, O.: Some aspects of indigenous education among the Chagga. In Middleton, J. (Ed.).: *Fron Child to Adult: Studies in the Anthropology of Education*. Austin, TX: University of Texas Press, 1970, pp. 91-108.

Schloesser, H.L: Psychiatric treatment of abusing mothers. *Child Abuse and Neglect*, 1:31-37, 1977.

Shah, J.H.: Kidnapped children in India. *International Journal of Offender Therapy and Comparative Criminology*, 20(2):186-89, 1976.

Simpson, K.: The battered baby syndrome. *Royal Society of Health Journal*, 87:168-70, 1967.

Smith, S.M. et al.: Social aspects of the battered baby syndrome. *British Journal of Psychiatry*, 125:568:82, 1974.

Spinetta, J.J., and Rigler, D.: The child abusing parent: A psychological review. *Psychological Bulletin*, 77:296-304, 1972.

Spinetta, J.J., and Rigler, D.: The child abusing parent: A psychological review. In Williams, G.J., and Money, J. (Eds.): *Traumatic Abuse and Neglect of Children at Home*. Baltimore: The Johns Hopkins University Press, 1980.

Stampoulis, M.: Bearing in their minds the memories of the reformatory. *National Herald Greek American Daily*, 68:233-36, 1983.

Steele, B.F., and Pollock, C.B.: A psychiatric study of parents who abuse infants and small children. In Helfer, R.E., and Kempe, C.H. (Eds.): *The Battered Child*. Chicago, University of Chicago Press, 1968.

Tauber, E.E., Meda, C., and Vitro, V.: Child ill treatment as considered by the Italian criminal law and civil codes. *Child Abuse and Neglect*, 1:149-57, 1977.

Tevoedjre, I.: Violence and the child in the adult world in Africa, *Child Abuse and Neglect*, 5:495-98, 1981.

Tornudd, M.: Misshandle are born (child battering). *Barnvard Och Ungdomskydd*, 23:1821, 1948.

Tsiantis, J., Kokkevi, A., and Agathanos-Marouli, E.: Parents of abused children in Greece: Psychiatric and psychological characteristics. *Child Abuse and Neglect*, 5:281-85, 1981.

Turnbull, C.M.: *The Mountain People*. New York: Simon and Schuster, 1972.

Vesterdal, J.: Handling of child abuse in Denmark. *Child Abuse and Neglect, 1*:193–98, 1977.

Wasserman, S.: The abused parent of the abused child. *Children, 14*:175–79, 1967.

White, R.B., and Cornely, D.A.: Navajo child abuse and neglect study: A comparison group examination of abuse and neglect of Navajo children. *Child Abuse and Neglect, 5*:9–17, 1981.

PART II

Part II of the book examines the etiology of various forms of abuse and neglect and its impact on the child. Chapter 3 discusses the epidemiology of physical abuse and possible contributing factors related to parents, the environment and the maltreated child. The impact on the unborn child as a result of maternal use and abuse of alcohol and drugs is also discussed, as well as child homicide and infanticide. Chapter 4 delves into the etiological explanations of child sexual abuse. It defines the various forms of sexual maltreatment and it examines its occurrence within and outside the family. Such factors as social, emotional, psychological and developmental are considered as they contribute to sexual victimization of children. Chapter 5, through an extensive review of the literature, delineates etiologies contributing to neglectful conditions. Since this is rarely done and usually neglect is viewed as part of the child abuse syndrome, it clarifies for the reader misconceptions regarding etiological dynamics in such cases. One of the most neglected areas in the literature of child abuse and neglect is that of emotional maltreatment which is the subject of Chapter 6. Knowledge in this area from researchers and practitioners alike in terms of etiology and treatment is limited. In this chapter an effort is made to define and differentiate this form of child maltreatment from other forms which have received considerable attention in the literature. Because of the complex and often intangible nature of emotional maltreatment, identification and treatment become formidable jobs. The author, therefore, raises many thought-provoking questions regarding these issues. Finally, the impact of abuse and neglect on the developing child from infancy to late childhood are all brought together in Chapter 7. The review of the literature is quite extensive. Without global generalizations the authors discuss analytically the severe impediments physical and sexual abuse and neglect create to the physical and emotional growth of the child.

CHAPTER 3

ETIOLOGY OF PHYSICAL ABUSE

Kristine A. Siefert

The true magnitude of the problem of physical abuse is unknown; estimates of incidence have varied from thousands of cases to millions. The *National Analysis of Official Child Neglect and Abuse Reporting, 1981* (American Human Association, 1983) analyzed abuse officially reported to state departments of social service in 1981 and estimated that 94,619 cases of confirmed physical abuse occurred during that year. This figure is problematic, however, in that not all states differentiate cases into abuse, neglect, and combined abuse and neglect, nor do they distinguish between sexual and physical abuse. Moreover, definitions of what constitutes reportable abuse vary from state to state. It is only recently that researchers have begun to address the problems of physical abuse, sexual abuse, neglect and emotional abuse as epidemiologically distinct entities. The recognition that cases of child maltreatment are not a homogeneous phenomenon has important implications for intervention, for only if specific etiologic factors are identified can effective measures for prevention and treatment be developed and implemented. This chapter examines the epidemiology and etiology of various types of physical abuse, analyzes factors that have been identified as causal or potentially causal of physical abuse generally, and presents a developmental approach to risk based on children's age-specific vulnerabilities.

TYPES OF PHYSICAL ABUSE

Physical abuse can be defined as any nonaccidental action that causes physical injury or harm to a child. Some common types of injuries inflicted on children are bruises and lacerations, head and eye injuries, fractures and dislocations, and abdominal injuries. Bruises on the buttocks, lower back

37

and thighs are likely to be inflicted, as are bruises resembling strap marks, slap or grab marks, and bruises that are unusual in shape. Nonaccidental injuries to the head and eyes include subdural hematomas and retinal hemorrhages caused by violent shaking or skull fractures following a blow or being hit or thrown against a wall. Fractures and dislocations can also be manifestations of abuse, particularly when there are multiple bone injuries at different stages of healing. Inflicted injuries to the abdomen, usually caused by a kick or punch, are particularly dangerous. Such injuries include ruptured internal organs, intestinal perforation, internal bleeding, and traumatic pancreatitis (Schmitt, 1980). Recently, other forms of physical abuse have been recognized as significant causes of childhood morbidity and mortality. Some of the types of abuse that are receiving increasing amounts of attention are fetal alcohol syndrome, addiction during pregnancy, child homicide, inflicted burns, and intentional poisoning of children.

Fetal Alcohol Syndrome

Over the past decade, it has become increasingly evident that certain maternal behaviors are associated with significant neonatal mortality and morbidity (Mackenzie, Collins and Popkin, 1982). Fetal alcohol syndrome, a pattern of multiple congenital abnormalities that occurs in varying degrees in children of mothers who chronically ingest alcohol during pregnancy, is now the third most commonly recognized cause of birth defects. It is characterized by prenatal growth retardation, which results in low birth weight and subsequent postnatal growth retardation; central nervous system dysfunction, including mental retardation; a characteristic facial appearance including a flat nasal bridge, epicanthic folds and malformed eyes; and increased frequency of major anomalies such as cardiac defects, cleft palate, ocular abnormalities, and limb deformities. The relationship between the amount of alcohol ingested and pregnancy outcome is not fully understood, but it appears that binge drinkers and moderate drinkers as well as chronic alcoholics risk damage to the fetus, ranging from fully identified fetal alcohol syndrome to low birth weight. Children born to alcoholic women have a 30 to 50 percent risk of fetal alcohol syndrome, and recent studies indicate that 10 percent of women who drink as little as 1-2 ounces of absolute alcohol per day in the first trimester produce infants with recognizable abnormalities. It is estimated that as many as one in every fifty newborns will have sustained some alcohol-related damage (National Research Council, 1982; Wright, 1981).

Although the effects of fetal alcohol syndrome are permanent, abstinence or a reduction in alcohol intake even as late as the third trimester lowers the risk of damage to the fetus. In most cases endangerment of the fetus is inadvertent, and information about the effects of alcohol are sufficient to curtail maternal drinking during pregnancy. However, the question arises of what should be done when maternal alcohol abuse continues even after the mother has been warned of the possible consequences of her behavior. This situation raises a host of complex, ethical, and legal issues which must be addressed (Mackenzie, Collins, and Popkin, 1982; Wright, 1981). Although there is currently little legal or medical guidance available, the fact that the cause of fetal alcohol syndrome is known indicates that intervention must focus on prevention as well as on treatment once the problem has occurred.

Until recently, problem drinking in women has received little attention or concern. Alcoholism has been considered a man's disease, and most prevention and treatment programs have been designed to address the problems of men. However, research has identified differences between women and men alcoholics that have implications for intervention. Compared to men, women alcoholics have lower self-esteem, a higher incidence of serious depression, are more likely to drink alone and to conceal their drinking, are more likely to abuse legal drugs, and are more likely to be physically abused. Women metabolize alcohol differently than men, becoming intoxicated more quickly at similar doses. Women are more stigmatized by alcohol abuse than men, and this can pose a barrier to seeking help. Finally, alcoholism treatment programs designed for men do not meet women's needs for treatment of the abuse of legal drugs, for counseling for victims of incest and battering, for child care and child guidance, and for prenatal care (Beckman and Kocel, 1982). If fetal alcohol syndrome is to be prevented, programs that meet the special needs of the women who abuse alcohol must be developed.

Addiction During Pregnancy

Drug addiction during pregnancy also poses a major threat to the developing fetus. The problem of chemical dependency in pregnancy appears to be increasing, and it is currently estimated that 10 percent or more of children in metropolitan areas are at risk (Lawson and Wilson, 1979). Infants born to opiate-addicted mothers may experience a potentially life-threatening withdrawal syndrome and are at high risk for prematurity, low birth weight and other complications related to the addict's life-style and to lack of prenatal care. Infants of mothers on methadone maintenance also experience a withdrawal syndrome, but the risks of recidivism and detoxification are thought to outweigh those of methadone withdrawal (Black and Mayer, 1980; Jacobs, Lurie and Cuzzi, 1983).

The problem of addiction during pregnancy raises the same issue of fetal abuse and the same medical and ethical dilemmas as the problem of maternal alcohol abuse during pregnancy, but it is compounded by the fact that opiate use without prescription is illegal. This, combined with the poverty that is characteristic of the addict's life-style, poses a formidable barrier to prenatal care. As is the case with fetal alcohol syndrome, intervention in addiction during pregnancy must focus on prevention as well as on treatment once damage to the fetus, as evidenced in perinatal morbidity, has occurred. This means that the causes as well as the consequences of maternal drug abuse must be addressed. In a study of heroin-addicted women, Binion (1982) found that the onset of drug use was related to unresolved problems in the family, especially in adolescence. To escape problems in the home, the women turned to early sexual activity, drug use, street life, and running away. Binion also found that adolescent women who became heroin addicts did not have positive achievement experiences in school and hypothesized that the resulting feelings of low self-esteem are causal antecedents of heroin use for those women. In another study, Colten (1982) found that addicted mothers were characterized by feelings of lack of control over their children's outcomes and by a pervasive sense of inadequacy as parents. These feelings appeared to reflect the attitudes that society holds toward addicted mothers. Preventive and interventive programs must take these findings into account and meet the special needs of addicted mothers in a nonjudgmental and nonpunitive way if services to this high-risk population are to be effective.

Child Homicide

Homicide is one of the five leading causes of death for children aged one to eighteen in the United States, accounting for one of every twenty deaths in that age group in 1978. The child abuse literature has focused on infanticide and filicide as forms of fatal child abuse, but recently researchers have taken the position that nonfilicidal child homicide also represents child abuse. Studies utilizing data from the Federal Bureau of Investigation's Uniform Crime Reporting System have identified four different types of child homicide: neonaticide, filicide, infanticide and nonfilicidal child homicide (Christoffel, 1984; Jason, 1983; Jason, Gilliland and Tyler, 1983). The findings of these studies differ from those of previous research, in that they show child homicide by parents to constitute a relatively small proportion of overall child homicide. This may be due to the small numbers of homicides studied by prior investigators; for example, 83 victims by Myers (1970) and 140 victims by Kaplun and Reich (1975).

Neonaticide

Three percent of child homicide victims in 1976 to 1979 were less than seven days of age. The majority of offenders were the victims' parents and were female; bodily force rather than weapons tended to be used (Jason, Gilliland, and Tyler, 1983). Studies of parents who commit neonaticide have consistently observed that the parents are nonpsychotic, are relatively young, and predominantly single mothers or women separated from their husbands. These women are likely to have concealed their pregnancy and not to have sought prenatal care or care at the time of delivery. There is consensus among researchers that the newborn is killed primarily for social or economic reasons (d'Orban, 1979; Myers, 1970; Resnick, 1970). Resnick (1970) suggests that the availability of abortion may be a preventive factor; Jason, Gilliland and Tyler (1983) observe that neonaticide is the only type of child homicide with a greater rate of occurrence in rural areas and speculate that this may reflect the unavailability or social unacceptability of abortion. If this is the case, it is logical to assume that access to effective contraceptive measures may also be a factor in prevention.

Infanticide

Nine percent of child homicide victims in 1976 through 1979 were between seven days and one year old. Unlike neonaticide, a slight majority (52%) of the assailants were male. The majority of the assailants were parents or stepparents of the victim. As with neonaticide, bodily force rather than weapons were likely to be used (Jason, Gilliland and Tyler, 1983). Infants are more likely to suffer central nervous system injury than older child homicide victims; research suggests that infanticide occurs when caretakers become frustrated with difficult infant behavior. The frustration erupts into violence and the infant is biologically vulnerable to fatal attack (Christoffel, 1984).

Filicide

In 1976 to 1979, 29 percent of all homicides of children under 18 were committed by the victim's parent or stepparent; 52 percent of these assailants were the victim's mother or stepmother (Jason, Gilliland and Tyler, 1983). The majority of child homicides by parents occurred before the victim was three years of age and were characterized by ill-defined precipitants and by the use of bodily force rather than weapons (Jason, 1983). Earlier studies of filicide identified maternal psychosis as a major etiological factor; Resnick (1969) classified 67 percent of the mothers he studied as psychotic compared with 44 percent of the fathers and noted that depression was found twice as often (71%) in mothers as compared with fathers (33%). Myers (1970) found that the majority of mothers he studied were overtly psychotic at the time of the child's murder but noted that most fathers or stepfathers were judged sane and appeared to have committed the filicide as the result of an intense rage reaction elicited by the child's misbehavior or continued crying. In light of current knowledge of gender-related bias in psychiatric diagnosis, as well as refinement in the diagnostic criteria for the major mental disorders, the validity of the finding of psychosis as a major etiologic factor in these studies is open to question.

A more recent study examined 140 child homicide victims in New York City (Kaplun and Reich, 1976). Of the 112 victims who could be identified, two-thirds were killed by their parents or cohabitees. Sixty-six of these victims' families were known to public welfare. Diagnosed psychosis in the offenders was rare; in 81 percent of the cases, alcoholism and narcotic use, assaultiveness and involvement in criminal activities were found. In 90 percent of the cases, there was a previous history of child maltreatment. The majority of victims' families lived in areas of severe poverty; two-thirds of the victims were illegitimate. The methods used in the homicides were mainly beating and kicking, suggesting that the murder was committed in an episode of impulsive rage. These findings are supported by those of d'Orban (1979), who studied 89 mothers who were charged with the murder or attempted murder of their children. Psychosis was diagnosed in only 14 of the subjects, and a large number of cases (36 of the 83 cases in which the outcome was fatal) were classified as "battering mothers," who killed impulsively in angry response to the behavior of the victim. Battering mothers were likely to have been separated from one or both parents before age 15, were likely to have been themselves battered by their husbands or cohabitees, and were likely to have experienced housing and financial problems. Eighty-nine percent of the victims of battering mothers were under three years of age. All of the victims died as a result of severe physical assault, usually beating or being thrown into a wall or to the ground. Most battering mothers sought medical attention but initially denied inflicting the injuries. In seven of the battering cases, husbands or cohabitees were also charged with murder. d'Orban notes that the outstanding feature of this group was the severe stress that characterized the mothers' lives and the chaos and violence of their home background. In forty-seven percent of the cases, there was a previous history of battering the victim or a sibling.

The findings of these latter two studies are consistent with the observations that fatal child abuse and filicide appear to be overlapping categories (Jason, Gilliland and Tyler, 1983), and that children who fail to meet their parents' unrealistic developmental expectations may receive fatal punishment (Christoffel, 1984).

Nonfilicidal Child Homicide

Between 1976 and 1979, 6 percent of child homicides were committed by a family member other than the victim's parent or stepparent, 35 percent by an acquaintance, and 10 percent by a stranger. The assailant was undetermined in 23 percent of the cases. As the age of the victim increased, the offender became less likely to be a family member; when the victim's age reached three, the majority of homicides occurred outside the family. By the victim's age of 12 years, child homicide resembled homicide of adults and was characterized by extrafamilial violence, by a precipitating argument or by occurrence while the child was committing a crime, and by the use of guns or knives. In 42 percent of child homicides, the assailant was under 21 years old (Jason, 1983; Jason, Gilliland and Tyler, 1983). Jason and her colleagues consider nonfilicidal homicide a form of child abuse and note that prevention would involve increasing parental, neighborhood societal responsibility for children.

Inflicted Burns

Inflicted burns are a common form of physical abuse of children. A 1970 study found that burns were the primary diagnosis in over 10 percent of cases of child abuse reported by Cook County Hospital in Chicago and a secondary diagnosis in an additional 7 percent of the cases. Moreover, more than 4 percent of all burn victims under 10 years of age were found to be abused, and abuse was suspected in another 4 percent of the cases (Stone et al., 1970). A more recent study (Hight, Bakalar and Lloyd, 1979) found that 16 percent of all children admitted to a burn center from 1972 to 1977 had non-accidental burns, and of 1,518 cases of child abuse treated during this period, 9 percent were caused by inflicted burns. Tap water burns are particularly likely to be non-accidental; one study found abuse in 28 percent of scald burns, and other studies support this finding (Feldman et al., 1978).

Most victims of burn abuse are under four years of age. Infants and toddlers are at highest risk, with abuse peaking in the 13–24 months range (Hight, Bakalar and Lloyd, 1979; Feldman, 1980). Families of children with inflicted burns are characteristically from the lower economic classes, although probable reporting bias must be kept in mind. Researchers have documented a high incidence of broken homes, absence of a primary caregiver, severe environmental stress, inappropriate expectations of children and poor parent-child relationships in families of burn victims (Bakalar, Moore, and Hight, 1981; Feldman, 1980). The high number of inflicted burns occurring during the toddler period and the family characteristics noted above suggest that such injuries may result when an unsupported and highly stressed parent is faced with a child who is developmentally unable to meet the parent's unrealistic demands.

Intentional Poisoning

Intentional poisoning as a form of child abuse has received little attention in the literature. This is probably due to lack of recognition, as recent studies suggest that abuse by poisoning is common. Shnaps et al. (1981)

presented a case of a child poisoned by her mother and reviewed the literature; fifteen other such cases were found. Dine and McGovern (1982) presented seven cases of intentional poisoning and reviewed an additional forty-one cases. Some important differences between child abuse by poisoning and physical abuse by a caretaker acting impulsively in response to a child's irritating behavior have been noted, leading to the suggestion that this form of child abuse be called "the chemically abused child" (Shnaps et al., 1981). Child abuse by poisoning is likely to occur within the same age range as other physical abuse (i.e. the preschool years) but is usually carefully planned and manipulative. In many cases, the poisoning has been going on for several months and is continued by the abuser—usually the child's mother—after the child is hospitalized for treatment of symptoms of obscure origin. The mother is frequently described as cooperative with the hospital staff, pleasant and concerned about the child's symptoms. A high incidence of serious mental disorders has been noted in these parents, and Shnaps et al. (1981) suggest that chemical abuse may represent an escape from the parent's own problems and a means of eliciting attention and support that the parent is unable to obtain elsewhere.

ETIOLOGICAL FACTORS: A REVIEW

It is apparent from the review of various types of physical abuse that despite the numerous studies that have been undertaken over the past two decades, the etiology of this problem is not fully understood. Confusing and conflicting findings have resulted from varying definitions of physical abuse and the failure to separate physical abuse from neglect, sexual abuse, and emotional abuse as well as from the failure to examine specific types of physical abuse separately. The use of small and nonrandom samples, the retrospective collection of data, the use of proportions rather than population-based rates, and inadequate controls are additional problems that have characterized research in this area. The various theories that have been proposed to explain physical abuse range from the purely intrapsychic to the purely environmental. Most current approaches conceptualize physical abuse as a multiple determined phenomenon, with characteristics of the abusing parent or caretaker, the vulnerable child and the environment in which they interact all contributing to the abusive event (Kempe and Helfer, 1980). This section examines some of the parent, child and environmental factors that have been considered in attempting to understand the etiology of physical child abuse.

Parent Factors

Early studies of the etiology of physical abuse focused on the personality characteristics of the abusing parent or caretaker. Abusing parents were described as having a variety of psychological disturbances ranging from immaturity and dependence to frank psychosis. The majority of these studies relied on "professional opinions" rather than on rigorous criteria for determining the presence or absence of a given mental disorder (Spinetta and Rigler, 1972). Currently, there is general agreement that the incidence of severe psychopathology among abusing parents is similar to that of the general population (Steele, 1975). It should be noted, however, that in cases where the parent or caretaker does suffer from psychosis or a severe personality disorder, the child must be considered at high risk.

A personality characteristic frequently cited as a causal factor in physical abuse is dependence to the extent that the parent's or caretaker's emotional needs remain unmet. This leads the parent to turn to the child for nurturing in what Morris and Gould (1963) first termed "role reversal." When the child is unable to meet the parent's needs, the parent becomes frustrated and strikes out at the child in rage. Closely related to this is the theory that premature or inappropriate expectations of the child by the parent are a critical factor in physical abuse. The unrealistic developmental expectations cannot be met by the child, and parental frustration and aggression result (Spinetta and Rigler, 1972). This hypothesis, which has gained wide acceptance, has been challenged recently by Kravitz and Driscoll (1983), who found no significant differences in expectations of abusing and non-abusing parents and suggested that abusers may react more intensely to a violation of developmental expectations than nonabusers.

Inappropriate developmental expectations of the child may be a factor in the finding that young maternal age is associated with an increased risk of physical abuse (Leventhal, 1981). Elster, McAnarney and Lamb (1983) observe that the cognitive immaturity of adolescent parents seems to impede the development of realistic expectations of child rearing and produces a self-centeredness that prevents the adolescent parent from giving the infant's needs precedence over his or her own.

The parents' or caretaker's own experience of nurturing in childhood is also considered an important etiological factor in physical abuse. The "generational hypothesis" assumes that the child who is abused will in turn abuse his or her own children, thus transmitting the violence from generation to generation (Helfer, 1980; Straus, Gelles, and Steinmetz, 1980). The empirical basis for this view has been questioned, however; Jayaratne (1977) notes the "definitional confusion, poor methodology, clinical assumptions" and apparent investigator bias associated with the generational hypothesis.

Dependence on alcohol and drugs has been cited earlier as a direct cause of fetal abuse. Abuse of alcohol and drugs by the parent or caretaker is also associated with later child abuse. The relationship between alcohol abuse and violent behavior is well established, and families in which one or both parents abuse alcohol are at high risk of physical abuse. Drug addiction appears more likely to lead to neglect, although a combination of abuse and neglect is found in many drug- and alcohol-abusing families (Black and Mayer, 1980).

Two parental risk factors for physical abuse that have received relatively little attention in the child abuse literature are Huntington's disease and maternal illness during pregnancy. Huntington's disease is an inherited progressive degenerative disease of the central nervous system which includes antisocial behavior among its symptoms. Pearlstein, Brill, and Mancall (1982) report the case of a nine-year-old child who was physically abused as well as neglected by her mother, who suffered from Huntington's disease. The authors reviewed the literature and found a number of references to abuse and neglect in Huntington's disease families; one author estimated an incidence of abuse in excess of 10 percent. In addition to the problems attributable to the organic illness itself, environmental stresses caused by the illness and the child's resulting vulnerability are thought to be factors contributing to abuse in families with Huntington's disease.

Maternal gestational illness has also been associated with severe physical abuse. In a follow-up study of 346 infants discharged from a special care nursery, ten (3.5%) were found to have been severely abused (tenBensel and Parson, 1977). The abused infants were compared with control group of infants who had not been abused during the three-year follow-up period. The control group was matched on birth weight to within 100 grams. A number of variables were studied, including lengthy nursery hospitalization, infrequent maternal visits, maternal-infant separation in the first six months of life, illness in the infant's first year, maternal gestational illness, and postpartum separation. Significant differences between the abusing mothers and the control groups were found only for maternal illness during pregnancy and postpartum separation, suggesting that these factors may be causal or contributing variables in the etiology of physical abuse.

Child Factors

The role played by the child in physical abuse is controversial, as it is difficult to separate the effects of abuse from preexisting characteristics of the child that may have contributed to the abusive situation. Some characteristics of the child that have been implicated as possible etiological factors in abuse include prematurity and low birth weight, physical illness or handicap, difficult infant temperament, and developmental deficits resulting from faulty parenting in early childhood.

An increased risk of abuse in children who have been born preterm or small for gestational age or who have suffered serious illness requiring hospitalization in the neonatal period has been well documented (Siefert et al., 1983). Investigations of etiological factors in the abuse of these children has focused on three major areas: biological, or child factors, environ-mental factors and family factors. Studies of biological factors as potential contributors to abuse have observed that premature and low birth weight infants may be more difficult to care for than full-term infants (i.e. more fussy and irritable and thus frustrating for the caretaker). This may be the result of anoxia or central nervous system dysfunction. A study compared abuse and nonabused children from a low socioeconomic group with respect to birth weight, Apgar scores (the Apgar score is a measure of infant health at the time of birth) and developmental quotients (Goldson et al., 1978). Significant relationships were found between low birth weight and poor performance on developmental testing in both the abused and nonabused groups, and between lower Apgar scores and abuse among both low birth weight and normal birth weight children. This suggests that both abuse and subsequent poor developmental performance in low birth weight infants may be related not only to low socioeconomic status but also to biological characteristics of the child. Another study compared 46 post-term infants and 59 normal infants (Field et al., 1978). The mothers in this sample were white, had more than one child, were middle class and were high school graduates. Multiple assessments at four-month intervals during the first year of life showed that the premature infants continued to exhibit delays in motor and mental development. This research also sup-ports the hypothesis that the premature infant's biological characteristics contribute to his or her risk of abuse.

Other researchers report conflicting findings, however. In a study of the effects of birth weight on mother's mood, concern about the baby and acceptance of the baby, Smith et al. (1969) found no significant differences between mothers of low birth weight infants and mothers of infants of normal birth weight. Another investigator found few significant differences between premature and full-term infants in the meantime for acquisition of a series of developmental milestones in the first two years of life (Sugar, 1977). These studies suggest that while certain characteristics of pre-term and low birth weight infants may contribute to abuse, other factors must intervene to enhance or suppress the effects of biological impairment in determining outcome. Family characteristics have been found to influence the likelihood of abuse, and environmental factors such as prolonged parent-infant separation due to the newborn's hospitalization in a neonatal intensive care unit with restricted visiting hours have also been implicated (Siefert et al., 1983).

Children with handicaps, mental retardation and congenital anomalies are at greater than usual risk of abuse (Friedrich and Boriskin, 1976), and a high incidence of physical illness in children who were subsequently battered to death has been observed. d'Orban (1979) found that in many of the cases of child homicide he studied, the child's crying, screaming, vomiting, feeding problems or incontinence precipitated fatal battering. These behaviors were frequently the result of the child's ill health. Similarly, infant temperament appears to play a role in abuse. The infant who is difficult to care for or who does not meet the parents' expectations may inhibit the process of parent-infant attachment. A cycle of disturbed parent-child interactions may ensue, producing developmental deficiencies in the child that increase the likelihood of abuse (Helfer, 1980). It should be noted, however, that the majority of parents cope well with the task of caring for a premature, handicapped or "difficult" child, and that the characteristics of the child do not alone explain abuse.

Environmental Factors

Despite Gil's (1970) identification of poverty and social inequity as major determinants of physical abuse, the role of environmental factors in the etiology of this problem has only recently received extensive attention. Many studies of the psychological attributes of abusing parents and characteristics of abused children have noted poverty, social isolation, and stress as the contexts within which abuse occurs but have minimized the explanatory significance of these environmental variables. While the likelihood of both reporting and labeling bias must be kept in mind, current research nevertheless provides impressive evidence for the hypothesis that physical abuse of children is more prevalent in families of low socioeconomic status. Straus, Gelles and Steinmetz (1980) surveyed a nationally representative sample of 2,143 individual family members to determine the magnitude and correlates of family violence. While violence was common across social class, certain types of child abuse were twice as prevalent in families of lower socioeconomic status.

Physical child abuse is highly correlated with the stresses that accompany poverty, such as poor housing, and unemployment and underemployment. Social isolation is a stress that has been implicated as an important etiologic factor in child abuse, particularly for single-parent families (Sze and LaMar, 1981). However, stress in middle-class families—financial problems, sexual difficulties and role conflict, for example—is also associated with high rates of domestic violence (Straus, Gelles, and Steinmetz, 1980). As noted earlier, parent-child separation in the neonatal period is an environmental stress associated with increased risk of abuse in premature and low birth weight infants. The relationship between these various environmental stresses and child abuse is not yet fully understood. It is interesting to note that in a study of 100 randomly selected case records of abused children, Sze and LaMar (1981) found that environmental factors appeared to play a significant role in first incidents of reported child abuse, while psychological factors were more important in repeated offenses.

A final environmental factor that appears to play a significant role in the etiology of physical child abuse is what has been referred to as "the culture of violence." The acceptability of physical punishment as a means of disciplining children varies across class and between racial and ethnic groups, but our culture generally condones violence as a way of resolving disputes and achieving goals. Efforts to modify the abusive behavior of individuals and families are likely to be ineffective as long as the larger context within such behavior occurs supports and even promotes physical violence.

IMPLICATIONS FOR PREVENTION AND TREATMENT

The review of parent, child and environmental variables investigated as possible causes of physical child abuse suggests that there are multiple determinants of outcome that interact with each other in various ways, parental or caretaker psychopathology can be an etiological factor in physical abuse across age groups and must be recognized and treated where it exists. However, it appears that psychopathology is a significant causal factor in a minority of cases of physical abuse. Poverty, employment, poor housing, low education and a culture that supports violent behavior are factors that are strongly associated with physical abuse of children in all age groups. Although not all children from impoverished environments are abused, it is clear that prevention and treatment programs must address these environmental contributors if they are to be effective. There are also risk factors that are consistently associated with physical abuse at different stages of the child's development. In pregnancy, the fetus is vulnerable to the damaging effects of maternal abuse of alcohol and drugs. This implies the need for public education, early detection, and for treatment programs that meet the special needs of the chemically dependent woman. Unwanted pregnancy is a risk factor for neonaticide, suggesting that access to effective family planning may be a preventive measure. In infancy, efforts to promote parent-infant attachment and parent education can be undertaken to modify the risks of bonding failure due to neonatal separation, "difficult" infant temperament, and parental immaturity and lack of experience. Maximizing social supports for struggling young families during the stressful period of infant care would also appear to be a critical measure in the prevention and treatment of physical abuse.

Research suggests that in early childhood, modification of parents' and caretakers' unrealistic expectations of child development is needed to reduce the likelihood of physical abuse. Education, early detection, and treatment are also indicated to address risks related to inappropriate methods of punishment, child behavioral problems, and developmental deficits. In later childhood and adolescence, children are at higher risk of extrafamilial violence, often at the hands of their peers. Increased supervision and public education are interventions that would modify this risk. In addition, environmental measures such as gun control can be expected to reduce the incidence of physical abuse, particularly child homicide, in this age group. Adolescence is a period of heightened vulnerability to physical abuse within as well as outside the family. Parents need education and support for the difficult task of parenting an adolescent, a task that is often made even more difficult by the parents' own developmental crisis of middle age.

It is apparent that there are no simple answers to the question of the etiology of physical child abuse. Nevertheless, knowledge of the specific risk factors that can converge to produce an abusive situation at different stages of the child's development provides a basis for designing appropriate measures for prevention and treatment. As research addressing this problem becomes more rigorous, empirically based interventions of increased effectiveness can be anticipated.

REFERENCES

American Human Association: *Highlights of Official Child Neglect Reporting* (Annual Report, 1981). Denver, CO: AHA, 1983.

Bakalar, H., Moore, J., and Hight, D.: Psychosocial dynamics of pediatric burn abuse. *Health and Social Work, 6*(4):27-32, 1981.

Beckman, L., and Kocel, K.: The treatment delivery system and alcohol abuse in women. *Journal of Social Issues, 38*(2):139-151, 1982.

Binion, V.: Sex differences in socialization and family dynamics of female and male heroin users. *Journal of Social Issues, 38*(2):43-57, 1982.

Black, R., and Mayer, J.: Parents with special problems: Alcoholism and opiate addiction. In Kempe, C., and Helfer, R. (Eds.): *The Battered Child*. Chicago: University of Chicago Press, 1980.

Christoffel, K.: Homicide in childhood: A public health problem in need of attention. *American Journal of Public Health, 74*(1):68-70, 1984.

Colten, M.: Attitudes, experiences and self-perceptions of heroin-addicted mothers. *Journal of Social Issues, 38*(2):77-92, 1982.

Dine, M., and McGovern, M.: International poisoning of children—an overlooked category of child abuse. *Pediatrics, 70*(1):32-35, 1982.

d'Orban, P.: Women who kill their children. *British Journal of Psychiatry, 134*:560-571, 1979.

Elster, A., McAnarney, E., and Lamb, M.: Parental behavior of adolescent mothers. *Pediatrics, 71*(4):494-503, 1983.

Feldman, K.: Child abuse by burning. In Kempe, C., and Helfer, R. (Eds.): *The Battered Child*. Chicago: University of Chicago Press, 1980.

Feldman, K., Schaller, R., Feldman, J., and McMillon, M. Tap water scald burns in children. *Pediatrics, 62*(1):1-7, 1978.

Field, T. et al.: A first-year follow up of high risk infants. *Child Development, 49*:119-131, 1978.

Friedrich, W., and Boriskin, J.: The role of the child in abuse: Review of the literature. *American Journal of Orthopsychiatry, 46*:580-589, 1976.

Gil, D.G.: Violence against children. In *Physical Child Abuse in the United States.* Cambridge, MA: Harvard University Press, 1970.

Goldson, E., Fitch, M., Wendell, T., and Knapp, G.: Child abuse: Its relationship to birthweight, apgar score and developmental testing. *American Journal of Diseases of Children, 132*:790-793, 1978.

Helfer, R.: Developmental deficits which limit interpersonal skills. In Kempe, C., and Helfer, R. (Eds.): *The Battered Child.* Chicago: University of Chicago Press, 1980.

Hight, D., Bakalar, H., and Lloyd, J.: Inflicted burns in children: Recognition and treatment. *Journal of the American Medical Association, 242*(6):517-520, 1979.

Jacobs, P., Lurie, A., and Cuzzi, L.: Coordination of services to methadone mothers and their addicted newborns. *Health and Social Work, 8*:290-298, 1983.

Jason, J.: Child homicide spectrum. *American Journal of Diseases of Children, 137*:578-581, 1983.

Jason, J., Gilliland, J., and Tyler, C.: Homicide as a cause of pediatric mortality in the United States. *Pediatrics, 72*(2):191-197, 1983.

Jayarante, S.: Child abusers as parents and children: A review. *Social Work, 22*:5-9, 1977.

Kaplun, D., and Reich, R.: The murdered child and his killers. *American Journal of Psychiatry, 133*(7):809-813, 1976.

Kempe, C., and Helfer, R. (Eds.): *The Battered Child,* 3d ed. Chicago: University of Chicago Press, 1980.

Kravitz, R., and Driscoll, J.: Expectations for childhood development among child abusing and nonabusing parents. *American Journal of Orthopsychiatry, 53*(2):336-344, 1983.

Lawson, M., and Wilson, G.: Addiction and pregnancy: Two lives in crisis. *Social Work in Health Care, 4*(4):445-457, 1979.

Leventhal, J.: Risk factors for child abuse: methodologic standards in case-control studies. *Pediatrics, 68*(5):684-690, 1981.

Mackenzie, T., Collins, N., and Popkin, M.: A case of fetal abuse. *American Journal of Orthopsychiatry, 52*(4):699-703, 1982.

Morris, M., and Gould, R.: Role reversal: A necessary concept in dealing with the battered child syndrome. *American Journal of Orthopsychiatry, 33*:288-299, 1963.

Myers, S.: Maternal filicide. *American Journal of Diseases of Children, 120*:534-536, 1970.

National Research Council. *Alternative Dietary Practices and Nutritional Abuses in Pregnancy.* Washington, D.C.: National Academy Press, 1982.

Pearlstein, L., Brill, C., and Mancall, E.: Child abuse in Huntington's disease. *Pediatrics, 70*(4):630-632, 1982.

Resnick, P.: Child murder by parents: A psychiatric review of filicide. *American Journal of Psychiatry, 126*(3):73-82, 1969.

———: Murder of the newborn: A psychiatric review of neonaticide. *American Journal of Psychiatry, 126*(10):58-64, 1970.

Schmitt, B.: The child with non-accidental trauma. In Kempe, C., and Helfer, R. (Eds.): *The Battered Child.* Chicago: University of Chicago Press, 1980.

Shnaps, Y., Frand, M., Rotem, M., and Tirosh, M. The chemically abused child. *Pediatrics, 68*(1):119-121, 1981.

Siefert, K., Thompson, T., ten Bensel, R., and Hunt, C.: Perinatal stress: A study of factors linked to the risk of parenting problems. *Health and Social Work, 8*:107-121, 1983.

Smith, N. et al.: Mothers' psychological reactions to premature and fullsize newborns. *Archives of General Psychiatry, 21*:177-181, 1969.

Spinetta, J., and Rigler, D.: The child-abusing parent: A psychological review. *Psychological Bulletin, 77*:296-304, 1972.

Steele, B.: Psychodynamic factors in child abuse. In Kempe, C., and Helfer, R. (Eds.): *The Battered Child*. Chicago: University of Chicago Press, 1975.

Stone, N., Rinaldo, L., Humphrey, C., and Brown, R.: Child abuse by burning. *Surgical Clinics of North America, 50*(6):1419–1424, 1970.

Straus, M., Gelles, R., and Steinmetz, S.: *Behind Closed Doors: Violence in the American Family*. New York: Anchor Press, 1980.

Sugar, M.: Some milestones in premature infants at 6 to 24 months. *Child Psychiatry and Human Development, 8*:67–80, 1977.

Sze, W., and La Mar, B.: Causes of child abuse: A reexamination. *Health and Social Work, 6*(4):19–25, 1981.

ten Bensel, R., and Parson, C.: Child abuse following early post-partum separation. *Journal of Pediatrics, 90*:490–491, 1977.

Wright, J.: Fetal alcohol syndrome: The social work connection. *Health and Social Work, 6*(1):5–10, 1981.

CHAPTER 4

ETIOLOGY OF NEGLECT

Walter Baily and Thelma Baily

Child abuse is a slightly easier concept to understand than child neglect. Most of us know what bruises, burns, and injuries look like. We can also appreciate in our mind's eye the hostile behavior which caused the injuries. We also have a little better grasp of the contributing factors to the act of violence. Not so with neglect. There are almost no actions, just inactions. The child shows few physical signs of neglect, unless there is severe malnutrition, unattended diaper rash, etc. Personality deficits and impairments are not as readily noticed as a burn or a bruise. Neglect is never a single incident or two; it is a continuum of incidents. The neglect may be related to one or two areas of a child's life, such as inadequate nutrition, lack of emotional nurture, or a total lack of supervision. More often, the neglect occurs in several areas of the child's life. But once again, all of these factors may not lead to a clearly observable bruise or cut in the child's skin, unless the child swallows a household poison from lack of supervision or suffers frostbite from insufficient clothing. Just as it is difficult to be precise about the caretaker's behaviors in neglect and to envision the concept of neglect, it is equally difficult to be precise about the multiple factors and the interactions among them which lead to the neglect of children.

INTERACTION OF VARIABLES

Giovannoni (1982, p. 30) observes that the existing research "does not clarify the nature and direction of the relationships among the variables and their relationship to the occurrence of the various manifestations of mistreatment. The correlates themselves are perhaps best thought of as a chain; with the addition of each link, there is an expected increase in the probability of the occurrence of mistreatment. However, it is not known which links are more important than others in breaking the chain." The correlates of neglect can also be depicted as a cobweb. One or more of the strands can be broken to reduce or eliminate the neglect, but the remainder of the webbing is intact. If the strands are repaired, then the neglect reoccurs. Since most cobwebs are only two dimensions, a three-dimensional structure is preferable. However, this still remains a static concept, and neglect, as in all behavior, is interactional. Giovannoni states the linkage most clearly: "To say that one is dealing with 'multiple causes' oversimplifies the matter. Rather, one is dealing with multiple and diverse effects that are associated with different configurations of the same variables." For practical purposes then, there may be twenty-five factors which contribute to neglecting behavior. One parent who has or is exposed to most of the characteristics will neglect, but the next parent will not. It is the peculiar or unique interaction of all the variables which result in the neglect or, conversely, in the non-neglect of the child. Although it is accurate to say that we do not know exactly why neglect occurs, we nevertheless have substantial knowledge about many factors.

RESEARCH STUDIES

There are three general lines of investigation to acquire knowledge on the causes of neglect: economic, ecologic and individualistic. Studies can also be categorized as sociological, parental deficiency and child deficiency. The latter schema, which includes child characteristics, would apply more often to abuse than to neglect, since neglecting families invariably neglect all the children. In contrast, abusing families more often respond negatively to one child. It is important to recognize that neglect and abuse also occur together.

In delineating the etiology of neglect, five research studies are considered plus findings from several other researchers. We examine first some of the populations used. In the late 1960s, Giovannoni and Billingsley (1970) studied 186 neglecting families in the Los Angeles area. They interviewed white, black and Hispanic parents. Neglecting families had more children than non-neglecting parents; more households were headed by a female; there were recent marital problems; and there was less money available to be used for the children.

Wolock and Horowitz (1970) studied numerous characteristics in neglecting families. They examined 380 white, black and Hispanic families known to the AFDC program in northern New Jersey. Neglect only was reported in 246 families and both neglect and abuse in another 106 families. Most of the families in the study were large, often with female heads; there was not always enough food in the house; occupancy was often rated at more than one person per room; some had gone without heat in the winter or had previously been evicted from their homes, and almost half lived in what they described as a crime-ridden or run-down neighborhood. Mal-treating families also were found to be larger and the children were spaced closer together.

Black and Mayer (1980) studied the adequacy of child care in 200 addicted families; 92 were alcoholics and the remainder were opiate addicts. Although abuse occurred in about one-fourth of both groups, children in all of the families were exposed to some neglect. Serious neglect existed in 28 percent of the alcoholic-related families and 32 percent of the opiate-addicted ones.

Kotelchuck and Newberger (1983) studied forty-two families with non-organic failure to thrive (FTT) children and compared them to a control group of families who also had a child admitted to the hospital. Families were matched for race, age and similar socioeconomic status. Most of the families were white, one-third of them received income maintenance or Medicaid, and almost three-fourths of the FTT children were under age one.

The most extensive investigations of neglect have been conducted by Polansky (1981) and his associates, first in Appalachia in the late 1960s and in Philadelphia a decade later. In Philadelphia, a group of forty-six neglecting families were compared to non-neglecting families. Both groups were all white and matched for socioeconomic status. Family size in the neglect group was much larger than in the caring parents' group, and the mean age of children was about the same. While recognizing that all their studies on neglect are based on white families, Polansky and his associates believe that research on other groups would support the same conclusions. The researchers discovered that, in spite of some differences in the charac-teristics of their study population, the features found in the parents were typical of those in other research projects.

As noted earlier, the variables contributing to neglect interact with each other, and they cannot be placed in mutually exclusive categories. Some of the causes, such as experiences in childhood, began years ago; others are more recent in their effects upon parental behavior. We begin with societal values and attitudes and then consider proverty, the social context, early life experiences, parent knowledge, parent isolation and alienation, and characteristics of the mother.

FACTORS CONTRIBUTING TO NEGLECT

Societal Values and Attitudes

Gil (1979) condemns negative, hostile and dehumanizing societal beliefs, values and attitudes which shape both individual and organizational behaviors toward children. These widespread attitudes result in abusive acts toward children, and Gil implies that they result also in neglect. He describes three levels in which the behaviors are found: in the child's own home, in institutional and community services, and in the societal readiness and sanction to use "force in general, and in adult-child relations in particular." A higher value is placed on parental rights than on children's rights. Gil defines other factors which contribute to maltreatment, such as stress and frustration which reduce individual self-control. The major source of desperate feelings derives from poverty and the many deprivations related to it. People's feelings of alienation, particularly from the workplace, also contribute to maltreatment. Various forms of individual psychopathology are a last factor which also contributes to the inadequate and abusive care of children.

Poverty

Numerous authors affirm that poverty is a key cause of neglect. Gil (1981, pp. 299–300) states that "poverty is a major source of insecurity, frustration, and stress, and that poor parents have fewer options than affluent ones for dealing with these and for making alternative child care arrangements. Poor households have less space, and this may lead to further stress." Pelton (1981) takes the position that poverty is one of the major causes of *both* abuse and neglect. Although he does not overlook the psychological effects of poverty, he maintains that environmental defects must be met prior to any psychological services. Garbarino (1981, p. 239) points out that "we must consider the possibility that some 'causes' of child maltreatment are relevant to only some cases, while others are present in most if not all cases. Thus, serious psychopathology is thought to be a 'cause' in only about 10 percent of the cases, while 'inadequate' income (as much a social as an economic concept) seems to be implicated in most cases. We should try to incorporate this notion of causality into our thinking." Sudia (1981, p. 275) observes that all research agrees that "maltreating families are overwhelmingly poor and have multiple problems." Data show that the median income of neglecting families ($4,633) is lower than that of abusing families ($5,361) and this represents only 29 percent of median family income. Polansky (1981) agrees with others that poverty does expose parents to additional stresses which may impair their capacities to care for children. However, not all parents in extreme poverty are neglectful; those mothers "who are not are little whort of heroic." Kotelchuck and Newberger (1980) did not find that low income was a significant factor in their study; however, the number of cases on public welfare was very small. Wolock and Horowitz (1979) considered all the characteristics of neglecting families such as family size, housing, and stress factors and then described them as the "poorest of the poor."

The following case reveals a number of the characteristics of the neglecting family. Miss Joyceman was young, had children by three fathers, became pregnant when she was herself a child, finished the seventh grade, lived as a child at a poverty level, was unable to recognize her own children's needs, avoided caring for them, and stated that she was "out on business" when asked why she was not with them. She lived near a poverty level until the insurance was received. The short improvement in child care suggests that she could do better if she had more resources. We do not know the impact of the father's departure, since he contributed little to the personal care of the children. The mother became a female head of household, on public welfare, similar to the situation of many neglecting parents.

Miss Joyceman, nineteen years old, and her four children, five, four, three and two years old, were referred to us when the third child was one year old. The father of the two oldest children and Miss Joyceman set up housekeeping shortly after the third child (fathered by another man) was born. The father primarily supported the family, and food stamps were received. The parents had many fights and separations, and the care of the children deteriorated. Referral came from the police when the youngest was found alone, dirty and naked. The child was placed in temporary foster care. At the time of placement the apartment was dilapidated and there were several broken windows. The sink was stopped up, the refrigerator barely worked, and all children slept in one bed with broken springs. The gas was turned off, and mother cooked, whenever she did, on a two-burner hot plate.

In subsequent visits, the children were found frequently alone or in the care of a younger sibling, one of them ten years old. On one of the visits, the youngest child picked up and was trying to eat an earth-covered string bean vine. Mother was not the least concerned. The parents received a $5,000 insurance payment for the father's work-related injury. Shortly thereafter, the father left home. We encouraged, and the mother found, adequate housing with utilities. She also bought two cots for sleeping. Her child care skills appeared to improve, and she spent more time with the children. Once the money ran out, the situation deteriorated again. Many workers have given this family their best shot. We have also used homemaker, public health nursing, and a small day care home. We are now petitioning for care of all the children.

Social Context

The ecological aspect of neglect, or of any behavior, is difficult to document. Garbarino and Gilliam (1980) use the term in order to understand "the way the organism and its immediate environment (the ecological niche) affect and respond to each other. This process of "mutual adaptation and accommodation" means that interactive behaviors are shifting, sometimes subtly and sometimes drastically. Polansky (1981) attempted originally to determine the social ecology of parents, but he and his associates discovered that they were not dealing with interactions between parents and the environment but deficiencies in the characters of the parents, primarily the mother. In the Wolock and Horowitz study (1979), maltreating parents saw the neighborhood as more unfriendly than non-neglecting parents did. Almost one-half described their neighborhood as crime-ridden or run-down, and one-third stated they were socially isolated and that people do not help each other. Lack of social supports for parents and their chaotic lives could lead to substantial stress and disrupted relationships (Black and Mayer, 1980). For example, substance-addicted parents may experience the following: frequent illness and repeated separations of parents and children; illicit activities related to opiate addictions which result in imprisonment; deaths of friends or relatives due to overdoses or severe alcoholic intake; arrests of parents through murder or illegal activities; and automobile accidents related to addictions. The authors discovered that the degree of poverty combined with the lack of social supports was one of the three most important factors correlated with the neglect of children.

Giovannoni and Billingsley (1970) concluded that the severely deficient income and material resources available caused great parental stresses, and these stresses "may have deleterious effects upon their capacities to care adequately for their children." Polansky (1981) and his associates developed a six-part classification of family, friend and neighborhood supports available to families. About one-third of the neglecting mothers scored in the lowest category, whereas only a few of the control mothers did. Even when two-parent neglecting families were considered, one-fifth of them scored in the lowest division, compared to just a few in the control families.

Kotelchuck and Newberger (1983, p. 324) found that there was no difference between the experimental and control groups on measures of current stress: factors such as "maternal perceptions of financial, legal, medical or marital problems." However, there was less "perceived positive support for mothers of FTT children from family and neighbors." The FTT mothers did not like their neighborhoods, and they also believed that the neighborhood was unfriendly. The authors observed that an FTT child, due to behavior and feeding problems, can cause maternal stress and disrupt mother-child interactions. The mother's behavior may be the "consequence, not the cause, of FTT" (1983, p. 327). Black and Mayer (1980, p. 111) found the addicted mother to have a precarious role. "Addicted women...are more likely to be poor and to have a spouse with a drug or alcohol problem than addicted men." In addition, the female parent is the primary caretaker, both in two-parent and in single parent families, (and) any interference in her functioning is likely to affect the children, especially if financial and social support is not available.

Early Life Experiences

The childhoods of neglecting parents, particularly the mothers, have been filled with distress and unhappiness. The incidence of major deprivations, which range from 60 percent to 16 percent in the groups studied, include: being raised by substitute caretakers; raised partly out of the natural home; living on welfare; having no or few clothes; being hungry, physically beaten, *severely* beaten, sexually abused, and neglected; feeling unwanted; not sure of being wanted; the presence of a heavy drinker in the home; and an unhappy childhood (Wolock & Horowitz, 1979; Giovannoni & Billingsley, 1979; Polansky and others, 1981). The factors which show the highest correlations to current neglect include: being raised by someone other than parents, having no decent clothes, being badly beaten, being sexually abused, the feeling of being neglected, and not feeling wanted as a child. Many children experience one or more of these factors, and it is obvious that a feeling of being unwanted can correlate highly with concrete experiences, such as the fact of few clothes or severe physical beatings.

Polansky (1981) hypothesized that neglectful parents will come from a disorganized and inconsistent home. However, abuse was reported by more than half of the neglect mothers but less than 20 percent of the control group. It can be speculated that a child who is abused may later abuse, but the person may also become inadequate. It is theorized that the abusing experience is later diffused through the personality. In a further examination of serious pathology in the neglectful mother's family of origin, the results are grim although impressionistic. Of twenty-four neglecting mothers without fathers, sixteen described severe problems in both parents, nine fathers severely beat the mothers, and thirteen had fathers who abused alcohol.

Sullivan, Spasser and Penner (1977), in the extensive Bowen Project in Chicago, found that parents who were deprived in childhood did not have normal growth-producing experiences, remained fixated at an early emotional level, and tried desperately to fill their unmet needs. Giovannoni and Billingsley (1970), in contrast to the others, found only minimum evidence that earlier life experiences led to later neglectful behavior.

Parental Knowledge

Cantwell (1980) pointed out that neglect is caused by parental lack of knowledge, judgment and motivation. Parents may: (1) be unaware that a young infant has to be fed every three or four hours, (2) have no knowledge of how to prepare a meal, or (3) not know the nutritional content of foods. Developmental stages are unknown to the neglecting parent, and they are uninformed about ways to encourage learning. Parents may fail to recognize a child's need to be seen by a physician, and they fail to understand that every child must receive emotional nurture. Black and Mayer (1980) indicate that most opiate addicted parents are young and have had little opportunity to learn parenting skills. Newberger and Cook (1983, p. 521), in a study of sixteen mothers with developmentally delayed children, suggest that "the developmental maturity of parents' awareness of children and the parental role may be importantly implicated in parental . . . dysfunction." Polansky et al. (1981) recognizes that neglectful parents show fewer areas of competence, but he would attribute this more to their character structures than to a clear lack of knowledge.

Gabarino and Gilliam (1980, p. 29), commenting that research supports the thesis that neglecting parents have a lack of knowledge and unrealistic expectations about children, state that "parents appear to have had little chance to rehearse the role of caregiver. They often were maltreated as children, did not have pets on which to practice being a parent, and have a history of social impoverishment. It is little wonder that they have trouble learning the role of parent." In contrast to the above findings, Wolock and Horowitz (1979, p. 189) found no difference between maltreating and control groups on "child-rearing knowledge, attitudes, and practices."

Isolation and Alienation

A parent who feels isolated or isolates herself may not be able to reach out to obtain social supports, even if the latter are readily available. Stresses within the family can reduce one's ability to even go out of the house. All studies reveal feelings of isolation and alienation from the larger community. Wolock and Horowitz (1979) discovered that neglecting parents had fewer outside contacts with both relatives and friends. Parents described themselves as social isolates and revealed that they did not have friends or relatives whom they could call upon when in need. The authors found that isolation was one of four factors which contributed most to neglect. They note that "participation in social network offers a family entree into a system of interpersonal and emotional exchanges" (p. 189). In a similar way, Gabarino and Gilliam (1980, p. 31) indicate that "social isolation is the weak link that is responsible for abuse and neglect. Isolation from potent, prosocial support systems places even the strong and competent in jeopardy, and often sends the weak or incompetent over the edge when stresses from within and outside the family conspire." Kotelchuck (1982, pp. 78–79) found "social isolation and unhappy maternal childhood" as the major risk factors for both abuse and neglect. Social isolation is both an inherent psychological stress and an absence of help for the mother.

In a schedule designed to determine the extent of isolation of parents, it was found that neglecting parents were more socially isolated than parents in the control group. Almost half of the neglecting mothers "rarely or never visited with their brothers and sisters." In contrast, almost all the control mothers visited relatives. Two-fifths of the neglect fathers rarely or never visited with siblings, in contrast to about one-fifth of the non-neglect. This isolation from family did not appear to be related to the recent arrival in the community. Although adequate care parents reported some change of residence, neglecting parents reported three times as many moves. But these were not interstate moves, only local. A question raised is whether their moves made them more isolated or whether "their lack of ties made it easier for them to move" (Polansky et al., 1981, p. 90).

Polansky further discovered that neglectful parents felt far more alienated from their community than those who do not neglect. Consistent with feelings of being alienated from the community, those who neglect their children have few, if any, memberships in formal organizations, including religious affiliations. Recognizing that participation in formal organizations might be difficult for persons who feel isolated and alienated, neglecting parents, both mothers and fathers (when they were together), were studied for their informal relationships, such as coffee with a friend. Again, the same pattern held consistent: the neglectful parent had significantly less outside contacts than the parents who cared adequately for their children (Polansky et al., 1981).

Regarding the social activities of neglecting mothers during their own adolescence, it was found that their participation scores were about half those of the control group. Fathers also had a difference in scores but not as much. Further analysis determined that there was a significant correlation between mothers' extent of feelings of futility and their adaptation as adolescents. It was concluded that the mothers especially "were starting to fall outside the mainstream already in adolescence. Lack of participation, in other words, was not a new thing in their lives" (Polansky et al., 1981, p. 95).

Observations of neglecting parents led Polansky to conclude that the isolation from others and from helping networks is a general pattern in their lives, not related just to the failure to use help for the children. These features are indicators of problems in their character structures. The deficiencies can be viewed as interactions which lead only downward in the ability to cope with problems. The mother can give little or nothing to someone else, and, in turn, the self-imposed isolation and alienation causes others to withdraw. This leads to a helplessness in neglecting parents which is both objective and subjective: "to be unable to manage for oneself *and* to have no one else to turn to must magnify the feeling of helplessness..." (Polansky et al., 1971, p. 96).

Characteristics of the Mother

Polansky and his associates may be best known for their delineation of the features of the parent with the apathy-futility syndrome:

> The door was finally opened by Mrs. Hall, a very tired looking woman dressed only in a sheer, dirty cotton nightgown (at 1:30 p.m.). She was extremely obese, disheveled and generally dirty; she greeted me passively. Although only age 23, she looked 35 to 40. I later learned that she was 8 months pregnant, but due to her size it was not apparent. The furnishings of the apartment were shabby. The shades were pulled down, making it quite dark. The kitchen floor was littered with bread crusts, and there was a penetrating odor of stale food and urine. The cribs in the adjacent bedroom were both dirty and in poor repair. Mother sat quietly on the couch and answered my questions in an unanimated manner. She seemed oblivious to the severity of Ralph's injury to his hand.

Child protective staff are quite familiar with the ways in which parents like Mrs. Hall conduct themselves. They are passive, have little expression and are generally withdrawn. They are disorganized in thinking and in behavior and are equally disorganized in caring for children. They seldom oppose suggestions, and they seldom change. A description of the apathy-futility features is listed below, but we first consider some other data which relate to this character problem.

By use of a Maternal Characteristics Scale, an assessment was made of four features of mothers: relatedness, impulse control, confidence, and verbal accessibility. A comparison of the two groups revealed differences which were highly significant: neglecting mothers were lacking in all four areas. In other measures of parents, high scores on two segments of the Childhood Level of Living Scale—physical care and psychological care— were positively associated with the mother's *absence* of apathy-futility, absence of impulsivity, verbal accessibility, workmanship, and capacity for object relations. "The data strongly implied that there was a substantial relationship between maternal character and the poor caliber of care focal children were receiving." Similar but not as strong correlations were found on fathers (Polansky et al., 1981, pp. 104–107).

The neglecting mother's character seems to have consequences for the selection of a mate. "More mature women had chosen husbands whose character was better suited for fatherhood." However, when a mother needed a strong husband to compensate for her own deficiencies, it was likely that the father's lacks would be the same as hers. Furthermore, the "more impulse-ridden the mother, the more likely she was to be living fatherless" (Polansky et al., 1981, p. 143).

Using a variety of assessment schedules, parents were classified according to standard diagnoses. Among the 45 mothers, the following types were found: none were mentally retarded, two had psychosis, two neurosis and none was essentially normal. The major personality problem among the remaining mothers was character disorder, with a large majority classified in either the apathy-futility syndrome or the impulse-ridden character. The major pattern in the apathy-futility syndrome is described as (Polansky et al., 1981, pp. 39–40:

1. A pervasive conviction that nothing is worth doing. The feeling of futility predominates, as in the schizoid personality.
2. Emotional numbness sometimes mistaken for depression. It is beyond depression; it represents massive affect-inhibition from early splitting in the ego.
3. Interpersonal relationships typified by desperate clinging; they are superficial, essentially lacking in pleasure, and accompanied by intense loneliness.
4. Lack of competence in many areas of living, partially caused by the unwillingness to risk failure in acquiring skills.
5. Expression of anger passive-aggressively and through hostile compliance.
6. Noncommitment to positive stands; even the stubborn negativism is a last-ditch assertion that one exists.
7. Verbal inaccessibility to others and a related crippling in problem solving because of the absence of internal dialogue.
8. An uncanny skill in bringing to consciousness the same feelings of futility in others; this is used as a major interpersonal defense against efforts to bring about change.

Other characteristics which can be added to the classification include concrete thinking, all-or-none viewpoints, conversion reactions, and "psychosomatic illnesses due to an inability to resolve life's problems or express feelings verbally" (Polansky et al., 1980, p. 40). They usually have no capacity for self-assessment, as if that ability never developed. Not every person with this syndrome has all of these characteristics, but even if there is a variation, it is likely that "the same underlying pathology has been at work" (Polansky, p. 40).

Neglecting behavior, according to Polansky, results from a character disorder of the personality, invariably that of the mother; this "character disorder" affects all facets of the mother's relationships and life. The definition of a typical neglecting mother, which emerged from the Appalachian study and was essentially confirmed in the Philadelphia research phase, is as follows:

She is of limited intelligence (IQ below 70), has failed to achieve more than an eighth-grade education, and has never held public employment. She married the first or second man who showed interest in her, and he proved to be ill-equipped in education and in vocational skills. She has at best a vague, or extremely limited, idea of what her children need emotionally and physically. She seldom is able to see things from the point of view of others and cannot take their needs into consideration when responding to a conflict they experience. She herself has grown up in a family in which her parents were retarded or showed deviant or criminal behavior (Polansky et al., 1981, p. 43).

At completion of the research, Polansky et al. (1981, p. 109) described neglecting parents as follows:

These parents were certainly functioning on a level far better, say, than that of regressed psychotics or severely retarded adults. But their standard for comparison was other adults of similar cultural background who were also caring for young children. The assessement by the research caseworkers, which was corroborated by the case judges, depicted a group of people with a model personality: less able to love, less capable of working productively, less open about feelings, more prone to living planlessly and impulsively, but also susceptible to psychological symptoms and to phases of passive inactivity and numb fatalism. The image is one of men and women who do not cope well with life.

The Faranelli case discussed below reveals the long-standing problems associated with some families. Parental behavior changes slightly on occasion, but the change may be related only to great outside pressure. A multitude of services were provided, but the agency still had to intervene frequently. This excerpt from the case record does not show the exasperation of some workers who made many attempts to sustain the Faranelli's. It must be acknowledged that we do not have the knowledge and skill to change some families, and some families will never change. A few families will be known to child protection agencies for more than one generation, and the community may have to support families during the entire child-rearing period.

Our agency has worked with the Faranelli family for thirteen years. The first intervention was with Leonard who was admitted to the hospital for malnutrition and dehydration. The mother was wearing little more than rags; there was no food in the house, nor was there any heat. Linda and Tony looked pathetic and were shivering under a thin blanket. All three children were placed in foster care and remained there for four years while efforts were made to help the parents perform better. Mrs. F made many promises, and Mr. F stood by her and nodded his head in agreement.

The children were returned home one at a time so that the parents could adjust to their needs. These services have been offered: homemaker, day care, a sheltered workshop, Bates Creek Specialized School, the state school, family and individual counseling, food stamps, transportation, Medicaid, Lincoln Boys Club and welfare. Despite the services rendered, sometimes very extensively, it was not uncommon to enter their home and find dressers without drawers (their clothing remained unfolded and unhung, scattered and in piles), urine-stained mattresses without sheets, an empty unclean refrigerator, furniture with slashed and burned seats, walls which were dirty and had holes in the sheetrock, broken hinges on the kitchen cabinets, holes in the flooring, food and garbage scattered about the house, and garbage heaped in the yard.

There were occasional drastic changes and improvements, but these were short lived and prompted only by the agency initiation of legal proceedings. Our last neglect petition was filed when we learned that Melinda, the youngest child, had had eight different placements with relatives, distant relatives and non-related persons, all within four months. Both parents have limited intelligence and cannot recognize the childrens' needs.

Polansky and his associates also reported that neither outright psychosis nor severe mental retardation was found among neglecting parents. However, the parents had little ability to test reality, to solve problems and to conceive of anything conceptually. In general, they found people who were functioning at an immature level and with little integration of mental processes. As the title to their book indicates, neglecting parents are "damaged people."

SUMMARY

Child neglect is the failure to provide for the needs of a child. It is seldom a conscious avoidance of responsibility but is an inability to perform. The existing research does not indicate precisely the relationships among variables. They interact with each other, and neglect results from different configurations of the same factors.

The following variables primarily contribute to, but may also be correlates of, neglect: hostile and negative societal values and attitudes toward children; poverty, including both low income and insufficient material resources; the physical and social "character" of the neighborhood; parental feelings of isolation and alienation from the community; availability and use of community and family social supports, both formal and informal; substance addictions and serious mental and physical health problems; parental experiences as children which were destructive, neglectful, abusive or isolating; parental knowledge of children's needs and developmental stages; parental knowledge of the role of a parent; the number of children and their spacing; the presence of one or both parents and their relationships; the characteristics of a child, particularly with the failure-to-thrive condition; the intelligence of one or both parents; a serious character disorder such as apathy-futility or impulsivity in either parent but especially in the mother; and stress, which usually results from poverty but may be associated with all other factors.

REFERENCES

Black, R., and Mayer, J.: Parents with special problems: Alcoholism and opiate addiction. In Kempe, C., and Helfer, R. (Eds.): *The Battered Child*. Chicago: University of Chicago Press, 1980.

Cantwell, H.B.: Child neglect. In Kempe, C., and Helfer, R. (Eds.): *The Battered Child*. Chicago: University of Chicago Press, 1980.

Garbarino, J.: An ecological approach to child maltreatment. In Pelton, L. (Ed.): *The Social Context of Child Abuse and Neglect.* New York: Human Sciences Press, 1981.

Garbarino, J., and Gilliam, G.: *Understanding Abusive Families.* Lexington, MA: D.C. Heath and Co., 1980.

Gil, D.G.: Unraveling child abuse. In Bourne, R., and Newberger, E. (Eds.): *Critical Perspectives on Child Abuse.* Lexington, MA: D.C. Heath and Co., 1979.

Gil, D.G.: The United States versus child abuse. In *The Social Context of Child Abuse and Neglect.* New York: Human Sciences Press, 1981.

Giovannoni, J.: Prevention of child abuse and neglect: Research and policy issues. *Social Work Research and Abstracts, 18*:3, 1982.

Giovannoni, J., and Billingsley, A.: Child neglect among the poor: A study of parental adequacy in families of three ethnic groups. *Child Welfare, 49*:4, 1970.

Kotelchuck, M.: Child abuse and neglect: Prediction and misclassification. In Starr, R. (Ed.): *Child Abuse Prediction,* Cambridge, MA: Ballinger Publishing, 1982.

Kotelchuck, M., and Newberger, E.: Failure to thrive: A controlled study of familial characteristics. *Journal of the American Academy of Child Psychiatry, 22*:4, 1983.

Pelton, L. (Ed.): Child abuse and neglect. In *The Social Context of Child Abuse and Neglect.* New York: Human Sciences Press, 1981.

Polansky, N. and others.: *Damaged Parents.* Chicago: University of Chicago Press, 1981.

Sudia, D.: What services do abusive and neglecting families need? In Pelton, L. (Ed.): *The Social Context of Child Abuse and Neglect.* New York: Human Sciences Press, 1981.

Sullivan, M., Spasser, M., and Penner, G.: *Bowen Center Project for Abused and Neglected Children.* Washington, D.C.: U.S. Department of Health, Education, and Welfare, 1977.

Wolock, I., and Horowitz, B.: Child maltreatment and maternal deprivation among AFDC-recipient families. *Social Service Review, 53*:1, 1979.

CHAPTER 5

ETIOLOGY OF EMOTIONAL MALTREATMENT

Elizabeth Elmer

INTRODUCTION

Paradoxically, although there is common agreement that children suffer as much or more from emotional abuse as from physical mistreatment, the literature contains far less discussion of "torture without hitting," as it has been called. Why this should be so is unclear. Both physical abuse and physical neglect seem more clear-cut than emotional mistreatment. Indicators of these abound, for example, cuts, bruises, and lacerations may be associated with physical abuse, while neglected children often appear bedraggled and malnourished and their environments deteriorated. In both physical abuse and neglect some children may require medical attention, and some perpetrators of physical abuse may confess to mistreatment of the child, which are rare occurrences with respect to emotional abuse. Nevertheless, most writers in this area seem preoccupied with various aspects of physical mistreatment, almost to the exclusion of emotional abuse and neglect.

Actually, we have no commonly accepted definitions for any form of abuse (Giovannoni and Becerra, 1979), although physical abuse in its grossest forms probably comes closest to achieving agreement. Thus, protective workers and others concerned with the welfare of children carry out their jobs in a haze of uncertainty, a never-never land where each state has its own (usually ambiguous) definitions and judges must often interpret distressingly broad legal formulations according to their individual experience. How can one study, adjudicate, or treat such a will-o'-the-wisp? Yet, for the child, the family, and society the stakes are very high. The child may face detachment from his family, perhaps life among strangers. His safety and healthy development may be threatened. The family suspected of maltreatment may be subjected to uninvited authoritarian intervention, to shame from neighbors and relatives, to appearances in court, even to loss of their children. Because of the failure to define offenses against children, society gambles with the good of the next generation as well as with the integrity of its most basic institution: the family. Despite these major problems, productive work on definitions has moved little in some years.

One of the most poorly understood and defined concepts is emotional maltreatment. In this chapter I will draw on the thoughts of others to suggest a working definition solely for the purpose of providing a common base for the reader. Discussion will then focus on some of the effects on children, possible etiological factors, and general implications for social workers excluding discussion of individual treatment, which will be addressed in a later chapter.

What is Emotional Maltreatment?

Any definition of emotional maltreatment should be framed in relation to other forms of maltreatment (i.e. physical abuse, physical neglect, and sexual abuse). Kinard (1979) sets out clear differentiations (which still must be interpreted by protective workers and others). In abbreviated form, Kinnard sees physical abuse as deliberately inflicted injuries, physical neglect as the endangerment of health or safety because of the inadequate provision of care such as shelter, food, and supervision. Emotional abuse Kinard describes as injury to the psychological self with intent to punish, while emotional neglect is the deprivation of psychological nurturance, a "lack of emotional involvement between parent and child" (Kinard, 1979, p. 83). I believe it is useful to distinguish between emotional abuse and emotional nelgect, as they appear to stem from quite different motives.

Until recently, sexual and physical abuse were lumped together, but gradually these two offenses have been identified as separate entities. The National Center on Child Abuse and Neglect defines sexual abuse as "any act of a sexual nature upon or with a child" (1978, p. 9). Sexual abuse may include elements of physical abuse (e.g. the use of force) and of emotional abuse (e.g. the use of threats).

Giovannoni and Becerra (1979) note that defining abuse sets forth the limitations of parental authority, while defining neglect sets forth the minimum expectations of parents. Clarity of definitions would therefore signify agreement on a fundamental issue—the parameters of acceptable parenting behavior in our society.

It seems possible to combine the definitions of Kinard with the concepts of Giovannoni and Becerra to say that the most blatant emotional abuse is the assertion of parental authority in extreme form, resulting in psychological injury. Examples include forcing the child to conform in every respect with the parents' wishes, requiring impossible standards of perfection, etc. Such goals are pursued through all-out assault on the child's individuality by denigrating him, debasing his or her achievements, comparing the child to others, always to the index child's disadvantage. This has been called "soul murder," the "deliberate attempt to interfere with another person's identity, joy in life, and capacity to love" (Shengold, 1978, p. 419). Certainly, this corresponds with Kinard's statement that emotional abuse is psychological injury with the intent to punish.

Again, combining Kinard's with Giovannoni and Becerra's statements, it could be said that extreme emotional neglect is the absence of parental involvement at a critical period in the child's life. The absence of involvement is difficult at any time, but there are life states when such absence places the child in a virtually untenable position. An example is the nonabused infant whose mother verbalizes and shows in her behavior a revulsion for physical contact (Main, 1981). The need of infants for such contact has been repeatedly documented; when it is impossible for whatever reason, its absence is thought to contribute to key difficulties in bonding (Klaus and Kennell, 1970), a basic step in the mother-child relationship.

Lesser forms of emotional mistreatment are of course more prevalent than the extreme forms. At the Parental Stress Center, where we attempt to help abused babies and their families, we have observed a parent hiding a favored toy or an important transitional object, then relishing the child's distress. At a later age, the failure to keep promises tells the child that he or she is not entitled to the consideration given to other persons. Again, many a child is repeatedly subjected to threats—to call the police and have him or her thrown in jail; to be beaten or put out for adoption—and although the threats are most often empty, they have the effect of impressing the child with his powerlessness and total reliance on the whim of the parent. Further, the eliciting of fears, groundless though they may be, also contributes to an abusive atmosphere (Herzberger, Potts, and Dillon, 1981).

Although the behaviors described above are milder than other possible forms of emotional abuse, they achieve much the same objectives: psychological injury through downgrading, interference with the child's joy of life, and emphasis on the child's helplessness.

The different forms of maltreatment tend to overlap; thus, the child who is physically abused is likely to be emotionally mistreated as well (Shengold, 1978; Giovannoni and Becerra, 1979; Kinard, 1979; Herzberger, et al., 1981). Garbarino (Reference Note 1) goes even further: He holds that emotional abuse is implicit in any physical attack. When the views of physically abused children themselves were sought, however, it was learned that a high proportion felt loved and wanted despite the bodily assault (Herzberger et al., 1981). Although the author of this chapter recognized the real limitations of their study, they felt justified in suggesting that physical and emotional abuse are distinct phenomena with consequences that may be quite different.

A word should be said about the question of "deliberate intent," a phrase that frequently appears in definitions of the various forms of maltreatment (for example, see Kinard, 1979). Intent is notoriously difficult to assess as demonstrated in criminal trials where its presence or absence is a major factor in establishing the level of guilt. In questions of maltreatment, it is the opinion of the author that intent should take second place to the effect on the child. Deliberate intent, if it can be determined, should affect the treatment plan, not the determination of maltreatment per se. Most perpetrators display an exquisite ability to rationalize what they are doing to the child. The parent, anxious to mold the child to preconceived expectations, feels justified in criticism, sarcasm, harassment —anything to get the child to stop crying, to perform better in school, etc. Such a parent seems incapable of perceiving the effects on the child. Instead, the parent concentrates on the goals for the child and sees his or her parental behavior as benignly instrumental in attaining them.

It is relatively easy to think of examples of emotional maltreatment and to analyze possible effects on the young victim. In practice there are many impediments to achieving consensus on the meaning of emotional abuse or neglect. A major source of difficulty is differences of opinion regarding the aims of child rearing. For example, a number of parents want nothing more than an obedient, docile child, while other parents place high value on a creative, spontaneous child. With such dissimilarities in desired outcome, there could be little agreement on how to get there.

Agreement on a legal definition of emotional maltreatment is even more elusive. One reason is the possible "sleeper effect." The negative results of chronic emotional maltreatment are subtle and may be imperceptible on a day-to-day basis. Because the effects are cumulative over a prolonged period, they are difficult to connect with particular parent behaviors. Many other individuals, groups, and events may have affected the child, leaving parental treatment as only one possible factor in the child's condition.

Legitimate differences in values and the general lack of knowledge about the outcome of different modes of child rearing are two of the many reasons that reputable groups have been unable to arrive at a mutually acceptable definition of emotional maltreatment. Differences in philosophy are also apparent, for example, the child as the principal concern versus the need to guard the rights of the parents. There is also the matter of professional identification of the group which is developing definitions and standards: Attorneys tend toward restrictive, narrowly defined language, while social workers and sociologists take a more expansive, sweeping approach. Unanimity is very far away; much time and effort will have to be expended on the problem of standards before workable, fair definitions can be wrought.

Effects on the Child

To the casual observer, physical abuse may seem harder to bear than emotional maltreatment. For a small child, to be attacked by your big protector, your caregiver, must seem an almost unbelievable event. Especially would this be true if the attack involved a weapon—a stick, an electric iron cord, in some instances even a gun or a knife. Nevertheless, several researchers report that the pain of emotional insult is more damaging than assault against the body (for example, see Garbarino, Reference Note 1).

Theoretically, many characteristics of childhood make "torture without hitting" exceedingly hard for the age group 0–5 years. Think of a child's world: Physically bounded by the walls of the home, the young child has not yet ventured far into the world outside. Even a trip to the grocery store can be undertaken only with an older person. Dependence on the parent, although lessening year by year, is still great up to school age.

During these early years the child gradually acquires the concept of himself as an individual, separate from all others. He then begins to assign himself some value as a person (self-esteem). The nature of the assigned value—positive or negative—depends largely on the child's interaction with adult caregivers. If they are "good enough" caregivers, a child incorporates a positive value. Recognition for his achievements helps the youngster extend his efforts and adds substance to his rudimentary self-esteem.

But suppose the parents rarely smile or encourage the child; instead his efforts are greeted by frowns and criticisms: "Why can't you *ever* do things right?" Or the caregiver verbalizes distaste for the child: "Take off—you make me sick." Inexperienced, naive, the child absorbs the idea that indeed he or she *is* incapable of behaving correctly. The parents' cutting remarks and corresponding actions are perceived as rejection which the child somehow deserves. Bear in mind that the child has no basis for comparing the parent with other adults because he is still encompassed by the cocoon of the family. His only knowledge of parental behavior is what he is experiencing.

Young children are prone to a number of fears: fears of abandonment, injury, loss of love. Emotional maltreatment plays into these frightening feelings, arousing even more anxiety and emphasizing the child's helpless-

---

*For an excellent discussion of the complications of standard setting, see Giovannoni and Becerra (1979, pp. 78–94).

ness. As if this were not enough, many parents do not allow the young victim to register his distress. He may not question, complain, or even verbalize his state of mind. It's like the emperor's new clothes: Everyone subscribes to the myth in order to avoid the ire of the ruler.

The repeated suppression of feelings is apt to lead to inability to recognize one's own reactions; thus the normal range of emotions is compressed and distorted. Shengold (1975) describes a family breakfast table with an unpeeled banana at each place. The father comes late and goes round the table squeezing and spoiling each piece of fruit. When the youngest child begins to cry, his father silences him and ridicules the child's upset behavior. As the older children and the mother have not complained and the father's outburst was directed only at him, the sobbing five-year-old is led to believe that the father's behavior is normal; it is the child's reaction that must be faulty.

Understandably, as similar events occur, the child's fragile self-esteem begins to wilt. Insofar as he blames himself for the attacks, he experiences hatred of self. The aggression that rightfully should be aimed at the victimizer is instead directed inward at himself, the victim. One result may be prolonged depression; another may be self-punitive behavior (e.g. an excessive number of accidents or, more direct, self-mutilation).

The younger the child, the more likely is aggression to be outer directed. Main (1981) reports several studies of infants and toddlers whose mothers expressed strong distaste for physical contact with their children and who were cold, unexpressive, hostile, and rigid. Although anxiously attached to their mothers, the babies reacted to reunion after separation (in the Ainsworth Strange Situation) with affectless rejection, turning away and ignoring the mothers' attentions. This was in contrast to children with more nurturing backgrounds, who reacted to reunion with relief and increased proximity-seeking. The avoidant infants were found to behave in similar fashion with other adults attempting to engage them in play during the same session. The investigator also learned that the observed avoidance behavior was associated with marked aggression toward caregivers in a day care situation. Main suggests that these rejected infants were already showing beginning signs of difficulties in relationships outside the home.

Main's detailed studies document very early interpersonal problems associated with early maternal rejection. The findings are the more impressive because there was no evidence of unusual infant behavior in the first few months of life (e.g. excessive crying, marked anger, or aversion to being held—behaviors that, if present, might have provoked the caregiver's hostility).

Probably, infants and very young children are especially vulnerable to emotional maltreatment, just as this age group is especially vulnerable to morbidity and mortality because of physical attack. Fortunately, many children are older when maltreatment begins; presumably they have a better chance to come through it relatively intact. A case in point is Rudyard Kipling, who was valued and warmly nurtured until age six, then inexplicably exposed to merciless maltreatment by a surrogate mother.*

Rudyard Kipling was born in Bombay in 1865, the much wanted first child of an affluent English couple. The father, an important Sahib, was a distinguished artist, artisan, and teacher who had an extraordinary ability to acquire and retain knowledge and a lively, active curiosity. He was the head of an art school.

The young boy was treated like a prince by the two servants who provided daily care, his nurse and his bearer. Between them, they saw that every wish was granted. The parents remained in the background as did many others of means during the Victorian era. Nevertheless, Kipling felt himself his mother's undisputed favorite during the first six years of life.

When Kipling was almost six, he and his two-and-one-half-year-old sister were taken to England to begin their formal education. The children were lodged with a family strange to them, the Holloways, composed of a retired sea captain (who soon died), his wife, and a son six years older than Kipling. Mrs. Holloway, called "Aunty Rosa" by the children, was a tyrannical, narrow-minded, religious fanatic who shortly became Kipling's chief persecutor. When she finished with beating and harassing the boy, her son Harold took over.

It is not known why Kipling's parents made the arrangement with the Holloways. A large number of well-to-do relatives resided in England, and it might have been possible for the children to live with one of them while attending school. Instead, the Kiplings found the Holloways through a newspaper advertisement. In fact, there are a number of unknowns related to the children's move to England. According to later letters, the parents made no explanation for the move, nor did they inform the children that the parents would return to India without them. Shengold suggests that this behavior demonstrated the lack of empathy for children so prevalent in the Victorian era. We do know that the children were devastated by the abandonment; Kipling never recovered from the feeling of being betrayed by his mother.

Aunty Rosa, apparently jealous of Kipling's superior intelligence compared to Harold, began a regime of regular beatings for the six-year-old. Kipling's sister Trix was never beaten, but Aunty Rosa attempted to woo Trix away from Kipling, which would have left him completely unsupported. Fortunately, Trix was not to be wooed; instead she stood by Kipling and shared mutual memories of the idyllic past.

Trix and Kipling were made to play in a basement den which had no heat and was perpetually damp. It smelled like mushrooms; mildew appeared in two days on the playthings. The children called the Holloway house the "House of Desolation."

Harold and Aunty Rosa cross-examined Kipling every day about his activities in school. If there was any contradiction in his account, Aunty Rosa punished him severely, then Harold had his turn. Kipling learned to be wary and sensitive

*This is a summarized version of the case found in Shengold (1975).

to his persecutors' moods and temper. He also learned to lie to avoid beatings, a skill that he later identified as the foundation of his literary career.

When he arrived in England at age six, Kipling did not know how to read or write. Aunty Rosa taught him and he gradually found an unexpected refuge in books. When "The Woman," as Aunty Rosa was called, discerned the importance of reading to the boy, she deprived him of it. Kipling's response was to read in secret, by poor light. Little by little his eyes began to fail and ultimately he could hardly see to read. His school work began to suffer causing "The Woman" to take away the small amount of study time he was granted. His school reports became so poor that he pitched one instead of bringing it home, then said he had never received it. The lie was soon discovered and led to a round of beatings by both Aunty Rosa and Harold. The final blow was being sent to school by way of the busiest streets with a placard reading "LIAR" hung on his shoulders.

Kipling later wrote that his sanity was probably saved by the yearly one-month visits to a kindly aunt. When this relative began to suspect that Kipling was having some kind of eye difficulty, she sent a physician to the Holloways. He found the boy to be half blind, with which Aunty Rosa accused Kipling of "showing off"; his punishment this time was segregation from Trix. But at last Kipling's mother became alarmed. She traveled to England and removed the children from the "House of Desolation." They had lived there for six long years.

Interestingly, Kipling never told on Aunty. As he explained it, children accept whatever happens to them because it appears "eternally established." Shengold believes Kipling's silence related more to unresolved anger against his parents for deserting him and to the need to deny the whole Holloway experience in the interest of maintaining a positive image of parents.

Note that Kipling experienced at least four types of maltreatment. First was desertion by hitherto loving parents who left a small boy (and an even smaller girl) alone in a strange home in a strange country at school-entering time. Most six-year-olds would be expected to deal with only one of these experiences, starting school. Kipling's parents withdrew their support at a critical period, causing Kipling to endure what this chapter has identified as emotional neglect. Later, both Aunty Rosa and Harold inflicted vicious physical abuse, while emotional abuse was evident in the public shaming of Kipling following the report card incident. Finally, the inattention to Kipling's growing eye problem constituted physical neglect, thus placing Aunty Rosa in the unenviable position of virtuoso in child maltreatment. It is remarkable that Kipling was able to survive psychologically. Possible contributing factors were the benign early years, the unflagging support of his sister, and his great intellectual gifts.

Thoughts Concerning the Origins of Emotional Mistreatment

Since little systematic research exists about any phase of emotional maltreatment, motivation is a matter of conjecture, clinical experience, and related theory.* There does seem to be some agreement that perpetrators have at least two traits in common: a pervasive sense of worthlessness and underlying feelings of rage. These two emotions are blended together in such a way that which came first cannot be determined. The sense of worthlessness results in an insatiable need to establish control. (Whether the right word is control, authority, or power is unclear.) Similarly, Cohn (See Reference Note 2) found that physically abusive or neglectful parents had an overwhelming urge to control even the least important facet of their children's lives. The push toward control can be observed in abusive behavior far less pathological than Aunty Rosa's. For example, the parent mentioned earlier who hid the baby's favorite toy delighted in eliciting distress, thus demonstrating her control of the child's emotional responses.

The underlying rage of the emotional abuser is more primitive and much stronger than run-of-the-mill anger. This may be part of the intent to hurt which is frequently mentioned in definitions of emotional abuse (Kinard, 1979). It is also possible that the true object of the rage and the effort to hurt is the abuser himself. In bringing shame or ridicule on the child, the abuser may be symbolically punishing himself, a dynamic that has also been observed in physically abusive parents. It's the old story: the child is "the victim of the victim."

Not all emotionally abusive parents are as cruel as Kipling's Aunty Rosa, nor do all have such intractable problems, of course. Some loving and kind parents may be hypersensitive to particular developmental stages (Martin, 1982), causing an uncharacteristic spurt of ill feeling and behavior against the unwitting offender. One such stage may occur around 18-24 months, when most boys and girls play randomly with dolls or tools, tea sets or trucks. If parents have strong sex stereotypes about toy choices, this can be quite upsetting. (Interestingly, boys playing with dolls seem more disturbing to parents than girls playing with traditionally masculine objects) (Fein, Johnson, Kosson, Stork, and Wasserman, 1975). Teasing and belittling usually force the child's interest away from inappropriate toys and the emotional abuse ceases.

A parent's ability to cope with the growing child is far from uniform across time, events, and personal stresses. Martin (1976) writes that professionals have paid too little attention to the idiosyncratic reaction of caregivers to different stages of development and to the unexpected, acute difficulties that parents may face as the child progresses from one to another life period. For example, some parents may be quite content with

---

*I am indebted to my colleagues at the Parental Stress Center for helpful discussions of abusers' motivations.

the dependent infant but annoyed, even angry, with the fumbling assertiveness of the two-year-old. Sexual exploration, teenage definace, the
beginning of heterosexual interest—these are examples of possible crisis
points. Martin (1976) speaks only of battering as a response to developmental changes, however, this author believes that emotional abuse may
be similarly triggered.

Parents reacting to these sensitive periods have no conscious wish to
punish or hurt the child. If they consider their motives at all they would
probably label their behavior as "normal," the flavor of victimization in
their actions escaping them altogether.

Besides being a reaction to normal child development, emotional maltreatment may be part of a response to difficult life events. Martin (1982)
suggests that grief following the birth of a defective child may lead to the
parents' psychological withdrawal from the infant. Presumably, this would
compound the original problem by adding difficulties in the important
early bonding.

A fair amount of speculation in the literature has concerned how the
child may provoke physical abuse; this is also a reasonable question in
relation to emotional mistreatment. For the perpetrator, the most relevant
child characteristics are probably powerlessness and dependence on the
parent, making the child a prime target for the parents' need to exercise
complete control. The child is further ensnared by his normal intense need
for a good parent, which damps down the impulse to question or complain and fosters the delusion that the parent is indeed loving and protective (Shengold, 1978). (It will be recalled that Kipling kept to himself the
traumatic story of his life with Aunty Rosa, and that Shengold attributed
his silence to his desire to preserve the image of good parents who would
not expose a child to cruelty and meanness.) In addition, as mentioned
above, the young child's contacts with persons outside the family are
limited and, therefore, objective comparisons of adult behavior are also
restricted.

Some Unanswered Questions

As this chapter has developed, I have been tantalized by questions that
suggest how much we still have to learn concerning the whole phenomenon
of child maltreatment. Some of the unanswered questions have to do with
differences between physical and emotional maltreatment while others
concern differences in the dynamics underlying the victimization of disparate groups.

As suggested above, we need to clearly separate physical abuse, physical
neglect, emotional abuse, and emotional neglect. Beyond the differences in
definitions, what do they have in common and what elements are different?

Of course, this is an exercise in futility since few investigators distinguish between emotional abuse and emotional neglect, and those who do will utilize different definitions. Some of the questions of interest concern the perpetrator. For example, are there differences in the demographic characteristics of physical abusers compared to emotional abusers? Or emotional abusers compared to emotional neglectors? Are there differences among the four groups in psychological makeup, environmental stresses, supportive networks? What trigger mechanisms work to provoke what form of maltreatment? If maltreatment of any kind begins in early childhood, is it likely to continue throughout the child's development? Contrariwise, is it apt to cease as the child matures? Or does one form of maltreatment shift to another with the passing of time? As noted above, several investigators have reported physical abuse accompanied by emotional maltreatment; thus, it would seem that the dynamics for the two forms must be similar. This is not a safe assumption. Since definitions are so ambiguous, many cases of all kinds go unreported; it is quite likely that emotional abuse, if not accompanied by physical maltreatment, is grossly underreported. The reported cases that include both physical and emotional maltreatment may represent only one segment of emotional maltreatment.

The answers to these questions would help make important decisions about the perpetrators' treatability and the outlook for the child who lives with maltreatment. We also need to know more about the outcome of emotional maltreatment. Although various opinions hold that this form is tremendously damaging to the child, what is the data base for such opinions?

Another kind of question addresses differences and similarities among victimized groups. The history of civilization shows there have always been such groups—in ancient Greece, the slaves; in most Western societies, women; and in our own country, blacks as well as women. Children have traditionally had such little value that one could hardly call them victimized; rather, until a few hundred years ago they tended to be almost totally disregarded. Looking back over what we know of centuries past, a march toward equality for all groups seems evident, though excruciatingly slow. One wonders whether the snail-like progress will ultimately extend to children and establish rights that have long appeared a contradiction in terms. Surely, the focus of the last twenty years on child maltreatment has incidentally forced a new and healthy consideration of the status of children.

Implications for Social Workers

Sorting out the tangles of emotional mistreatment suggests the involvement of social workers in a number of ways; I would like to concentrate on three major areas of need: definitions, assessment, and advocacy. As implied throughout this chapter, the failure to set acceptable standards for child mistreatment daily causes multiple problems. For the sake of every segment of the puzzle, we need to push for clarification of definitions. This means paying attention to questions of legal language, attending hearings on proposed changes in the law, being willing to accept compromises in order to progress, and examining the results of current ambiguities in the laws and regulations.

The second important area for social worker involvement in the question of maltreatment is assessment. By no means a new social worker activity, the assessment process needs to be widened and deepened to address the child's status as well as the parents' behavior. An estimate of the child's status should include not only an evaluation of physical well-being but also some assay of emotional health, particularly when the alleged maltreatment includes emotional abuse or neglect. This is not easy to do. For the preschool child it requires observation by a skilled professional; for the older child, interviews and psychological tests should be added.

I am quite aware of the burden that this involvement would impose on a group of workers already stretched beyond reason. To deny the need for better child assessment, however, will not make it go away; only by including the need in planning for the future will we have any chance of eventually meeting it.

Finally, this brief essay on emotional maltreatment highlights the significant role of the social worker as an advocate for children: to pick up on the needs of children as a group. Part of our heritage is to extend help and heart to the individual child or family; we tend to be less sensitive to common needs of the group. Focusing attention on what is good for all children will help reduce maltreatment while also contributing to a better world for the young.

REFERENCE NOTES

1.   Garbarino, James: "Defining Emotional Maltreatment: The Message is the Meaning." Unpublished paper, 1979.
2.   Cohn, M.: "Assessment of Risk in Child Abusing and Neglecting Parents." Unpublished doctoral dissertation, California School of Professional Psychology, Los Angeles, 1978.

REFERENCES

Fein, G., Johnson, D., Kosson, N., Stork, L., and Wasserman, L.: Sex stereotypes and preferences in the toy choices of 20-month-old boys and girls. *Developmental Psychology, 11*:527-528, 1975.

Giovanonni, Jeanne M., and Becerra, Rosina M.: *Defining Child Abuse.* New York: The Free Press, 1979.

Herzberger, S.D., Potts, D.A., and Dillon, M.: Abusive and non-abusive parental treatment from child's perspective. *Journal of Consulting and Clinical Psychology,* 49:81-90, 1981.

Kinard, E.: The psychological consequences of abuse for the child. *Journal of Social Issues,* 35:82-100, 1979.

Klaus, M.H., and Kennell, J.: Mothers separated from their newborn infants. *Pediatric Clinics of North America,* 17:1015-1037, 1970.

Main, M.: Abusive and rejecting infants. In Frude, N. (Ed.): *Psychological Approaches to Child Abuse.* Totowa, NJ: Roman and Littlefield, 1981.

Martin, H.P.: The clinical relevance of prediction and prevention. In Starr, R.H. Jr. (Ed.): *Child Abuse Prediction.* Cambridge, MA: Ballinger Publishing Co., 1982.

Martin, H.P.: Which children get abused? High risk factors in the child. In *The Abused Child.* Cambridge, MA: Ballinger Publishing Co., 1976.

National Center on Child Abuse and Neglect. *Interdisciplinary glossary on child abuse and neglect.* Washington, D.C.: U.S. Department of Health, Education, and Welfare, 1978, p. 9.

Shengold, L.: Assault on a child's individuality, a kind of soul murder. *The Psychoanalytic Quarterly,* 47:419-424, 1978.

Shengold, L.: An attempt at soul murder. *The Psychoanalytic Study of the Child,* 30:683-724, 1975.

CHAPTER 6

ETIOLOGY OF SEXUAL ABUSE

Stephen J. Bavolek

The widespread sexual use and abuse of children by adults is well documented in the religious and cultural histories of nations around the world. For thousands of years, children have been made to sexually interact with adults for a variety of reasons which range from increasing good luck before a hunt to curing venereal disease (Meiselman, 1978). Throughout the ages, societies have rationalized, legalized, outlawed, defended and condemned sex between adults and children. Clearly, no other type of adult-child interaction has created so much interest as well as anxiety, fear, myth, taboo, and guilt.

An etiological examination of sexual abuse is quite an arduous task. Sexual abuse is a complex phenomenon. Despite classifying all sexual activity between adults and children as sexual abuse, the nature of the relationship between the victim and perpetrator, as well as the intent of the perpetrator and type of sexual abuse committed, all contribute essential factors to the problem. The motivation of a stranger to engage children in sexual activity is considerably different from the motivation of a parent or sibling. The type of treatment provided, as well as the strategies employed to prevent the problem, differ in the two situations; yet both are recognized as sexual abuse.

Let us begin the examination of the etiology of sexual abuse by defining the problem.

DEFINITION

Sexual abuse, like other forms of child abuse, is a process; one way in which human beings interact with each other. As a process, sexual abuse is an interaction where children are exploited for sexual gain. From a process viewpoint, sexual abuse varies in intensity (the nature of the sexual abuse), frequency (how often it occurs), and complexity (the people involved and their intent). For example, some children experience rape by a stranger one time; other children experience sexual intercourse with their mother or father or other relative for a period of months; and still other children are involved in prostitution or pornography over a period of years. From a social sense, intensity, frequency and complexity shouldn't be criteria used in the determination of sexual abuse, but they are. Whether certain actions are defined as sexual abuse is often largely dependent upon the existing values of the society generally and of the social service and legal systems specifically.

May (1978) places possible sexual offenses under two categories: non-touching and touching sexual offenses. Non-touching offenses may include verbal sexual stimulation, such as frank discussions about sexual acts intended to arouse the child's interest or to shock the child; obscene telephone calls; exhibitionism; voyeurism; and allowing children to observe or listen to the act of sexual intercourse. Touching offenses, according to May, include fondling; vaginal, oral or anal intercourse or attempted intercourse; touching of the genitals; incest; prostitution; and rape.

Summit and Kryso (1978) identified a spectrum of behaviors that range from loving sensuality to abusive sexuality. At one end of the spectrum are behaviors that most would identify as variations of normal behavior. At the other extreme are the more bizarre and apparently malicious acts that most would agree are clearly criminal and demanding of aggressive intervention. Most state child abuse and neglect statutes, however, do not include all types and categories of sexual abuse offered by May or by Summit and Kryso.

Variations of values and categories notwithstanding, it becomes apparent that a number of terms are used to describe sexual abuse, of which many are used interchangeably. These terms have different legal and clinical interpretations and, therefore, represent different aspects of adult-child sexual abuse. An initial prerequisite for examining the etiology of sexual abuse is the ability to clearly define and differentiate among the terms.

Sexual abuse is a generic term used to define all types of adult-child sexual activity.

Sexual assault is often used in state statutes to define varying degrees of adult-child sexual activity. Sexual assault charges are based on the type of sexual activity that occurred between the perpetrator and victim which result in a fine and/or imprisonment.

Sexual exploitation is another generic term used to describe adult-child sexual activity. The sexual exploitation of children is commonly referred to in cases involving child prostitution and/or child pornography.

Sexual molestation is often used to describe adult sexual advances towards children in the form of verbal sexual abuse, exhibitionism, voyeurism, and fondling of the genitals. The term may or may not be meant to indicate sexual intercourse.

Incest is a technical term used to describe sexual activity between persons related by blood, who would be legally prohibited from marrying. Incest commonly is meant to refer to sexual activity between family members and relatives. In a technical sense, sexual activity between a stepparent and a stepchild is sexual abuse, not incest. However, because a stepparent/stepchild relationship most often closely resembles a biological parent/child relationship, sexual activity between stepparent and stepchild is often referred to as incest.

Sexual abuse is perpetrated by total strangers, adults known by the children prior to the abuse, peers, parents, and siblings. The ensuing discussion of the etiology of sexual abuse will examine offenses perpetrated by others outside the immediate family (non-familial sexual abuse) and offenses perpetrated by members within the family (familial sexual abuse or incest).

NON-FAMILIAL SEXUAL ABUSE

Adult Offenders

Sexual abuse of children perpetrated by complete strangers accounts for only a small percentage of the total sexual abuse cases reported each year. At least half, and possibly as many as 80 percent, of all child victims are sexually abused by people known to the child prior to the abuse (Burgess and Holmstrom, 1975). Parents, parent-substitutes, and relatives account for 30 to 50 percent of all cases (DeFrancis, 1969). In general, studies indicate that over one-third of the assaults on children are reported to occur in the childrens' homes, while 20 percent occur in the homes of the offenders (Peters, 1976).

Studies that have focused on developing a profile of sexual abusers indicate most offenders are male, around thirty years of age, with some high school training and an adequate job history (Jaffe, Dynneson, and ten Bensel, 1975). Swanson (1968) found half of the offenders in his study had been charged with at least one criminal complaint prior to the offense and two-thirds were described as having some personality disorder. Hayman and Langa (1971) suggest excessive alcohol misuse plays an important role in the sexual abuse of children.

Several theories are offered in describing the motivation of non-familial perpetrators to engage in sexual activity with children. In cases where the perpetrators are known to the children but are outside the boundaries of the families, the adults' position of dominance, bribes of material goods, threats of physical violence, or a misrepresentation of moral standards may induce cooperation from the children (DeFrancis, 1969). In participating in the sexual activity, children often cooperate out of a need for love, affection, attention, or a sense of loyalty to the adult perpetrators. Weiss, Rogers, Darwin, and Dulton (1955) suggest children may engage in sexual activity with adults to defy parental figures or to express anger about chaotic home lives. DeVine (1980) indicates the lack of adequate supervision by parents and the failure to set proper controls for childrens' behavior may be contributing factors to sexual abuse. To this end, DeFrancis (1969) found 41 percent of the families in his study showed behavior indicative of psychosocial disturbances.

Costell (1980) suggests sexual abuse offenses against children and adolescents occur both in circumstances where the offenders' behaviors are expressions of abnormal sexual preferences and in situations where normal preferred sexual outlets are thwarted. In the former instance, the offenders simply prefer sexual activity with children. Pedophiles are adults who engage in non-aggressive heterosexual or homosexual behavior with children. In situations where normal preferred sexual outlets are thwarted, incest often results. In father-daughter incest cases, fathers choose their daughters for sexual activity usually when their preferred partner (their wife) has rejected them and an accepting partner (their daughter) is available.

Juvenile Offenders

Adolescents who commit sexual offenses against other children receive far less attention in research than offenses committed by adults. From what is known about adolescent offenders, two profiles emerge. The first type of adolescent offenders may show signs of immature psychosexual development. Costell (1980) indicates some adolescents simply do not progress beyond childhood sexual play and exploration. Their sexual activity with other children is an extension of earlier permissable developmental sexual curiosity and play.

The other type of adolescent offenders are classified in a more serious light. In these cases, their sexual behavior may be an early manifestation of pedophilia or aggressive sexual behavior. Force, control and aggression are typical responses of these offenders. By adult sexual assault standards, such behavior is typically classified as rape.

FAMILIAL SEXUAL ABUSE

Incest is the most emotionally charged and socially intolerable form of sexual abuse and, for a great majority of people, it is easily the one type of sexual abuse that is the most threatening and difficult to understand and accept. It is also the most difficult type of sexual abuse to detect, because incest, by its very nature, tends to remain a family secret. Incest can take various forms. Sibling incest, or sexual activity among young children, is generally accepted as normal developmental play. Incest between older children is less acceptable and perhaps indicative of dysfunction in healthy social and emotional development. Sexual activity between children and adults, particularly parental figures, causes the greatest stigma and appears to have the greatest psychological impact on the victim. In adult-child incest, the problem becomes nearly intolerable for society when the incest is homosexual in nature (i.e. mother-daughter or father-son).

A discussion of the causes of incest cannot occur under any general framework, for the various types of incest are unique onto themselves. The motivation of a father to perpetuate sexual activity with his daughter or son is vastly different from the motivation of a mother, sister or brother to initiate intrafamilial sexual activity. Aside from the universal multi-problematic notion of incestuous families, not much else can be generalized to describe the various types of incest. Therefore, an examination of each of the various types of incestuous activities will occur. The discussion will be limited to members of the nuclear family: father, mother, daughter and son.

FATHER-DAUGHTER INCEST

Father-daughter incest is the most frequently reported type of incestuous relationship, as well as the most researched, discussed and treated form of sexual abuse (May, 1978). There are many factors that contribute to the development of father-daughter incest although insufficient in themselves to cause the incest. It is generally recognized that in father-daughter incest, a triad of participation occurs among the father, mother and daughter. Each has a role to play in the development and perpetration of the incest without which the incest would not occur. The examination of the triad describes how and why father-daughter incest occurs.

The Father

Incestuous fathers are characterized as average to below average in intelligence, very timid and cautiously passive in social relationships outside their families. Spencer (1978) reports a high number of incestuous fathers are from lower socioeconomic levels. This finding supports the earlier research of Weinberg (1955), who found 67 percent of the families he investigated were in the low socioeconomic bracket, and the work of Kaufman, Peck, and Tagiuri (1954), who noticed that the incestuous fathers in their sample came from poverty backgrounds typically characterized by inadequate housing and little education. Giaretto (1976), however, suggests that incestuous fathers are not to be confined to any one socio-economic group and that incestuous fathers involved in this treatment program are typically professionals, semi-professionals, and skilled blue-collar workers.

An examination of the characteristics of incestuous fathers reveals two distinct and differing profiles. The first profile describes incestuous fathers as socially isolated, self-centered, and introverted with a weak, ineffective personality (Luther & Price, 1980). Weinberg (1955) suggests the introvertive personality leads to an extreme intrafamilial orientation with little or no outside contacts. Coupled with sexual and emotional immaturity and the unwillingness of the father to seek a sexual partner outside the nuclear family (Roth, 1978), the fathers turn to their own daughters for self-gratification.

Brown (1979) reports incestuous fathers lack a strong masculine identity, often the result of a domineering and over-controlling mother and a corresponding weak or absent father who demonstrated little warmth and understanding during early periods of development. This lack of identity, coupled with a concomitant low self-esteem, may be greatly magnified during a period of mid-life adjustment, often referred to as "middlescence" (Summit and Kryso, 1978). During middlescence, all semblence of sameness is gone. Some men seek a re-endorsement of youth and masculine vitality via love affairs with younger women. Due to their extreme intrafamilial orientation described earlier, however, incestuous fathers seek to have their sexual needs met within their marriage. When attempts to rekindle their love affair with their wives fail, the oldest daughters are often used as objects for sexual gratification. Attempts to re-establish their self-worth and self-identity are made through their incestuous relationships with their daughters. Despite efforts to continue the incest, the affair almost always ends during the adolescent years when the daughters begin to struggle for independence and seek to establish close relationships with their peers (Molnar and Cameron, 1975).

Controlling and possessing their daughters sexually fulfills a fantasy of social and emotional competence which, in turn, allows them to avoid dealing with their feelings of inadequacy and anger toward women in general. Summit and Kryso (1978) suggest that incestuous fathers exhibit a lack of impulse control due to stress and poor superego development. Unable to stop or control their actions, the incest continues. Within the context of the weak, socially isolated personality type of incestuous fathers, Burgess and Holmstrom (1978) suggest that incest occurs on a level they call pressured sex. In a case of pressured-sex incest, physical force or the threat of physical force is seldom the vehicle by which incest occurs.

Father-daughter pressured-sex incest usually involves a process of conditioning by the father toward the daughter. There is frequent body contact and caressing by the father, evolving into genital contact and play which exists for a period of time before culminating in actual coitus. These actions may be stimulated by the habitual absence of the wife due to work or social recreations, loss of the wife by divorce, separation or death, or inordinate amounts of time spent with the daughter due to long-term unemployment of the father. Pressured-sex incest may further develop as an outgrowth of the sexual rejection of the husband by the wife, which in turn promotes a reversal of family roles that condones the daughter as the sexual substitute mate for the father (Bavolek, 1984).

Some cases of pressured-sex incest are masked by the belief that it is a father's duty to teach the daughter the facts of life. As an educational practice, fathers righteously believe that sexual activity with their daughters is the best technique to teach sex education. Still other fathers believe that sexual activity with their young daughters will lessen the predictable neurotic anxieties regarding sex that are common to adult men and women. Believing in the motto "Sex by eight or else it's too late," members of the Rene Guyon Society actively promote sex between fathers and their daughters and view such activity as therapeutic (Densen-Gerber, 1980).

The second profile describes incestuous fathers as chronically brutal, demanding and alcoholic (Sarles, 1975). Weinberg (1955) describes incestuous fathers as having psychopathic personalities characterized by indiscriminate promiscuity who, in turn, are unable to form any tender attachment with their wives and children and view them as sexual objects. Burgess and Holmstrom (1978) refer to this type of incest as "forced sex," whereby perpetrators are generally psychopathic with problems of alcohol and chemical dependency. Marcuse (1923) identified chronic alcoholism as a primary descriptor of incestuous fathers in one of the earliest research studies regarding incest. Since that early work, the relationship between alcoholism and incest has been repeatedly discussed as a contributing factor to incest (Meiselman, 1978; Tormes, 1968). Lukianowicz (1972) in his study of twenty-six incestuous fathers found fourteen were diagnosed as inadequate psychopaths, five as aggressive psychopaths, and four as alcoholics. The fathers present to the world a picture of a "stable" home but perpetrate incredible violence, threats, and abuse (May, 1978). Baker (1978) found incestuous fathers as domineering and exhibiting extreme dominance over their wives as well as rigid, restrictive, and over-protective parenting practices toward daughters with whom they chose to initiate sexual contact.

The Mother

The mother who operates within a father-daughter incestuous family is commonly characterized as passive, infantile, dependent, possessing a poor self-image, emotionally immature, and depressed (Luther and Price, 1980; Pittman, 1976). She feels worthless as a mother and as a woman, is unhappy in her marriage, and grows increasingly disenchanted with her husband. She rejects the sexual role of a wife and the maternal role as a mother. A mother-daughter role reversal occurs in which the mother assumes with her daughter the relationship she wishes she had with her own rejecting mother (Pittman, 1976). Her general denial of sexuality makes it easy for her to deny the sexually charged intimacy she has encouraged, perhaps unknowingly, between her husband and daughter. Sarles (1975) indicates that a mother in a father-daughter incest family promotes the relationship by abandoning and frustrating her husband sexually or by actually altering the living arrangements to foster the incest.

Once the incestuous relationship is in place, the mother will usually tolerate the incestuous activity with little or only token protest or she will use denial to reject any thoughts of the incest. She may be motivated to deny the reality of incest because she had a hand in unconsciously setting up the incest situation and wishes it to continue in order to relieve her of her sexual role in the marriage (Meiselman, 1978). More commonly, the denial may be the result of avoiding divorce, loss of financial support, humiliation in the community and legal proceedings against her husband. Tormes (1968) describes eight cases in which mothers who were told about or actually witnessed the incest and who denied or ignored the activity. Emotional and economic dependency on the husbands and a concurrent emotional rejection of the daughters provided the necessary ingredients for the mothers to allow the incestuous relationships to continue.

The Daughter

The daughter who falls victim to her father's sexual advances can be of any age. Luther and Price (1980) suggest that the average onset of the incestuous activities occurs when the girls are between the ages of eight and fifteen. Bavolek (1984) suggests that the girl is usually approached between the ages of six to nine years, and by the time the relationship has reached the critical stage of awareness outside the family, she is in adolescence. The girl is often the oldest of several children (Maisch, 1972), usually of average intelligence, although subnormal intelligence of the daughter may be present in some cases (Luther and Price, 1980). The emergence of the daughter as the central female figure of the household plays a key role in the development and perpetuation of the incestuous activity (Roth, 1978). Set up by her mother to assume the role of lover and surrogate wife to the husband, coupled with subtle or overt rejection by the mother of the daughter's beauty, youth and energy, the daughter is available prey for her father's sexual advances. Unknowingly, the daughter may contribute to her own demise through her normal developmental physical growth and increasing curiosity toward sex (Summit and Kryso, 1978). Although the father should be approving, admiring and responsive to her growing sexual attraction, and harmless to flirt with, he instead uses the opportunity to satisfy his own deteriorating identity and image.

During the time the incest is occurring, the daughter may feel depressed, unattractive, unloved, inadequate, and guilty. She may demonstrate emotionally immature behaviors or may exhibit precocious, maturationally advanced behaviors. Confused about love and sex, the child may be completely preoccupied with sex or may completely avoid the topic. Sarles (1975) suggests that the incestuous relationship may span several months to several years. During this time, the daughter is usually passive and seldom complaining. Believing that the incest is her fault, afraid to report the incest for fear of reprisal from her father or mother, or because of a compromised agreement made with the father to not sexually abuse remaining daughters, the victim often allows the incest to continue (Williams, 1981).

MOTHER-SON INCEST

Incest between mother and son is regarded as being the least common and most intensely taboo form of heterosexual incest (Meiselman, 1978). Although there may be instances in which the son has sex with his mother without serious emotional disturbance, according to May (1978) it appears that serious emotional disturbance must be considered a likely factor in all cases of mother-son incest. Due to the nature of the relationship, theorists are quick to point out the role of repressed incestuous feelings of the son towards the mother. In psychoanalytic theory, the son, caught up in his oedipal fantasies, wishes to destroy his father and marry his mother. In light of the fact that the oedipal stage of development is important to the continued personality growth of the son, the association of psychopathology with mother-son incest is common (Weinberg, 1955).

There are two types of mother-son incest: mother initiated and son initiated. In mother-initiated cases, Justice and Justice (1979) suggest the characteristics of the mother may be similar to the characteristics of fathers in father-daughter incest cases. She may deeply love her son and rationalize incest as the highest expression of that love. In some cases, mother-son incest occurs under the guise of sex education or personal hygiene. Still in other cases, the mother may be shut off from the world and turn to her son for human contact, or she may be promiscuous and share sex with her son along with other males. Alcoholism, relatively little age discrepancy between mother and son, the lack of other sexual objects available to the son, and a general history of incest in the family are other characteristics contributing to mother-son incest (Wahl, 1960). Berry (1975) describes the case of a young boy who slept with his mother since early childhood that included periodic genital examinations "to make sure everything was all right."

Weinberg (1955) provides a differing profile of the mother: one of severe instability, serious emotional disturbance, or psychosis. Lukianowicz (1972) reports of a young schizophrenic mother who perpetrated incest with her eleven-year-old mentally retarded son. Frances and Frances (1976) suggest that in families where mother-son incest exists, a strong symbiotic relationship exists where one or both of the partners are psychotic with a clear lack of psychic differentiation.

In son-initiated cases of mother-son incest, the son is almost always classified as seriously emotionally disturbed, brain damaged, or psychotic. Kubo (1957) recounts a case history of a young brain-damaged boy who initiated repeated sexual activity with his mother. Weinberg (1955) discusses the case of an adolescent who raped his mother after he had witnessed her in sexual activities with other men. Medlicott (1967) describes the case of a young man in the early stages of a paranoid schizophrenia who attempted sexual intercourse with his mother after hearing voices. Unlike most cases of mother-initiated incest, when the son initiates the behavior, it is usually an extension of the psychopathology he is currently experiencing.

FATHER-SON INCEST

Although father-son incest is rarely recognized, it is the most common form of homosexual incest reported. Justice and Justice (1979) suggest the rare accounts of father-son incest may be due to the double stigma it causes: incest and homosexuality. Characteristic traits of the father generally suggest that it is the father who almost always initiates the sexual behavior. He may be alcoholic or using alcohol to justify the behavior, may have had strong homosexual desires since childhood, and may have experienced or witnessed incest during early childhood (Meiselman, 1979). In these relaships, the father's usual behavior toward his son may be aggressive, infantilizing, and controlling (Langsley, Schwartz, and Fairbairn, 1968). Berry (1975) suggests the primary stimulus for father-son incest may be the father's own unresolved adolescent sexual conflicts. Generally, he has no history of severe emotional disorders prior to the incestuous relationship with his son (Berry, 1975), and unlike the psychopathic personality described in some father-daughter incest cases, the father feels guilt and depression after realizing the emotional damage caused to his son (Raybin, 1969). Langsley et al. (1968) describe a case involving a twenty-year-old man hospitalized following the use of LSD in which the sexual activity with his father began at age twelve and involved mutual genital manipulation. The father himself was the victim of a similar experience involving mutual masturbation with his father and seduction by an uncle.

Like the incestuous daughter, the incestuous son generally does not resist the father, despite feeling damaged, dirty and worthless (Justice and

Justice, 1979). In contradistinction to cases of father-daughter incest, father-son incest is usually short-lived, ending when the son begins to develop strong negative feelings towards his father and their relationship.

MOTHER-DAUGHTER INCEST

Like father-son incest, mother-daughter incest occurs, but it is rare (May, 1978). Meiselman (1978) suggests that female homosexual relationships within the nuclear family are the most understudied area of incest research. The occurrence of mother-daughter incest focuses on the speculation that the mother is expressing deep-seated repressed homosexual feelings (Lidz and Lidz, 1969) or that, to avoid any further contact with her husband, she chooses to initiate sexual activity with the daughter as a prelude for future father-daughter incest. Since very little is known, however, about mother-daughter incest, speculation rather than empirical findings are the rule.

SIBLING INCEST

As a type of sexual abuse, sibling incest receives a lot less attention in the literature, in research, and in clinical practice than the two parent-child types of incest, despite the relatively high frequency of its occurrence. Although father-daughter incest is the most frequently reported type of incest (De Francis, 1969), sexual activity among siblings is believed by many to be the most frequently occurring type of incest (Weiner, 1964). Finkelhor (1979) found heterosexual and homosexual activity among siblings to be greater in occurrence than father-daughter incest.

Sibling incest may be defined as either heterosexual or homosexual activities among brothers and sisters that exceed allowable and normal developmental sexual play and experimentation. The reported types of sexual activities among siblings appear within the full range of sexual behaviors commonly reported in father-daughter and mother-son cases. Such sexual activity ranges from genital inspection and fondling to sexual intercourse and rape. Unlike the two types of parent-child incest, however, in discussing sibling incest, a differentiation is needed between normal allowable sexual activities which occur among and between brothers and sisters and sexual activities that are deemed inappropriate. To this end, attempts to define sibling incest have to take into account several important factors, such as: (1) the age of the children engaging in the sexual activity; (2) the intent of the sexual activity; (3) the duration of the sexual activity; and (4) the type of sexual behavior experienced by both siblings.

Age

The age of the siblings involved in the sexual activity will, to a large extent, determine the degree in which the sexual behavior is allowable or incestuous. The younger the children, generally speaking, the less stigma there is on sexual activities that would otherwise be defined incestuous. Child nudity, sleeping and bathing with siblings or parents, watching siblings or parents dress and undress, asking sex-related questions, exhibiting their genital areas, or masturbating in open view of other family members are permissible behaviors in a large number of families. Such behaviors are viewed by many parents and professionals as normal, healthy and developmental which the child will eventually refine. These same behaviors, however, exhibited by older children become less acceptable and are more likely to be stigmatized as incestuous. The determining incestuous criterion in this situation is not the type of behavior displayed but the age of the siblings participating in the behavior.

In cases of reported sibling incest, older children almost always initiate the act with younger children (May, 1978). Meiselman (1978) and Justice and Justice (1979) report that in cases where one sibling is substantially older than the other, the younger sibling often perceives the relationship and sexual activity as exploitive and unpleasant. In heterosexual incest between brother and sister, the older brother is often perceived by the younger sister as a father figure. The resulting feelings of the sister toward the sexual activity are more likely to resemble the feelings of a daughter in father-daughter cases. In reported cases of sibling incest where the ages of the participants were closer and where the incestuous act did not result in pregnancy, there appears to be little evidence of harmful effects to either of the participants.

Intent

The intent of the sexual activity between and among brothers and sisters is another critical factor in defining sexual behavior as developmentally appropriate and incestuous. Much of the sexual behavior which takes place among young children seems to be motivated primarily from natural curiosity. This behavior often occurs in the context of a game that is designed to provide children with a mutually permissible mechanism by which their sexual curiosity can be expressed. Both children freely participate, and the intent of the game is usually limited to playful examination and manipulation of body parts. The game "Doctor" is a good example of playful natural curiosity. In the game, one child play acts the role of a physician; the other, the role of a patient. Since the normal range of the doctor's actions usually requires an examination of the patient's body, the patient is usually required by the doctor to remove his/her clothing. The goal of the game is usually accomplished at this point, whereupon the patient redresses and then takes the turn of being the doctor. If discovered, the children will respond with feelings of shame and guilt. If the parents react too harshly, deep-seated feelings that sex is shameful, dirty and evil may be reinforced (May, 1978). These feelings may become so integrated into the perceptions of sex that they may be a lifelong problem.

Whereas most sex-related games played between siblings is natural curiosity with a willingness by both siblings to participate in the activity, in many cases of sibling incest the intent is exploitive or the participation of one sibling is usually by force or coercion. Finkelhor (1979) found that 30 percent of sibling incest identified in his study involved coercion in the form of force or the threat of force. Santiago (1973) reports an in-depth case history of one sister who expressed revulsion at her brothers. In her case, the sexual activity took place when two of her older brothers issued serious threats and made it clear that they intended the sexual contact to be humiliating to her. Meiselman (1978) describes the reactions of two sisters who were forced to have sexual intercourse with their brother as rape. In both of these instances, the sexual activity was neither of mutual interest nor mutual participation of all siblings involved.

The concepts of intent and mutual participation play an important role in determining the extent of the psychological trauma experienced by siblings in reported incest cases. In numerous case histories which appear in the literature, sisters very seldom express the disgust towards their brothers that daughters express towards their fathers (Eist and Mandel, 1968; Weinberg, 1955). Meiselman (1978) suggests that sisters are more likely than daughters to experience conscious sexual pleasure in the incestuous act. Such a response is not unlikely, in that more sisters than daughters mutually participate or even initiate the sexual activity (Weinberg, 1955).

Duration

Normal developmental sexual play between siblings is usually transient and common to a particular period of development. As children continue to mature and become more social, their sexual interests extend to members within their own peer group.

In cases of sibling incest and in particular brother-sister incest, the sexual activity may range from a few isolated incidents over a period of months to continual sexual activity over a period of years. In a case history presented by Santiago (1973), a sister had sexual relations with her younger brother for several years in childhood and early adolescence. In comparison to father-daughter incest, where daughters are often prevented from leaving the relationship, brother-sister incest is less enduring, unless the sister is genuinely cooperative.

Type

The type of sexual activity displayed by the siblings contributes substantially to the perceptions of the activity by parents and professionals as either normal and permissible or incestuous. As mentioned earlier, sexual abuse, like all other forms of child abuse and neglect, exists on a continuum of degree. When viewed on a continuum, sexual intercourse, anal intercourse, oral-genital intercourse, rape and sadomasochistic sexual behavior rank high on the list of unacceptable sibling sexual activity, usually without regard to the age of the children, intent or duration of the activity. In the same light, however, nudity, masturbation, genital fondling and inspection may be more acceptable types of sexual activities with regard to the age of the children, intent, and duration. It is clear that what may be acceptable sibling sexual activity in one circumstance may not be acceptable in another. Sexual activities between children which appear on the lower end of the continuum, then, are less likely to be stigmatized as incest. Activities which appear at the upper end of the continuum have a greater likelihood of being classified as incestuous.

An understanding of the causes of sibling incest requires an examination of three types of sexual activities among siblings: brother-sister, brother-brother, and sister-sister.

BROTHER-SISTER INCEST

Several types of families have been described in cases where brother-sister incest has occurred. It is suggested that unique characteristics of the family structure serve as catalysts for the escalation of normal sexual play between siblings into incest. In her case studies, Meiselman (1978) found in families where brother-sister incest occurred that children lacked adult supervision, particularly with regard to their sex play. In this family type, the father is either physically or symbolically absent (Weinberg, 1955). That is, he lacks the ability to control his adolescent son due to his own weak personality structure, alcoholism, or old age. When this occurs, the oldest son is often elevated to the role of "father" (Kubo, 1959). The ensuing sexual activities which occur with his sister are clinically comparable to actual father-daughter incest. The younger sister, victimized by her older brother, is left feeling guilty and exploited. In comparison, when siblings are more comparable chronological ages, the resulting feelings carry less psychological trauma.

Weinberg (1955) describes families in which brother-sister incest occurs as exhibiting little regard or concern for the children's sex play. In these families, parents speak openly about sex with their children and do little to prevent the children from seeing them engage in sexual intercourse. The sexual knowledge and overt stimulation is manifested in children attempting to replicate the adult sexual activity. As such, children involved in sexual intercourse may be simulating adult behavior.

In other families where brother-sister incest has occurred, the attitudes toward sex displayed by the parents follow a very fundamental, puritanical prohibition against any activity or discussion regarding the topic. In these households, information provided to the children presents nudity, masturbation, intercourse, and genital observation as dirty and unacceptable. Meiselman (1978) suggests that such attitudes only tend to increase rather than decrease the sexual curiosity of the children. Children engage in sexual activity as a result of the intense pressure to avoid all sexual contact and the intrigue surrounding such a delightfully "forbidden" subject.

In some families with brother-sister incest, incestuous experiences between the father and the daughter may have been occurring prior to or duing the initial stages of the brother-sister affair. Weinberg (1955) describes five cases of combined father-daughter and brother-sister incest where the daughter was engaged in sexual activities with her father prior to the incest with her brother. In this instance, the promiscuous behaviors of the sister led to the initiation of sex with her brother.

Raphling, Carpenter, and Davis (1967) also describe a family situation in which the father had engaged in sexual behavior with his daughter first and then encouraged his sons to do the same. Meiselman (1978) found father-daughter incest to be a precursor in eight cases of brother-sister incest.

BROTHER-BROTHER INCEST

Finkelhor (1979) found homosexual incest between brothers to occur almost as often as heterosexual incest between brothers and their sisters. Yet, despite the apparent frequency of the act, brother-brother incest is rarely reported and little is known about the behavior. With the few clinical reports cited in the literature, speculation exists that brother-brother incest results either from prior sexual stimulation by the father (Raybin, 1969) or homosexual interests between the brothers (Cory, 1963).

SISTER-SISTER INCEST

Similar to incest between brothers, sister-sister incest is a relative unknown in the field. Reported cases of incest between sisters is extremely rare. Two theories are offered as rationale for the absence of information on sister-sister incest. First, affection and physical contact between sisters is more acceptable and therefore carries less stigma and psychological trauma resulting in fewer actual cases reported. Second, incestuous activities between sisters is a rare occurrence and therefore relatively unreported in the literature. In either instance, little is known about sister-sister incest.

CHILD PORNOGRAPHY

Child pornography, also known as "kiddie porn" and "chicken porn," is often considered a more perverse form of sexual abuse. Child pornography is defined as films, photographs, magazines, books, and motion pictures which depict children under a certain age involved in sexually explicit acts, both heterosexual and homosexual (Densen-Gerber, 1980). According to Densen-Gerber, in 1977 there were at least 264 different magazines produced in America each month that depicted sexual acts among children and adults. In 1978, Congress passed legislation to amend the Mann Act, which makes illegal the use of children under age sixteen in the production of pornographic materials mailed or transported in interstate commerce.

Many of the more than one million American children who run away from home each year become involved in child pornography (U.S. House of Representatives, 1977). Often victims of physical or sexual abuse at home, these children seek an escape from the intolerable conditions of home life. From this population, adults who seek to exploit children in pornography are able to attract willing participants through the promise of food, money, shelter, drugs, etc. Other children exploited in pornography are recruited from the offender's own family or from other families (Lloyd, 1979). Parents are willing to sell their children for a few hours of work which may result in several hundred dollars profit.

The profile of the child pornographer is unlike the stereotyped image of the "dirty old man." The vast majority of adults who engage children in pornography may be parents who are drug addicts, pornographic performers themselves, prostitutes or, more frequently, parents having incestuous relationships with their children which they wish to memorialize in photographs or movies. Summit and Kryso (1978) suggest adults who engage in child pornography need to explore whatever is considered the most forbidden sexual activity. They want to record their achievements and put their fantasies into action; such activity seems to heighten the excitement.

CHILD PROSTITUTION

Child prostitution, sometimes referred to as "child sex for sale," is sexual abuse for profit. Children as young as seven years of age engage in sexual activities with adults or other minors without the threat of force. Child prostitution differs from other forms of sexual abuse due to the element of payment usually in the form of drugs, gifts, clothing, money, food, or other items. Historically, children have been used as objects for adult sexual gratification since antiquity (De Mause, 1974). Boy brothels existed in almost every city in Greece and Rome for adults who could not afford their own personal boy slave (Scott, 1976). In more recent times in the United States, peghouses were common in San Francisco in the late 1800s. Derived from a Midwest custom, boys were required to sit on greased wooden pegs to dilate their anuses (Bullough, 1976). Although outlawed in all fifty states, child prostitution today is clearly a vestige of our cultural history.

Children engage in prostitution for a variety of reasons. Like those involved in pornography, a substantial number of child prostitutes are runaways. Many leave homes to escape physical and/or sexual abuse, some because they are bored and unchallenged, still others because their families have become too distant and preoccupied. Runaways turn to prostitution for survival which ultimately will lead them to lives characterized by drug and alcohol abuse.

Although no one has counted, the number of girls and boys involved in prostitution is probably equal. Fisher (1982) suggests that there are differences between adolescent males and females involved in prostitution. Many males are gay-identified; most females are not. While most males are independent free-lance hustlers, most females have pimps or operate from massage parlors and escort services. Gay-identified males indicate they find prostitution exciting; non-gay-identified males and females indicate a strong dislike for the sexual activity. Whereas females prostitute for money and exhibit negative self-images, males often prostitute for excitement and adventure and view themselves and their activities as acceptable.

Densen-Gerber (1980) suggests that the buyers of "child sex for sale" are almost exclusively men from all classes and races. Many are married, although they often feel inadequate and are unable to meaningfully relate to peer sexual partners. Unresolved oedipal conflicts, along with attempts to gain power and control over the love object, result in using children for sexual self-gratification (Bavolek, 1984). Lloyd (1976) suggests that many adult male users of children describe their activity as a substitute father-son relationship. In this instance, adult users of children appear to be seeking in their relationship with the prostitute the love and affection lacking from their own developmental period with their parents.

CONCLUSION

A thorough examination of sexual abuse clearly suggests that the causes of the phenomenon are as varied as the act itself and as complex as the individuals perpetrating the act. It is clear that social, emotional, psychological and developmental factors all contribute an important role in the occurrence of sexual abuse. In many instances, sexual abuse is a learned behavior, the result of years of "teaching" children through observation, modeling and direct experiences to exploit others for sexual self-gain. In other instances, sexual abuse is a manifestation of an earlier developmental period of deprived appropriate parental touch and nurturing and restrictive healthy exploration and questioning of one's own sexual identity and sexuality. And, unlike other types of aberrant social behaviors, sexual abuse does not always involve the identification of an obvious "villian;" that is, an individual whom the victim or victims can emphatically demand punishment.

From a developmental perspective, punishment through incarceration of a perpetrator hardly seems intent on reconstructing the family, teaching appropriate family role responsibilities, or reducing the initial occurrence of sexual abuse. Yet, incarceration is a usual course of action for dealing with sexual abusers in many communities. Research has taught us that for some, excessive punishment is the only action that can be taken to protect the victim and others from continued abuse. However, for the vast majority of sexual abuse cases, education, treatment, and training do more to modify abusive behaviors than punishment.

It is generally assumed that the solution of most social problems lies in the examination of their etiologies. Within the context of this thought, work towards the reduction of child sexual abuse should be directed.

REFERENCES

Baker, S.: *Sexual Abuse of Children*. Mendocino, CA: Lawren, 1978.

Bavolek, S.: *A Handbook for Understanding Child Abuse and Neglect*. Roselle, IL: Schaumburg Publications, Family Development Assoc., 1984.

Berry, G.W.: Incest: Some clinical variations on a classical theme. *Journal of American Academy Psychoanalysis, 3*:151–161, 1975.

Brown, S.: Clinical illustrations of the sexual misuse of girls. *Child Welfare, 4*:435–442, 1979.

Bullough, V.L.: *Sexual Variance in Society and History*. New York, Wiley, 1976.

Burgess, A.W., and Holmstrom, L.L: Sexual trauma of children and adolescents: Sex, pressure, and secrecy. *Nursing Clinics of North America, 10*:551–563, 1975.

Burgess, A.W., and Holmstrom, L.L: The child and family in court process. In *Sexual Assault of Children and Adolescents*. Lexington, MA: Lexington Books, 1978.

Cory, D.W.: Homosexual incest. In Masters, R.E.L. (Ed.): *Patterns of Incest*. New York: Julian Press, 1963.

Costell, R.M.: The nature and treatment of male sex offenders. In *Sexual Abuse of Children: Selected Readings*. Washington, D.C.: U.S. Department of Health and Human Services, 1980.

De Francis, V.: *Protecting the Child Victim of Sex Crimes Committed by Adults*. Denver: American Humane Association, 1969.

De Mause, L.: *The History of Childhood: The Evolution of Parent-Child Relationships as a Factor in History*. London: Souvenir Press, 1974.

Densen-Gerber, J.: Child prostitution and child pornography: Medical, legal, and societal aspects of the commercial exploitation of children. In *Sexual Abuse of Children: Selected Readings*. Washington, D.C.: U.S. Department of Health and Human Services, 1980.

De Vine, R.A.: Incest: A review of the literature. In *Sexual Abuse of Children: Selected Readings*. Washington, D.C.: U.S. Department of Health and Human Services, 1980.

Eist, H.I., and Mandel, A.U.: Family treatment of ongoing incest behavior. *Family Process*, 7:216-232, 1968.

Finkelhor, D.: *Sexually Victimized Children*. New York: Free Press, 1979.

Fisher, B.: *Adolescent Prostitution: A Study of Sexual Exploitation, Etiological Factors, and Runaway Behavior with a Focus on Adolescent Male Prostitutes*. San Francisco: URSA, 1982.

Frances, V., and Frances, A.: The incest taboo and family structure. *Family Process*, 15:235-244, 1976.

Giaretto, H.: Humanistic treatment of father-daughter incest. In *Child Abuse and Neglect: The Family and the Community*. Cambridge, MA: Ballinger, 1976.

Hayman, C.R., and Lanza, C.: Sexual assault on women and girls. *American Journal of Obstetrics and Gynecology*, 109:480-486, 1971.

Jaffe, A.C., Dynneson, L., and ten Bensel, R.W.: Sexual abuse of children: An epidemiologic study. *American Journal of Disabled Children*, 129:689-692, 1975.

Justice, B., and Justice, R.: *The Broken Taboo*. New York: Human Sciences Press, 1979.

Kaufman, I., Peck, A.L., and Tagiuri, C.K.: The family constellation and overt incestuous relations between father and daughter. *American Journal of Orthopsychiatry*, 24:266-267, 1954.

Kubo, S.: Researches and studies on incest in Japan. *Hiroshima Journal of Medical Science*, 8:99-159, 1959.

Langsley, S.D., Schwartz, M.N., and Fairbairn, R.H.: Father-son incest. *Comprehensive Psychiatry*, 9:218-226, 1968.

Lidz, R.W., and Lidz, T.: Homosexual tendencies in mothers of schizophrenic women. *Journal of Nervous and Mental Disorders*, 149:229-235, 1969.

Lloyd, R.: *Boy Prostitution in America—For Money or Love?* New York: Vanguard, 1976.

Lloyd, R.: *Obscene But Not Forgotten*. McCann: New York, 1979.

Lukianowicz, N.: Incest. *British Journal of Psychiatry*, 120:301-313, 1972.

Luther, S.L., and Price, J.H.: Child sexual abuse: A review. *Journal of School Health*, 50:161-165, 1980.

Maisch, H.: *Incest*. Translated by C. Bearne. New York, Stein & Day, 1972.

Marcuse, M.: Incest. *American Journal of Urology*, 16:273-281, 1923.

May, G.: *Understanding Sexual Child Abuse*. Chicago: National Committee, 1978.

Medlicott, R.W.: Parent-child incest. *Australia and New Zealand Journal of Psychiatry*, 1:180-187, 1967.

Meiselman, K.C.: *Incest*. San Francisco: Jossey-Bass, 1978.

Molnar, G., and Cameron, P.: Incest syndromes: Observations in a general hospital psychiatric unit. *Canadian Psychiatric Association Journal*, 20:373-377, 1975.

Peters, J.J.: Children who were victims of sexual assault and the psychology of offenders. *American Journal of Psychotherapy*, 30:398-412, 1976.

Pittman, F.S.: Counseling incestuous families. *Medical Aspects of Human Sexuality*, (April):57-58, 1976.

Raphling, D.L., Carpenter, B.L., and Davis, A.: Incest: A genealogical study. *Archives of General Psychiatry*, 16:505-511, 1967.

Raybin, J.B.: Homosexual incest. *Journal of Nervous and Mental Disorders, 148*:105-110, 1969.

Roth, R.A.: *Child Sexual Abuse: Incest, Assault and Sexual Exploitation.* Washington, D.C.: National Center, 1978.

Santiago, L.P.: *The Children of Oedipus: Brother-Sister Incest in Psychiatry Literature, History, and Mythology.* Roslyn Heights, NY: Libra, 1974.

Sarles, R.M.: Incest. *Pediatric Clinics of North America, 22*:633-642, 1975.

Scott, G.R.: *A History of Prostitution.* London: Laurie, 1976.

Spencer, J.: Father-daughter incest: A clinical view from the corrections field. *Child Welfare, 11*:581-590, 1978.

Summit, R., and Kryso, J.: Sexual abuse of children: A clinical spectrum. *American Journal of Orthopsychiatry, 48*:237-251, 1978.

Swanson, D.: Adult sexual abuse of children. *Disorders of the Nervous System, 29*:677-683, 1968.

Tormes, Y.N.: *Child Victims of Incest.* Denver: American Humane Association, 1968. U.S. House of Representatives, Committee on Judiciary, Subcommittee on Crime. Hearing: March 8, 1977.

Wahl, C.W.: The psychodynamics of consummated material incest: A report of two cases. *Archives of General Psychiatry, 3*:188-193, 1960.

Weinberg, S.K.: *Incest Behavior.* New York: Citadel, 1955.

Weiner, I.B.: On incest: A survey. *Excerpta Criminology, 4*:137-155, 1964.

Weiss, J., Rogers, S., Darwin, P., and Dulton, J.: A study of girl sex victims. *Psychiatry Quarterly, 29*:1-27, 1955.

Williams, B.G.: Myths and sexual child abuse: Identification and elimination. *The School Counselor, 11*:103-110, 1981.

CHAPTER 7

THE IMPACT OF MALTREATMENT
ON THE DEVELOPING CHILD

Spyros Monopolis and Richard M. Sarles

INTRODUCTION

There is little doubt that physical and sexual abuse of children is all too common. There is also little doubt that such abuse evokes public outrage and substantial professional concern. Such responses by professional and lay groups are often tainted by an "apple pie and motherhood" motif, that is, abuse cannot be good for children. The scientific and commercial literature have, with ever-increasing frequency and number, attempted to document and verify this hypothesis that abuse of children is detrimental to their optimal growth and development.

This view is shared with strong conviction by the authors of this chapter. Clinical experience has proven time after time that exploitative physical and/or sexual abuse may be a powerful contribution to major psychiatric and psychosocial behavioral disturbances. To believe otherwise appears antithetical to all accepted theories of human development.

Previous chapters acknowledge that there are multiple variations in the spectrum of child abuse, which include: emotional and nutritional deprivation; inadequate care; emotional neglect; and physical, emotional and sexual abuse. In order to adequately address this broad spectrum of abuse, we have chosen to use the term "maltreatment syndrome" (Fontana, 1973). The phenomenon of child maltreatment has a complex multifactorial etiology and medical, psychological, social, educational, as well as legal implications. Yet, the existing unitary theories appear to be inadequate in gaining a better understanding of the problem and consequently developing more effective prevention and treatment services. Various investigators therefore have developed more comprehensive theories in order to address the individual, family, and societal parameters (Garbarino, 1975; Newberger

100

et al. 1977; Starr, 1978) or an ecologic theory in order to help organize the multiple and complex variables (Bittner and Newberger, 1981).

Unfortunately, well-controlled studies of the various emotional, cognitive, and social consequences of child maltreatment on the victim are lacking. The existing case reports, empirical studies, or data on small groups of children are usually limited in scope, focus on rather brief periods of time, and commonly do not have control groups. Newberger et al. (1983) point out that the available studies usually have small sample size, employ imprecise definitions, show inadequate matching between study and control groups, and usually their conceptual framework is limited to the psychodynamic theory. Consequently, these reports are frequently difficult to interpret, compare, or generalize. These factors become more impressive and worrisome when one attempts to explore and classify the impact of child maltreatment according to its forms (emotional abuse or neglect, emotional or nutritional deprivation, inadequate care, physical or sexual abuse), or its relationship to time consequences (acute/ short term, chronic/long term), or the various stages of child development at the time of the occurrence of maltreatment (infancy, preschool, latency, adolescence). In addition, the environment in which the maltreatment took place (natural home, foster home, relatives' home; institution; chaotic, noncaring, "sick," violent family or reasonably well-functioning, caring, supportive family) further confounds the problem.

It is difficult to distinguish the impact of maltreatment per se from the impact of other concomitant factors such as parental psychopathology, chaotic family environment, unemployment or job instability, low socioeconomic factors, high mobility, drug and alcohol abuse, and divorce (Martin, 1976a). Also, the equipment of the child, such as individual differences in behavior (Brazelton, 1973) and temperament (Alexander et al., 1958), inherent strength of basic drives (Freud, 1937/1964a), variations in the capacity to adapt to the environment and intelligence (Martin, 1976a), plays a role in the subsequent development of children who have been abused.

In this chapter we will focus primarily on the direct impact of maltreatment of the developing child. Our goal is to examine and review the scientific literature concerning physical and sexual abuse of children and adolescents. We will try to critically evaluate the professional literature in an objective fashion in the hopes of providing substance to our clinical belief and experience that abuse is detrimental rather than an "apple pie and motherhood" mentality.

Impact of Neglect

Parental neglect in the form of deprivation (physical or emotional), inadequate care (psychological, physical, medical, educational, social), separation, or malnutrition has been the focus of many studies. Most authors agree on the wide range of implications of neglect on the physical, psychological and social development of children.

Brenneman (1932), Bakwin (1942), and Ribble (1943) wrote about the child's need for maternal stimulation, the loneliness of children deprived for their mothers and the correlation of effects of hospitalization to inadequate mothering. Spitz (1945), Goldfarb (1945), Spitz and Wolf (1946), and Bakwin (1949) suggested that deprivation of mothering in institutions may be related to behavior problems, neurologic disturbances, mental retardation, or even death.

Bowlby (1951) emphasized the crucial importance of maternal deprivation on the mental health of the child. The lack of loving care, warmth, intimacy, and a continuous relationship with the mother (or permanent mother-substitute) has ill effects on the child's development. Partial deprivation leads to anxiety, feelings of revenge, guilt, depression, disturbance of psychic organization, neurosis, and instability of character. Complete deprivation has even a more deleterious impact on personality development, leading to an inability to form relationships.

Coleman and Provence (1957) and Prugh and Harlow (1962) emphasized that "masked deprivation" (significant maternal deprivation in children living with their family of origin) has a severe impact on the development of the child. Yarrow (1961) indicated that "deviant maternal care" may occur in cases of hospitalization, maternal separation, multiple mothering, or distortions in the mother-child relationship (all of which can be observed in child maltreatment). Furthermore, "psychological malnutrition" as exemplified by high-strung authoritarian parenting and inadequate approval of children shows a significant correlation with behavior problems such as later school failure, truancy, stealing, and destructiveness (Talbot, 1963). The adequacy of mothering seems to be more important than the physical abuse per se. Abused children who experience adequate parenting do better than those who suffer from emotional neglect as well. This adequate parenting may be a "most important parameter of the abusive home in terms of making prognostic statements and planning treatment" (Martin, 1976a).

Failure to thrive (Martin, 1972; Martin and Beezley, 1974), undernutrition (Elmer, 1967; Birrell and Birrell, 1968), symptoms of neglect such as poor hygiene, inadequate well-baby care, and insufficient care for illness (Gregg and Elmer, 1969) have been frequently encountered among abused children.

Various authors have emphasized the significant impact of undernutrition, poverty, poor medical care, chaotic family environment, and socioeconomic level of the family. On the development of perception, language, memory, thinking and learning (Hurley, 1969; Wortis, 1970a; Wortis, 1970b; Birch and Gussow, 1970; Drillien, 1964; Werner et al., 1967), it has also been pointed out that several factors such as failure to thrive (Martin and Beezley, 1974), maternal deprivation (Rutter, 1974), the emotional milieu of the child (Martin, 1976a), the abusive environment (Baron et al., 1970), and their own families (Coleman and Provence, 1957) may contribute, predispose, or cause the neurologic impairment of abused children.

Impact of Physical Abuse

The concepts presented in this section refer to either physical abuse or abuse in general. These two terms are used interchangeably, reflecting their customary use in the literature ("abuse" connoting "physical abuse") and also that the prototype of the impact of physical abuse applies by and large to most types of maltreatment.

The impact of physical abuse on the developing child has been extensively studied. It appears to be multidimensional and may present with psychological components, behavioral patterns and personality characteristics, cognitive aspects, and neurological consequences.

Abused children may present with psychological impairment, behavioral problems, disturbed emotional-cognitive-social development and physical disabilities. In many cases early disturbances may complicate further development in later childhood and adolescence or even adulthood in the form of personal dysfunction and interpersonal difficulties. Psychopathology is not uncommon.

Psychological Components of Physical Abuse

Green (1983) considers the actual or threatened acute physical or psychological assault as equivalent to a *traumatic neurosis*, often accompanied by ego disorganization/regression, narcissistic injury, a painful affective state, primary defense mechanisms, compulsion to repeat the trauma, severe panic, and a feeling of helplessness. The trauma induced by the abuse is consistent with Freud's concept of traumatic neurosis and the breaching of the stimulus barrier of the child (Freud, 1920/1955; Freud, 1926/1959). Furthermore, a review of the "diagnostic features" of child maltreatment reveals the wide spectrum of its impact on the child. Green (1983) suggested that in most cases of child abuse the DSM-III* criteria for *post-traumatic stress disorder* are satisfied:

1. A recognizable stressor (the short- and long-term results of abuse).
2. Re-experiencing of the trauma is observed (recurrent dreams and intrusive recollections of the abusive experience).
3. Reduced involvement with the external world is noted (constriction of affect, detachment).
4. Traumatic symptoms-consequences of the abuse are clinically evi-

dent (e.g. disturbance of sleep, hypervigilance, avoidance of situations or activities which may lead to exaggeration of symptoms of repetition of the trauma, e.g. they tend to exhibit phobic, pain-dependent or hyperaggressive behavior in situations that resemble or symbolize the abuse).

Other authors also emphasize the traumatic nature of the maltreatment. Kris (1956) suggests that the actual physical assault with the inherent threat of destruction and/or abandonment may be perceived by the abused child as an overwhelming trauma, as a "shock" trauma. Khan (1963) argues that the inadequacy of maternal care, the scapegoating, the underlying harsh and punitive parenting, and the eventual neurological damage from physical abuse would be the components of a "strain" or "cumulative" trauma.

According to Green (1983), the following *primitive defense mechanisms* can be observed among abused children: avoidance, distancing behavior, raising of sensory thresholds, denial, projection and splitting. These defenses are reinforced by the denial of the abusive episodes by the parents, threats of additional punishment, the child's effort to protect himself, and the fear of retaliation or annihilation if the child would acknowledge the reality of the situation.

It is hypothesized that the use of denial, projection, and splitting allows the child to maintain a "good parent" fantasy, in that the parental malevolence is projected and displaced onto others or onto the child himself. The latter experiences splitting of self-representation into "good" and "bad" parts which seems similar to the adult borderline personality organization (Kernberg, 1975). Abused children frequently avoid eye contact, may exhibit "frozen watchfulness" (sitting passively and immobile but alert and hypervigilant so as to watch for any danger) (Ounstead et al., 1974), or avoid their parents (George and Main, 1979). Green (1983) suggested that these behaviors may be precursors of denial, projection, and splitting observed in some of these children in later childhood.

Abused children may show a tendency for *repetition of the trauma* in dreams, fantasies, play, and object relationships. They may act either as helpless and overwhelmed passive victims or actively repeat the original traumatic experience by assuming an active, aggressive role in fantasy or play with peers. Other evidences of this repetition may be seen through self-destructive activity, through behavior that may provoke attack, or through accident-proneness (Green, 1983). This situation resembles Freud's concept of "fixation to trauma" (1939). Green (1983) suggests that this may be viewed as a primitive defense mechanism with an adaptive quality. Through this, the child may actively master a passive dangerous situation. Greenacre (1967) sees the repetition compulsion as a defense for survival.

Impaired self-concepts, depressive affect or self-destructive behavior may be frequently encountered among abused children. These situations may be secondary to the child's scapegoating, which induces self-blame and the feeling that he deserves the punishment. Projection or externalization may be manifested by some scapegoated abused children. Also, it is not uncommon to observe isolation, denial or gradual constriction and numbing of affect (Green, 1983). Johnson and Morse (1968) found that abused children were unresponsive, negativistic, stubborn, and depressed. Goldston (1965) noticed that they were apathetic, unappealing, fearful, with a poor appetite and a blunting for human contact. Green (1968) reported that physically abused schizophrenic children showed a high incidence of self-mutilation. He also suggested that the impact of child maltreatment refers to ego functions, identifications, cognitive functions, object relationships, and libidinal organization. Abused children show: low frustration tolerance, impulsivity, suspiciousness and mistrust of adults, tendency to control, manipulate and exploit objects, need for immediate gratification, exaggerated aggression, preference to use motor activity for expression, tendency to provoke others, violent fantasies, pseudoindependence, and precocious achievements in some areas. Fear, feelings of worthlessness, helplessness, depression, self-reproach, "bad" self-image, and a sense of guilt are common. Aggressive fantasies and activities represent defenses against these painful states. The anger toward the abusing adult is displaced on others such as teachers, peers and siblings or against themselves as suicidal behavior. Further punishment and rejection by adults follow these behaviors and a vicious cycle ensues with repetition of the original trauma. Galdston (1971) described *violent behavior* among boys who had been abused which was unpremeditated, purposeless and unpredictable, whereas girls appeared to be more withdrawn and involved in autoerotic activities. Abused children appear to have marked difficulty with *impulse control* and the *control of anger* (Elmer et al., 1971). Sandgrund et al. (1974) found that abused children exhibited problems with impulse control, body image, reality testing, thought processes, defenses, object relations, and overall ego competency. Low self-esteem was frequent and often accompanied by self-destructive behavior. Although in most cases the above abnormalities represented the impact of the emotional and physical trauma on the normal development of the child's adaptive ego functions, in some situations the defects preceded or even precipitated or contributed to the abuse.

According to Green (1980), adolescence plays a significant role in the psychosocial development of the abused child. On the one hand, the impact of the traumatic experiences interferes with the developmental tasks of adolescence, and adolescence itself may further aggravate the vulnerability of the abused child. Low self-esteem, chronic anger, fear and distrust of adults, and pathological identification with violent parental models disrupts individual development and future relationships with others. *"Acting-out" behavior* is enhanced resulting in assaultive, antisocial, delinquent acts and self-destructive or suicidal behavior. The latter is the manifestation of the abused children's *self-perception as victims* which may be a reflection of parental wishes for the child's disappearance or destruction (Green, 1983). According to Sabbeth (1969), this may be a significant etiological factor in adolescent *suicide*. Chaotic sexual behavior is frequently seen among girls. Cognitive impairment continues and academic performance deteriorates, not infrequently resulting in dropping out of school. Pathological object relationships result in further deterioration of the psychosocial adjustment of adolescents (Green, 1980).

The stage of basic trust (Erikson, 1950) is often not achieved, and abused children frequently become involved in *abusive adolescent relationships*, repeating the traumatic experiences of their childhoods and thus maintaining their roles as "victims." Martin (1972) noted that abused children lack basic trust, tend to be loners, are shallow and suspicious, have poor peer relationships and may perpetuate the abusive behavior as adults. Dyadic relationships follow the "angry parent/bad child" model. Human relationships are perceived as interactions between aggressors and victims. In this fashion, violence among adolescent victims of maltreatment is an *adaptive coping mechanism* in the context of a threatening and dangerous world.

Chronic abuse may lead to the development of *primary identification with the aggressor, impaired impulse control, and a proneness toward violence*. The fears of helplessness and annihilation induced by the traumatic experience are replaced by a sense of power and omnipotence when the abused child identifies with the aggressor. The same mechanism may also represent a displacement of the child's rage toward the abusive parent, as well as means for counteracting painful affects and relieving tension. Furthermore, the imitation of parental impulsive and aggressive attitudes may eventually lead to aggressive and assaultive behavior as the main way for object relationships (Green, 1983). Alfaro (1973, 1977) found that 10 to 30 percent of victims of maltreatment showed juvenile misconduct, Steele (1970) stated that abused children tend to exhibit juvenile delinquency, and Schmitt and Kempe (1975) indicated that in cases without treatment abused children tended to become "juvenile delinquents and murders, as well as the batterers of the next generation. Duncan (1958), Satten et al. (1960), and Tanay (1969) have also suggested a relationship between child abuse and subsequent violent behavior.

Parke and Collmer (1975) believe that children who have grown up in an abusive and violent environment have an increased tendency to become *abusive parents and spouses*. Sarles' (1976) argument is that if violence in the home is viewed by the child as a method of problem solving, the child may then incorporate this value. Also, the mechanism of identification with the aggressor (the parent who is also a model for the child's superego formation) seems to play a significant role in this context (Steele, 1970). When abused adolescents become parents, they are likely to continue the vicious cylce of maltreatment toward their own children by identifying with their own abusive parents and projecting onto their children their own deficiencies, incompetence, and unmet gratification needs (Green, 1980). Other authors have also reported that abusive parents tend to present with a history of emotional or physical abuse or neglect (Steele and Pollock, 1974; Holter and Friedman, 1968a; Melnick and Hurley, 1969; Wasserman, 1967). Oliver and Taylor (1971) reported the multiple case of five generations of abused children in one family pedigree.

It appears that abusive parents repeated the abusive (parenting) attitudes, behavior and methods they were exposed to when they were growing up. This is compatible with the notion that parents often parent as they were parented (Sarles, 1976) and that "violence breeds violence" (Silver et al., 1969).

Behavioral Patterns and Personality Development of Maltreated Children

Yates (1981) in an elaborate study of fifty abused children two weeks to six years of age observed three distinct patterns of behavior: (A) *Destructive children* (they destroyed property, disobeyed rules, were assaultive toward other children; their ego functions were limited; they reacted to their parents with recriminations, screams, or violent affection; some were restless and hyperactive; they showed overt identification with the aggressor; not infrequently they elicited abusive fantasies in their caretakers; most of them were boys; subsequent abuse, repetitive problems in foster homes, failures at school, and legal involvement occurred more frequently in this group; enuresis, extreme restlessness, cruelty to animals and children, fire setting, and vandalism were also observed; they exhibited poor peer relationships, as well as paranoid, borderline, or overly depressive features). (B) *Frightened children* (most of them were girls; initially they appeared passive, withdrawn, anxious; they avoided contact, they seemed compliant, and remained in bed; they were fussy, obstinate, compulsive stealers, picky eaters; deficiencies in ego functions, growth, speech, cognition were less pronounced than those in group A; they were less restless than group A; they had underlying identification with the aggressor; they also exhibited borderline, paranoid or depressive features; they were perceived as "hyperactive" because of underachievement, attention deficit and immaturity). Other authors reached comparable conclusions (Martin and Beezley, 1974; Martin, 1976a). (C) *Private children* (the children of this group were pleasing, attractive and appeared very bright; on the other hand they were manipulative and had poor peer relationships; in some areas they exhibited precocious ego functions, while in others (e.g. object relations) they exhibited serious defects; some cognitive skills were very advanced, they did well at school, they adapted well in foster homes, and they showed good impulse control, attention span, ability to tolerate frustration and to sublimate in autonomous functions; they demonstrated lack of separation anxiety, mild behavior problems, and had no transitional object; they seemed to be able to predict the behaviors of adults toward them, and their reactions to parents were guided by their parents' needs as opposed to their own; their internal emptiness was masked by their precocity and charm; their obeying rules and pleasing adults was an adaptive mechanism toward an environment perceived as threatening; their ego appeared "fluid" and there was an "as-if" quality of the self; they either did not value relationships or the latter had no affectual significance for them.

In a follow-up study of fifty-eight abused children six to thirteen years old, more than half showed an impaired capacity to enjoy life, exhibited psychiatric symptomatology (enuresis, tantrums, hyperactivity, bizarre behavior) or had a low-self-esteem, school difficulties, withdrawal, opposition, hypervigilance, compulsivity, or pseudomature behavior (Martin and Beezley, 1976). These authors also noted several interesting factors: school learning problems and psychiatric manifestations were observed frequently in the same child; neither the age of the onset of abuse nor the type of injury inflicted on the children appeared to correlate with the observed behavior; the environment of the child after the abuse seemed to have a significant correlation with the current functioning of the child, in that the extent of psychopathology was related to the instability and impermanence of the child's current home. Consequently, the authors emphasized that "events and parental behavior after the incident of abuse play an important role in psychopathology and personality development of abused children." These authors suggested that the physical abuse itself is less significant in regard to adverse developmental effects as compared to deprivation, rejection, chaotic environment, unrealistic expectations and distorted perceptions by parents, separation, hospitalization, foster home placement and frequent changes of living environment. Finally, Martin and Beezley argued that abused children show a variety of personality traits and act as "chameleon" in their attempt to adjust to various situations and environments. Their behaviors may be a developmental delay, a problem, a distortion, a symptom, an adaptive/coping mechanism, or a combination of these.

Cognitive Aspects of Physical Abuse

Other consequences of abuse may be a *compromised ability for learning.* Many authors have noted increased incidence of mental retardation among abused children from 20 to 60 percent (Sandgrund et al., 1974; Martin and Beezley, 1974; Morse et al., 1970; Martin and Rodeheffer, 1976; Elmer and Gregg, 1967; Gregg and Elmer, 1969; Martin, 1972; Gil, 1970). Quite frequently, it is difficult to ascertain whether the mental deficit preceded the abuse, whether the abuse was responsible for mental deterioration, or whether the impaired mental ability was secondary to the abuse. In the latter, physical abuse may lead to cerebral damage resulting in mental deficiency. Conversely, various "psychosocial impediments" may contribute to the possibility of mental retardation: unpredictable, non-nurturing environment; reduced opportunities for learning; impaired stimulation; inadequate support; preoccupation with fears, anxiety, fantasy world; mental energies focused on survival; danger of age-appropriate performance and non-performance (Martin and Rodeheffer, 1976; Martin, 1976a).

Martin and Beezley (1974), on the other hand, state that some abused children demonstrate above-average or even superior intelligence, explaining this phenomenon as the children's need to acquire information, to be perceived as capable, and to sublimate their aggressive and libidinal drives into learning.

Neurological Sequelae of Physical Abuse

Various authors have noticed a variety of neurological signs among abused children: these included spasticity, paresis, impaired cranial nerve function, paraplegia, focal signs, deficiency in proprioceptive, tactile, kinesthetic or haptic perception, blindness, hyperactivity, dysparaxia, delay in motor skill acquisition, gross or fine motor incoordination, hyperreflexia, exaggerated startle response, and increased muscle tone. In some cases, the neurological deficits were related to the physical abuse; in others there was no history of head trauma. Often, it is difficult to ascertain whether neurologic disturbance exists prior to the abuse (congenital). Green (1983) noted that children with neurological impairment are more vulnerable to the traumatic impact of physical abuse. He argued that the CNS dysfunction interferes with the cognitive, adaptive, and defensive functions of the ego and therefore makes it more difficult for the child to respond to the traumatic experience. Martin (1976) stated that 20 to 50 percent of physically abused children would be expected to have a "significant impairment of neurological function."

The abused children's *inhibitions of speech and motility* may be a consequence of learned avoidance (to protect themselves from further abuse) (Green, 1983) or may be an adaptation to the abusive environment (Martin, 1976b). This phenomenon would be in accordance with A. Freud's (1971) concept that certain ego functions of children are inhibited as an adaptive mechanism in the face of external danger. The observed speech and language disorders consist of delayed speech development and/or problems in articulation and expression. Problems of motor development consist of motor clumsiness (Kempe, 1976), transitory, reversible disorders in body tone, coordination and reflexes (Martin, 1976b), and inhibition of age-appropriate motor acts (e.g. crawling, walking, reaching, "getting into things") (Green, 1983). Language retardation was also reported by Martin (1972) and Smith and Hanson (1974). Blager and Martin (1976) found that younger abused children demonstrated more striking delays and deficits in speech and language, while older children had learned substantive but not communicative language. The former could be possibly explained by the inadequate stimulation of language and/or adaptation to the abusive environment. The latter could be understood in the context of not having a significant adult role model and/or a dangerous environment for risk taking (Gray and Wise, 1959; Mysak, 1966).

Neurologic dysfunction or damage relate to emotional growth and development. Psychiatric disturbances show a significant relationship with organic brain disorders (Rutter et al., 1970). Since defense mechanisms, impulse control and social behavior, as well as psycholinguistic abilities and perceptual awareness, rely upon the intactness and maturation of the central nervous system, some of the developmental disturbances of abused children may be related to neurologic impairment as opposed to noxious environmental factors (Martin, 1976).

IMPACT OF ABUSE IN SPECIAL SITUATIONS

The effect of maltreatment on infants is an area of recent interest. Unfortunately, most of the available studies suffer from the lack of control groups. Kempe (1976) found that abused infants less than six months of age were irritable, had a high-pitched cry, were hard to satisfy, had difficulties with feeding, and showed motor and social developmental delays. Between six and twelve months of age their social responsiveness was impaired, they did not exhibit separation anxiety, and they showed "frozen watchfulness" (intense scanning of the environment with parallel immobility and motor passivity). Gaensbauer and Sands (1979) observed affective and social withdrawal, unpredictable and shallow affective expression, diminished ability for pleasure, proneness toward sadness, distress, anger, and weak attachment to caregivers.

In a controlled study, George and Main (1979) made similar observations in abused infants and toddlers. Children one to three years of age harassed their caregivers and threatened to assault or did assault them and were less likely to respond to their friendly overtures. Evidence indicates that the attachment of the abused child to his mother is seriously compromised; this fact may explain the notorious difficulties of abused children adjusting to various caregivers such as foster parents, institutional staff, and teachers (Green, 1980).

Children with various conditions (e.g. unwanted; having physical problems such as prematurity, birth defects, serious illness or physical handicap; exhibiting behavioral and/or emotional disturbances such as being irritable, demanding, never sleeping, always crying, having colic, showing teething problems, having difficulties with toilet training, being hyperactive, showing slow development, suffering from mental retardation or even being extremely bright) appear to be in higher risk for abuse. Therefore, the impact of maltreatment is more severe (Kempe and Helfer, 1972; Holter and Friedman, 1968a; Wasserman, 1967; Smith et al., 1973; Sarles, 1976). An additional aggravating factor is the fact that these children have to deal and cope with a situation which is perceived as unacceptable by their environment or a handicapping condition. These "special," "different" children are clearly vulnerable to the usual vicissitudes of psychosocial development in the context of the average home and even more so in an abusive home.

Another issue of great significance for the development of the abused children is the impact of the *primary effects of maltreatment*, such as physical injuries and disabilities, malnutrition and illness, neurological damage, intellectual dysfunction, behavioral disorders and emotional disturbances (*secondary impact of maltreatment*). In most of those situations the available data (clinical empirical, and research) are limited.

IMPACT OF SEXUAL ABUSE

Sexual Abuse in General

Although the sexual abuse of minors has always been known, only recently has it started to draw the serious attention of health professionals, child protective and social services, the legal system, the press, and society at large.

The impact of sexual abuse on the developing child has been the focus of many studies. It appears that the majority of authors recognize the occurrence of both short- and long-term ill effects that may range from adjustment reactions, to somatic symptoms, to overt psychopathology, to serious developmental disturbances, and deleterious socioeducational sequelae.

The evaluation of the consequences of sexual abuse on children is difficult due to a variety of reasons. Sexual abuse and physical abuse often coexist. Thomas (1968) found a high frequency of paternal violence (65%) directed toward family members in cases of incest. DeFrancis (1969) noted coexistence of neglect (79%) and/or physical abuse (11%) among sexually abused children, and Martin (1976a) described the coexistence of sexual and physical abuse in preadolescent and adolescent girls.

The multifactorial etiology of sexual abuse is another major consideration in the assessment of its impact: relationship to the perpetrator, the nature of the sexual activity (genital manipulation, exhibitionism, sexual play, masturbation, fellatio, intercourse, etc.), conditions of the sexual contact, the use of force, the age difference between perpetrator and child, the child's resistance of compliance, perception of the sexual abuse by the child, the presence of physical injury, the age and developmental stage of the child, the pretraumatic level of adjustment and functioning of the child, the affective nature of the abusive relationship, the use of threat by the perpetrator, the collusion and non-protectiveness by mother, as well as the type of the sexual abuse (isolated-extrafamilial, isolated-intrafamilial, short term, long term) (Mrazek and Mrazek, 1981; Sarles, 1981).

In addition, studies on the impact of child sexual abuse have serious methodological problems, such as lack of control groups, unclear definition of "child sexual abuse," compilation of cases as opposed to research groups, lack of follow-up, biased selection of study groups, retrospective studies depending on recollection of past events, single case reports with a tendency to generalize conclusions, use of non-standardized psychiatric interviews, court reports, material from therapy sessions, agency reports, and non-specific and global assessment of adjustment (Mrazek and Mrazek, 1981).

A further serious concern is whether sexual abuse of children is causally related to later disturbances in development or whether these children were already presenting with various problems.

In this context the majority of the available literature must be reviewed with caution and the various consequences of child sexual abuse considered as tentative or possible (Mrazek and Mrazek, 1981). Furthermore, Sarles (1981) suggested that our understanding of child sexual abuse is based primarily on the more seriously disturbed cases, that the incidence of psychological disorders among all victims of incest is unknown, and the impact of family dysfunction, alcoholism, and physical abuse complicate the effects of sexual abuse.

Short-Term Impact of Sexual Abuse

Several papers in the literature proposed that there is *little or no evidence of harmful effects of sexual abuse of children*: Rasmussen (1934) suggested good adjustment on the part of children; Bender and Blau (1937) stated that sexual abuse may be psychologically harmless; Rascovsky and Rascovsky (1950) found no evidence of damage; Bender and Grugett (1952) stated that there was no need for correction or attention; Kinsey et al. (1953) argued that such experiences contributed favorably to psychosexual development; Yorukoglu and Kemph (1966) found that children were not severely damaged; Burton (1968) reported no particular detrimental effects; and Gibbens and Prince (1963) and Lempp (1979) found lack of subsequent disturbance.

However, many other authors reported *a variety of ill effects.* Various *psychological and behavioral manifestations* were described: regressive symptoms (thumbsucking, nailbiting, enuresis, encopresis) (Green, 1980), sleep problems including nightmares (Peters, 1976), fears and phobias (Sarles, 1981), anxiety states and acute anxiety neuroses (Bender and Blau, 1937; Meiselman, 1978), loss of self-esteem, pessimistic or callous attitude (Bender and Blau, 1937), guilt or shame (DeFrancis, 1969; Rosenfeld et al., 1977), depression (Ferenczi, 1932/1949; Kaufman et al., 1954; Nakashima and Zakus, 1977), suicidal ideation (Forbes, 1972; Mehta et al., 1979), impulsive, self-damaging behavior (Dixon et al., 1978), tendency to withdraw from activities of normal childhood (Bender and Blau, 1937), various behavior problems and delinquency (Maisch, 1972; Nakashima and Zakus, 1977), facade of maturity and capacity for responsibility (Kaufman et al., 1954), character disorder (Maisch, 1972), and obesity (Meiselman, 1978). In the area of *interpersonal relationships,* sexually abused children were frightened by contact with adults (Kinsey et al., 1953; Peters, 1976), showed increased seeking of affection from adults (Burton, 1968), developed hostile, dependent relationships with older women (Kaufman et al., 1954), demonstrated bewilderment in regard to social relations (Bender and Blau, 1937), were shocked by parental reaction to the discovery of the assault (Landis, 1956), ran away from home (Kaufman et al., 1954; Browning and Boatman, 1977), and had homicidal ideation (Dixon et al., 1978). Sexually abused children showed also *disturbance in their psychosexual development*: increased masturbatory activity (Isaacs, 1933; in Mrazek and Mrazek, 1981) rush into heterosexual activities (Moses, 1932—reported by Mrazek and Mrazek, 1981), prostitution (James and Myerding, 1977), homosexuality (Kaufman et al., 1954; Heims and Kaufman, 1963; Meiselman, 1978), pregnancy (Mehta et al., 1979), promiscuity, molestation of younger children (Meiselman, 1978), impaired feminine identification (Heims and Kaufman, 1963), desperation secondary to the inability to control sexual urges (Bender and Blau, 1937), and purposeless and non-enjoyable sexual acting out (Rabinovitch, 1952–1953; Kaufman et al., 1954). *School problems* have also been reported among sexually abused children: truancy (Peters, 1976), learning disorders (Kaufman et al., 1954; Browning and Boatman, 1977), and mental retardation (Bender and Blau, 1937).

Long-Term Impact of Sexual Abuse

According to some authors, sexual abuse may induce *no long-term effects*: Lukianowicz (1972) reported normal development among victims of sexual abuse without neurotic, psychotic or personality disorders; the same author and Meiselman (1978) found no sexual problems; Raskovsky and Raskovsky (1950) suggested that the sexual abuse experience may reduce the possibility of psychosis in seriously depressed persons.

However, other authors described some of the short-term effects of child sexual abuse becoming chronic but also other problems developing. The following *psychological and behavioral disturbances* have been reported: non-integrated identity (Katan, 1973), neurosis (Meiselman, 1978), chronic depression (Weiner, 1964; Rosenfeld et al., 1977), low self-esteem and sense of helplessness (Steele and Alexander, 1981), psychosis/schizophrenia (Barry, 1965; Peters, 1976), suicidal ideation (Rhinehart, 1961), homicide (Brown, 1963), character disorder (Lewis and Sarrell, 1969; Lukianowicz, 1972), masochism (Meiselman, 1978), somatic symptomatology (Goodwin and DiVasto, 1979; Meiselman, 1978), and obesity (Meiselman, 1978). *Interpersonal relationships* can also be affected on a chronic basis: social isolation and difficulty in establishing close human relationships (Steele and Alexander, 1981), fear of or conflict with sex partner or husband (Meiselman, 1978), and conflict with parents or in-laws (Herman and Hirschman, 1977). There are also various references to the long-term effects of sexual abuse on *psychosexual adjustment*: problematic sexual relationships (Rosenfeld et al., 1977), various sexual dysfunctions (Lukianowicz, 1972), prostitution (Flugel, 1953; James and Meyerding, 1977), sexual molestation of children (Raphling et al., 1967; Reichenthal, 1979), aversion to sexual activity (Greenland, 1958; Magal and Winnik, 1968), illegitimate pregnancies (Malmquist et al., 1966), homosexuality (Medlicott, 1967; Gundlach, 1977), involvement with other incestuous relationships (Raybin, 1969), impulses to sexually assault children (Armstrong, 1978), and not protecting one's own children from sexual abuse (Katan, 1973). Female drug addicts, women with significant sexual problems, and prostitutes presented frequently with a history of sexual abuse or incest in childhood (Giaretto, 1976). Many of the sexually abusive parents had been sexually abused as children (Rosenfeld et al., 1977).

In contrast to the "tentativeness" of the clinical and research reports on the impact of child sexual abuse, Melanie Klein (1932) suggested that seduction or rape of a child by an adult may have serious impact on the development of the child. Also, Anna Freud (1981) considered sexual abuse more harmful than "any other form of abuse." She directed our attention to the "disastrously" disruption of the normal sequence in the child's sex organization and the possible lasting harmful effect on later sexual behavior. She distinguished cases with an "insatiable longing for repetition" or with "massive defense activity, denial, repression, inhibition, etc." against sexuality which results in frigidity or impotence later in life.

In regard to the extent of the impact of sexual abuse on the child, it appeared that the degree of disturbance was greater the closer the relationship between victim and perpetrator, and genital contact was associated with a poorer prognosis (Landis, 1956; Gibbens and Prince, 1963). Steele and Alexander (1981) suggested that younger children may be more vulnerable to psychic trauma secondary to sexual abuse because the stimulation may be overwhelming for their ego. Adolescents, especially when there is no concurrent violence or undue coercion, are less likely to experience harmful consequences.

Specific Situations of Sexual Abuse

In cases of *father-daughter incest*, the impact on the victims ranged from no apparent ill effects to promiscuity, psychopathic traits, frigidity, frank psychiatric symptoms (Lukianowicz, 1972); depression, learning difficulties, sexual promiscuity, running away, somatic complaints (Kaufman et al., 1954); frigidity, promiscuity, depression (Rosenfeld et al., 1977); impaired mothering, tendency to repeat childhood traumas, self-directed aggression, difficulty integrating libidinal and aggressive drives, poor sense of identity (Katan, 1973); behavior problems, school problems, delinquency, depression (Nakashima and Zakus, 1977); and prostitution (Flugel, 1953; James and Meyerding, 1977).

Mother-son incest may not result in ill effects for the child as in the case of healthy ego functions developed prior to the incest (Yorukoglu and Kemph, 1966) or may lead to problems in identification and tendency to repeat the traumatic experience (Shengold, 1963) or psychosis (Lukianowicz, 1972; Wahl, 1960).

Father-son incest may result in further homosexual experiences among the victims (Raybin, 1969; Machotka et al., 1967), male prostitution (Steele and Alexander, 1981), or sexually abusing their own sons (Langsley et al., 1968). Raybin (1969) and Raphling et al. (1967) reported homosexual incest and multiple incestuous relationships respectively over three generations.

In the case of *mother-daughter incest*, Lidz and Lidz (1969) described three cases in all of which the daughters became schizophrenic.

Various effects of *uncle-niece incest* have been reported: Lukianowicz (1972) described the victims as normal; Browning and Boatman (1977) observed pseudomaturity and seductiveness.

Aunt-nephew incest produced no significant sequellae on the victims (Lukianowicz, 1972).

Grandfather-granddaughter incest has led to promiscuity (Lukianowicz, 1972).

In cases of *sibling incest*, Bender and Blau (1937) suggested that these children do not appear to develop feelings of guilt and do not show evidence of psychological harm. Lukianowicz (1972) found the majority to be free from neurosis, psychosis or personality disorders, while a few became aggressive psychopaths. Bonaparte (1953) noted some promiscuity, Sloane and Karpinski (1942) observed promiscuity and guilty feelings among sisters, and Finkelhor (1980) found that about one-third of sibling single sexual experiences were described as positive and one-third as negative.

Rape

Shock, fear, embarrassment, disbelief, and rage, in that order, constitute the immediate emotional reactions to rape. Adolescents may describe themselves as "used," "dirty," or "violated." The rape victims may withdraw from peers; sleep problems and nightmares are often noted, and school performance may deteriorate. They may be afraid that the rapist will harm them, and occasionally phobic reactions may develop including fear of leaving home, fear of strangers, fear of dark, etc. (Sarles, 1981).

Psychological disturbances and psychosomatic complaints may persist. The defense mechanism of denial may be used in the form of wearing sloppy clothes to hide their sexuality and appear less attractive (Felice et al., 1978). The long-term impact of rape is not well documented.

Prostitution

Prostitution may be either a direct form of sexual abuse of children or one of its consequences. Its direct impact is difficult to ascertain because of the many other factors involved which accompany or may have preceded and led to prostitution: poor self-image; low self-esteem; alcohol and drug abuse; runaway; family history of sexual and/or physical abuse, conflict, alcoholism; lack of intimate relationships; depression (Sarles, 1981).

Prostitution does not seem to be related to any specific personality pattern or psychopathology. Some girl prostitutes follow role models (a relative or close friend prostitute) (Gray, 1973).

While girl prostitutes suffer frequently from violence, threats, force or rape by their "protectors," boy prostitutes seem to enjoy more clothing, feeding and entertainment (Sarles, 1981). Some investigators reported that male prostitutes become derelicts, pimps, drug addicts, and/or alcoholics (Gandy and Deisher, 1970). Others described well-adjusted, healthy, married men who were prostitutes as boys (Lloyd, 1976).

The long-term impact of prostitution on boys and girls is unknown.

Pornography

This form of exploitation of boys and girls as young as toddlers has recently become the focus of major concern of parents, professionals, and authorities. Documentation on the specific emotional and developmental impact of this form of sexual abuse of children is still limited.

Recently, various authors addressed the physical, psychological, behavioral and social consequences of child pornography, as well as treatment implications (Schoettle, 1980a; Schoettle, 1980b; Burgess et al., 1981; Burgess et al., 1984). Children developed a variety of symptoms such as difficulty sleeping, nightmares, mood swings, withdrawal, peer fighting, declining academic performance, stealing, drug and alcohol abuse, sexual anxiety, gender confusion, avoidance behavior, depression, and guilt.

CONCLUSION

The maltreatment of children has been well documented since earliest recorded history. There has been an explosion of knowledge regarding physical and sexual abuse of children over the past quarter century. Probably more is known today about the various forms of child maltreatment than ever before, and, in general, children are better protected and represented in today's world than at any other time. Yet, abuse is still rampant and although we know more we still know very little.

The authors have attempted in this chapter to critically review the professional literature regarding maltreatment. Personal clinical experience taught us that maltreated children are at greater risk for severe impediment to physical and emotional growth and development. We know that violence begets violence, that abusing parents (both sexual and physical abuse) basically were abused themselves as children, that criminals charged with violent crimes were usually abused as children, that 75 percent of prostitutes were sexually abused as children, and that almost all cases of multiple personality were sexually abused as children. We know that the abused children we see in clinical settings are often depressed, lack basic trust in others, and are overanxious and aggressive. We "know" that maltreatment of children cannot be good for them in spite of the criticism of the poorly controlled studies and the multitude of confounding factors in most scientific views of the maltreatment syndrome.

REFERENCES

Alexander, T., Chess, S., and Birch, H.G.: *Temperament and Behavior Disorders in Children.* New York: New York University Press, 1968.

Alfaro, J.: Report on the feasibility of studying the relationship between child abuse and later socially-deviant behavior. New York: New York Assembly Select Committee on Child Abuse, 1974.

Alfaro, J.: Report on the relationship between child abuse and neglect and later socially-deviant behavior. Draft of a paper presented at a Symposium Exploring the Relationship Between Child Abuse and Delinquency. Seattle: University of Washington, July 21-22, 1973.

Anthony, E.J., and Benedek, T. (Eds.): *Parenthood: Its Psychology and Psychopathology.* Boston: Little, Brown and Co., 1970.

Armstrong, L.: *Kiss Daddy Goodnight: A Speak-out on Incest.* New York: Hawthorn, 1978.

Bakwin, H.: Loneliness in infants. *American Journal of Diseases of Children, 63*:30-40, 1942.

Bakwin, H.: Emotional deprivation in infants. *Journal of Pediatrics, 35*:512-521, 1949.

Baron, M.A., Bejar, R.L., and Sheaff, P.J.: Pediatric manifestations of the battered child syndrome. *Pediatrics, 45*:1003-1007, 1970.

Barry, M.J.: Incest. In R. Slovenko (Ed.), *Sexual Behavior and the Law.* Springfield, IL: Thomas, 1965.

Bellak, L.: Acting out: Some conceptual and therapeutic considerations. *American Journal of Psychotherapy, 17*:375-389, 1963.

Bender, L., and Blau, A.: A reaction of children to sexual relations with adults. *American Journal of Orthopsychiatry, 7*:500-518, 1937.

Bender, L., and Grugett, A.E.: A follow-up report on children who had atypical sexual experiences. *American Journal of Orthopsychiatry, 22*:825-837, 1952.

Birch, H.G., and Gussow, J.D.: *Disadvantaged Children: Health, Nutrition, and School Failure.* New York: Grune and Stratton, 1970.

Birrell, R.G., and Birrell, J.H.W.: The maltreatment syndrome in children: A hospital survey. *Medical Journal of Australia, 2*:1023-1029, 1968.

Bittner, S., and Newberger, E.H.: Pediatric understanding of child abuse and neglect. *Pediatric Review, 2*:197-207, 1981.

Blager, F., and Martin, H.P.: Speech and language of abused children. In H.P. Martin, and C.H. Kempe (Eds.), *The Abused Child.* Cambridge, MA: Ballinger, 1976, pp. 67-82.

Bonaparte, M.: *Female Sexuality.* New York: International University Press, 1953.

Boyer, L.B.: On maternal overstimulation and ego defects. *The Psychoanalytic Study of the Child, 11*:236-256, 1956.

Bowlby, J.: Maternal care and mental health. *Bulletin of the World Health Organization, 3*:355-534, 1951.

Brazelton, T.B.: *Neonatal Behavioral Assessment Scale.* Philadelphia: Lippincott, 1973.

Brenneman, J.: The infant ward. *American Journal of Diseases of Children, 43*:577-584.

Brown, W.: Murder rooted in incest. In Masters, R.E.L. (Ed.): *Patterns of Incest.* New York: Julian, 1963.

Browning, D.H., and Boatman, B.: Incest: Children at risk. *American Journal of Psychiatry, 134*:69-72, 1977.

Burgess, A.W., Groth, A.N., and McCausland, M.P.: Child sex initiation rings. *American Journal of Orthopsyciatry, 51*:110-119, 1981.

Burgess, A.W., Hartman, C.R., McCausland, M.P., and Powers, P.: Response patterns in children and adolescents exploited through sex rings and pornography. *American Journal of Psychiatry, 141*:656-662, 1984.

Burton, L.: *Vulnerable Children.* London: Routledge and Kegan Paul, 1968.

Caffey, J.: On the theory and practice of shaking infants: Its potential residual effects of permanent brain damage and mental retardation. *American Journal of Diseases of Children, 24*:161-169, 1972.

Coleman, R., and Provence, S.A.: Developmental retardation (hospitalism) in infants living in families. *Pediatrics, 19*:285-292, 1957.

Daniel, J.H., Newberger, E.H., Kotelchuck, M., and Reed, R.B.: Child abuse screening: Limited predictive power of abuse discriminants in a controlled study of pediatric social illness. *International Journal of Child Abuse and Neglect, 2*:247-259, 1978.

DeFrancis, V.: *Protecting the Child Victim of Sex Crimes Committed by Adults.* Denver: American Humane Association, Children's Division, 1969.

Dixon, K.N., Arnold, L.E., and Calestro, K.: Father-son incest: Underreported psychiatric problem? *American Journal of Psychiatry, 135*:835-838, 1978.

Drillien, C.M.: *The Growth and Development of the Prematurely Born Infant.* Edinburgh: Livingston, 1964.

Duncan, G.M.: Etiological factors—First degree murder. *Journal of the American Medical Association, 168*:1755-1758, 1958.

Elmer, E.: *Children in Jeopardy.* Pittsburgh: University of Pittsburgh Press, 1967.

Elmer, E.: *Fragile Families, Troubled Children: The Aftermath of Infant Trauma.* Pittsburgh: University of Pittsburgh Press, 1977.

Elmer, E., and Gregg, G.S. Developmental characteristics of abused children. *Pediatrics, 40*:596-602, 1967.

Elmer, E., Gregg, G.S., Wright, B., and Reinhart, J.B. *Studies of Child and Infant Accidents.* DHEW Publications No. (HSM) 72-9042, Rockville, MD: National Institute of Mental Health, 1971.

Erikson, E.H.: *Childhood and Society.* New York: W.W. Norton, 1950.

Felice, M., Grant, J., Reynolds, B., Gold, S., Wyatt, M., and Heald, F.P.: Follow-up observations of adolescent rape victims. *Clinical Pediatrics, 17*:311-315, 1978.

Ferenczi, S.: Confusion of tongues between adult and child. *International Journal of Psychoanalysis, 30*:225-230, 1949. (Original work published in 1932.)

Finkelhor, D.: Sex among siblings. *Archives of Sexual Behavior, 9*:195-197, 1980.

Flugel, J.C.: *The Psychoanalytic Study of the Family.* London: Hogarth, 1953.

Fontaan, V.J.: The diagnosis of the maltreatment syndrome in children. *Pediatrics, 51*:780-782, 1973.

Forbes, L.M.: Incest, anger, and suicide. In Berkovitz, I.H. (Ed.): *Adolescents Grow in Groups.* New York: Brunner/Mazel, 1972, pp. 104-107.

Freud, A.: The ego and the mechanisms of defense. *In the Writings of Anna Freud, 2.* New York: International Universities Press, 1971. (Original work published in 1936.)

Freud, A.: A psychoanalyst's view of sexual abuse by parents. In Mrazek, P.B. and Kempe, C.H. (Eds.): *Sexually Abused Children and Their Families, 34*: Oxford: Pergamon Press, 1981.

Freud, S.: Beyond the pleasure principle. In Strachey, J. (Ed. and Trans.): *The Standard Edition of the Complete Psychological Works of Sigmund Freud, 18*:3-64, 1955. London: Hogarth Press. (Original work published in 1920.)

Freud, S.: Inhibitions, symptoms and anxiety. In Strachey, J. (Ed. and Trans.): *The Standard Edition of the Complete Psychological Works of Sigmund Freud, 20*:75-175, 1959. London: Hogarth Press. (Original work published in 1926.)

Freud, S.: Analysis terminable and interminable. In Strachey, J. (Ed. and Trans.): *The Standard Edition of the Complete Psychological Works of Sigmund Freud, 23*:240-246, 1964a. London: Hogarth Press. (Original work published in 1937.)

Freud, S.: Moses and Monotheism. In Strachey, J. (Ed. and Trans.): *The Standard Edition of the Complete Psychological Works of Sigmund Freud, 23*:1-137, 1964b. London: Hogarth Press. (Original work published in 1939.)

Gaensbauer, T.J., and Sands, K.: Distorted communication in abused-neglected infants and their potential impact on caretakers. *Journal of the American Academy of Child Psychiatry, 18*:236–250, 1979.

Galdston, R.: Violence begins at home. *Journal of the American Academy of Child Psychiatry, 10*:336–350, 1971.

Gandy, P., and Deisher, R.W.: Young male prostitutes: The physician's role in social rehabilitation. *Journal of the American Medical Association, 212*:1661–1666, 1970.

Garbarino, J.: A preliminary study of some ecological correlates of child abuse: The impact of socioeconomic stress on the mother. *Child Development, 47*:178–185, 1975.

George, C., and Main, M.: Social interactions of young abused children: Approach, avoidance, and aggression. *Child Development, 50*:306–318, 1979.

Giaretto, H.: Humanistic treatment of father-daughter incest. In Helfer, R.E., and Kempe, C.H. (Eds.): *Child Abuse and Neglect: The Family and the Community.* Cambridge, MA: Ballinger, 1976.

Gibbens, T.C.N., and Prince, J.: *Child Victims of Sex Offenses.* London: Institute for the study of Treatment and Delinquency, 1963.

Gil, D.G.: *Violence Against Children: Physical Child Abuse in the United States.* Cambridge, MA: Harvard University Press, 1970.

Giovacchini, P.L.: Effects of adaptive and disruptive aspects of early object relationships upon later parental functioning. In Anthony, E.J., and Benedek, T. (Eds.): *Parenthood: Its Psychology and Psychopathology.* Boston: Little, Brown and Co., 1970, pp. 525–538.

Goldfarb, W.: Effects of psychological deprivation in infancy and subsequent stimulation. *American Journal of Psychiatry, 102*:18–33, 1945.

Galdston, R. Observations on children who have been physically abused and their parents. *American Journal of Psychiatry, 122*:440–443, 1965.

Goodwin, J., and DiVasto, P.: Mother-daughter incest. *Child Abuse and Neglect, 3*:953–957, 1979.

Gray, D.: Turning out: A study of teenage prostitution. *Urban Life and Culture, 1*:401–425, 1973.

Gray, G.W., and Wise, C.M.: *The Bases of Speech.* New York: Harper and Row, 1959.

Green, A.H.: Self-destructive behavior in physically abused schizophrenic children. *Archives of General Psychiatry, 19*:171–179, 1968.

Green, A.H.: Self-destructive behavior in battered children. *American Journal of Psychiatry, 135*:579–582, 1978.

Green, A.H.: *Child Maltreatment.* New York: Jason Aronson, 1980.

Green, A.H.: Dimension of psychological trauma in abused children. *Journal of the American Academy of Child Psychiatry, 22*:231–237, 1983.

Green, A.H., Voeller, K., Gaines, R.W., and Kubie, J.: Neurological impairment in maltreated children. *Child Abuse and Neglect, 5*:129–134, 1981.

Greenacre, P.: The influence of infantile trauma on genetic patterns. In Furst, S.S. (Ed.): *Psychic Trauma.* New York: Basic Books, 1967, pp. 108–153.

Greenland, C.: Incest. *British Journal of Delinquency, 9*:62–65, 1958.

Gregg, G.S., and Elmer, E. Infant injuries: Accident or abuse? *Pediatrics, 44*:434–439, 1969.

Gundlach, R.H.: Sexual molestation and rape reported by homosexual and heterosexual women. *Journal of Homosexuality, 2*:367–384, 1977.

Heims, L.W., and Kaufman, I.: Variations on a theme of incest. *American Journal of Orthopsychiatry, 33*:311–312, 1963.

Helfer, R.E., and Pollock, C.B.: The battered child syndrome. *Advances in Pediatrics, 15*:9–27, 1967.

Herman, J., and Hirschman, L. Incest between fathers and daughters. *The Sciences,* (October 1977), pp. 4–7.

Holter, J.C., and Friedman, S.B.: Principles of management in child abuse cases. *American Journal of Orthopsychiatry, 38*:127–136, 1968a.

Holter, J.C., and Friedman, S.B.: Child abuse: Early case findings in the emergency department. *Pediatrics, 42*:128-138, 1968b.

Hurley, R.: *Poverty and Mental Retardation: A Causal Relationship.* New York: Random House, 1969.

James, J., and Meyerding, J.: Early sexual experience and prostitution. *American Journal of Psychiatry, 134*:1381-1385, 1977.

Johnson, B., and Morse, H.: Injured children and their parents. *Children, 15*:147-152, 1968.

Kagan, J., and Moss, H.A.: *Birth to Maturity: A Study in Psychological Development.* New York: Wiley, 1962.

Katan, A.: Children who were raped. *The Psychoanalytic Study of the Child, 28*:208-224, 1973.

Kaufman, I., Peck, A.L., and Taguiri, C.K.: Family constellation and overt incestuous relations between father and daughter. *American Journal of Orthopsychiatry, 24*:266-277, 1954.

Kempe, R.: Arresting or freezing the developmental process. In Helfer, R.E., and Kempe, C.H. (Eds.): *Child Abuse and Neglect, The Family and Community.* Cambridge, MA: Ballinger, 1976, pp. 64-73.

Kempe, H.C., and Helfer, R.E.: *Helping the Battered Child and His Family.* Philadelphia: Lippincott, 1972.

Kernberg, O.: *Borderline Conditions and Pathological Narcissism.* New York: Aronson, 1975.

Kahn, M.: The concept of cumulative trauma. *The Psychoanalytic Study of the Child, 18*:286-306, 1963.

Kinsey, A.C., Pomeroy, W.B., Martin, C.E., and Gebbard, P.H.: *Sexual Behavior in the Human Female.* Philadelphia: Saunders, 1953.

Klein, M.: *The Psychoanalysis of Children.* London: Hogarth Press, 1932.

Kris, E.: The recovery of childhood memories. *The Psychoanalytic Study of the Child, 11*:54-88, 1956.

Landis, J.T.: Experiences of 500 children with adult sexual deviation. *Psychiatric Quarterly, Supp., 30*:91-109, 1956.

Langsley, D.G., Schwartz, M.S., and Fairbairn, R.H.: Father-son incest. *Comprehensive Psychiatry, 9*:218-226, 1968.

Lempp, R.: Psychologic damage to children as a result of sexual offenses. *Child Abuse and Neglect, 2*:243-245, 1979.

Lewis, M., and Sarrell, P.M.: Some psychological aspects of seduction, incest and rape in childhood. *Journal of the American Academy of Child Psychiatry, 8*:606-619, 1969.

Lidz, R.W., and Lidz, T.: Homosexual tendencies in mothers of schizophrenic women. *Journal of Nervous and Mental Disease, 149*:229-235, 1969.

Lloyd, R.: *For Money or Love: Boy Prostitution in America.* New York: Vanguard, 1976.

Lukianowicz, N.: Incest I: Paternal incest II—Other types of incest. *British Journal of Psychiatry, 120*:301-313, 1972.

Machotka, P., Pittman, F.S., and Flomenhaft, K.: Incest as a family affair. *Family Process, 6*:98-116, 1967.

Magal, V., and Winnik, H.Z.: Role of incest in family structure. *Israel Annals of Psychiatry, 6*:173-189, 1968.

Maisch, H.: *Incest.* London: André Deutsch, 1972.

Malmquist, C.P., Kiresuk, T.J., and Spano, R.M.: Personality characteristics of women with repeated illegitimacies: Descriptive aspects. *American Journal of Orthopsychiatry, 36*:476-484, 1966.

Martin, H.P.: The child and his development. In Kempe, C.H. and Helfer, R.E. (Eds.): *Helping the Battered Child and His Family.* Philadelphia: Lippincott, 1972, pp. 93-114.

Martin, H.P.: Factors influencing the development of the abused child. In Martin, H.P.

and Kempe, C.H. (Eds.): *The Abused Child.* Cambridge, MA: Ballinger, 1976a, pp. 139-162.

Martin, H.P.: Neurologic status of abused children. In Martin, H.P. and Kempe, C.H. (Eds.): *The Abused Child.* Cambridge, MA: Ballinger, 1976b, pp. 67-82.

Martin, H.P., and Beezley, P.: Prevention and the consequences of child abuse. *Journal of Operational Psychiatry, 6:*68-77, 1974.

Martin, H.P., and Beezley, P.: Personality of abused children. In Martin, H.P. and Kempe, C.H. (Eds.): *The Abused Child.* Cambridge, MA: Ballinger, 1976, pp. 105-111.

Martin, H.P., and Rodeheffer, M.: Learning and intelligence. In Martin, H.P. and Kempe, C.H. (Eds.): *The Abused Child.* Cambridge, MA: 1976, pp. 93-104.

Martin, H.P., Beezley, P., Conway, E.F., and Kempe, C.H: The development of abused children. *Advances in Pediatrics, 21:*25-73, 1974.

Medlicott, R.W.: Parent-child incest. *Australia and New Zealand Journal of Psychiatry, 1:*180-187, 1967.

Mehta, M.N., Lokeshwar, M.R., Bhatt, S.S., Athavale, V.B., and Kulkarni, B.S.: "Rape" in children. *Child Abuse and Neglect, 3:*671-677, 1979.

Meiselman, K.C.: *Incest: A Psychological Study of Causes and Effects with Treatment Recommendations.* London: Jossey-Bass, 1978.

Melnick, B., and Hurley, H.B.: Distinctive personality attributes of child abusing mothers. *Journal of Consulting and Clinical Psychology, 33:*746-749, 1969.

Morse, W., Sahler, O.J., and Friedman, S.B.: A three-year follow-up study of abused children. *American Journal of Diseases of Children, 20:*439-446, 1970.

Mrazek, P.B., and Mrazek, D.A.: The effects of child sexual abuse. In Mrazek, P.B. and Kempe, C.H. (Eds.): *Sexually Abused Children and Their Families.* Oxford: Pergamon Press, 1981, pp. 235-243.

Mysak, E.D. *Speech Pathology and Feedback Theory.* Springfield, IL: Charles C Thomas, 1966.

Nakashima, I.I., and Zakus, G.E.: Incest: Review and clinical experience. *Pediatrics, 60:*696-701, 1977.

Newberger, E.H., Haas, G., and Mulford, R. Child abuse in Massachusetts. *Massachusetts Physician, 321:*31-35, 1973.

Newberger, E.H., Reed, R.B., Hyde, J.H., and Kotelchuck, M.: Pediatric social illness: Toward an etiologic classification. *Pediatrics, 50:*178-185, 1977.

Newberger, E.H., Newberger, C.M., and Hampton, R.L.: Child abuse: The current theory base and future research needs. *Journal of the American Academy of Child Psychiatry, 22:*262-268, 1983.

Oliver, J.E., and Taylor, A.: Five generations of ill-treated children in one family pedigree. *British Journal of Psychiatry, 119:*473-480, 1971.

Ounstead, C., Oppenheimer, R., and Lindsay, J. Aspects of bonding failure: The psychotherapeutic treatment of families of battered children. *Developmental Medicine and Child Neurology, 16:*446-456, 1974.

Parke, R.D., and Collmer, C.W.: Child abuse: An interdisciplinary analysis. In Hetherington, E.M. (Ed.): *Review of Child Development Research, 5:*509-590. Chicago: University of Chicago Press, 1975.

Peters, J.: Children who are victims of sexual assaults and the psychology of offenders. *American Journal of Psychotherapy, 30:*398-421, 1976.

Prugh, D.C., and Harlow, R.G. Masked deprivation in infants and young children. In *Deprivation of Maternal Care: A Reassessment of Its Effects* (Public Health Papers, No. 14, pp. 9-30). Geneva: World Health Organization, 1962.

Rabinovitch, R.O.: The sexual psychopath. *Journal of Criminal Law and Criminology, 43:*610-621, 1952-1953.

Raphling, D.L., Carpenter, B.L., and Davis, A.: Incest: A genealogical study. *Archives of General Psychiatry, 16:*505–511, 1967.

Rascovsky, M.W., and Rascovsky, A.: On consummated incest. *International Journal of Psychoanalysis, 31:*42–47, 1950.

Rasmussen, A.: Die beteutung sexueller attentate auf kinder unter 14 jahren fur die entwicklung von geistekrankheiten und charakteranomalien. *Acta Psychiatrica et Neurologica, 9:*351–360, 1934.

Raybin, J.B.: Homosexual incest. *Journal of Nervous and Mental Disease, 148:*105–110, 1969.

Reichenthal, J.A.: Letter to the editor: Correcting the underreporting of father-son incest. *American Journal of Psychiatry, 136:*122–123, 1979.

Rinehart, J.W.: Genesis of overt incest. *Comprehensive Psychiatry, 2:*338–349, 1961.

Ribble, M.A.: *Rights of Infants: Early Psychological Needs and their Satisfaction.* New York: Columbia University Press, 1943.

Rice, E.P., Ekdahl, M.C., and Miller, L.: *Children of Mentally Ill Parents.* New York: Behavioral Publications, 1971.

Rizley, R., and Cicchetti, D. (Eds.): Developmental perspectives on child maltreatment. *New Directions of Child Development, 11,* 1981.

Rodeheffer, M., and Martin, H.P.: Special problems in developmental assessment of abused children. In Martin, H.P. and Kempe, C.H. (Eds.): *The Abused Child.* Cambridge, MA: Ballinger, 1976.

Rosenfeld, A.A., Nadelson, C.C., Kreiger, M., and Blackman, J.H.: Incest and sexual abuse of children. *Journal of American Academy of Child Psychiatry, 16:*327–339, 1977.

Rutter, M.: Children of sick parents: An environment and psychiatric study. (*Maudsley Monograph* No. 16.) London: Oxford University Press.

Rutter, M.: *The Qualities of Mothering: Maternal Deprivation Reassessed.* New York: Aronson, 1974.

Rutter, M., Graham, P., and Yule, W.: *A Neuropsychiatric Study in Childhood.* Philadelphia: Lippincott, 1970.

Sabbeth, J.: The suicidal adolescent. *Journal of the American Academy of Child Psychiatry, 8:*272–286, 1969.

Sandgrund, A., Gaines, R.W., and Green, A.H.: Child abuse and mental retardation: A problem of cause and effect. *American Journal of Mental Deficiency, 79:*327–330, 1974.

Sarles, R.M.: Child abuse. In Madden, D.J. and Lion, J.R. (Eds.): *Rage, Hate, Assault, and Other Forms of Violence.* New York: Spectrum, 1976, pp. 1–16.

Sarles, R.M.: Sexual abuse in the adolescent. In Moss, A.J. (Ed.): *Pediatrics Update: Reviews for Physicians.* New York: Elsevier, 1981, pp. 73–86.

Satten, J., Menninger, K., Rosen, I., and Mayman, M.: Murder without apparent motive: A study in personality disorganization. *American Journal of Psychiatry, 117:*48–53, 1960.

Sattin, D.B., and Miller, J.K.: The ecology of child abuse within a military community. *American Journal of Orthopsychiatry, 41:*675–678, 1971.

Schmitt, B., and Kempe, C.H.: Neglect and abuse of children. In Vaughn, V. and McKay, R. (Eds.): *Nelson Textbook of pediatrics* (10 ed.). Philadelphia: Saunders, 1975.

Schoettle, U.C.: Child exploitation: A study of child pornography. *Journal of the American Academy of Child Psychiatry, 19:*289–299, 1980a.

Schoettle, U.C.: Treatment of the child pornography patient. *American Journal of Psychiatry, 137:*1109–1110, 1980b.

Shengold, L.: The parent as sphinx. *Journal of the American Psychoanalytic Association, 11:*725–751, 1963.

Silver, L.B., Dublin, C.C., and Lourie, R.S.: Does violence breed violence? Contributions from a study of the child abuse syndrome. *American Journal of Psychiatry, 126*:404–407, 1969.

Sloane, P., and Karpinski, E.: Effects of incest on the participants. *American Journal of Orthopsychiatry, 12*:666–673, 1942.

Smith, S.M., and Hanson, R.: 134 battered children: A medical and psychological study. *British Medical Journal, 3*:666–670, 1974.

Smith, S.M., Hanson, R., and Noble, S.: Parents of battered babies: A controlled study. *British Medical Journal, 4*:388–391, 1973.

Sperling, M.: The clinical effects of parental neurosis on the child. In Anthony, E.J. and Benedek, T. (Eds.): *Parenthood: Its Psychology and Psychopathology*. Little, Brown and Co., 1970.

Spitz, R.A.: Hospitalism: An inquiry into the genesis of psychiatric conditions in early childhood. *The Psychoanalytic Study of the Child, 1*:53–74, 1945.

Spitz, R.A. The effect of personality disturbances in the mother on the well-being of her infant. In Anthony, E.J. and Benedek, T. (Eds.): *Parenthood: Its Psychology and Psychopathology*. Boston: Little, Brown and Co., 1970.

Spitz, R.A., and Wolf, L.M.: Anaclitic depression: An inquiry into the genesis of psychiatric conditions in early childhood. *The Psychoanalytic Study of the Child, 2*:323–342, 1946.

Starr, R.H.: Controlled study of the ecology of child abuse and drug abuse. *International Journal of Child Abuse and Neglect, 2*:19–28, 1978.

Steele, B.J.: Violence in our society. *The Pharos of Alpha Omega Alpha, 33*:42–48, 1970.

Steele, B.J., and Alexander, H.: Long-term effects of sexual abuse in childhood. In Mrazek, P.B. and Kempe, C.H. (Eds.).: *Sexually Abused Children and their Families*. Oxford: Pergamon Press, 1981, pp. 223–234.

Steele, B.J., and Pollock, C.B. A psychiatric study of parents who abuse infants and small children. In Helfer, R.E. and Kempe, C.H. (Eds.): *The Battered Child* (2 ed.). Chicago: University of Chicago Press, 1974.

Talbot, N.B.: Has psychological malnutrition taken the place of rickets in contemporary pediatric practice? *Pediatrics, 31*:909–918, 1963.

Tanay, E.: Psychiatric study of homicide. *American Journal of Psychiatry, 125*:1252–1258, 1969.

Thomas, W.: *Child Victims of Incest*. Denver: American Humane Association, Children's Division, 1968.

Wahl, C.W. The psychodynamics of consummated maternal incest. *Archives of General Psychiatry, 3*:188–193, 1960.

Wasserman, S.: The abused parent of the abused children. *Children, 14*:175–179, 1967.

Weiner, I.B. On incest: A survey. *Excerpta Criminologica, 4*:137–155, 1964.

Werner, E.E., and Smith, R.S.: *Kauai's Children Come of Age*. Honolulu: University of Hawaii Press, 1977.

Werner, E., Simonian, K., Bierman, J.M., and French, F.E. Cumulative effect of perinatal complications and deprived environment on physical, intellectual, and social development of preschool children. *Pediatrics, 30*:490–505, 1967.

Wortis, J.: Poverty and retardation: Social aspects. In Wortis, J. (Ed.): *Mental Retardation*. New York: Grune and Stratton, 1970a, pp. 262–270.

Wortis, J.: Poverty and retardation: Biosocial factors. In Wortis, J. (Ed.): *Mental Retardation*. New York: Grune and Stratton, 1970b, pp. 271–279.

Yarrow, L.J.: Maternal deprivation—toward an empirical and conceptual re-evaluation. *Psychological Bulletin, 58*:459–490, 1961.

Yates, A.: Narcissistic traits in certain abused children. *American Journal of Orthopsychiatry, 51*:55–62, 1981.

Yorukoglu, A., and Kemph, J.P.: Children not severly damaged by incest with a parent. *Journal of the American Academy of Child Psychiatry, 5*:111–124, 1966.

PART III

Part III of the book deals with medical, legal and ethical aspects of child maltreatment. Various issues often arise in the course of identification and treatment of such cases. Knowledge and familiarity of these issues and their implications in practice are prerequisites for effective work of social workers and other professionals. Chapter 8 discusses the physician's role and the complex (at times) diagnostic process to be followed in determining the presence of various forms of child abuse and/or neglect. It specifically delineates the "medical risk factors for abuse" and it considers comparatively abuse and neglect of the child. The chapter, written in a plain, understandable language, helps the reader realize the enormous and complex issues involved in differentiating organic from nonorganic child-maltreatment conditions. The need for cooperation among medical personnel, social workers, and other professionals in the medical setting is emphasized.

Chapter 9 provides the reader with the legal framework of child protection as it has come to exist presently. It discusses the protective agency's responsibilities related to identification and treatment services as they are mandated by federal and state laws and the increased nationwide quality of such services as they are manifested in increased reporting and reduction of child fatalities. This chapter further discusses the evolution of judicial roles and court proceedings which guarantee a better due process and fundamental fairness now than in the past. In addition, the chapter provides a list of guidelines for effective court testimony.

Chapter 10, with an extensive introduction to the history of moral philosophy, considers ethical issues of child maltreatment in its proper perspective. It focuses on such social work activities as those related to advice-giving in child care and removing children from their homes, which raises such ethical issues related to use of authority, the individual's self-determination, the role of the state and the social worker's role conflicts. The authors discuss these issues considering teleological and deontological ideas, and they propose that a blend of these two schools of thought could provide the social work practitioner and other professionals a proper balance between the interests of the individual and society.

CHAPTER 8

MEDICAL ASPECTS
OF CHILD ABUSE AND NEGLECT

Charles Felzen Johnson

INTRODUCTION

Although child abuse is considered to be an affliction that dates back to antiquity (Solomon, 1973), it has only received serious medical attention since 1946, when Doctor John Caffey (1946), a radiologist, reported the frequent association of chronic head injuries and multiple fractures of long bones in children who had been abused. Despite the appearance of over 800 publications about child abuse in the scientific literature between 1973 and 1980 (National Library of Medicine, 1975, 1980), a textbook dedicated to medical aspects of child abuse (Ellerstein, 1981), and laws requiring professionals to report, physicians (McDonald, 1979) and dentists (Beaver and McClendon, 1979) have been reluctant to report child abuse. It is apparent that laws that require physicians to report suspected child maltreatment may not affect their reporting behavior (Silver, 1967). In 1981, of the 16,314 cases of suspected child abuse reported to the Ohio Central Registry for Child Abuse, only 202 (1.2%) were made by physicians.

Factors which influence reporting behavior by physicians in private practice include: attitudes toward what constitutes acceptable discipline; seriousness of the injury; presence of other injuries; physician familiarity with the family; appropriateness of parental concern about the child; compatibility of the history and physical examination, and the child's behavior (Morris, Johnson, and Clasen, in press). The injuries suffered from the results of inappropriate discipline may not be equated with reportable child abuse by the private physician.

The physician in private practice may be unjustly accused of not reporting child abuse cases (Johnson, 1983). In a recent survey of 58 practicing physicians, a low incidence of child abuse in private practice was claimed. In addition to this perception, other reasons for not reporting included a fear of losing patients, the need for certainty of diagnosis and a lack of confidence in community agencies (Morris et al., 1983). The pediatricians surveyed indicated that they filed an average of three abuse reports a year compared to less than one report per year for the family practitioners. The difference in reporting may not be due to unwillingness to report; it may only reflect the larger number of children seen by pediatricians. Of the 58 physicians interviewed, 70 percent stated that they had reported either no cases or only one case in the past year. This is in contrast to the 20 to 30 cases reported each year by the emergency room physicians or abuse team physicians at a children's hospital (Children's Hospital, Child Abuse Program, 1984). Clearly, the reporting experience of most physicians is limited. Despite an average exposure of one or two lecture hours on the topic of child abuse in medical schools and in pediatric residency programs in the state of Ohio (Ohio Chapter American Academy of Pediatrics, 1984), the physicians surveyed did not equate a lack of awareness of child abuse as a major reason for a failure to report.

What significance do these studies of physician's experiences and attitudes have for the social worker who is seeking assistance to help delineate the etiology of an injury? The social worker must realize that unfamiliarity with child abuse and its manifestations, and discomfort with dealing with parents who may have abused their children (Sanders, 1972), will vary from physician to physician. A lack of knowledge or reporting experience may be further complicated by a reluctance to become involved because of financial considerations imparted by the length of time required to perform an adequate examination and the minimal financial compensation for a possible court appearance. Concern about the skills and motivation of a physician may necessitate referral of the child, by the social worker, to a regional center with an experienced child abuse team.

SUSPICION VS. DIAGNOSIS: THE PHYSICIAN AS DETECTIVE

Among the reasons given by physicians for not reporting child abuse are perceived problems in defining abuse (Silver, 1969). Physicians are not alone in feeling most comfortable recognizing and recording the obvious and uncontroversial. The role of the physician is to suspect child abuse as a possible cause in the evaluation of any injury. This is a major responsibility, considering the number of injuries sustained by children. It was estimated, in 1967, that 1,750,000 infants had sustained a fall in the first year of life (Kravitz, Driessen, Gomberg and Kovach, 1969). An estimated 15,000,000 children are injured annually (Izant and Hubay, 1966). A busy emergency room in a children's hospital may see as many as 26,000 injuries a year. Studies have indicated that as many as 10 percent of injured children seen in an emergency room have been abused; another 10 percent may have been neglected (Holter and Friedman, 1968). Audits of inpatient charts indicate that 60 percent of the charts have inadequate information to rule out abuse as a cause of the injury (Solomon, 1973). The need to rule out abuse as a possible cause for every injury can be facilitated by stamping, in the patient's chart, that the injury is or is not compatible with the history and development of the child.

Parents rarely come to a physician or social worker with an injured child and confess that they had purposely caused the injury. The differentiation between accident and intentional injury or failure to protect (neglect) is the frustrating challenge to the physician. When a child dies of multiple trauma or under unusual circumstances, an autopsy may clarify the cause of death (Palmer and Weston, 1976); however, it may not be possible to differentiate certain causes of death, such as smothering, from sudden infant death syndrome. Intentional poisoning may cause unusual symptoms and death; the cause may elude detection.

The physician, who is comfortable when "playing detective" in the search for a cause of disease, may be angered when the social worker or court demand a definitive cause-and-effect statement about sexual abuse. Physicians are often less upset by probability and possibility statements about the cause of an injury than the social worker or court. This is a reality in the "science" of medicine. Too often the evaluation of the cause of an injury cannot be definitive. This is not a reflection of the competence of the physician but a problem in the evaluation of any injury which has not been witnessed. Could the injury have occurred in the manner that the parents describe? Is the child at an age which would allow the child to have injured him/herself? Children with developmental problems and chronic disease (Klein and Stern, 1971; Johnson, in press) are at increased risk for being abused. Twin birth, which may be associated with prematurity and delayed development (Groothius et al., 1982) is also associated with increased abuse risk. These conditions stress families; physicians, involved in the complicated medical care, may be unaware of the increased risk factors. Hospital and clinic social workers who are sensitive to these issues can help prevent abuse and neglect through counseling (Johnson, 1983). Medically sophisticated parents with effective communication skills may give a credible explanation that supports an accidental cause of an inflicted injury.

THE CREDIBLE STORY: A CASE EXAMPLE

During my residency training there was not one lecture on the subject of child abuse. My fellow residents were dedicated to "saving the lives" of children who were ravaged by genetic and infectious disease. Pediatric residents treated many children who were poisoned and injured. We generally considered these potentially lethal events to have been accidental. We were naive in our belief that all parents were concerned about the welfare of their children. It would have been a discomforting shock to imagine that a parent would PURPOSEFULLY cause an injury to a child, much less poison him/her. One case had a profound effect on my naivety. A six-month-old child was admitted to my service with crops of one-inch, perfectly circular, red lesions all over her body. The circles surrounded a central "target" circle. For days we did laboratory tests to determine if this was infectious or allergic in origin. The lesions began to clear and she was sent home. Two weeks later she reappeared with a new crop. Luckily our attending physician, or pediatric supervisor, was a wise and sophisticated practitioner who reminded us that no biologically induced lesion has a perfect geometric shape. Only man makes perfect geometric shapes. An object had caused the leisons. We concluded that the child had been burned with an automobile cigarette lighter. It was a sickening experience to tell the mother that the lesions must have been inflicted. The mother confessed, but I had little compassion for the emotional problems that were eventually uncovered that had led to her actions. Munchausen's syndrome by proxy—or injury caused by a caretaker which mimics disease (Dine and McGovern, 1982)— is a relatively newly described form of child abuse.

After residency, I entered the army for three years of general pediatric practice. I saw many children with accidental injuries but none as severe as the unconscious two-month-old child admitted to the hospital with a skull fracture. The mother was an attractive, sophisticated wife of a lieutenant. She was mortified by what had occurred due to her negligence—she had forgotten to put the crib rail up and the child had rolled out of bed. That evening, as I was making "bedtime" rounds, I heard loud voices coming from the child's room. The father was yelling that he was going to tell the doctor what really had happened. I entered the room and asked for an explanation. The father related that the mother, in a fit of anger and frustration, had thrown the baby against the wall. I was shocked. I had not doubted the original story. I had not considered that two-month-old babies cannot roll over, how far the baby fell or whether the floor was carpeted or not. There was no way to medically differentiate the consequences of a fall from being thrown. Something hard had to come in contact with the baby's head. It could have been a hand-held object, the wall or the floor.

Would I have been more suspicious if the father was an enlisted man or the mother less articulate in her profession of guilt?

PATHOGNOMONIC INJURIES: ARE THERE ANY INJURIES THAT ARE DIAGNOSTIC OF CHILD ABUSE?

To fully investigate the etiology of an injury, one would need to be an expert in physics and familiar with the patterns of inflicted injury in child abuse (Johnson and Showers, in press). What happens as the result of trauma depends upon many factors. In physical trauma one would need to know the force applied, the shape of the object and the particular characteristics of the tissue involved. Few studies have been done to help the physician determine if the force required to cause the injury is consistent with the story given by the family. It is unusual for an infant to fall out of bed and sustain a skull fracture or any permanent damage (Kravitz et al., 1969; Helfer, Slovis and Black, 1977). Familiarity with studies of how injuries occur may help the physician gain credibility during testimony about the possible cause of an injury; although, in one study, 95 different instruments were used to perpetuate abuse (Johnson and Showers, in press).

Certain parts of the body, such as the eyes, are more easily injured. The susceptibility of the area may vary with the age of the child. The head, because of the thinness of the skull, poor internal brain support, delicacy of brain blood vessels and size relative to the rest of the body, makes the infant's brain more vulnerable to even mild trauma such as shaking (Caffey, 1972, 1974). The older child is less likely to be seriously injured and may be able to divert a blow or escape. The susceptibility of the child's bones to injury will also vary with age. The growing portion, which is at the ends of the bones, may be separated by twisting forces (metaphyseal injury). Spiral fractures occur from a twisting motion. Parents will often state that the twisting motion resulted from the child catching the leg in a crib rail and rolling over or fixing the foot in the crack between pillows on a couch and then falling. It is not possible for the physician to tell if the injury was purposeful unless the child cannot roll or stand. Subdural hemorrhages, or bleeding under one of the coverings of the brain, with retinal hemorrhages and no signs of external trauma should suggest shaking. Although there are no pathognomonic injuries that result from child battering, any fracture in a child under one year of age should be investigated with suspicion, as one study has indicated that 56 percent of all such fractures are nonaccidental (McClelland and Kingsbury, 1982). Bruises or lacerations caused by looped cords or belts, human bites, bruises and fractures in various stages of healing (which suggest multiple trauma), immersion burns and cigarette burns should suggest child abuse. Bilateral injuries and injuries to the genitalia, which are generally protected by the diaper, should also be viewed with suspicion. The shape of a mark as well as its age may suggest that the injury is nonaccidental. Circumferential injuries about the wrists or ankles may indicate that the child has been tied, and marks from choking are distinctive (Ellerstein, 1979). The type of injury and instrument used may vary with the age and race of the child (Johnson and Showers, in press).

CLUES THAT SUGGEST ABUSE ARE SUBTLE: THE BODY HAS A LIMITED REPERTOIRE WHEN REACTING TO INJURY

Generally, if the burn or impact injury is slight and the child is not especially sensitive to trauma (such as in hemophilia), only redness results. Blood vessels are dilated in reaction to a mild insult and the overlying skin becomes red. This is referred to as erythema. If the force is more severe, tiny blood vessels will rupture. On the surface this manifests itself as a bruise. Deeper bleeds cause swelling and are called hematomas. Bruises and hematomas are the most frequent manifestations in child abuse in studies emanating from hospitals (Johnson and Showers, in press; Johnson, in press). Bruises on dark-skinned children may be less apparent than on fair-skinned children.

Workers dealing with child abuse need to know that bruises change color with time and can be dated to ascertain if the injury is in keeping with the history given by the caretaker. Bruises of different colors indicate injuries of different ages. The new bruise is reddish-blue and changes to green by five to seven days and yellow by eight to ten days. Bruises resolve in two to three weeks. Fractures may also be dated (Swischuk, 1981). The pattern of a burn injury may suggest a specific instrument such as an iron or hot fork. The scald burn resulting from intentional submersion in hot water, which usually occurs during toilet-training time, is typical (Lenoski and Hunter, 1977). There is a distinct delineation between the normal and burned tissue. There are no splash marks suggesting a fall into the water. The buttocks may be the only area burned. Areas that are pressed against the container or flexion folds may not be as severely burned. The child's developmental stage must be considered. One must determine if the child could have crawled into the tub, reached the stove top, or turned on the hot water. Drawing the pattern of the burn on a doll may help determine how it occurred. It is impossible to crawl into a tub of hot water and not burn the bottom of the feet or get splashed in attempts to escape. Hands burned from accidental placement under a hot water faucet do not have a distinct burn line. Rarely will a child place two hands in a pan of hot water or keep them there long enough to sustain a third-degree burn. Ten seconds are needed to cause a full thickness (third-degree) burn when the water temperature is 136 degrees (Moritz, 1947). One must determine the maximum temperature of the household water. These investigations may be best performed by the police. It is helpful if the physician can guide the investigator. The presence of other injuries suggest a purposeful burn (Ayoub and Pfeifer, 1979). It may not be possible to distinguish if water was spilled on the child or poured; however, social information may suggest risk for nonaccidental injury (Bakalav, Moore and Hight, 1981). Because a burn suggests premeditation and is associated with family violence and social disruption, intensive intervention is needed in nonaccidental burn injuries. The initial mortality may be as high as 40 percent and reabuse is common (Ayoug and Pfeifer, 1979).

IT HELPS WHEN THE CHILD CAN TALK

Despite what may be obvious, many professionals in their examination of a child will not separate the child from the parent to ask the child's story. Some children above two years of age, depending upon their developmental level, may be able to identify an abuser. By three years of age, with three-word sentences, the child may be able to explain the event.

Ask the older child what happened. A four-year-old child, with burns on the tops of both hands, after being admitted to the hospital, told the nursing staff that his father had poured hot water on his hands. A fourteen-year-old who, upon hospital admission, agreed that hot cereal had fallen on his head by accident waited until after a week to state that his father had poured the cereal on him.

It is appropriate to continue to clarify the etiology of a suspicious injury after the first history has been taken. Older children may be afraid initially to relate the truth. They may be fearful of retribution or removal from the family. The hospital social worker, able to establish rapport over time with children who have suffered injuries, may be more successful than the physician in clarifying the history.

There are characteristic marks which result from a slap to the face (e.g. a looped cord, a cigarette burn or a geometric object such as a fork) that belie other explanations by the parent. Parents may claim that the typical slap mark was due to the child pressing against the crib rail or falling onto an object. Injuries to the mouth or frenulum in a bottle-fed baby should suggest trauma from forced feeding. The astute investigator will be familiar with common inflicted injuries and be able to support their conclusions, if necessary, in court. It would be harmful to the family, and the physician's reputation, to mistake common impetigo for cigarette burns. Photographs are indispensible in the investigation. Close-up photographs taken with a special Polaroid camera will guarantee an immediate record. Supplemental slides taken with a quality 35-mm camera will be more distinct and color correct. The social worker, responsible for guaranteeing that established protocols are followed, is the most reliable person to take and file the photographs. The physician must consider unusual injuries or accidents as possible abuse. Abuse may be manifest as an unusual injury. Until recently, penetrating injuries of the body have been considered unusual in child abuse (Cameron, 1977); however, blunt abdominal injuries from fists or other objects are reported in the surgical literature (McCort and Vaudagna, 1964; Grosfeld and Ballantine, 1976; Philippart, 1977). The child's abdomen is not as well protected as that of an adult; trauma to the abdomen may result in rupture of the liver or spleen or bleeding into the bowel wall that may cause intestinal obstruction (Maull, 1978). Lymphatic damage may cause chylous ascites, or enlargement of the abdomen due to lymphatic fluid leakage. Compression of the child's chest may cause hemorrhage into the retina of the eye (Tomasi and Rosman, 1975). The physician's concern with lifesaving procedures, or establishing the diagnosis of a chronic disease (Johnson, in press), may interfere with the consideration of abuse.

Covert parental actions may result in what is mistaken for disease states in the child. This is referred to as Munchausen syndrome by proxy (Meadow, 1977). Munchausen syndrome describes actions by an often seriously disturbed adult which result in the creation of a disease state that defies diagnosis and treatment in the adult. Munchausen syndrome by proxy occurs when an adult creates a disease state in a child. The parent may give the child dangerous amounts of a food substance (Dine and McGovern, 1982; Pickel, Anderson and Holliday, 1970) such as salt, or medications such as insulin (Bauman and Yalow, 1981) or tranquilizers (Watson, Davies and Hunter, 1979). Parents may be quite clever in their covert attacks on the child. An unusual series of near-fatal infections in a child was eventually found to be caused by the mother injecting stool into the child's intravenous fluid line. Seizures and apnea have been caused by a mother injecting a hydrocarbon into a child's intravenous fluid line (Saulsbury, Chobanian and Wilson, 1984). The ultimate result was blindness, cerebral palsy, and developmental delay. Polle syndrome occurs when a parent with Munchausen syndrome also creates a disease in their child (Verity, Winkworth and Burman, 1979). Reports of unusual symptoms being intentionally caused have come from hospital records. The number of children who are poisoned and never reach the doctor is unknown. A summary of risk factors that should be considered by the physician may be found in Chart 1 (Johnson, 1983).

CHART 1

Medical Risk Factors for Abuse

Infant
   Any bruises—especially about the face
   Immersion or "dunking burn"
   Small burns in series (cigarette, lighter)
   Any fracture (56% are "nonaccidental" under 1 year)
   Mouth-tooth-frenulum injury (consider force feeding)
   Subdurals and/or retinal hemorrhages (shaking or hitting)
   Failure-to-thrive—consider neglect in differential diagnosis

Child
   Bruises or lacerations on posterior surfaces
   Bruises or lacerations with unusual marks (belt, loop, teeth)
   Clustered bruises (multiple swats)
   Bruises or fractures of different ages
   Any unusual burn (pattern, rope)
   Tooth injuries, nose and face injuries
   Metaphyseal (twisting) fractures
   Periosteal injury (twisting or pulling)
   Spiral fractures (twisting or pulling)
   Circumferential injury (from binding)

General Considerations
   Is child at risk? (abnormal, seen as abnormal)
   Is family at risk? (stress, resources, drugs, attitudes, skills)
   Any injury to external genitalia or rectum?
   Discrepant/varying history (child's, parents', others')
   Injury not consistent with child's development (i.e. foot burn in
      pre-ambulatory child, head injury in pre-crawling or rolling
      child)
   Series of injuries or poisoning (also consider neglect)
   Delay in seeking medical attention
   Unusual religious practices (on part of parents)
   Injury to abdominal contents from blunt or sharp trauma (fist, foot)
   Injury not in keeping with history (i.e. multiple fractures from
      minor fall; multiple burns from falling hot object, such as an
      iron)
   Bilateral injuries
   Venereal disease(s)—16 percent of sexually abused males have pre-
      vious history of child abuse
   Poor hygiene, no concern of parents for child, child is a manage-
      ment problem

ABUSE VS. NEGLECT:
ARE ALL ACCIDENTS THE PARENTS' RESPONSIBILITY

If parents are to be considered ultimately responsible for a child's welfare, any breach in this responsibility should be considered neglect. Neglect implies an act of omission—a failure to protect or serve the child's needs. Abuse is generally easier to define than neglect, although professionals have been shown to disagree about what constitutes appropriate discipline and when the consequences should be reported as abuse (Morris et al., in press). For example, spanking the bottom with an open hand resulting in a *red mark* was considered inappropriate discipline by 45 percent of 58 physicians, whereas spanking resulting in a bruise was considered inappropriate by 86 percent. Only 1 percent would have filed an abuse report on the child with the reddened bottom, but 25 percent would have reported the child with the bruise. More serious injuries, injury locations on other than the buttocks and use of an instrument or fist, resulted in higher percentages. Striking a child with a fist was considered inappropriate by 100 percent of the physicians, and 86 percent would report the caretaking perpetrator for abuse.

Though emotional, physical and medical neglect are associated with intentional trauma (Lauer, Broeck and Grossman, 1975), there have been no studies about physician attitudes toward neglect and reporting behavior; however, one would speculate that even wider discrepancies would be found in definition and reporting of neglect. Health care situations in which a lack of compliance results in serious or permanent repercussions to the child's health present less of a problem in definition (Bross and Meredyth, 1979). Dental neglect was carefully defined in a report that indicated that 50 percent of abuse cases exhibited injury to the teeth and jaws. Since only a small number of cases of suspected abuse were reported by dentists (Bensel and Wardking, 1975), it is likely that reporting neglect will be "similarly neglected."

If the child's life or welfare is endangered by caretaker neglect, there will be little resistance to filing of a report and evoking action to provide for the child's welfare (Bross, 1982). A medical statement which indicates that the child is in danger is necessary along with careful documentation that the parent has been informed of what is needed to provide for the child's care. If the parent is unable to comply for emotional, intellectual, religious or economic reasons, a different "level" or type of neglect may be implied in contrast to the situation where the parent understands and has resources but refuses to comply. The court may view the former as child endangering. From the child's point of view, the cause of the neglect is immaterial. The child's welfare may be at stake when the parent's religion will not allow a medical procedure. The state law may not label the situation as neglect even though an emergency court order may be necessary to perform a procedure. One must be familiar with the individual state laws and their interpretation in order to facilitate serving the child. Careful documentation is necessary. A chart that indicates what was communicated, the time frame for compliance and the parents' understanding of the instructions for each episode will make it easier to bring court action if necessary to assure compliance. Each missed appointment should be charted. The consequences of a lack of compliance must be indicated by a physician. Lack of control due to missed urine testing in a child with diabetes, and seizures resulting from missed anticonvulsant doses, are convincing. Blood levels of certain medications such as antibiotics and anticonvulsants can be obtained to clarify compliance. Standards for care of each disease process, including well-baby visits, have been developed by physicians and hospitals to facilitate recognizing and documenting neglect (Cantwell, 1978). Repeating the above exercise in each community is an excellent way to sensitize professionals to the problem.

NON-ORGANIC FAILURE TO THRIVE (NO FTT): THE ARCHETYPE OF NEGLECT THAT CAN RESULT IN THE DEATH OF A CHILD

A variety of problems can interfere with a child's ability to gain weight. The most common cause of failure to gain adequately is non-organic, or due to inadequate caloric intake. Charts are available which are used to follow a child's weight gain when the child is seen for well-baby examinations. If a child begins to fall away from the expected curve of weight gain, this is considered failure to thrive. During an acute illness, a child may temporarily fall away from the growth curve. When the child recovers, the weight quickly approximates the curve. In chronic illness the child's weight may not approximate the curve. If the child's weight gain is insufficient for a period of months, an effect on linear growth may be seen. Eventually, the brain, which is spared in early malnutrition, begins to suffer and head circumference fails to increase as expected. Persistent movement away from the growth curve may ultimately result in developmental retardation from a lack of brain nourishment and increased susceptibility to infection and death.

The cause of the failure to thrive dictates the treatment. If the cause is organic, such as diabetes, insulin would reverse the disease process and weight gain would ensue. The parent did not "cause" the diabetes—the cause was "organic." Failure to give the insulin would result in re-emergence of the disease, with weight loss and possible death. The parents in this instance would be considered neglectful. If they overdosed the insulin to purposefully injure the child, this would be abuse and a form of

Munchausen's syndrome by proxy. Blood insulin and sugar and urine sugar levels help establish the diagnosis.

Non-organic failure-to-thrive implies that no disease state is present in the child. To reach that conclusion requires a basic work-up to eliminate probable organic causes. Once an organic cause is ruled out, the physician should entertain a diagnosis of NO FTT. The child who has received inadequate calories due to poor feeding techniques on the part of the parent or from inadequate calories in the formula will respond with weight gain after a few days of hospitalization. A child who has been seriously emotionally neglected, force-fed, or abused may have a delay of several weeks before weight gain occurs. The gain in weight in the hospital establishes the diagnosis. Inadequate calories in the formula may be caused by ignorance in formula preparation or insufficient income to purchase an adequate diet for the child. Financial assistance and instruction with support in a follow-up clinic, supplemented by visiting nurse services, may be sufficient to assure weight gain. If the parent's intellectual capacity is limited, support and follow-up must be intense. The community will need to decide if the child's needs can be met by the limited parent. Because of the potential for serious and permanent effects, continued weight loss should not be the sole criterion for removal from the home. Emotional neglect may be difficult to separate from NO FTT. It has been suggested that the term "maternal deprivation" be substituted for NO FTT (Gagan, 1984). Infants require stimulation, in addition to calories, to develop. An emotionally disturbed or intellectually handicapped parent may not be able to provide adequate stimulation. The neglected child may become apathetic and disinterested in food. Of great concern is the parent who dislikes the child and either neglects to feed the child or forces eating so that the child will finish as quickly as possible. The child who is force-fed may develop an aversion to the bottle, associating it with a painful experience. The parent may deny any "inappropriate" behavior and in a manner similar to the abusing parent. Close observation of the parent-child interaction in the hospital or home is necessary to document this behavior. This can be performed by a trained social worker, nurse, or physician. Loss of weight in a developing baby may have as serious an effect on the baby's future as a blow to the head resulting in a brain hemorrhage. Failure to thrive (Goldson, Cadol, Fitch and Umlauf, 1976) and abuse (Klein and Stern, 1971) are seen more frequently in prematures. Routinely, involvement of a social worker with these high-risk babies may prevent abuse and neglect. If a decision cannot be made about the adequacy of the feeding or parenting skills and prolonged hospitalization is not possible, then temporary placement in an experienced foster home may be a lifesaving alternative to a return home on a "trial basis."

CIA GAO: ABUSE, NEGLECT OR CULTURAL TRADITION?

Every family has accepted health practices that have evolved from tradition and not medical science. These home remedies are attested to by adult family members, with children often serving as the unwilling victims. Generally, the remedy does not cause any harm and , since most illnesses of children (and adults) are self-limited, seems to be associated with "cure." I am a living testimony to the efficacy of chicken soup. But it is not humorous, or harmless, when the treatment of a potentially serious disease, such as strep throat, is avoided in lieu of a non-dangerous but ineffective treatment. The home remedy may also be dangerous. Can ignorance be allowed to treat disease when the child's welfare is in danger? Certainly not. Education may avert tragedy.

Some individuals will resist medical treatment for their children for religious reasons. This may require a court order to provide treatment. The physician must forcefully attest to the need for treatment. What if the parent has not had access to education or scientific approaches to medical care because they have just come to this country? Cia Gao is a treatment used by recently arrived immigrants from Vietnam and Cambodia who may not have been exposed to European medicine (Muecke, 1983). They rub coins on the backs, necks or chests of children with respiratory ailments to bring about a cure. The skin is abraded and reddened. Should this attempt to help be reported as abuse? Should the failure to acquire proper attention be construed as neglect? Aggressive approaches and abuse reports on the part of child welfare agencies or the physician may result in fear, anger, and confusion on the part of the parents. Professionals must learn the health idiosyncracies of new immigrants, offer early instruction in proper medical care, and involve agencies and individuals who speak the language and understand the culture in order to affect appropriate care and compliance.

A CASE REPORT OF CULTURAL COLLISION AND CATASTROPHE: NEGLECT VS. CULTURAL IDIOSYNCRACY

A young oriental couple, recently arrived in this country, were apprised that their infant had bilateral retinoblastomas—eye cancers that can spread to the brain and cause death. They refused to allow the eyes to be removed surgically. An emergency court order was obtained to perform the surgery. Friends and relatives created a diversion while the parents fled with the child. A police search was instituted. Professionals were furious and frustrated. The social service agency serving immigrants accused the professionals of heavy handedness and lack of understanding. The parents had believed that removal of the eyes would endanger the child's spirit or soul. They believed that they were acting in the child's best interest. The story had a happy ending. The parents found help and understanding in another community, agreed to the surgery and the child's life was saved. What if the couple were not immigrants and had refused the surgery because they believed that a life of blindness was not in the best interest of the child?

Issues of neglect often intersect with questions of medical ethics. This is especially significant in the field of neglect of the unborn child (Bross and Meredyth, 1979) and professional abuse of children (Polier, 1975). A team approach to problem solving is an inestimable value in delineating complicated issues of neglect when religion or culture clash with the recommendations of medical science. Careful follow-up is needed with close communication between the physician and social worker. There is evidence that unnecessary and potentially dangerous cultural practices, such as circumcision, persist in our own culture despite efforts to educate parents (Herrera, Cochran, Huerrera and Wallace, 1983). The physician must primarily represent the child while maintaining compassion for the parent. The social worker, serving as an advocate for the parent, facilitates entry into service.

SEXUAL ABUSE: INCREASING INCIDENCE OR INCREASING RECOGNITION?

While physicians may vary in their definition of physical abuse and willingness to report, there is a probably lesser reluctance to recognize and report sexual abuse. The types of sexual abuse are less well known than the bruises, fractures, and burns of physical abuse. For example, how many professionals know that frottage is a form of sexual gratification and not French for "cheese"? We are just becoming aware of the incidence of sexual abuse in males (Showers, Farber, Joseph, Oshins, and Johnson, 1983). Although we may tolerate various degrees of injury suffered in the name of "attempts to discipline," we are less tolerant when we suspect that an adult is using a child for sexual gratification. Possibly that adult misbehavior, imbedded in our mores, results in more anguish and anger. Because the most common form of incest is between siblings, differentiating sex play from sexual abuse may be difficult (Loredo, 1982). Sex play may be defined as sexual interaction between children not greater than four years in age difference and *without force*. There are exceptions to the definition, and the physician may be frustrated by a police officer who claims that any sexual contact involving a child is sexual abuse, since minors cannot give consent. A physician may be reluctant to report sexual interactions between children that suggest "normal sexual curiosity and experimentation between children," although there may be coercion and trauma in what superficially appears to be innocence (Sgroi, Porter and Blick, 1982). Because the common perpetrator of sexual abuse of either sex child is a male (Showers et al., 1983) and is known to the family and child, it is not unusual for the mother to come to the physician having discovered something "unusual" about the child's genitalia, such as bleeding or pain. The child also may have shocked the mother with a statement about advances of a relative or friend. The mother then comes to the physician with a vengeance seeking "proof." Alternatively, the mother may not believe the child for a variety of reasons, which may include a realization that the consequences of the act may mean dissolution of a marriage or other relationship. The more dependent the relationship, the less likely it may be for the mother to believe the child. The physician's role is to believe the child.

The child generally enters the medical system through the emergency room when the abuse has resulted in an injury or was perpetrated by a stranger. The emergency-room physician may object to considering a sexual abuse examination to be a true emergency. An examination is needed in order to determine safe placement of the child. Alternatively, the child may present in the physician's office for examination of medical complaints, such as a chronic urinary infection or vaginal discharge, which may be related to sexual abuse. The naive or unsuspecting physician may pursue a host of laboratory tests to determine the etiology of the problem and never consider sexual abuse. A culture report of a venereally transmitted disease may shock the physician into realization (White, Loda, Ingram, and Pearson, 1983). Gonorrhea, syphilis and chlamydia infections are rarely, if ever, transmitted in a non-venereal manner. There is controversy over the non-sexual transmissibility of less common venereal diseases such as venereal warts, ureaplasma, mycoplasma, candida, trichomonas and herpes of the genitalia. It is possible for a child to "auto innoculate" herpes from a "cold sore" on the lip to the genitalia. It is also possible for the infection to come from an infected adult. The incubation period (time needed for the disease to manifest itself) in the unusual venereal diseases may be several months after the contact. Prudent policy would be to report any venereal infection as suspect sexual abuse unless there is definite proof of non-venereal transmission.

The emergency room is not the ideal place to examine a child who has suffered acute or chronic sexual abuse. The examination requires special skill and sensitivity on the part of the medical examiner. A child who has just been traumatized in the genital area may resist examination by a male or female physician. The sense of urgency that permeates the emergency room may further disquiet the child and parents. Crowding the hospital social worker, emergency-room nurse, children services worker, and a police officer into a small room to hear the child's story may be self-defeating. Ideally, a room with a one-way mirror would allow all the individuals to hear the child's story for documentation while fostering a semblance of tranquility. The emergency room should be equipped with the anatomically correct dolls, drawing materials, and dollhouses that facilitate obtaining a history of sexual abuse from a young child.

The physical findings in child sexual abuse can be documented by a routine physical examination, photographs, and supplementary x-rays or laboratory work. There may be no unusual physical findings in a child who has been molested. The physical indicators will depend upon the parts of the body involved in the sexual abuse. There may be rectal bleeding or pain with passage of stool or urine. Foreign bodies may cause infection or obstruction. There may be associated trauma of the breasts or buttocks.

The physician will also need to follow a protocol established to obtain "evidence" (Daniels, 1979). The protocol for an acute episode will be similar to the protocol for a rape investigation. The physician will need to obtain evidence from the child's clothing as well as body. Special containers and preparations are needed to identify sperm. Cultures must be obtained from all orifices, even if the child claims that she/he was only finger manipulated. The child will need to return to a physician for reculture and testing for syphilis, depending upon the time that has elapsed since the episode.

Pediatricians do not tend to routinely examine the genitalia of young girls; consequently their knowledge of the normal girl's genitalia may be inadequate. Further studies are needed to establish norms to assist the physician in this assessment, although the children services worker, police and court may insist on comments about the normality of the hymen and patency of the vaginal orifice. Unless the child has been brutalized in an attempt to enter the vagina or rectum, there will not be evidence that satisfies the court. The perpetrator may have simply entered the introitus, or chamber that is beneath the labia which can admit an adult fingertip. The prepubescent female's vaginal opening is but 0.4 mm in diameter (Cantwell, 1983). This would not admit an adult's little finger without causing pain and dilatation. The opening size may vary with the child's position and muscle tension. If the incident took place some time prior to the examination and was a single episode, the anatomy may have returned to normal. The physician's frustration over demands by non-medical professionals have to "proof" of sexual abuse, in addition to the child's story, may result in reluctance to become involved in evaluations. There is no evidence that preadolescent children, unless prompted by an adult, possibly in a custody battle, can or will invent a detailed story that includes description of the perpetrator's genitalia and the products of ejaculation. Sexually abused children may present with a variety of behavior problems at home or in school. Unfortuantely, sexual abuse is not often considered as a cause (Sgroi et al., 1982).

HELPING THE PHYSICIAN HELP YOU

It has been estimated that an abused child who is returned to his/her parents without intervention has a 50 percent chance for reabuse and a 10 percent chance of being fatally injured (Green and Haggery, 1968). Knowledge of this should provide sufficient motivation for physicians to maximize their skill in identifying and reporting child abuse. Physicians' lack of compliance in providing medical assistance in child abuse evaluation may frustrate and anger the social worker. Probably the worst approach to a reluctant physician, especially a young physician, is to aggressively tell the physician what to do or what you think, even when you are right. The physician may be threatened by any non-medical person who appears to (or does) have more medical knowledge than he/she does. Tact and support will result in more cooperation. It is helpful to have standardized reporting forms for physical abuse, sexual abuse, neglect and failure to thrive. This will guarantee that, at least, the printed portion of the report will be legible. It will also insure that all the information that is needed to process a report has been collected. The form should clarify the physician's responsibility to: (1) collect a detailed history, (2) perform a complete physical examination, (3) order appropriate laboratory tests, (4) request appropriate consultations, including social services, (5) indicate discrepancies between the history and all injuries, (6) document neglect and state possible consequences, (7) determine the need for emergency medical and protective services, (8) report suspicions to appropriate authorities, (9) determine the need for hospitalization and follow-up, (10) maintain rapport with parents, and (11) maintain rapport with social workers. The program at the Children's Hospital in Columbus, Ohio uses such standardized reports, even though we evaluate over 800 abused children a year. The report that is detailed and complete will often preclude appearance of the physician in court. Providing this information to the physician may increase compliance.

Ideally, the evaluation of any child with a complicated problem should be evaluated by a specialist. Smaller communities may not have a pediatrician, much less a pediatrician who is experienced and comfortable in the evaluation of an abused child. If the community recognizes an expert, other physicians may take advantage of the situation by referring all cases to them. Because the time required for the examination and courtroom appearance is rarely adequately compensated, it may be economically unwise for a single physician to become involved with all evaluations. The local medical society may be able to respond to the need by developing a call list of physicians who will rotate the responsibility. The physicians on the call list, the local prosecutor, a member of the children's protective services team and a representative of the police department may be able to develop a team approach to evaluation that rivals that found in a larger city with its children's hospital and a child abuse team. The development of such services may need to be encouraged by the local children services department.

Each specialty has its own jargon and camaraderie. By working together as teammates, physicians and social workers can gain confidence in each others' skills and potentials for serving children and their families. This requires social worker visibility and assertiveness relative to his/her contributions. Social workers are generally trained in group dynamics and communication skills. These skills can be used profitably in the interest of abused children, when applied to the physician. The physician needs to express his/her distress over the realization that all children are not loved or protected by their parents and may be abused. It is helpful to know that social workers and community social service agencies are as concerned and frustrated. This sensitive communication, devoid of mutual recrimination, will generate the ideal partnership for the protection of and service to children.

REFERENCES

Ayoub, C., and Pfeifer, D.: Burns as a manifestation of child abuse and neglect. *American Journal of Diseases of Children, 133*:910-14, 1979.

Bakalav, H.B., Moore, J.D., and Hight, D.W.: Psychosocial dynamics of pediatric burn abuse. *Health and Social Work, 6*(4):27-32, 1981.

Bauman, W.A., and Yalow, R.S.: Child abuse: Parental insulin administration. *Journal of Pediatrics, 99*:588-591, 1981.

Beaver, H., and McClendon, E.: The dentist's responsibility in child abuse and neglect. *Journal of the Michigan Dental Association, 61*:133-36, 1979.

Bensel, R.W. ten, and Wandking, K.J.: Neglect and abuse of children: Historical aspects, identification and management. *Journal of Dentistry for Children, 12*:348-58, 1975.

Bross, D.C.: Medical care neglect. *International Journal of Child Abuse and Neglect, 6*:375-81, 1982.

Bross, D.C., and Meredyth, J.D.: Neglect of the unborn child: An analysis based on law in the United States. *International Journal of Child Abuse and Neglect, 3*:643-50, 1979.

Caffey, J: Multiple fractures in long bones of children suffering from chronic subdural hematoma. *American Journal of Radiology, Radium Therapy, and Nuclear Medicine, 56*:163-71, 1946.

Caffey, J.: On the theory and practice of shaking infants. *American Journal of the Diseases of Children, 124*:161-73, 1972.

Caffey, J.: The whiplash shaken infant syndrome: Manual shaking by the extremities with whiplash-induced intracranial and intraocular bleedings, lined with residual permanent brain damage and mental retardation. *Pediatrics, 54*:396–403, 1974.

Cameron, T.M.: Rarity of non-accidental penetrating injury in child abuse: Letter to the editor. *British Medical Journal, 1*:375–76, 1977.

Cantwell, H.B: *Standards of Neglect*. Denver: Denver Department of Social Services, 1978.

Cantwell, H.B.: Vaginal inspection as it relates to child sexual abuse in girls under thirteen. *International Journal of Child Abuse and Neglect, 7*:171–76, 1983.

Children's Hospital Child Abuse Program. *Annual Report*. Columbus, OH: Children's Hospital, 1984.

Daniels, J.S.: Emergency department management of rape. *The Ohio State Medical Journal, 51*–352, June 1979.

Dine, M.S., and McGovern, M.E.: Intentional poisoning of children: An overlooked category of child abuse: Report of seven cases and review of the literature. *Pediatrics, 70*:35–35, 1982.

Ellerstein, N.: *Child Abuse and Neglect: A Medical Reference, 3*. New York: John Wiley and Sons, 1981.

Gagan, R.J.: The families of children who fail to thrive: Preliminary investigations of parental deprivation among organic and non-organic cases. *The International Journal of Child Abuse and Neglect, 8*:93–103, 1984.

Goldson, E. et al.: Non-accidental trauma and failure to thrive: A sociomedical profile in Denver. *American Journal of the Diseases of Children, 130*:490–92, 1976.

Green, M.I., and Haggery, R.J. (Eds.): *Ambulatory Pediatrics*. Philadelphia: W.B. Saunders Company, 1968.

Groothius, J.R. et al.: Increased child abuse in families with twins. *Pediatrics, 70*:769–73, 1982.

Grosfeld, J.L., and Ballantine, T.V.: Surgical aspects of child abuse (Trauma-X). *Pediatrics, 5*(1):106–20, 1976.

Helfer, R.E., Slovis, T.L., and Black, M.: Injuries resulting when small children fall out of bed. *Pediatrics, 60*:533–35, 1977.

Herrera, A.J. et al.: Parental information and circumcision in highly motivated couples with higher education. *Pediatrics, 71*:233–34, 1983.

Holter, J.C., and Friedman, S.B.: Child abuse: Early case finding in the emergency department. *Pediatrics, 42*:128–38, 1968.

Izant, R.J., and Hubay, C.: The annual injury of 15,000,000 children: A limited study of childhood accidental injury and death. *Journal of Trauma, 6*(1):65–74, 1966.

Johnson, C.F.: Physician abuse in child abuse. *The Bulletin of the Academy of Medicine for Columbus and Franklin County, 49*:157–60, 1983.

Johnson, C.F.: Sudden infant death syndrome vs. child abuse: The teenage connection. *Journal of Pedodontics, 7*:196–208, 1983.

Johnson, C.F.: Bruising and hemophilia: Accident or child abuse? Manuscript submitted for publication, 1984.

Johnson, C.F., and Showers, J.: Injury variables in child abuse. *The International Journal of Child Abuse and Neglect*, in press.

Klein, M., and Stern, L.: Low weight and the battered child syndrome. *American Journal of the Diseases of Children, 122*:15–18, 1971.

Kravitz, H. et al.: Accidental falls from elevated surfaces in infants from birth to one year of age. *Pediatrics, 44*:869–76, 1969.

Lauer, B., Broeck, E., and Grossman, M.: Battered child syndrome: Review of 130 patients with controls. *Pediatrics, 53*:67–70, 1975.

Lenoski, E.F., and Hunter, K.A.: Special patterns of inflicted burn injuries. *The Journal of Trauma, 17*:842–46, 1977.

Loredo, C.M.: Sibling incest. In Groi, S.M. (Ed.): *Clinical Intervention in Child Sexual Abuse.* Lexington, MA: Lexington Books, 1982, pp. 177-189.

Maull, K.: Selective management of posttraumatic intramural hematoma of the duodenum. *Surgical Gynecology and Obstetrics, 146:*221-24, 1978.

McClelland, C.Q., and Kingsbury, G.H.: Fractures in the first year of life: A diagnostic dilemma. *American Journal of the Diseases of Children, 136:*26-29, 1982.

McCort, J., and Vaudagna, J.: Visceral injuries in battered children. *Radiology, 88:*424-28, 1964.

McDonald, A.E.: Child abuse: Problems of reporting. *Pediatric Clinics of North America, 26:*785-91, 1979.

Meadow, R.: Munchausen syndrome by proxy: The hinterland of child abuse. *Lancet, 2:*343-45, 1977.

Moritz, A.R., and Henriques, F.C.: Studies of thermal injury: II. The relative importance of time and surface temperature in the causation of cutaneous burns. *American Journal of Pathology, 23:*695-98, 1947.

Morris, J.L., Johnson, C.F., and Clasen, M.: To report or not to report: Physicians' attitudes toward discipline and child abuse. *American Journal of the Diseases of Children,* in press.

Muecke, M.A.: Caring for Southeast Asian refugee patients in the U.S.A. *American Journal of Public Health, 73:*431-38, 1983.

National Library of Medicine. Child abuse literature search #75-29. August, 1973-December 1975 (353 citations).

National Library of Medicine. Child abuse literature search #80-23. January 1975-December 1980 (463 citations).

Ohio Chapter of the American Academy of Pediatrics Subcommittee on Child Abuse Education. *Education Committee Report,* 1984.

Palmer, C.H., and Weston, J.T.: Several unusual cases of child abuse. *Journal of Forensic Sciences, 21:*851-55, 1976.

Philipart, A.I. Blunt abdominal trauma in childhood. *Surgical Clinics of North America, 57:*151-63, 1977.

Pickel, S., Anderson, C., and Holliday, M.A.: Thirsting and hypernatremic dehydration: A form of child abuse. *Pediatrics, 45:*54-59, 1970.

Polier, H.J.: Professional abuse of children: Responsibility for the delivery of services. *American Journal of Orthopsychiatry, 45:*357-62, 1975.

Sanders, R.W.: Resistance to dealing with parents of battered children. *Pediatrics, 50:*653-57, 1972.

Saulsbury, F.T., Chobanian, M.C., and Wilson, W.G.: Child abuse: Parenteral hydrocarbon ingestion. *Pediatrics, 73:*719-21, 1984.

Showers, J. et al.: The sexual victimization of boys: A three-year study. *Health Values: Achieving High Level Wellness, 7*(4):15-18, 1983.

Sgroi, S.M., Porter, F.S., and Blick, L.C.: Validation of child sexual abuse. In Groi, S.M. (Ed.): *Clinical Intervention in Child Sexual Abuse.* Lexington, MA: Lexington Books, 1982, pp. 39-79.

Silver, L.B.: Child abuse laws—are they enough? *Journal of the American Medical Association, 199*(2):65-68, 1967.

Silver, L.B.: Child abuse syndrome: The "gray areas" in establishing a diagnosis. *Pediatrics, 44:*594-600, 1969.

Solomon, T.: History and demography of child abuse. *Pediatrics (Supplement), 51:*773-76, 1973.

Swischuk, L.E.: Radiology of the skeletal system. In Ellerstein, N.S. (Ed.): *Child Abuse and Neglect: A Medical Reference.* New York: John Wiley and Sons, 1981, pp. 253-73.

Tomasi, L.G., and Rosman, P.: Purtscher retinopathy in the battered child syndrome. *American Journal of Diseases of Children, 129*:1335-37, 1975.

Verity, C.M., Winkworth, C., and Bierman, D.: Polle syndrome: Children of Munchausen. *British Medical Journal, 5*:422-23, 1979.

Watson, J.B.G., Davis, J.M., and Hunter, J.L.P.: Non-accidental poisoning in childhood. *Archives of Diseases of Children, 54*:145-44, 1979.

White, S.T. et al.: Sexually transmitted diseases in sexually abused children. *Pediatrics, 72*:16-21, 1983.

CHAPTER 9

THE LEGAL FRAMEWORK
FOR CHILD PROTECTION

Douglas J. Besharov

INTRODUCTION

In 1960, no state had a law that required the reporting of child abuse. In 1960, few communities had specialized child protective agencies. In 1960, most juvenile courts saw themselves as social service-like agencies responsible for helping parents and children with their problems. And, in 1960, few parents were provided with legal representation or accorded other due process rights. All this changed over the past twenty-five years. This chapter seeks to describe these changes and how they came about.[1]

PAST INDIFFERENCE

Child abuse and child neglect are not new phenomena. "The maltreatment of children is as old as recorded history," notes Professor Sanford Katz. "Infanticide, ritual sacrifice, exposure, mutilation, abandonment, brutal discipline and the near slavery of child labor have existed in all cultures at different periods and have been justified by disparate beliefs—that they were necessary to placate a god, to expel spirits, to maintain the stability of race or simply to inculcate learnings. Practices viewed today as victimizing children were accepted for long periods in civilized communities as 'in the best interest' of society."[2]

Over the centuries, new attitudes slowly developed about the needs of children—and their right to be protected from abuse and neglect. Many of the original thirteen colonies, for example, had laws against certain forms of child maltreatment.[3] Similarly, the first specialized "child protective

148

agency," the New York Society for the Prevention of Cruelty to Children, was founded in 1875.[4] By the early 1920s, most states had passed specific laws against child maltreatment, often within the context of their newly established juvenile courts.[5] And, by the late 1930s, rudimentary networks of public and private child welfare agencies had emerged in most states.[6]

Nevertheless, until the 1960s, child abuse and child neglect remained largely hidden problems, handled by poorly funded and uncoordinated agencies far from public view. If they were recognized at all, they were seen only in terms of a few isolated cases. People might have known that particular parents were "pretty hard on their children," but they did not realize that there were tens of thousands of such parents.

It was easy for the general public and policymakers to underestimate the magnitude of child maltreatment. Few abused or neglected children were reported to the authorities. Even children with serious (and suspicious) injuries went unreported. A 1968 study in Rochester, New York, for example, revealed that 10 percent of all the children under five treated in a hospital emergency room fell into the "battered child syndrome" and another 10 percent were neglected. The researchers concluded that, had it not been for their study, most of these cases would not have been reported.[7] Two years later, a study in nearby Auburn, New York determined that of 195 hospital emergency-room cases, twenty-six (or approximately 13%) involved children with suspicious injuries" which should have been reported. None were.[8]

Reporting was so haphazard that even many murdered children were not reported. A 1972 study by the New York City Department of Social Services, for example, found that "many children known to the medical examiner's offices (as suspected abuse fatalities) have not been reported to the (central) registry as neglected or abused."[9] This was not simply a problem of keeping statistics. When fatalities go unreported, the siblings of these dead children are left unprotected.

MANDATORY REPORTING LAWS

In the early 1960s, a small group of physicians, led by Doctor C. Henry Kempe, became convinced that the only way to break this pattern of indifference was to *mandate* certain professions to report. In 1963, they persuaded the United States Children's Bureau to promulgate a model law that required physicians to report children with a "serious physical injury or injuries inflicted...other than by accidental means."[10] The response of states to this model law was far beyond anything expected. In the short span of four legislative years, all fifty states enacted reporting laws patterned after it, "In the history of the United States, few legislative proposals have been so widely adopted in so little time," according to the late Dean Monrad Paulsen.[11]

This first generation of state reporting laws only mandated the reporting of children with serious inflicted injuries, that is, "battered children." In 1975, however, the U.S. Congress passed the federal Child Abuse Prevention and Treatment Act.[12] The federal act made special grants available to states which expanded their laws to require the reporting of *all* forms of child maltreatment. To obtain these grants, over forty-five states broadened their mandatory reporting laws. As a result, almost all states now have laws which require—under threat of civil and criminal penalties—medical, educational, social work, child care and law enforcement professionals to report physical abuse, sexual abuse and exploitation, physical neglect, and emotional maltreatment. These laws also have provisions which encourage all persons—including friends, neighbors, and relatives of the family—to report suspected maltreatment.[13]

These mandatory reporting laws, and associated public awareness campaigns, have been strikingly effective. In 1963, about 150,000 children came to the attention of public authorities because of suspected abuse or neglect.[14] By 1972, an estimated 610,000 children were reported annually.[15] And, in 1982, more than 1.3 million children were reported.[16] These statistics led President Carter to say: "One of the most serious blights on the prospects for the children of our country is child abuse and the damage that results from it."[17]

Many people ask whether this vastly increased reporting signals a rise in the incidence of child maltreatment. While some observers believe that deteriorating economic and social conditions have contributed to a rise in the level of abuse and neglect, there is no way to tell for sure. So many maltreated children previously went unreported that earlier reporting statistics do not provide a reliable baseline against which to make comparisons. However, one thing is clear: The great bulk of reports now received by child protective agencies would not have been made but for the passage of mandatory reporting laws and the media campaigns that accompanied them.

FRAGMENTED INVESTIGATIVE RESPONSIBILITY

In 1960, few communities had organized programs to investigate reports of suspected child maltreatment and to take protective action when needed. Prior to the enactment of mandatory reporting laws, reports of suspected child abuse and neglect were handled by a variety of different agencies. Reports were made to police agencies, which could investigate the reports themselves or which could refer them to a child welfare agency or, if the family was on welfare, to a public assistance agency. Reports also were made to child welfare agencies (and to the few child protective agencies in existence), which could investigate the reports or refer them to the public assistance agency. Reports also were made directly to public assistance agencies, which, again, either investigated the reports themselves or referred them to police or child welfare agencies. Finally, schools, hospitals, social service agencies, and the full range of other community organizations—as well as friends, neighbors, and relatives—could report to any one of these agencies or bypass them entirely, going directly to court where they could file a child protective petition.

Early reporting laws reflected this system of shared—and divided— authority over reports. Most laws allowed mandated persons to report to either of two specified agencies (usually the police and the local social service agency); some gave reporters a choice between three or more agencies. And, attempting to cover all contingencies, a few laws *required* reports to two or more agencies.[18]

The flood of new cases caused by mandatory reporting laws soon demonstrated that this system of blurred authority did not work. What one study called "a patchwork system of delegated responsibility, often poorly defined, often based on vague and superficial considerations"[19] prevented the development of investigative expertise and encouraged administrative breakdowns. Doctor Ray Helfer complained at the time that this Balkanization of efforts meant that no one person was responsible for protecting the child.[20]

As reports were passed from agency to agency, important information about a child's condition was frequently lost—because it was not communicated to the "appropriate" agency. All too often, the result was a child's tragic death. In New York, for example, the State Assembly's Select Comitee on Child Abuse found that three-quarters of the child abuse fatalities in 1971 involved children previously known to the authorities.[21]

Even many reports that were "accepted" for investigation were, in actuality, simply ignored. Because of staff shortages and limited accountability, the protective staff in the capital city of one Western state, for example, had established what it called "the bank." Uninvestigated reports were "put in the bank." At one point, there were 140 cases in "the bank." Workers tried to screen cases, seeking to put aside only less serious or less urgent situations. Nevertheless, a random review of three cases revealed that two involved reports of generalized neglect and one, from a private physician, complained of a child's "severe malnutrition." Yet, six months after this report had been made, it had not been investigated. In other communities, other euphemisms, such as "the pending case load," were used to describe the uninvestigated cases stacked on the workers' desks.

SPECIALIZED "CHILD PROTECTIVE AGENCIES"

Child protective specialists were uniformly critical of the fragmented investigative responsibility which so weakened child protective efforts. Under the leadership of Vincent DeFrancis of the American Humane Association and Doctor Vincent J. Fontana of the New York Foundling Hospital, they advocated the designation of one, single agency to receive and investigate reports. In keeping with their commitment to non-punitive, therapeutic responses to child maltreatment, they urged that this centralized responsibility be vested in the child protective (or child welfare) staffs of public social service agencies.[22]

At first, child protective specialists (and their allies from the community and other professional fields) had great difficulty convincing states to reform their child protective programs. As late as 1973, only a handful of states had established comprehensive reporting and investigative systems, usually in the wake of a young child's tragic death and the sensational media coverage that followed it.

In New York state, for example, complacency over the plight of maltreated children came to an abrupt end in 1969, when the brutal murder of a young girl attracted intensive media coverage. For more than a month, New York City newspapers ran numerous front-page stories about Roxanne Felumero's death and the agency's (and judicial) mistakes that made it possible. Roxanne had been removed from her drug-addicted parents after repeated beatings. Subsequently, in the face of clear evidence that her parents were extremely disturbed individuals, Roxanne was returned home, where the beatings resumed. Because agency follow-up was so poor, no one noticed the bruises all over Roxanne's body. Eventually, Roxanne died from these beatings, and her parents dumped her body into the East River. A subsequent investigation performed by the judicial authorities found that: "If the Family Court and the complex of public and private agencies operating within it had functioned more effectively, Roxanne Felumero would probably not have met her tragic death."[23] As a result of the attention that this one case received, the New York State Legislature completely revamped the state's child protective system.[24]

Passage of the federal Child Abuse Prevention and Treatment Act in 1974 speeded the creation of specialized child protective agencies. In state after state, federal encouragement (especially grant money) together with recurrent media coverage of child fatalities (or other serious cases) spurred legislative and administrative action. Now, almost all major population centers have specialized "child protective agencies." Usually housed within the public child welfare agency, child protective agencies receive and investigate almost all of the 1.3 million reports of suspected child maltreatment made each year. Especially in larger communities, these agencies receive reports twenty-four hours a day via highly publicized "hotlines" and initiate investigations on the same day or shortly thereafter.[25]

The actual organization of child protective agencies varies widely from state to state and from community to community within the same state. But these differences are less substantial than they seem. All child protective agencies perform essentially the same functions. They receive and screen reports; they investigate reports and determine whether child protective information is needed; they determine what protective measures and treatment services are needed and seek the parents' consent for them; and, finally, if the parents do not agree to the agency's plan, they may seek court authority to impose such measures.[26]

Without exception, child protective agencies have adopted a therapeutic response to the problems of child abuse and neglect. Nationwide, less than 5 percent of substantiated cases result in a criminal prosecution.[27] Based on their investigation of the home situation, the child protective agency in charge will decide what kinds of mental health and social services a family needs and then helps the family to obtain them. Many of these services, such as financial assistance, day care, respite care and crisis nurseries, or homemaker care, are concrete efforts to relieve the pressures and frustrations of parenthood. Other services, such as infant stimulation programs, parent aides, and parent education programs, are designed to give parents specific guidance, role models, and support in child rearing. In addition, individual, group, and family counseling and mental health services are used to ease the tensions of personal problems and marital strife.[28]

This is not meant to suggest that existing investigative and treatment services are sufficient. The expansion of service programs, though substantial, has not kept pace with the rapid and continuing increase in reported cases. There has been chronic shortage of those mental health and social services needed to meet the deep-seated treatment needs of both parents and children.[29].

Recent budget cuts at the federal level have only aggravated these problems. Past expansions of services were facilitated by federal financial support provided under Title XX of the Social Security Act. Until the late 1970s, most states had not yet reached the ceiling in their Title XX allotments, the major federal social service funding program, and so they were able to obtain 75 percent federal reimbursement for their increased expenditures.[30] (Thus, federal expenditures just for "child protective services" rose from a few million dollars a year in 1960 to over $325 million in 1980.)[31] These funds are now under great pressure, as states and localities are called upon to shoulder an increased share of social service expenditures. Consequently, even communities that had developed strong child protective systems are having difficulty keeping up with constantly increasing case loads.

Child protective programs have grave weaknesses.[32] Nevertheless, one must be impressed by the steady increase in their scope and quality. Nationwide, there now exists a basic infrastructure of laws and agencies to protect endangered children—and it has made a difference. Increased reporting and specialized child protective agencies have saved many thousands of children from death and serious injury. In New York state, for example, after the passage of a comprehensive reporting law which also mandated the creation of specialized investigative staffs, there was a 50 percent reduction in child fatalities—from about 200 a year to under 100.[33] Similarly, Ruth and Henry Kempe report that in Denver, the number of hospitalized abused children who die from their injuries has dropped from 20 a year (between 1960 and 1975) to less than one a year.[34]

COURTS AS SOCIAL AGENCIES

When juvenile courts were first established at the turn of the century, they were intended to be the center of society's efforts to help children and families in trouble. Cases were to be brought before "fatherly" judges who, in a relaxed legal setting, would decide what treatment services were needed and then arrange for their delivery.[35] In most communities, probation departments, mental health clinics, alcohol treatment programs, and various other individual and family counseling programs were seen as court, or at least court-related, services; often, they were housed in the court building itself and funded under the court's own budget. As late as 1962, one state legislative committee described its juvenile court as a "special agency for the care and protection of the young and the preservation of the family."[36]

Juvenile court judges were expected to be, in effect, robed social workers. As one observer put it in 1927, the methods that judges were to use were "those of social case work, in which every child is studied and tried as an individual."[37]

To perform this role, judges needed freedom to depart from many existing procedural and constitutional safeguards. They needed freedom to discover the underlying causes of the family's problems, freedom to make use of social and psychiatric reports, and freedom to fashion flexible and innovative treatment plans. To give judges this freedom the rules of court procedure and evidence were substantially relaxed, the presence of counsel was discouraged, and hearings were held in an informal atmosphere.

The doctrine of *parens patriae* was used to justify this departure from standard court procedures. The term *parens patriae*, a Latin phrase, when translated literally means "father of his country." The concept apparently was first used by English kings to justify their intervention in the lives of the children of their vassals—children whose position and property were of direct concern to the monarch. However, because the king justified his intervention by claiming to protect the children, the term grew to mean the sovereign's general obligation to look after the welfare of children in the kingdom since they are helpless. Thus, in 1828, the children of the Duke of Wellesley were removed from him because of his dissolute behavior.[38] When he was on the New York Court of Appeals, Chief Judge Cardozo described the concept of *parens patriae* as the responsibility to do "what is best for the interest of the child. He (the judge) is to put himself in the position of a 'wise, affectionate, and careful parent and make provision for the child accordingly."[39]

Unfortunately, most juvenile courts have never been given the opportunity to put this ideal into practice. From their inception, they have been denied the personnel, facilities, auxiliary services and operating funds they have requested as necessary for them to meet their responsibilities: "Even in the larger cities where juvenile courts are presided over by experienced judges having an interest in, and sympathy for, the problems of juveniles, staffs are usually quite inadequate to handle the work load and to provide the kind of services for juveniles which the juvenile court ideal originally envisioned."[40]

Furthermore, the emphasis on the rehabilitative aspects of the juvenile court's mission obscured the court's judicial role. In their good-faith attempt to help those coming before them, many judges overlooked the need for sufficient and legally admissible evidence before assuming jurisdiction. Moreover, because most petitioners were not legally trained, cases were often inadequately prepared and presented. To fill the resultant gaps in proof, judges frequently elicited the bulk of testimonial and documentary evidence. (It was not unusual for judges to adjourn a case after giving the petitioner precise instructions on what additional witnesses or evidence should be brought to the court.) Having sought evidence against a respondent, it was difficult for judges to weigh it dispassionately, to keep an open mind until the moment of judgment and then sit back and apply the presumption of innocence as they considered all the evidence. (Even if they could, the need to maintain the appearance of impartiality, as well as its reality, would argue persuasively against such practices.) The parents' own lack of legal representation only aggravated these problems. Thus, the informality of juvenile court proceedings often meant that parents were denied an impartial consideration of the charges against them.

THE "JUDICIALIZATION" OF COURT PROCEEDINGS

The *Gault* decision[41] marked a revolutionary and dramatic change in the way juvenile courts handled young people accused of crimes and other forms of misbehavior. In recent years, there has been an equivalent shift in the way juvenile courts handle child protective cases. But because this change was not signaled by a particular case or singular event, it has escaped widespread attention.

The steady, twenty-year expansion of child protective agencies (described above) has made the juvenile court no longer the center of community responses to child abuse and neglect but, rather, the apex, the last stop, in an elaborate pre-court process that takes great pains to avoid formal court action. Child protective agencies seek to use the formal apparatus of the court "only as a last resort." Even if there is sufficient evidence to establish court jurisdiction, they may not file a petition if the parents voluntarily accept services. Only when the parents refuse to accept the child protective worker's decision about the need for services (or to place a child) or when the worker believes that the court's authority will be needed to make the service plan work is court action initiated.[42] Nationally, less than 20 percent of all cases of confirmed child abuse or neglect reach the court.[43]

This avoidance of court action (what the juvenile justice calls diversion) is a recognition that most families can be helped without the stigma and stress of formal court action. It is also a recognition that the expansion of child protective agencies has left the juvenile court out of the mainstream of treatment services: "There has been an expansion of welfare service programs apart from the court but of particular significance to its clientele. Except in certain states the court is no longer a major source of public services available to youth in trouble, and it may have little voice in how these services are provided even for cases coming before it."[44]

One New York case, *Commissioner of Social Services* vs. *Honan*, illustrates the degree of change that has taken place. In this case, the judge, concerned about the possible agency mishandling of one case in which the parent had abducted a child, ordered officials of the local Department of Social Services "to provide the court with a statement of the names of children in their care who are now unaccounted for or who have been on a prior occasion unaccounted for."[45] While appreciating the judge's concern, an appellate court vacated his order on the grounds that, under the state's Child Protective Services Act of 1973, "local departments of social services are given the responsibility for child protection and for safeguarding against child abuse and neglect; and Family Court has no power to deprive such departments of the responsibility."[46]

While this shift of basic treatment responsibility away from the court has made it even more difficult for judges to help the families coming before them to get needed services, it has also had beneficial effects. Vesting treatment responsibility with the court tended to make judges more concerned about the social aspects of the case. In one sense this was good and reflected the highest aspirations of the juvenile court movement; nevertheless, to the extent that it caused judges to pass over the need for clear proof of the allegations before assuming jurisdiction over the family, it obscured the court's judicial role and denied to parents the impartial consideration of the charges made against them.

Thus, the expansion of child protective agencies has allowed the full recognition of the judicial nature of the court's role, namely; to impose, in proper cases, and usually against the wishes of parents, a treatment or protective measure when voluntary adjustments are refused or are insufficient.[47] The New York Family Court Act describes this newly clarified purpose of the juvenile court as: "to provide a due process of law for determining when the state ... may intervene against the wishes of a parent on behalf of a child so that his needs are properly met."[48]

Child protective agencies now must prove that a child is abused or neglected in accordance with the normal rules of evidence. If they cannot do so, the case will be dismissed. Juvenile court judges are now judicial decision makers, not robed social workers.

The increase in the formality of court proceedings, by the way, has led a growing number of states to provide attorneys to assist petitioners in the preparation and presentation of cases. In a few states, legislation requires the presence of an attorney to assist the petitioner. Such statutes generally require that an attorney be provided by a local public law officer—either the local criminal court prosecutor or the local county attorney or corporation counsel. In other states, the law merely provides that the judge may request the local public law official to assist the petitioner. In states where the law is silent on the subject, counsel is often made available through administrative arrangements with a local public law office—either criminal or civil. Occasionally, the local child protective agency uses its own internal legal staff or hires outside counsel to represent its workers.[49]

The "judicialization of court proceedings has not reduced the importance of the court's role, just its centrality. Those cases that do reach the court are often the most severe and require firm, speedy action. Thus, even though most child abuse and child neglect cases do not reach the juvenile court, the court is nevertheless the linchpin upon which the entire out-of-court system depends. Its processes set the tone and parameters for the activities of all non-judicial agencies that make up the child protection system and the juvenile justice system generally. For example, agencies quickly sense what types of cases the court will accept and they tailor their intake and decision-making policies accordingly. Thus, if the court will not adjudicate situations of drug addiction as child abuse or child neglect, community agencies not only will not initiate such proceedings but they also will tend to consider them not maltreatment for their own internal purposes.

Many child protective professionals are unhappy with the "judicialization" of court proceedings. This is a mistake. To protect children from harm caused by parents, child protective and law enforcement agencies need not violate due process and fundamental fairness. The array of protective workers, police officers, social workers, and prosecutors that the state typically musters in child protective proceedings should be sufficient to build a case against the parents; the assistance of a tolerant judge should not be needed to make their case stick.

REPRESENTATION FOR PARENTS

The benign purpose of child protective proceedings does not prevent them from being unpleasant—and sometimes counterproductive—intrusions into family life. A petition which alleges that a child is "abused" or "neglected" is an explicit accusation of parental wrong doing or inadequacy. As Justice Black described: "The case by its very nature resembles a criminal prosecution. The defendant is charged with conduct—failure to care properly for her children—which may be viewed as criminal and which in any event is viewed as reprehensible and morally wrong by a majority of society."[50]

Besides the stigma involved, a finding of abuse or neglect may encourage a criminal prosecution, may result in the removal of a child from parental custody and, ultimately, may result in the termination of their homes for over six years.[51] (During this time, efforts to reunite the family are often inconsequential.) Even if the child is not removed from the home, the parents may be placed under long-term court supervision and be forced to submit to court- or agency-sponsored treatment programs.

Some parents are willing, and a few are even eager, to relinquish their parental rights. But most parents, even inadequate or "bad" ones, do not want to do so. However, most parents strive to avoid a court adjudication of "child abuse" or "child neglect."

Without legal counsel, though, parents are at a severe disadvantage if they seek to contest the state's petition. As the American Bar Association points out: "Skilled counsel is needed to execute basic advocacy functions: to delineate the issues, investigate and conduct discovery, present factual contentions in an orderly manner, cross-examine witnesses, make objections and preserve a record for appeal.[52] Supreme Court Justice Stewart described some of the obstacles faced by unrepresented parents: "Expert medical and psychiatric testimony, which few parents are equipped to understand and fewer still do confute, is sometimes presented. The parents are likely to be people with little education, who had uncommon difficulty in dealing with life, and who are, at the hearing, thrust into a distressing and disorienting situation. That these factors may combine to overwhelm an uncounselled parent is evident...."[53]

The imbalance of the adversaries in child protective proceedings is striking. Marshalled against the unaided parent are "the full panoply of traditional weapons of the state."[54] In many states, the petitioning agency is represented by counsel.[55] But even if the agency is not represented, it "has access to public records concerning the family and to professional social workers who are empowered to investigate the family situation and to testify against the parent....(It) may also call upon experts in family relations, psychology, and medicine to bolster (its)...case."[56]

A 1968 study of child protective cases in New York City is apparently the only attempt to determine the effect that legal representation has on the outcome of court proceedings.[57] Although its methodology was flawed,[58] the study does tend to document the positive impact of counsel (see Chart 2). A later survey of family court judges who preside over termination proceedings confirm this finding. The study found that "72.2 percent of them agreed that when a parent is unrepresented, it becomes more difficult to conduct a fair hearing (11.1% of the judges disagreed); 66.7 percent thought it became more difficult to develop the facts (22.2% disagreed)."[59]

CHART 2

Disposition	Percentage Represented By Counsel	Percentage Not Represented By Counsel
Children placed outside the home	18.2	40.6
Discharged under court supervision	45.4	39.6
Discharged without court supervision	9.1	5.0
Petition dismissed after initial adjudication	9.1	3.0
Other	18.2	11.8

For all these reasons, the appointment of counsel to represent parents has, for many years, been recommended by most standard setting organizations, such as the American Bar Association,[60] the National Council on Crime and Delinquency,[61] and the U.S. Children's Bureau.[62]

Until the early 1970s, though, few indigent parents were provided with appointed counsel. Then, the growing formality of juvenile court proceedings, coupled with the heightened sensitivity of courts to the legal representation of indigents before the court (in large part encouraged by the *Gault* case),[63] led a number of courts to hold that indigent parents in child protective proceedings have a right to appointed counsel.[64] In 1972, the

New York Court of Appeals, for example, held that: "In our view, an indigent parent, faced with the loss of a child's society, as well as the possibility of criminal charges, is entitled to the assistance of counsel. A parent's concern for the liberty of the child, as well as for his care and control, involves too fundamental an interest and right to be relinquished without the opportunity for a hearing, with assigned counsel if the parent lacks the means to retain a lawyer."[65]

However, the case law was never unanimous, and a 1981 Supreme Court case made the parents' *constitutional right* to counsel even less clear.[66] In *Lassiter* vs. *North Carolina*[67] the Court held that an indigent mother did not have a right to appointed counsel in a termination proceeding in which she permanently lost custody of her child. Instead, ruled the Court, the parents' right to counsel must be determined on a case-by-case basis.[68] Most authorities assume that the Court would apply the same case-by-case rule to child protective proceedings since they involve a lesser state intrusion into parental rights. But no one is quite sure.

This uncertainty in the case law makes all the more surprising—and satisfying—the movement of state legislatures toward statutorily guaranteeing the appointment of counsel in child protective proceedings. At this writing, about 40 states legislatively mandate the provision of counsel.[69] In most of the remaining states, court decisions or administrative arrangements insure that parents are represented. Thus, almost all indigent parents who are called before juvenile courts are now provided with legal representation.

The presence of an attorney to guard the parents' rights undoubtedly makes it harder for the authorities to "win" child protective cases. But this is as it should be. State intrusion in family matters is an extreme remedy—which should be pursued only in accord with traditional American values of due process and basic fairness. If the child's interests require societal intervention, the petitioner, through sufficient planning and preparation, should be able to prove it in court. To protect children, the state needs no tools and needs no advantages greater than those it ordinarily possesses.

IMPLICATIONS FOR PRACTICE

No one should believe that the changes described in this chapter have made practice easier for social workers. Just the opposite. The formalization of child protective responsibilities and judicialization of court proceedings require social workers practicing today to master a series of investigative, legal, and administrative skills that their predecessors were able to ignore.

Heightened requirements for providing the need for court action, for example, have had the corollary effect of requiring social workers to be much better at discovering and preserving evidence. Similarly, the expansion of formal legal rules and rights to child welfare situations has had the corollary effect of requiring social workers to develop expertise in identifying and handling legal issues. As law professor Sanford Katz observed: "No professional group, other than lawyers, come in contact with so many 'pigeon holes' of law, such as domestic relations, criminal law, real property, evidence, procedures, and contracts, as do social workers."[70]

More importantly, the central aspect of social work decision making has changed. Social workers no longer enjoy all but unfettered discretion in doing what they deem is in the best interests of children and parents. Social work professors Stein and Rzepnicki provide an apt warning to all workers in the child welfare field:

> Moreover, social work practice in child welfare has changed markedly in recent years. Whether one considers the increased formality of juvenile court procedures, the growth of litigation against child-caring agencies, the interest in the disposition of a case is represented by separate counsel, the substantive case-planning requirements found in federal and state legislation, or the growing acceptance of 18-month dispositional hearings for children in placement, the trend toward a more legal approach to practice is clear.
>
> Workers can expect to have their decisions challenged by review boards or by attorneys representing children or their biological or foster parents, and to have to support their choices with factual evidence, not, as in the past, with impressions and judgments that are not supported by objective data.[71]

These added burdens have not been easily assumed by social workers already pressed to the limits by overwhelming case loads and the lack of adequate treatment services in the community. Clearly, there must be a comprehensive and sustained response from the profession. The adversary proceedings in court today may be quite different from what the social worker has experienced earlier or from what she or he was taught to expect. Often, the reality is a shock to the new social worker. When challenged in court, the social worker may feel that it is necessary to protect the child not only from the parents but also from the court. Schools of social work and responsible agencies could help by instructing social workers in courtroom procedures and by teaching them to present the facts of the case and the recommendations in a manner that will meet legal standards as well as benefiting the child.[72]

In this chapter, it has not been possible to do more than mention these problems. However, the following guidelines for effective testimony, prepared for the National Center on Child Abuse and Neglect, should be helpful:

- A witness should present a professional appearance and attitude in court. A witness's manner of dress, tone of voice, and facial expression all contribute to the judge's perception of the testimony. A worker who antagonizes the judge or any of the attorneys may prejudice the case and could be held in contempt of court. It is very important, therefore, to avoid being argumentative.
- CPS workers and other professionals who are testifying are permitted to bring notes to which they can refer during the hearing; notes are sometimes helpful in remembering specific dates and times. These notes, however, may be admitted as evidence.
- It is necessary to be as thoroughly prepared and as objective as possible regarding the case. Testimony should be limited to the facts, unless the witness is specifically asked for a professional opinion. For example, a CPS worker should testify: "I visited the family on Tuesday and Thursday of last week," rather than "a couple of days last week"; "I arrived at 12:30 p.m.," rather than "around noon"; and "food and dishes were scattered all over the kitchen," rather than "the house was a mess."
- The witness should be aware of the general rules of evidence before testifying, although these do change slightly depending on the type of hearing.
- The witness should answer only the question asked and should not volunteer additional information. It is important for the witness to understand the question asked and not to guess at an answer. All statements must be as accurate as possible. The witness should take time to think through both the question and the answer thoroughly before responding. If a "yes" or "no" answer is requested but cannot be accurately given, the witness should explain that this would be a misleading response and that the question cannot be answered in this way. Usually, the witness will be given an opportunity to explain the response more completely.

    Remember that witnesses have rights, too. Help can be sought in the form of a question to the judge if the witness feels the answer being sought would be misleading or untrue.
- During cross-examination, an attorney may try to confuse the witness in order to make the testimony appear inaccurate or biased. The witness should never respond to this angrily or in haste but should remain calm and answer the question as clearly and accurately as possible. If a witness becomes flustered, it is possible that inaccurate or misleading information may be given and the best interests of the child may not be served. The worker may ask the judge for help if the questions or manner of an attorney are confusing.

HINTS FOR TESTIFYING

- Dress appropriately.
- Prepare ahead of time.
- Don't memorize your testimony.
- Expect to feel anxious.
- Speak a little louder and slower than you feel is necessary.
- Be sincere and dignified.
- Speak clearly and distinctly.
- Use appropriate language.
- Answer the question that was asked.
- Let the attorney develop your testimony.
- If you don't know the answer to a question, say so. Don't guess.
- Don't make your testimony conform to other testimony you may have heard.
- When answering questions, look at the person asking the questions or at the judge or jury.
- Tell the truth.

How to survive cross-examination:

- Be careful about what you say and how you say it.
- Listen carefully to the question; don't answer it unless you understand it.
- If a question has two parts requiring different answers, answer it in two parts.
- Keep calm.
- Answer positively rather than doubtfully.
- If you are testifying as an expert, be prepared to reconcile or distinguish your opinion from opposing schools of thought.
- Don't close yourself off from supplying additional details.
- Don't allow yourself to be rushed.
- Don't get caught by a trick question.

SUMMARY

If any one word characterizes the legal framework for child protection over the last twenty years, it is "change." New reporting laws, new child protective agencies, new roles for juvenile courts, and new rights for parents all require change—change in attitudes, operating procedures, and personnel.

Such change does not come easily. Old ways die hard. And no change, no matter how needed, is accomplished without tension and trauma.

Even though many courts and social agencies have lost ground in the face of budgetary austerity; overall, things are better than they were in 1960. The changes that have been made should make us all proud and should encourage us to redouble our efforts for the future.

But whether or not one feels that all of the changes of the last twenty years were for the good, the truth is that they were inevitable, just as more change in the future is inevitable.

Child protective professionals from all disciplines must be ready to respond to more change, and they must be ready to help channel that change in constructive directions, as society seeks to improve further its ability to protect abused and neglected children.

REFERENCE NOTES

1. This chapter is necessarily selective. For example, in response to the federal Child Abuse Prevention and Treatment Act, over forty states have changed their laws or court procedures to provide for the independent representation of children. This is an important development which merits careful discussion. Unfortunately, space considerations make it impossible to address this and many other equally important subjects. For further information on the representation of children, *see* American Bar Association, *National Guardian Ad Litem Policy Conference Manual* (Young Lawyers Division, rev. ed., November 1981).

2. Katz, S., McGrath, M., and Howe, R., *Child Neglect Laws in America*, p. 3 (1976). *See also* Radbill, "A history of child abuse and infanticide," found in: *The Battered Child* (Helfer, R., Kempe, C.H., eds., 1974).

3. *See* Brenner, R., *Children and Youth in America* (1971).

4. *See* An Act for the Incorporation of Societies for the Prevention of Cruelty to Children, ch. 130, 1875 Laws 114.

5. *See generally* Lou, *Juvenile Courts in the United States* (1927); Mack, "The Juvenile Court," 23 *Harvard Law Review* 104 (1909).

6. *See generally* Kadushin, A., *Child Welfare Services* (1974).

7. Holter and Friedman, "Child Abuse: Early Case Finding in the Emergency Department," *Pediatrics*, Vol. 42, No. 1, July 1968.

8. Cited in: New York State Assembly Select Committee on Child Abuse, *Report*, p. 25 (April 1972); reprinted in *The Battered Child* (Kempe, C.H., Helfer, R., eds., 2nd Ed., 1974).

9. Initial Quarterly Progress Report to Criminal Justice Coordinating Council, Child Abuse Grant C55934 (January 1972, p. 8).

10. U.S. Children's Bureau, *The Abused Child—Principles and Suggested Language for Legislation on Reporting of the Physically Abused Child* (U.S. DHEW 1963).

11. Paulsen, "The Legal Framework for Child Protection," 6 *Columbia Law Review* 679, 711 (1966).

12. Act of January 31, 1974, Pub. L. No. 93-247, 88 Stat. 5, codified at 42 U.S.C. §§ 5101-5106 (Supp. V, 1975).

13. *See generally* Besharov, "The Legal Aspects of Reporting Known and Suspected Child Abuse and Neglect," 23 *Villanova Law Review* 458 (1977-1978).

14. U.S. Children's Bureau, *Juvenile Court Statistics*, p. 13 (U.S. DHEW 1966).
15. Nagi, S., *Child Maltreatment in the United States: A Challenge to Social Institutions*, p. 35 (1977).
16. U.S. National Center on Child Abuse and Neglect, *National Study of the Incidence and Severity of Child Abuse and Neglect*, p. 11 (DHHS 1981).
17. Quoted in: U.S. National Center on Child Abuse and Neglect, *Working Together: A Plan to Enhance Coordination of Child Abuse and Neglect Activities* 1 (U.S. DHHS 1980).
18. *See* Besharov, D., *Juvenile Justice Advocacy*, p. 130-131 (1974).
19. N.Y.C. Department of Social Services, Initial Quarterly Progress Report to N.Y.C. Criminal Justice Coordinating Council, Child Abuse Grant C-55734, at 10 (1972).
20. Helfer and Kempe, *The Battered Child*, ed.'s note to Chapter 2 (2nd ed., 1972).
21. New York State Assembly Select Committee on Child Abuse, *supra* n. 8, at 1-2.
22. *See, e.g.*, DeFrancis, V., *Child Protective Services: A National Survey* (1967); Fontana, J., *The Maltreated Child* (1964).
23. Report of the Judiciary Relations Committee of the Appellate Division of the First Department, quoted in: *New York Law Journal*, June 30, 1969, at 1, col. 4.
24. *See* New York State Assembly Select Committee on Child Abuse, *supra* n. 8, at pp. ii-v.
25. *See generally* U.S. General Accounting Office, *Increased Federal Efforts Needed to Better Identify, Treat, and Prevent Child Abuse and Neglect*, chap. 3 (1980).
26. *See generally* Besharov, "Representing Abused and Neglected Children: When Protecting Children Means Seeking the Dismissal of Court Proceedings," 20 *Journal of Family Law* 217 (1982).
27. *See* U.S. National Center on Child Abuse and Neglect, *National Analysis of Child Neglect and Abuse Reporting* (1978) p. 36, Table 28 (U.S. DHEW 1979).
28. *See generally* U.S. National Center on Child Abuse and Neglect, *Annual Analysis of Child Abuse and Neglect Programs* (DHHS 1980).
29. *Compare* DeFrancis, V., *Child Protective Services in the United States: A Nationwide Survey* (Amer. Humane Assoc. 1956); DeFrancis, V., *Child Protective Services: A National Survey* (Amer. Humane Assoc. 1967); *with* Hildenbrand, W., *et al.*, *Child Protective Services Entering the 1980's* (Amer. Humane Assoc. 1981).
30. *See, e.g.*, Benton, Field, and Millar, "Social Services: Federal Legislation vs. State Implementation," p. 72 (The Urban Institute, Washington, D.C., 1978), stating that: "The majority of (state administrators and federal staff surveyed) agreed that Title XX had the greatest positive impact on the children's protective service category."
31. U.S. Department of Health and Human Services, *Technical Notes: Summaries and Characteristics of States' Title XX Social Services Plans for Fiscal Year 1980*, p. 126 (undated report).
32. *See* Besharov, "Child Protection: Past Progress, Present Problems, Future Directions," 17 *Family Law Quarterly* 151 (1983).
33. New York State Department of Social Services, *Child Protective Services in New York State: 1979 Annual Report*, Table 8 (1980).
34. Kempe, R.S., and Kempe, C.H., *Child Abuse* 8 (1978).
35. *See, e.g.*, Lou, *supra* n. 5; Mack, *supra* n. 5.
36. Joint Legislative Committee on Court Reorganization, "The Family Court," 1962 McKinney's Session Laws 3420.
37. Lou, *supra* n. 5, at pp. 1-2.
38. *Wellesley* v. *Wellesley*, II Bligh, N.S. 124, 4 Engl. Rep. 1078 (1828).
39. *Finlay* v. *Finlay*, 240 N.Y. 429, 433-434, 148 N.E. 624, 626 (1925) (footnote omitted).
40. Clark, "Why Gault: Juvenile Court Theory and Impact in Historical Perspective," in *Gault: What Now for the Juvenile Court* 1, 10-11 (Nordin, ed., 1968).

41. *In re Gault*, 387 U.S. 1 (1967), required the appointment of counsel for indigent juveniles who face the possibility of commitment to secure institutions.

42. *See generally* Besharov, *supra* n. 26.

43. *National Analysis of Child Neglect and Abuse Reporting, supra* n. 27, at p. 36, Table 28.

44. Vinter, The Constitutional Responsibility of Court-Related Personnel, in *Gault: What Now for the Juvenile Court* 119, 122 (Nordin, ed., 1968).

45. 67 A.D. 2d 815, 816, 413 N.Y.S. 2d 532, 533 (4th Dept. 1979).

46. 67 A.D. 24 at 816, 413 N.Y.S. 2d at 534.

47. This is not to say that the *Gault* case did not also contribute to this change by establishing a general atmosphere in the court more sensitive to due process safeguards.

48. N.Y. Fam. Ct. Act §1011 (1983).

49. *See* Besharov, "The 'Civil' Prosecution of Child Abuse and Neglect," 6 *Vermont Law Review* 403 (1981).

50. *Kaufman* v. *Carter*, 402 U.S. 954, 959 (1971) (Black, J., *dissenting* from a denial of certiorari).

51. U.S. Children's Bureau, *National Study of Social Services to Children and Their Families* p. 120 (DHEW 1978).

52. *Amicus* Brief of the American Bar Association, *Lassiter* v. *Department of Social Services of Durham County, North Carolina*, No. 79-64323, 452 U.S. 18 (1981).

53. *Lassiter* v. *Department of Social Services of Durham County, North Carolina*, 452 U.S. 18, 30 (1981).

54. *Danforth* v. *State*, 303 A. 2d 794, 799, (Me. 1973).

55. *See* text at *supra* n. 49.

56. *Lassiter* v. *North Carolina, supra* n. 53, at 43 (Blackman, J., *dissenting*).

57. Note, "Representation in Child-Neglect Cases: Are Parents Neglected?" 4 *Columbia Journal of Law and Social Problems* 230, 241–242 (1968).

58. The representation by counsel was not random. Only parents who could afford to hire an attorney or who made the effort to obtain one from a legal aid or legal services agency were represented. Even without counsel, such parents would be more likely to prevail in a termination proceeding.

59. *Lassiter* v. *North Carolina, supra* n. 53, at 29, n. 5.

60. American Bar Association, Juvenile Justice Standards Project, *Standards Relating to Counsel for Private Parties*, Standard 2.3(b) (1980).

61. National Council on Crime and Delinquency, *Model Rules for Juvenile Courts*, Rule 39 (1969).

62. U.S. Children's Bureau, *Legislative Guide for Drafting Family and Juvenile Court Acts*, § 25(b) (1969).

63. *See supra* n. 41.

64. *See, e.g., Cleaver* v. *Wilcox*, 499 F. 2d 940, 945 (9th Cir. 1974) (case-by-case basis); *Davis* v. *Page*, 442 F. Supp. 258, 263 (S.D. Fla. 1977); *Smith* v. *Edmiston*, 431 F. Supp. 941 (W.D. Tenn. 1977); *In re Welfare of Myricks*, 85 Wash. 2d 252, 533 P. 2d 841 (1975); *Crist* v. *New Jersey Div. of Youth and Family Services*, 128 N.J. Super 402, 415, 320 A. 2d 203 (1974); mod. on other grounds, 135 N.J. Super. 573, 343 A. 2d 815 (1975); *State ex rel. Lemaster* v. *Oakley*, 157 W. Va. 590, 203 S.E. 2d 140 (1974); *Danforth* v. *State Dept. of Health and Welfare*, 303 A. 2d 794, 795 (Me. 1973); *In re Ella B.*, 30 N.Y. 2d 352, 334 N.Y.S. 2d 113, 285 N.E. 2d 288 (1972).

65. *In re Ella B.*, 30 N.Y. 2d 352, 356–57, 334 N.Y.S. 2d 133, 136, 285 N.E. 2d 288, 293, citations omitted.

66. *See, e.g., In re Robinson*, 8 Cal. App. 3d 783, 87 Cal. Reptr. 678 (1970), *cert. denied sub nom., Kaufman* v. *Carter*, 402 U.S. 964 (1971), denying the right to counsel in child

protective proceedings; *In re Joseph T.*, 25 Cal. App. 3d 120, 101 Cal. Reptr. 606 (1974). *Cf.*, *Potvin* v. *Keller*, 313 So. 2d 703 (Fla. 1975), where the parents requested state care for the child (in effect, *rev'd* by *Davis* v. *Page*, *supra* n. 64).

67. *See supra* n. 53.
68. *See* Besharov, "Terminating Parental Rights: The Indigent Parent's Right to Counsel after *Lassiter* v. *North Carolina*," 15 *Family Law Quarterly* 205 (1981).
69. U.S. National Center on Child Abuse and Neglect, *State Child Abuse and Neglect Laws—A Comparative Analysis*, pp. 76–77, Table I (DHHS 1983).
70. Katz, "The Lawyer and the Caseworker: Some Observations," *Social Casework* 42 (1961):14.
71. Stein, T., and Rzepnicki, T., *Decision Making at Child Welfare Intake: A Handbook for Practitioners* pp. 7–8 (1983).
72. U.S. National Center on Child Abuse and Neglect, *Child Protection: The Role of the Courts* pp. 57–58 (DHHS 1980).

CHAPTER 10

ETHICAL ISSUES

Shankar A. Yelaja and John Latimer

INTRODUCTION

At first glance it may not appear that child abuse and neglect would pose any complex ethical issues. After all, abusing and neglecting children is wrong and the state is justified in intervening to protect the interests of the child. But as one begins to study the problem, the issues become more complex. In order to put these ethical issues in a proper perspective, we will begin our discussion with a brief history of moral philosophy from its origins in ancient Greece to present contemporary ethical thought, thus using history as a basis to inform our discussion of the ethical issues surrounding child abuse and neglect.

One of the most persistent problems facing philosophers down through the ages has been the question of what is good and what is evil. The answers to this question have ranged from the claim of an absolute and ultimate measure of good and evil to the belief that both good and evil are relative to the conditions of time and place. The metaethical thinking about this problem has changed and evolved over the centuries. The codes of conduct or the applications of ethical standards and values that have appeared throughout history, commonly referred to as normative ethics, are derived from conclusions drawn in the area of metaethics. According to Reamer: "Formal theories of obligations...appeal to a logically necessary relation between ethical principle, so that to perform actions that contradict such principles is to be inconsistent or to contradict one's self" (Reamer, 1982, p. 18).

The absolutist position mentioned above is commonly referred to as denotology. Within this school of thought it is generally believed that the measure of good or evil is inherent within the structure of the universe. Man, through the development of reason, discovers these universal laws or they are revealed to him by the Creator of the universe. Deontological arguments are made concerning the metaethical questions and generally appeal for justification to either the will of God, conformity to the laws of nature, or conformity to human nature. The point being made is that these are absolute measures of good and evil that apply in all situations and at all times.

The relativist or teleological position suggests that the measure of good and evil depends upon time and place. The consequences of a particular act on the welfare of the group determines whether it is an ethical act. The most popular of the telelogical theories have been the utilitarian models. Social workers have historically relied on this framework in their ethical analysis of issues confronting social work practice.

Historical Development of Deontology

The early Greeks were among the first in recorded history to consider the question of good and evil. They generally perceived the universe as being in a state of harmony which was the result of a combination of opposites: good and evil. Man was enjoined to strive to understand this harmony which encompassed universal reason and to pattern his actions accordingly.

With the maturing of Greek thought and the contributions of Socrates, Plato and Aristotle, the belief in absolute and all-pervasive laws controlling the universe was modified.

Socrates maintained the belief that there needs to be a basic principle of right and wrong beyond the beliefs of any one individual. He was finally to understand that knowledge was the highest good and that a good life was one spent in search of a knowledge of good. He believed that nobody is voluntarily bad. Following Socrates, Plato held that reason was the highest good and that a good life was one ruled by reason. Such a life would be characterized by wisdom, courage and self-control. Pleasure, according to Plato, came as a result of a good life and was not sought as an end in itself.

Aristotle believed that the good for which all else was done was self-realization. Like Plato, this meant the full realization of one's reason. Reason lead one to be noble, just, honest, considerate and to exhibit a rational attitude marked by a balance of extremes. Such a person is driven to ethical acts from the depth of his own being.

The metaethical question of what is good is answered quite unequivocally by both Plato and Aristotle as being the full development of the faculty of reason. The normative question is of less importance. The implication being that at the end of the process (i.e. the development of reason), the ethical act is self-evident and the individual is compelled to carry it out. Disagreement about the ethics of an act then can occur only between two individuals, one or both of whom have not fully developed their reason. Therefore, every act is either right or wrong in an absolute sense. Reason does not determine the ethics of an act that merely reveals its inherent ethical quality.

The Judeo-Christian religious traditions also exerted strong influences on deontological thinking. Greek thought, under these influences, emphasized a greater distinction between good and evil. The soul or mind became the seat of good, while the body became the seat of evil. Because of this strong dualism, the development of one's faculty of reason, required to discover universal reason, depended upon removing oneself from the influence of the body and the world.

Christianity, historically, has been more pessimistic about man's ability, through the use of reason, to discover universal reason or the will of God. The sinful will of man, not as a result of ignorance as in Greek thought but as an inherent quality, was central to Christian moral philosophy. Man, then, could not be trusted to develop a system of normative ethics as was the case in Greek thought. A code of ethical conduct had to be given to man by God (i.e. the Sermon on the Mount and the Ten Commandments) and these were to be observed for individual as well as societal well-being and welfare.

The deontological elements of the Greeks were universal laws which could be discovered by human beings through the development of the faculty of reason; while Christian thinkers held that the will of God was absolute but that divine revelation was necessary for its dissemination.

Historical Development of Teleology

The origins of teleological thought can also be traced back to ancient Greece. The first blossoming of this school of thought occurred with the Sophists. They eschewed the idea of an absolute measure of good and evil and held the belief that morality was mere convention and that every individual should determine for himself what was good and what was evil.

The Epicureans, another group of Greek philosophers, espoused the view that the goal of human activity was pleasure and supreme good was happiness. The rightness of an act could be judged by its consequences: the balance of pleasure over pain.

More recent philosophers, including Thomas Hobbes and John Locke, held similar ideas to the Epicureans, both believing that good and evil are relative to the individual.

Teleological thinking evolved after Hobbes and Locke had begun to include a concern for the happiness of others as well as the individual. The metaethical systems within this school of thought began to incorporate a social element which had a marked effect on the normative systems being proposed. Utilitarianism was developed from this trend of thought by

Richard Cumberland. He called for a proper balance between the interest of the individual and society and believed that a good act resulted in the greatest good for the greatest number. John Stuart Mill, also a utilitarian, expanded on Cumberland's thoughts by ascribing different qualities to certain classes of goods. He contended that goods of the intellect were better than goods of the senses.

The pragmatic school of thought rose in an attempt to balance the strong social ethic which had developed with the older concern for the welfare of the individual. Dewey and James both emphasized that the individual must be considered an end in himself and not as a means to the collective good. They believed that the individual was a social product and, therefore, an act which enriches the life of the individual must also be enriching for the group. The individual and the group are tied together and the measure of good and evil becomes the individual.

The criticisms of teleology, and specifically of utiltarianism, have basically fallen into two areas. The first has to do with the functioning of the theory in practice. There have been problems with quantifying the good resulting from specific actions; with making comparisons between individuals with respect to whether a good is equally good for various individuals; with identifying good generally; and, finally, with assessing future consequences. However, the second area of criticism is far more serious. This has to do with the lack of concern and respect for the individual. Reamer suggests: "Technically it may permit subordination of the rights of a few individuals if a greater aggregation of good results" (Reamer, 1982, p. 23).

Wilkes is stronger in her opposition to utilitarianism and the values associated with it: "The values adhered to are instrumental to the purpose aimed at and are more than a means to an end.... All assume that values are instrumental to human purposes and all deny the fixed essence of human nature, a phenomenon Stephen Spender likens to the second fall of man" (Wilkes, 1981, p. 63).

Summary of the History of Moral Philosophy

The two fundamental schools of thought regarding moral philosophy, deontology and teleology, clearly have a long history. As well as the maturing of thought within each school which has occurred over time, there have been shifts in the popular appeal of the two positions throughout history. At the present time, the relativistic or teleological position seems to have gained dominance in the forms of situational ethics and the utilitarian models. However, it must be remembered that ethical models are refined over time to meet the ethical demands of the societies within which they have influence. The criticisms leveled against current ethical models are mounting which suggests that they are not meeting the needs of our changing society. What can be learned from this historical perspective is that an ethical theory must have the flexibility to adapt to changing conditions as well as an element of permanence that reflects an inherent humanness shared by all people in all places at all times.

Tillich addresses the same question in his study of ethics in the changing world. He asks: "Is there a possible solution beyond the alternative of an absolutism that breaks down in every radical change of history and the relativism that makes change itself the ultimate principle?" (Tillich, 1957, p. 154).

Tillich answers his own question by stating that the rationalistic-progressive solution of Western society as represented in the Bill of Rights is a partial answer. Some eternal principles are outlined which point the direction in which mankind must go: "Their theoretical and practical realization is always in a process towards higher perfection. In this way they are adaptable to every human situation" (Tillich, 1957, p. 153).

Tillich concludes, however, that these principles are not creative or comprehensive enough to allow the immovable element to unite with the power of change needed in an ultimate ethical theory. Tillich's ultimate answer lies in the principle of love: "Love, agape, offers a principle of ethics which maintains an eternal, unchangeable element but makes its realization dependent on continuous acts of a creative intuition" (Tillich, 1957, p. 154). Frankena, in proposing a tentative theory of moral obligation, states that two basic principles are required: that of beneficence or utility and that of justice. He goes on to suggest: "All our duties, even that of justice, presuppose the principle of benevolence though they do not all follow from it. To this extent, and only to this extent, is the old dictum that love is what underlies and unifies the rules of morality correct" (Frankena, 1963, p. 37).

What is implied by both Tillich and Frankena is an idea that again finds its root in ancient Greece in the writings of Democritus. The ethics of an act is determined to a large extent by the intention or motivation of the actor. This idea has been echoed many times by moral philosophers throughout history.

The Individual and the Process of Ethical Analysis

Downie and Telfer suggest that a moral nature is a characteristic endowment of human beings. One's life becomes meaningful as the result of one's moral judgments about the nature of the self and the activities which express that nature. They conclude that moral process leads to self-development.

Essentially, Tillich is in agreement with Downie and Telfer when he says that: "Every moral act is an act in which an individual self establishes itself as a person.... The moral act leads to self-realization" (Tillich, 1963, p. 20).

A final quote, in support of the point that the ethical process going on within the individual is as important as the final act, is provided by Ruth Wilkes. In supporting a belief of the ancient Greeks, she states that: "The good man performs the good action, the bad man performs the bad action. Becoming good is the first requirement and the rest follows" (Wilkes, 1981, p. 67).

Our findings to this point have a direct bearing on the process of ethical analysis in which one would engage concerning the problems of child abuse and neglect. What we have discovered is that there is no supreme ethical theory with which to resolve the ethics of this situation. Actually, it would be unfortunate if there were because of the importance of the ethical process to self-development and a meaningful life. Ethics in a changing world such as ours requires a blend of the relativist and absolutist positions, the teleological and deontological schools of thought, and social and individual ethics.

Child abuse and neglect, when discovered, result in the intervention in families' lives by social workers. These interventions range from the giving of advice about child care to the removal of children from homes. Many ethical issues are raised as a result of these interventions, including the problem of authority, the role of the state, conflicts of values about individuals' rights to self-determination, freedom and well-being, and social workers' role conflicts. At first glance it would seem obvious that a child's best interests are served by removal from his battering parents. However, Downie and Telfer suggest that "This would depend on a calculation of what he would gain and what he would lose by being taken away" (Downie and Telfer, 1980, p. 29). This is very much a utilitarian position. A thorough utilitarian analysis of the issues involved in the case for removal of a child from the home of abusing parents should serve to identify the ethical issues more clearly.

Teleological Factors Regarding Child Abuse and Neglect

There are three parties involved for which the good resulting from removal of the child must be weighed: the child, the parents and the state. The analysis begins by directing attention to the interests of the child. The probable consequences for the child of remaining in the home must be compared to the probable consequences of removal from that home. The social worker needs to know the past behavior of the parents and the effect of that behavior on the child. Some predictions must be made about the future behavior of the parents and the possible effect of this behavior on the child. The social worker then compares the consequences of the child remaining in the home with the possible consequences arising from placing the child in a foster home. Mnookin, in a very well-written chapter about foster care, states that:

> This would require predicting the effect of removing the child from home, school, friends and familiar surroundings as well as predicting the child's experience while in the foster care system. Such predictions involve estimates of the child's future relationship with the foster parents, the child's future contact with natural parents and siblings, the number of foster homes in which the child ultimately will have to be placed, the length of time spent in foster care, the potential for acquiring a stable home, and myriad other factors (Mnookin, 1979, p. 189).

Mnookin is quite right in concluding that often the decision to remove a child must be made by comparing an existing family with largely unknown alternatives.

Of equally serious concern in trying to predict the potential physical and psychological damage to the child, if he remains in the home, are the limitations of psychological theory in this regard. There is considerable debate about the effects of abuse and neglect in early childhood on personality development. Skolnick, for example, concluded as a result of her research that investigators have tended to overestimate the damaging effects of early childhood problems (Skolnick, 1973, p. 372).

Compounding the difficulties already mentioned with respect to calculating the benefits or damages accrued to the child, there is the question of values. Which good for the child should be of higher value than others? For example, is intellectual stimulation better than stability and security or is a child's spirituality of higher value than his economic productivity? Ultimately, the social worker must rely on his/her personal values to determine a child's best interests.

It is of paramount importance to this analysis that one has an understanding of the foster care system. Are there risks to the child as a result of foster care placement? Goldstein, Freud, and Solnit suggest that: "A child's placement should rest entirely on consideration for the child's own inner situation and developmental needs" (Goldstein, Freud, and Solnit, 1973, p. 106).

They emphasize that not enough consideration has been paid to the child's psychological well-being. Every child needs direct intimate and continuous care by a personally committed adult. They caution that the parents' right to freedom from state intervention should be respected except in serious cases of neglect and abandonment.

Other writers have pointed to problems with foster care that have a direct bearing on the concerns voiced by Goldstein et al. Finkelstein has referred to children in foster care as "children in limbo." She states that psychosocial problems evident in these chidlren can be traced to the lack of a sense of permanence which is essential for their growth. Hampson and Tavormina (1980) studied foster mothers and found among other things motivational problems. They recommended a more rigid screening of foster parents, attitude and motivation assessment, better matching of parents' abilities to the presenting problems of the child and better training of foster parents. These studies are far from conclusive, but they do point to the possibility of severe risks in foster care placement.

The difficulty of quantifying the net good to the child that can be expected to result from removal is clearly evidenced in the case of child abuse and neglect. In all but extreme cases, a utilitarian analysis will not produce a reliable decision. One is forced to make a decision in the face of a multitude of unknowns. These difficulties arise even before the effects on the parents and the state have been considered.

Parents will lose the goods of pleasure and satisfaction that a relationship with the child will bring them. Again, how is the value of these goods to be compared to the potential damage to the child? In addition to loss of goods, actual damage may be done to the parents.

From the point of view of the state, predictions must be made about the future effects on economic productivity of both the parents and the child. Emotional damage to both parties may demand the distribution of considerable resources in the form of mental and physical health care.

The utilitarian method is not useful as an exclusive method of ethical analysis in the case of child abuse and neglect. However, it does allow for change in decisions about child abuse and neglect as we become better able to quantify the effects on all parties concerned. The fact that there are so many unknown factors forces decisions to be made on other grounds. The personal values of the social worker become a dominant influence in the final decision.

Deontological Factors Regarding Child Abuse and Neglect

The deontological thinking of the social worker augments his/her teleological thinking. An individual's values and principles of right and wrong are ideally derived from his/her notions about human nature and philosophy of life. All groups that espouse ethical codes or statements on human rights also derive their conclusions from collectively shared beliefs about human nature and philosophy of life. As one enters into the ethical process, one's notions about human nature and philosophy of life evolve and can become somewhat distinct from the dominant group's ideas. One develops an evolving set of values which can be compared to the group's evolving values; in this case the code of ethics elucidated by the social work profession.

The values of the profession that have a direct bearing on child abuse and neglect are essentially the right to basic well-being and the right to the freedom required for self-determination. In addition, there is the question of the role of the state in ensuring these basic rights, especially when they conflict.

The individual may enter the deontological debate by comparing these two values espoused by the profession with his/her own beliefs about human nature and life. The root of the right to basic well-being is the right to life. This right is usually given first priority against the desires or rights of others. So, in the case of child abuse, if the right to life is threatened, the assurance of this right takes precedence and the ethical argument focuses on the means. However, if the issue is the quality of life or the degree of well-being, then the conflict of this value with the parents' right to freedom for self-determination becomes more difficult to resolve.

There have been a number of schools of thought that have called into question the whole concept of self-determination. The materialistic-mechanistic thoughts of Hobbes and his followers have held that human thought and action are determined by the laws of physics and chemistry. Behavioral psychology and many of the existentialists would question the whole idea of self-determination. There are strong economic, political, legal, religious and ideological forces shaping us. But if one were to adopt completely this idea of determinism, the whole question of ethics would be irrelevant. As Downie and Telfer correctly suggest "that which is not freely chosen is not an expression of our will and therefore we are not morally responsible" (Downie and Telfer, 1980, p. 127).

The importance attributed to the concept of self-determination depends upon how one resolves this issue of determinism versus free will. If one feels that to a large extent our thoughts and actions are determined by the forces of society, then one would attribute less importance to the value of freedom and self-determination. In a conflict between this value and the right of well-being, one would be inclined to sacrifice one person's right to freedom to ensure the well-being of another. In the case of child abuse and neglect, one would be inclined to condone intervention in families where less severe forms of neglect were occurring. If self-determination was given greater value, then only severe forms of neglect and abuse would call for intervention. Mnookin, judging from his following statement, would seem to place a high value on freedom and self-determination: "Removal would seem appropriate only when there are no means to protect the child within the home" (Mnookin, 1979, p. 196).

Once one begins to resolve the conflict of these two basic values, issues about the ethics of specific types of intervention begin to arise. Reamer addresses the problem of authority and asks the questions: "Under what circumstances are social workers obligated to intervene in the lives of others? What limits should we place on our interventions?" (Reamer, 1982, p. 42). In other words, after we have decided that it is ethical to intervene in the lives of the parents, what authority and role should be assumed by the social worker?

Giovannoni begins to answer this question by stating that the protective responsibility for children rests with the whole community and especially with all agencies serving children. Social work's involvement in the area of child abuse has evolved to the point where it functions in two broad roles: "On the one hand, they exercise the authority of the community to interfere in parent-child relationships, and on the other hand, they are expected to contribute to amelioration of the situation through rehabilitation of the parent-child relationship and/or the provision of substitute parental care" (Giovannoni, 1982, p. 106).

Two other issues are raised by Giovannoni in addition to the problem of authority: the role of the state and the conflict of social work roles. Actually, these issues are interrelated.

The social work profession has evolved under the tenet that members of society have an obligation to assist those in need. It is also argued by the profession that the state "must assume significant responsibility for its organization and distribution" (Reamer, 1982, p. 43). The private sector has shown historically that it will not provide adequately for those in need. There are those that argue, however, that it is ethically wrong for the state to assume this responsibility and they usually base their arguments on individuals' right to freedom. It has also been argued that members of society have an obligation to meet the needs of those less fortunate, but that this need should be met through the actions of private citizens and not by government.

There is another element to the problem of authority which involves the conflictual roles ascribed to the social work profession by the state. An individual social worker is usually responsible for both a social control function and a social support function as pointed out by Giovannoni. The danger of abuse of authority is very real in this situation. Families can be easily coerced into counseling relationships under the threat, whether expressed or not, of removing the child. The work of rehabilitation is seriously jeopardized under a system which encourages this kind of role conflict. This is a serious ethical problem, and Giovannoni urges that all therapeutic social services to families should come from other than the protective services and placement agencies.

As a means of understanding the values and issues involved in making a decision about removing a child from the parental home, consider the questions involved in the following case.*

---

*From Shankar A. Yelaja (Ed.): *Ethical Issues in Social Work*, 1982. Courtesy of Charles C Thomas, Publisher, Springfield, Illinois.

Mr. and Mrs. Johns had a son, Jonas, nine years of age, who the neighbors had reported was being physically abused. Mr. Johns was not reluctant to let me into his extremely spartan home and introduced me to his wife and son. Jonas was pale in color and seemed to walk with a slight stoop. He was short for his age, and although he did not seem unfriendly, intimidated, or fearful, he only answered the questions I put to him and did not attempt any conversation on his own.

In my discussion with Mr. Johns, I discovered that he ran his household in a very stoic manner, in strict compliance with what he took to be some vaguely defined religious edicts. The family ate a sparse diet of rice and beans. Each member was required, in a ritualistic manner, to perform a number of hours of physical labor and read from a religious text for a period of several hours. This particular religious text was unknown to me.

My discussion with Mrs. Johns disclosed that as a family they had a unique life together, each working to free themselves from some sort of communal sin and modeling their day-to-day life-style after some more primitive situation. They donated a very substantial part of their income to overseas charity and lived on as little money as possible. In order to sustain this life-style, they intentionally kept their distance from the rest of society.

It seems to me that there was a delicate balance between each member of this family; they had one goal they all agreed to and they all worked toward this goal. This life-style was so all-pervasive that it seemed as if no one member could survive on their own very long outside of this situation.

I was troubled by this life-style, however. That it was an unusual life-style did not bother me, but the effect of the diet and working schedule on young Jonas seemed to be severe. I did not have the immediate opportunity to consult with a psychiatrist on the possible adverse psychological effects this situation was having on Jonas' mental development, but I suspected the worst. At the very least, it looked as if the development of his individual autonomy was in jeopardy.

Still, it did not seem as if any family member was intentionally trying to directly harm Jonas. Was this particular family care insufficient for Jonas' well-being? Barring some possible nutritional problems, the answer was somewhat hard to determine since Jonas seemed not overly joyful but very content. He did not appear fearful of either of his parents, and I had no evidence that he had ever been beaten and suspected I would not find any. There was the religious (or was it pseudo religious) aspect to the case as well. These people did have the right to follow their religion, but did this right also include possible abuse of their child? This was not necessarily a case of maltreatment, although it could still be a case of mistreatment.

To take Jonas from this protective environment against his will and the will of his parents could prove detrimental to this family unit and traumatic to the child. This life-style had in some significant ways shaped his personality and outlook on life. I knew that the parents were unlikely to alter their somewhat dogmatic and severe life-style—it was a cocoon, their protection against the verities of the outside world.

This case raises many questions; however, the most significant ones are:

1. Does it make any ethical difference whether a case of child mistreatment shows evidence of intentional harm/neglect or not?
2. How far should the agents of society allow deviant life-styles to extend into areas of which some possible psychological harm may result to the children of these families, especially when these life-styles are based on some form of religion?

CONCLUSION

We have attempted to outline the major ethical issues involved in child abuse and neglect. At the same time, the suggestion was made that a blend of teleological and deontological ideas should be sought to allow for a proper balance between the interests of the individual and of society. One can only rehash this blend during the process of ethical analysis which in itself leads to self-realization.

REFERENCES

Costin, L.F.: *Child Welfare: Policies and Practice.* New York: McGraw-Hill, 1979.

Downie, R.S., and Telfer, E.: *A Philosophy of Medicine and Social Work Caring and Curing.* London: Methuen, 1980.

Finkelstein, N.E.: Children in Limbo. *Social Work, 25:* 100–105, 1980.

Frankena, W.: *Ethics.* Englewood Cliffs, NJ: Prentice-Hall, Inc., 1963.

Frost, S.E., Jr.: Basic Teachings of the Great Philosophers. Garden City, NY: Doubleday & Company, Inc., 1962.

Giovannoni, J.Mm: Mistreated children. In Yelaja, S.A. (Ed.): *Ethical Issues in Social Work.* Springfield, IL: Charles C Thomas, Publisher, 1982.

Goldstein, J., Freud, A., and Solnit, A.: *Beyond the Best Interests of the Child.* New York: The Free Press, 1973.

Hampson, P.B., and Tavormina, J.B.: Feedback from the experts: A study of foster mothers. *Social Work, 25:* 108–113, March 1980.

Hardman, D.G.: Not with my daughter you don't. *Social Work, 20:* 278–85, July 1975.

Mnookin, R.H.: Foster care—In Whose Best Interest? In O'Neill, O., and Ruddick, W. (Eds.): *Having Children: Philosophical and Legal Reflections on Parenthood.* New York: Oxford University Press, 1979.

Reamer, F.G.: *Ethical Dilemmas in Social Service.* New York: Columbia University Press, 1982.

Skolnick, A.: *The Intimate Environment, Exploring Marriage and the Family*. Boston: Little Brown, 1973.

Tillich, P.: *Morality and Beyond*. New York: Harper and Row Publishers, 1963.

Tillich, P.: *The Protestant Era*. Chicago: The University of Chicago Press, 1957.

Wilkes, R.: *Social Work with Undervalued Groups*. London: Tavistock Publications, 1981.

Yelaja, S.A. (Ed.): *Ethical Issues in Social Work*. Springfield, IL: Charles C Thomas, Publisher, 1982.

PART IV

Part IV of the book discusses the treatment process in cases of child maltreatment and the needed skills and services for effective child protection work. This part is also practice oriented and attempts to answer the myriad of questions practitioners could have in the handling of various forms of child maltreatment. Starting with investigation, it introduces the reader in a sequential fashion to various aspects of child protection interventions.

Chapter 11 deals with intake and the investigative assessment. Factors pertaining to investigation, which includes the report and the initial contact, are thoroughly discussed and analyzed. This chapter specifically directs social workers in areas of assessment and it defines their responsibilities in their role as an "investigator." Although the investigative assessment is part of the overall assessment process in cases of child abuse and neglect, it discusses separately the continuing assessment, which most of the time is another worker's responsibility, and helps the reader identify problems, issues and roles which tend to be different at the initial contact.

Chapter 12 defines continuing assessment and its dimensions as children and parents are involved in treatment. In this chapter, directives in assessment as they relate to parents and the child are discussed separately. This separation contributes to clarity of the issues that need to be understood as treatment interventions are initiated and carried out by the social worker. Because assessment in cases involving sexual abuse of children can be a complicated process, a separate section is devoted to this subject. Although assessment as part of the treatment process is briefly addressed in subsequent chapters, it is not redundant and in fact further enhances understanding of its critical place for effective service delivery.

Chapter 13 focuses on interviewing as a means of communication and a tool in treatment. Although the basic principles of effective communication are applicable in work with abusive and neglecting parents, because these clients are involuntary and often highly resistant, special skills are required. This chapter therefore discusses such concepts as relationship, self-determination, authority, and motivation and how their understanding can influence the worker's effective communication. It also provides the practitioner with specific interviewing techniques to overcome resistance and to direct the communication process during initial contacts. The last section of this chapter discusses various issues and techniques for interviews with the abused and neglected child and the sexually abused in particular.

Chapter 14 addresses critical areas in the provision of treatment services in cases involving physical abuse. To insure successful treatment, the author advocates the involvement of a host of well-coordinated community resources focusing on the needs of the entire family. The chapter delineates specific treatment objectives and ways to achieve them. Also discussed are how to work with character-disordered clients and mentally ill clients with interpersonal relationships problems. Individual and environmental stress, inadequate methods of discipline, emotional and social isolation, dysfunction around intimacy and sex, poor problem-solving skills and multiproblem families are addressed in this chapter. Treatment issues related to young children and adolescents are also discussed. The chapter reflects the author's long practice experience with physical abuse situations.

Chapter 15 addresses various issues in the treatment of sexual abuse cases. The author alerts the reader to the lack of knowledge regarding effective treatment methods and she discusses analytically the skills, knowledge and attitudinal changes essential for the workers' effective treatment of such cases. Among such essential elements discussed are feelings regarding sexuality, feelings toward those who sexually abuse children, prejudices and myths, and the significance of transference and countertransference during the treatment process. The approach to treatment is a humanistic one based on the assumption that incest is primarily the result of relationship problems. Several modalities are used to accomplish treatment objectives. The chapter analytically discusses these modalities and addresses the specific dynamics in all phases of treatment. The author's separate analysis of treatment dynamics and processes with children of various ages is a plus for this chapter.

Treatment of emotional maltreatment, often referred as emotional neglect and emotional abuse, is discussed in Chapter 16. The author recognizes the limitations of the existing knowledge base for interventions addressed to this aspect of child maltreatment. He proposes that a functional definition of the condition will require confirmations by psychiatrists, psychologists, pediatricians, and social workers, among others. The author identifies five types of families which are predisposed to psychological maltreatment of the child. This typology is the result of the author's own research and is helpful in understanding the dynamics of neglect cases and the specific steps to be undertaken in treatment.

In Chapter 17 the authors suggest that neglect cases are difficult to treat because the problems affecting the entire family are complex and are often chronic in nature. They propose and discuss a multimodal, multidimensional, and multidisciplinary approach characterized by coordination, intensity, continuity, and follow-up after termination of services. Many of the principles in treatment discussed in this chapter are also considered in other chapters. However, in this chapter these principles are brought together and they are analytically examined. Although their relevance to treatment of other forms of child maltreatment are important, in the treatment of child neglect these principles are paramount because of the multiplicity of problems, the families' proneness to crises, and the involvement of many disciplines and numerous supportive services.

Chapter 18 discusses the use of interdisciplinary teams in the treatment of child abuse and neglect cases. Since the team concept in its various forms has become the sine qua non of treatment interventions, the content of this chapter assists the practitioner in seeing his or her role in perspective. The authors present detailed information regarding size, composition, functions depending on the setting, roles and responsibilities of team members. The discussion centers on team process and the identification of problems and issues, giving the reader a realistic view of the obstacles which can negatively impact the team's effectiveness.

The last chapter in Part IV of the book focuses on the use of supervision in child abuse and neglect cases. The author approaches the topic with a well-balanced amount of theory and practice. He devotes considerable attention to discussing various issues related to supervision, consultation, functions to be performed by the supervisor, relationships of supervisor-supervisee and reciprocal responsibilities. His analytic discussion of the specialized tasks performed by the supervisor during the various phases of the treatment process from investigation to termination is informative and practical. Especially the emphasis placed on the assessment phase with a detailed description of diagnostic models will be found useful and pertinent in fulfilling supervisory responsibilities.

CHAPTER 11

INTAKE—INVESTIGATIVE ASSESSMENT

Chris M. Mouzakitis

INTRODUCTION

The investigative assessment is the first step in the helping process in cases involving abuse and/or neglect of children. It is one of the most difficult jobs protective services workers are called upon to perform when such cases are reported to the protective services agency. This is primarily because of: (1) the involuntary nature of this client population, since such persons as a rule do not seek help, and (2) the diversity and seriousness of their problems. Furthermore, these clients are resistive or are involved with social workers and other professionals out of fear that they may be persecuted or that they may lose their individual autonomy as parents, and out of their personal conviction that their parental rights should not be questioned (Hill, 1983). Such an attitude makes the investigative assessment difficult indeed.

It is during this beginning assessment process that many crucial decisions are made by the protective services workers that determine the entire course of the agency's involvement:

- whether a particular referral will be accepted
- whether the children's condition and safety will permit them to stay home or to be removed to a hospital or foster home
- whether to file a court petition
- whether to provide needed services to the parents and the entire family (Duquette, 1981).

This chapter examines the factors that influence the quality of the investigation, the handling of the report, the kind of assessments and decisions to be made at the initial contact, and the recording of the findings.

FACTORS PERTAINING TO INVESTIGATION

The effectiveness of the investigative assessment is determined by several factors: the workers' knowledge and skills, adequacy of time, adequacy of supportive services, and the agency's philosophical commitment.

Workers' Knowledge and Skills

Throughout the investigative assessment the workers are called upon to make informed and defendable judgments from the moment the report is received up to the final disposition of the case. The soundness of their judgment depends heavily on their knowledge of the dynamics of child abuse and/or neglect and of human growth and development. Collecting facts and their interpretation are possible only if the workers possess the knowledge and ability to understand the many configurations of human interactions and behaviors.

Communication skills and how to handle the behaviors of aggression, hostility, and passivity that the abusers and/or neglectors usually manifest are crucial for successful completion of a case. A thorough understanding of laws on child abuse and neglect and on agency policies and procedures is basic, since many decisions and actions must be made within certain prescribed legal limits. In addition, since the investigative assessment is not only a fact-gathering device but also an opportunity to assess the needs of the family, workers' knowledge of, and ability to use, community resources enhances their efforts in offering the services needed.

Adequacy of Time

The need for sufficient time to carry out an investigative assessment cannot be underestimated if it is to be completed successfully. Such factors as excessive case loads, mixed case loads, excessive time spent traveling, meeting emergencies, and court appearances all can limit workers' effectiveness. As a result, they tend to handle such cases superficially, avoid appropriate assessments of children and family, resort to expedient tactics, and become impatient and careless in following agency standards and other administrative procedures. Furthermore, lack of time forces workers to abbreviate their investigations, which may have negative legal and treatment implications.

Although the trend in urban areas is toward the establishment of separate investigative units, the practice of mixed assignments still is prevalent, especially in rural areas. Freeing investigative workers from other agency duties enables them to do a responsible job, to serve the abused children and the family better, and to protect themselves and the agency from possible liability.

Adequate Supportive Services

The workers' role during this process is not only to collect facts regarding the reported maltreatment but to also do an initial assessment and to begin the treatment process. The availability of supportive services enhances their helping stance. Abusive and neglecting parents are better convinced of the workers' intent to assist them, not only through words but through actions. Demonstrating their usefulness through the provision of concrete services is a most effective way workers can reduce parents' resistance and thus initiate a tentative treatment plan. Access to such services as homemakers, parent aids, emergency and foster care, and medical and legal services give workers a solid base to inform the parents and to involve them at the onset of the agency's inquiry.

The effectiveness of the investigative assessment also depends on such worker-supportive services as appropriate supervision, consultation, and use of multidisciplinary teams. Since an investigative assessment naturally leads toward a number of important decisions, supervision should be part of this process. Decisions regarding leaving or removing children from the home or taking a case to court should always be made through supervisory channels. Of course, there are exceptions, such as emergency removals of a child; however, the supervisor should always be kept informed about the status of cases.

Not all investigative assessments are completed in one visit. Many, especially in cases of sexual abuse, last a month and even longer. In such instances, a multidisciplinary team is of immense help in giving the workers direction on treatment issues. Unfortunately, such teams are not used extensively despite their acceptance (Kaplan and Zitrin, 1983).

AGENCY'S PHILOSOPHICAL COMMITMENT

Investigation is thought by many agencies to be a "police type" of involvement where only the hard facts of the alleged abuse and/or neglect are sought—nothing more. Unfortunately, this widespread misperception can have a negative impact. As a result, less qualified workers are assigned to investigatory work since it is a "nontreatment" activity. Those who are qualified but who are pressured into accepting such assignments feel demoted and tend to lack motivation and commitment to do the job.

There is nothing more inaccurate than considering the investigative process as only a fact-gathering activity. That is only one aspect of the process. The other aspect focuses on assessing feelings, attitudes, behaviors, and the psychological and environmental factors that possibly have contributed to the situation. A thorough assessment calls for a concerted effort for effective communication with the family, for building a relationship of trust, and for imparting the agency's helping stance.

This author's reference to the process as "investigative assessment" is purposeful to denote its dual focus. It can be defined as the process by which the validity or nonvalidity of the reported maltreatment is determined and an initial understanding of the children, the parents, and their situation is acquired that may lead to protective actions.

INTAKE

The investigative assessment in cases involving child maltreatment is part of what is traditionally known as intake. This refers to all activities and functions the protective services agency performs to substantiate or not substantiate a reported case of child abuse and/or neglect. There is a multiplicity of functions and purposes at intake:

- It provides the means by which the community can express its concern for children who may be in questionable substandard or dangerous situations.
- It provides an opportunity for the agency's functions and responsibilities regarding protection of maltreated children to be interpreted to the individuals and/or agencies who report such cases.
- It represents a commitment by the agency of its numerous resources to evaluate whether families and their children need services (Holder and Mohr, 1980).

The accomplishment of these functions and purposes, as discussed earlier, depends on the agency's philosophy and commitment and the preparedness of its staff to deliver such services.

An investigative assessment is underway at intake as soon as the agency receives a report by telephone or in writing that a child is abused and/or neglected. The focus of intake then is twofold: (1) validation of the report and (2) substantiation of the abuse. Intake consists of two phases: Phase 1 includes all the activities and procedures in validating the report; Phase 2 includes all the activities and procedures in substantiating or making a decision that the maltreatment of the child is not valid (Holder and Mohr, 1981).

Receiving and Assessing the Report's Validity

All states have laws requiring that the professionals who come into contact with children in performing their duties and all citizens who have knowledge and/or suspicion that children are abused and/or neglected must report such situations to the protective services unit of the department of social services (Duquette, 1981). In most states, persons who have such knowledge and fail to report it can be prosecuted and fined (Duquette, 1981).

The reports come to the protective services unit from, among others, private citizens, teachers, hospitals, mental health clinics, the police, and juvenile facilities. Most referrals come from nonprofessional individuals (American Humane Association, 1983). The sources of those from institutions as a rule are identifiable since the "reporters" disclose their names and place of employment. But in referrals by private citizens, their identities are not always known; indeed, many are anonymous. The anonymity results primarily from the reporters' fear of possible hostility from the parent(s), uncertainty as to the actual maltreatment the child may be experiencing, and fear of being involved with the agency, the police, and the court. Often, too, this is used as a way to get back at a person because of personal dislikes and disputes.

In institutional and/or professional referrals, the validation usually is not difficult because the professionals are willing not only to talk over the telephone but also to give specific information about their observations and examinations of children who come to their attention. It is a good practice for the intake worker to request that such referrals be made in writing, as it leaves no doubt as to the reasons why the reports were made and they also are valuable documents that can be used later if the case lands in court. Intake workers should seek personal contact with professional reporters to gather as much information as possible about the children's background and family. This information alerts protective service workers as to the overall dynamics operating in a particular case before the first meeting with the children and parents and/or caretakers. In cases of individuals' telephone referrals, the validation process similarly aims to collect as much information about the children's condition and the family and to assess the actual motivation of the caller for making the referral.

In all cases, the first step is determining the nature of the situation referred. What kind of child maltreatment it is? Is it sexual abuse? What kind of sexual abuse? Incest, sexual exploitation, sibling sexual involvement, sudden rape? Is it physical abuse; if so, what kind? How was it inflicted and by whom? Did the caller witness the abuse or hear about it from someone else? How long has it been going on? Is it a one-time occurrence or a chronic one? What is the child's present condition? The last point is a crucial one, and the intake worker should ask the caller to describe the victim's condition in detail. Immediate agency actions often are based on the caller's perception of the seriousness of the child's condition. In cases of neglect, similar questions are asked to determine the child's (or children's) situation.

As the second step, the intake worker should raise questions about the home and the family's background. Where does the family live? What is the home environment? Are the parents employed or unemployed? What are their names and ages? Does the caller have any personal contacts and/or know any family problems that may be contributing to the parents' maltreating behavior? Are there other children in the family? If so, who are they in terms of age and sex, and what possible effects does the parents' behavior have on them? Information about extended family members or possible family contacts with agencies should be ascertained.

All of this information helps the workers form an overall view of the situation and its seriousness. Specifically, it helps to determine whether the victim(s) are in immediate danger, to locate the family, to identify other sources of information, and to assess the caller's actual motivation. If the caller has a genuine concern about a situation, disclosure of the person's name and address should not leave any doubt as to real motives. However, when a caller refuses to disclose a name and address, the intake worker should try to ascertain whether the silence stems from fear of further involvement or out of vengeance toward the parents. The caller's real motivation can be detected easily by an astute intake worker from the kind of responses to the questions, the consistency of the responses, the tone of the caller's voice, and the question as to why the person is concerned enough to make the report.

In all cases, the workers must express the agency's appreciation and its intention to let the reporter know the outcome. Opinions on these issues are divided. Those who are against it claim that the principle of confidentiality is violated. Those who are for it claim that a call to the reporter indicating that the agency is inquiring into the specific allegations has no bearing on confidentiality (Holder and Mohr, 1981).

This author supports the second view, since such an acknowledgement to the reporter does not disclose any of the agency's findings. It simply indicates that the person's concerns about the children's situation have been taken into serious consideration. Such practice also is a good public relations strategy, demonstrates the agency's sincere commitment to the welfare of children, and encourages future reporting of such cases.

The trend to investigate all reports is a sound practice. However, once the validation process has been completed, its urgency should be determined. A report is considered urgent if: (1) the child is in need of medical care, (2) the child is alone in the house, (3) the child is fearful, (4) the child is young in age, (5) the child is injured, and/or (6) the parents' behaviors are reported to be threatening to the child (Holder and Mohr, 1980). If any one of these factors is present, an immediate investigative assessment of the child and the family is in order.

Reports characterized as nonurgent also should receive attention within twenty-four hours, not two or three days later as is the practice in many agencies. Reports thought to be not urgent, if investigated two or three days later, may be found to be not valid primarily because the specific factors that prompted the reporter's call are not easily detectable. On the other hand, long delays pose a risk to the child if an error was made in characterizing the reports as nonurgent.

INITIAL CONTACT

As indicated earlier, the investigative assessment commences not at the point of the home visit (initial contact) but at the point when the report reaches the agency's intake unit. The practice of separating the two as different entities is not logical since the second step naturally flows from the first. A good assessment provides the appropriate groundwork when the first contact with the family is initiated.

In rural communities, there is no separation of investigative responsibilities since the intake worker performs both and often is responsible for the treatment as well. However, in urban communities, these responsibilities generally are separated. One worker is assigned to receive referrals and do screening, a second to do the initial contact with the family and the assessment, and a third to carry on with continuing treatment.

It seems to this author that the rural model has continuity—most of the time out of necessity rather than by design—and can be effective in spite of the shortcomings often cited by some experts. On the other hand, the urban model, which has come about not so much out of necessity but by design, harbors more problems in terms of continuity and effectiveness of the investigative process. That is why it is stressed here that there is a need for the results of extensive assessment of the referral to be passed on to the investigative worker in order to limit the fragmentation of the process.

AREAS TO BE ASSESSED IN THE INITIAL CONTACT

The more knowledge the workers have about the report of the alleged abuse and/or neglect, the better they are equipped to anticipate possible reactions of the parents and the areas on which to focus the assessment. The kinds of parents' resistive reactions discussed in Chapter 13 on "Interviewing" also determines how successful the workers will be in covering certain areas and how extensively. Often, workers arrive at the first meeting with the parents or caretakers with an overloaded agenda that negatively affects the quality of their initial assessment. An in-depth understanding should be attempted later if the case receives continuing services. As a rule, no matter what the reported child maltreatment, the workers should aim to make a determination of the following critical areas:

1. the nature, extent, and seriousness of the abuse and/or neglect
2. the effect of the maltreatment on the child or children
3. the child's or childrens' idiosyncratic characteristics
4. the parents' and family's behaviors and attitudes toward the child or children
5. the parents' idiosyncratic characteristics
6. the ability of the parents to provide care and protection
7. the parents' awareness of the situation
8. the degree of the parents' motivation, or lack of it, to cooperate with the worker and/or agency
9. the probable effect of the investigative assessment on the parents' attitude and behaviors toward the child

NATURE, EXTENT, AND SERIOUSNESS OF THE CASE

This is the most critical area in the investigative assessment since the decision as to whether or not abuse and/or neglect is present is based on these findings. Positive findings immediately dictate that certain actions be taken, whereas negative findings require no further assessment and the investigation is terminated. Actually, the protective services agency has no right to stay involved in a case once the reported abuse and/or neglect is not substantiated.

The nature, extent, and seriousness of the maltreatment can be complicated at times, requiring patience, flexibility, and assertiveness from the workers. The situation becomes much more difficult if the parents present a wall of resistance and refuse to cooperate. For example, in instances of physical abuse, if the parents do not allow the workers to see and examine the children, the nature and extent of the abuse cannot be determined.

No conclusions should be made solely on the basis of what the parents say unless the workers are given the opportunity to see and personally examine the children (Faller-Coulborn and Stone, 1981). In such instances, parents and/or caretakers should be informed of the alternate routes workers can follow to require a personal examination. The seriousness of an apparently injured child's condition is difficult for the worker to ascertain without a systematic medical examination. The need for immediacy of such action should be communicated to the parents without hesitation if the child's removal to a hospital seems appropriate.

One controversial issue in cases of physical abuse is whether or not the workers should take pictures of the injured child. The rationale for doing so is that such pictures could be used later in court if the case follows that route. Although this is a sound reason, indiscriminate picture taking could create strong negative feelings in the parents toward the workers and the agency's efforts. It seems a better practice to take pictures only in cases where there is a strong corroboration that the parents will resist involvement with the agency. On the other hand, if the child's physical injury is serious and necessitates medical attention, pictures can be taken during the medical examination.

In cases of sexual maltreatment, depending on its type and the specific circumstances of its referral, the nature and extent of the abuse can be determined more easily than others. In most instances, the workers have direct access to the children either because one of the parents reported it or the children reported the situation to the agency or school authorities. Since the police are involved in all such cases, the steps that need to be taken usually are not thwarted by the parents' interference.

In cases of neglect, as is in instances of abuse, the children should be seen by the workers. In such cases the nature, extent, and seriousness of the neglect (although the report indicates inadequate care) may differ from child to child. It is not unusual in the same family to find one child with a failure-to-thrive syndrome and others hygienically and medically uncared for. Cases of neglect are not as clear-cut as are those of abuses involving bruises, punctures, lacerations, and broken bones. The neglect often is insidious and can be identified only on the basis of the behaviors or symptoms the children present, medical and psychological examinations, the parents' feelings and attitudes, and the general home condition. In many instances, however, the seriousness of the victim's condition is obvious, requiring immediate removal. In the majority of cases, a decision on removal is made only after many visits to the home and a series of medical and psychological examinations.

THE EFFECT OF MALTREATMENT ON THE VICTIMS

The effect of maltreatment should be assessed in conjunction with its nature, extent, and seriousness. A child who has suffered multiple injuries, head injuries, bone fractures, and severe malnutrition undoubtedly is fearful of the parents. In many instances, especially in cases involving incest, the children have been threatened by the perpetrators and are reluctant to talk or communicate their pain and feelings. Many such children, in spite of repeated abuse, present a picture of model youngsters—quiet, polite, willing, and responsive to the needs of the adults around them.

The impact varies, however. Although many such children are passive and withdrawn, others—especially the older ones—act out, are delinquent, and become belligerent (Okell-Jones, 1981). These behaviors usually are seen in children who are neglected. Those youngsters are unruly, loud, undisciplined, impulsive, and destructive to toys and objects. In many young children who have been repeatedly abused, neglected and deprived of emotional nurturing, workers will find conduct, habit, neurotic and psychoneurotic behaviors (Kellmer and Pringle, 1978; Martin, 1979).

Analyzing the probable effects of abuse and/or neglect at the point of the investigative assessment assists the workers in deciding the course of action to take. One course may be removal and immediate psychological and medical examination; another could require only a psychological and medical checkup while the children remain at home. Either course depends on the victims' welfare and safety as well as on other corroborative factors discussed later.

CHILDRENS' IDIOSYNCRATIC CHARACTERISTICS

Children generally are abused and/or neglected because of their parents' or other adults' inability to care and provide for them responsibly. The adults' own problems limit their capacity to meet their obligations toward the children; instead, they maltreat them (Maden and Wrench, 1977; Milner and Wimberly, 1980; Paulson et al., 1977). All experts in the field generally accept the fact that the children's own idiosyncratic characteristics (at times, unintentionally) can precipitate the maltreating behavior of the parents (Lynch, 1975; Martin, 1976; Smith, 1984).

Children who are mentally retarded, emotionally disturbed, and/or physically handicapped and difficult to handle for various reasons may be resented for their handicap by their own parents and/or caretakers. Such children require special care and constant attention and thus may become a burden that many parents refuse to bear; in the process, the parents reject and abuse them. Workers who do an investigation should take this "special child" factor into consideration in making initial decisions.

For example, a mentally limited child who has been found to be abused and/or neglected should never be left at home (even if the abuse is not serious) until the parents' feelings and intentions are assessed thoroughly. It is not uncommon for such children to experience further abuse and/or neglect and even death following the workers' departure.

PARENT AND FAMILY BEHAVIORS AND ATTITUDES

Many parents not only stubbornly refuse to accept any responsibility for a condition but they also blame the children. They are loud and defensive and feel that the children are their own property. This often is seen in cases involving physical and sexual abuse. Many such parents show no guilt or remorse for what they did and in many instances are passive, withdrawn, indifferent, or in a state of inertia—an attitude seen more frequently in neglect cases. Others are immature, childish and impulsive.

Such attitudes and behaviors also must be assessed to determine how the parents view the abuse and/or neglect and how they may react if a decision was made to leave the children at home. Both parents do not necessarily feel and behave in identical fashion. The workers therefore have to determine whether a nonabusing parent feels differently about the situation and, because of that, can exercise some control toward the other parent (perpetrator) to protect the children if the need arises.

Similar assessments have to be made in regard to other family members (siblings, uncles, aunts, and grandparents) if they are in the same household. In many cases, extended family members, especially if they live in the same household, should be considered as to whether they can provide protection.

PARENTS' IDIOSYNCRATIC CHARACTERISTICS

Abusive and neglectful parents may suffer from alcohol and drug addiction or from mental illnesses or be sociopathic (Faller-Coulborn and Ziefert, 1981). Although the occurrence of such conditions with child abuse and neglect is not any higher than in the general population (Wright, 1976), these conditions must be given serious consideration. However, the mere suspicion that the parents are alcoholics or addicts or emotionally not well should not weigh too heavily in any immediate drastic decision, such as removal of the victims, unless the conditions would place the children at risk after the workers depart. At the point of the initial contact it is difficult to assess how serious such conditions are and the factor of limited time prevents in-depth understanding.

These conditions should be viewed together with the parents' feelings and attitudes toward the children and their capacity to provide care and protection. Under no circumstances should a decision be made in favor of the parents if there is any suspicion that the children are at risk, because the workers think that an unfavorable decision will worsen the parents' condition and functioning.

THE PARENTS' AWARENESS OF THE SITUATION

The degree of the parents' awareness of what has happened and how the children have been affected by a particular neglectful and/or abusive situation becomes apparent as a result of their display of their feelings and their behaviors. Do they openly recognize that what they have done has caused the children pain and suffering? Are they aware that the home conditions are not conducive to the childrens' safety and welfare? What kind of emotions do they express? Do they say they are sorry and remorseful or are they angry toward the children and belligerent toward the workers? Are they passive, indifferent, and apathetic or do they express concern and interest for the childrens' welfare? These and other behaviors or feelings give the workers some understanding of the parents' perceptions of the situation and how they have been affected by it.

PARENTS' MOTIVATION—OR LACK OF IT—TO COOPERATE

The parents' motivation—or lack of it—is an important factor to be considered in an abusive and/or neglectful situation. It would be unrealistic, of course, for decisions to be guided solely by this factor. On the other hand, many abusive and neglecting parents—especially at the point of initial contact when they are overwhelmed with emotions and apprehensions about the situation—are resistive and unwilling to show their actual intent to work with the workers and/or agency. In many instances, their stating that they want to cooperate should not be taken at face value. They often show complacency in order to get rid of the worker and avoid the consequences of their actions (Martin, 1976).

The parents' degree of motivation can be assessed better not so much by what they say they will do to ameliorate a situation but rather by what they do immediately to bring about changes. For example, parents can demonstrate their motivation to be helpful if they voluntarily agree to take the child (or children) to the hospital for examination or if they act on specific suggestions by the investigators on clearing up unhygienic and hazardous household conditions. However, although motivation is a sign of good prognosis, decisions as to whether or not children will be removed from the home should depend on the type of the abuse and/or neglect and their condition.

EFFECT ON PARENTS' ATTITUDE TOWARD CHILDREN

It is not unusual for many parents who are exposed to the agency and community because of their abusive and/or neglectful behavior to vent their anger and hostility on the children. Many such parents feel that the children have betrayed them, especially if the situation came to the attention of social workers, police, and other authorities because of the youngsters' initiative. This often occurs in cases of sexual and physical abuse.

The parents construe the childrens' willingness to talk to strangers (social workers and counselors) not only as betrayal but also an intentional act to "get" them. Such parents may control their actual feelings while the workers are still in the home, but later they may intimidate the children with threats, further abuse, or may even kill. There are many reports of children who experience further abuse and even death by their parents upon the investigative workers' departure.

It is difficult to predict accurately what parents will do once the workers have left. One way to determine their possible subsequent behavior is to assess the children. Do the children appear to be fearful of the parents, withdrawn, avoiding any contacts with them? Do they express feelings of fear and apprehension as to what the parents may do? Another way is to note how the parents communicate with the children while the workers are still there. Are the parents indifferent, ignoring, avoiding any physical or verbal contact? Are there any signs of anger or disapproval in their tone of voice and facial expressions when they refer to the children and the condition? The slightest suspicion should lead to a decision to guarantee their protection.

INVESTIGATIVE DECISIONS

As a result of the workers' interaction with the parents and/or caretakers and assessment of these areas, certain decisions have to be made:

1. Is the reported child abuse and/or neglect valid?
2. Is police and court assistance needed?
3. Will the children remain at home?
4. Will the children be taken to a hospital or removed to an emergency shelter and/or foster home?
5. Are immediate and/or continuing treatment services needed?

If the case is found not to be valid, the investigation is terminated. An agency's insistence on remaining involved in such cases on unspecified grounds is illegal and gives the parents the right to seek legal action. A decision as to whether the police should be involved in a case of sexual abuse is beyond the workers' control because of its criminal nature.

In other types of maltreatment, the extent of involvement is an evaluation the workers have to make on the scene. If the parents do not allow entry into the home or refuse to cooperate with the workers to remove the children to a hospital for medical care or elsewhere for safety and protection, police assistance should be sought (Duquette, 1981). In such instances, however, the workers should try first to obtain a court order, if possible. If this is not possible because a judge is not available, then police assistance should be sought and a court order obtained the following day.

Many workers may hesitate to remove a child from a risky home situation without a court order, thinking that such action violates the parents' rights and poses the possibility of a malpractice lawsuit. Such hesitancy is not supported by court decisions, since the workers act in good faith and out of concern for the childrens' welfare. It is better then for workers to opt for the childrens' removal if there is the slightest doubt that the youngsters' welfare and safety are at stake.

CONDITIONS PROMPTING REMOVAL

In general, with due consideration of the childrens' ages, the overall home atmosphere and the parents' attitude (as discussed earlier), the following should be considered as indicators of high risk posing imminent danger to a child.

In neglect cases if: (1) the child is found to be alone, unsupervised, and unattended; (2) the child is in need of medical treatment; (3) housing conditions are hazardous and dangerous, such as lack of heat; (4) the parents are incapacitated and unable to provide care because of mental or physical illness and/or drug or alcohol abuse; and/or (5) there is violence in the home.

In abuse cases if: (1) the child's condition requires special attention; (2) the child needs immediate medical and/or psychiatric treatment; (3) the parents show no guilt and are belligerent and aggressive toward the workers; (4) one or both parents are psychotic; and/or (5) the parents are under the influence of drugs and/or alcohol.

Any of these factors justifies the workers' decision to remove the child. In cases of sexual abuse, although these factors may not be present, the removal should be attempted based only on the victim's statement if the alleged perpetrator continues to live in the house. If the perpetrator moves out voluntarily or through a court order and if the victim has the other parent's support, then the child should not be moved.

The removal of children from their parents and their familiar home environment is as traumatic and devastating as the maltreatment they had experienced. It thus behooves workers in decisions regarding removal to follow the least traumatic yet practical route for the childrens' protection. Leaving the perpetrators undisturbed at home, as often occurs with incestuous fathers, gives the children a feeling of being punished for what they were forced to do and a feeling of guilt and rejection from the family.

OTHER ISSUES DURING INVESTIGATION

The decision that a substantiated case of abuse and/or neglect will receive continuing treatment services is a crucial one during the investigative assessment. Normally, if a case is found to be valid, the worker at that point should offer services to meet the family's and the childrens' needs. Such immediate activity at the initial contact not only is useful in meeting the family's needs but also clearly indicates the agency's serious intent to be of service. Immediate help to the family members reduces anxiety, fear, and resistance that can result from their not knowing how the agency will handle their situation. However, the offering of such services should be carefully prioritized to help overcome the crisis; otherwise, it can create more anxiety and resistance.

For example, in a neglectful situation, immediate provision of a homemaker, food, clothing, and day care increases the parents' receptiveness of the agency's intent to help them than suggestions that they need psychological examinations and possibly counseling with an alcohol problem. Similarly, in abuse cases it may be useless to tell the parents that they need marital counseling and/or improvement of their parenting skills when they are fearful of possible court involvement. The abusive parent may be more receptive if the workers offer day care for the other children, financial assistance, and help to go through the court process if that is required.

The practice in many agencies of having the assigned investigative worker stay with a case until it is processed through the court, before it goes to a continuing treatment worker, is questionable. In many instances the worker carries the case for weeks and months, particularly in instances of sexual abuse. This author has direct knowledge of such cases that remained with the investigative worker for three to six months. The reason is that the court may not have decided the case because of legal entanglements. As a result, workers true to assigned investigative duties do nothing major to help the victim, the perpetrator, or the family. Their activity consists simply of making sporadic referrals to various agencies. If this actual situation in a metropolitan area is representative of practice in other parts of the country, there is no wonder why the rate of treatment success in sexual abuse cases is minimal.

RECORDING THE INVESTIGATIVE FINDINGS

The investigative assessment in most cases (except for sexual abuse) should be completed in one or two visits with the family and the findings immediately recorded and passed on to the continuing treatment worker. It is inexcusable to delay for several days the assignment of cases to treatment workers because the investigative assessment findings have not been recorded due to shortage of secretarial staff. This kind of delay breaks the continuity of services so necessary in such cases and creates resentments and doubts in the family as to the agency's sincerity in saying it wants to be of help.

Recording is essential for various reasons. First, it helps the continuing treatment worker develop an overall dynamic understanding of what is happening in a case. Second, it gives the supervisor an opportunity to express an opinion regarding the handling of the case and to direct the workers on issues that may require special attention. Third, it helps the court to decide what is best for the children and the family, if the case winds up there.

Recording of investigative assessments should be factual and inclusive of the workers' views, decisions, and recommendations. It could be organized under five subheadings: (1) referral and problem presented, (2) factual information, (3) assessment, (4) services provided, and (5) recommendations.

The most critical areas in this format are the second and third points: factual information and assessment. Factual information should be just that. It simply describes what the workers saw and heard from the children, parents, and others. The victim(s)' condition, reaction and behaviors of family members, their explanations of the situation, physical surroundings, and other disclosures from anyone involved in the family should be included (Bell and Mlyniec, 1972).

It is imperative to omit from the factual information any feelings and/or interpretations such as that the parent is immature, psychotic, or sociopathic. Such materials belong in the assessment when the workers express their professional viewpoint based on all the facts. Diagnostic conclusions with such strong characterizations should be avoided in the assessment unless the (evidence) facts strongly support them. Investigative recordings often reflect excessive diagnostic conclusions not justified by the facts. Thus, a diagnostic conclusion can misdirect the continuing treatment worker and its validity can be questioned by a judge if the record is subpoenaed or is included in a report to the court.

The assessment in the record should indicate precisely the workers' views as to whether abuse or neglect exists and, if it does, its extent and seriousness; an explanation of possible etiological factors; and an analysis of the parents' ability (or lack of it) to care for and provide for the children and the degree of their motivation to work with the agency. Finally, an explanation of the decision for leaving the children at home or removal to some other place should be included.

In general, an assessment during an investigation is a preliminary stage and aims to determine as to whether or not abuse and/or neglect exists and the possible etiology as a guide to providing the needed protection to the children, to meet the family's immediate needs, and to make explicit the agency's intent to provide continuing treatment services. A more thorough assessment of such cases is the responsibility of the continuing treatment worker, which is discussed in Chapter 12.

CONCLUSION

The investigation and initial assessment are inseparable processes in cases of child abuse and neglect when they are conducted by a protective service worker. Whereas investigation denotes efforts to gather concrete evidence in a case, assessment goes beyond the obvious facts into subtle etiologies, behaviors, and feelings, and attempts in its own fashion to meet needs and develop relationships within the context of anticipated continuing treatment. The protective service worker is expected to perform this unique function which requires ability to combine these two processes with flexibility and good judgment to complete the tasks of the initial contact.

A successful investigative assessment as defined in this chapter is not an all-encompassing, unstructured encounter but rather a well-defined process based on limited objectives and goals. The expectation that the investigative worker will achieve the impossible in terms of understanding problems and behaviors and of services to maltreating parents and maltreated children can negatively affect the quality of the practitioner's efforts as well as the quality of service.

Extensive assessments and the provision of continuing services are not and should not be the responsibility of the investigative workers. These are the responsibility of the continuing treatment worker who treats the children and the family.

REFERENCES

Highlights of Official Child Neglect and Abuse Reporting: Annual Report 1981. Denver: American Humane Association, 1983, p. 8.

Bell, C., and Myniec, W.J.: Preparing for neglect proceedings: A guide for the social worker. *Public Welfare, 32:* 28-29, 1974.

Duquette, D.N.: The legal aspects of child abuse and neglect. In K. Faller-Coulborn (Ed.): *Social Work with Abused and Neglected Children.* London: Collier Macmillan Publishers, 1981, pp. 117-24.

Faller-Coulborn, K., and Stone, J.B.: The child welfare system. In K. Faller-Coulborn (Ed.): *Social Work with Abused and Neglected Children.* London: The Free Press, 1981, pp. 101-102.

Hill, D.A.: The initial interview: Alliance building and assessment. In N.B. Ebeling and D.A. Hill (Eds.): *Child Abuse and Neglect.* Boston: John Wright, 1983, p. 45.

Holder, W., and Mohr, C. (Eds.): *Helping in Child Protective Services.* Englewood, CO: The American Humane Association, pp. 6-11, 100-106, 1980; pp. 7-10, 1981.

Kaplan, S.J., and Zitrin, A.: Psychiatrists and child abuse. II. Case assessment by hospitals. *Journal of the American Academy of Child Psychiatry, 22(3):* 257, 1983.

Lynch, M.: Ill health and the battered child. *Lancet, 7929,* 317-19, 1975.

Maden, M., and Wrench, D.: Significant findings in child abuse research. *Victimology,* 2:206-7, Summer 1977.

Martin, H. (Ed.): *The Abused Child.* Cambridge, MA: Ballinger, 1976.

Martin, H.: *Treatment for Abused and Neglected Children.* National Center on Child Abuse and Neglect, Children's Bureau; Administration for Children, Youth and Families. Office of Human Development Services, U.S. Department of Health, Education and Welfare, DHEW Publication No. (OHDS) 79-30199. August 1979, pp. 27-48.

Milner, J.S., and Wimberley, R.C.: Prediction and explanation of child abuse. *Journal of Clinical Psychology,* 36(4): 875-84, October 1980.

Okell-Jones, C.: Characteristics and needs of abused and neglected children. In K. Faller-Coulborn (Ed.): *Social Work with Abused and Neglected Children.* London: The Free Press, 1981, pp. 79-83.

Paulson, M., et al.: Parent attitude research instrument (PARI): Clinical vs. statistical inferences in understanding abusive mothers. *Journal of Clinical Psychology,* 33(3): July 1977.

Pringle, K.M.: The needs of children. In S.M. Smith (Ed.): *The Maltreatment of Children.* Baltimore: University Park Press, 1978, pp. 221-244.

Smith, S.L.: Significant research findings in the etiology of child abuse. *Social Casework,* 65(6): 341, June 1984.

Wright, L.: The "sick but not slick" syndrome as a personality component of parents of battered children. *Journal of Clinical Psychology,* 32(1): 41-45, January 1976.

CHAPTER 12

CONTINUING ASSESSMENT

Chris M. Mouzakitis

INTRODUCTION

The investigative assessment and/or intake was analyzed in the previous chapter. This chapter discusses assessment as the step in the process following initial contact. At the initial contact, workers attempt to decide whether or not the reported abuse and/or neglect is valid. They also decide the seriousness of the abusive or neglectful situation and whether or not the children will remain in the home. They acquire a rough understanding of the parents and determine the degree of their motivation to work with the practitioners.

This is the most difficult part of the workers' involvement because whatever they do is within the confines of limited time, pressure, and high emotions. In this assessment subsequent to the investigation, the continuing treatment worker develops a comprehensive understanding of the situation and, in a systematic way, determines its basic etiology and provides treatment.

This chapter addresses the nature of assessment and related issues and areas to be included during the continuing protective services workers' involvement with parents and children.

ASSESSMENT

Assessment is an essential aspect of the child protection casework process, for without it, all other phases of the helping process—study (intake), treatment, and termination—cannot exist. It is not possible to speak about the intake phase of the process without implying that an assessment is at work. Similarly, in treatment, assessment is ever present. Practitioners cannot assume the responsibility of a treatment role unless they are able to understand the clients' problem.

The ultimate goal of assessment is to understand the nature of the clients' problem and its dynamic aspects. The clients' environment, previous life experiences, social and cultural factors, pathologies, adaptive and nonadaptive behaviors, attitudes and feelings, and their interrelationships are all concerns of assessment (Holis, 1970). According to Cohen (1980), the interaction among the individual's biological, psychological, and social experiences provide a guide for clinical (social work) intervention.

Unfortunately, in current social work practice with abused and neglected children, assessment for various reasons is done poorly so treatment interventions can be incongruous to the actual dynamics of a case. As a result, workers fail to address in treatment the actual issues related to the abusive and neglectful situations and cases are untimely terminated to the detriment of both parents and children (Mouzakitis, 1983). The reasons for this can be attributed to excessive demands placed upon the workers by the agencies in terms of work loads and to their limited training in this specialized field of practice.

CHARACTERISTICS OF ASSESSMENT

An assessment must be based on pertinent facts. This is of utmost importance if workers are to do a relevant, meaningful assessment. When they enter a child abuse and neglect situation they are flooded with all kinds of facts as a result of their own observations and on the basis of what the clients communicate. Unless the workers can discuss which facts are pertinent, their diagnostic assessment may not reflect an accurate understanding of the situation. Pertinent facts have such characteristics as consistency pervasiveness, and duration.

For example, if a parent constantly neglects to feed a child, that is a pertinent fact to be taken into consideration, as contrasted with a mother who has once neglected to do so. The question could be raised, how do workers know whether certain facts are pertinent, especially at the initial contact? The answer is that they will not know until they have an opportunity to visit regularly with the parents and the children. Assessment based on sparse, impressionistic information could lead to the wrong course of treatment. Assessments therefore should be tentative at first, without implying that the workers should remain detached from the family during this period by not offering needed services.

An assessment is a continuing dynamic process. As long as workers are involved with a case of child maltreatment, they are engaged in a continuing assessment. Diagnostic impressions may have to be modified because of new facts that emerge later. Such new facts could be better insight into the clients' idiosyncratic characteristics or related to changes they have made as a result of the workers' efforts. A reassessment then has to be made, along with new diagnostic formulations and new treatment plans. Workers often make thorough assessments and congruous treatment interventions but fail to reassess the situations as they move along in attempting to implement objectives that have become irrelevant to the clients' new reality.

For example, if the worker diagnosed Ms. Jacobs (not her real name) as being a neglectful mother and as a result provided all kinds of supportive services—homemakers, a visiting nurse, day care for the children, transportation, and counseling—did the practitioner reassess the situation three months later? Such a re-evaluation may disclose that Ms. Jacobs, although an inadequate mother, has become less neglectful. As a matter of fact, it may be learned that she has acquired a few homemaking skills and developed some awareness of her children's needs. She no longer is resistive and cooperates with the practitioners and others. This new insight for the workers paves the way for revised treatment plans pertinent to Ms. Jacobs' reality.

As indicated earlier, the assessment is biopsychosocial. However, it cannot be accomplished by the workers alone. The assistance of such other disciplines as psychiatry, psychology, medicine, and education, among others is required. In moving along in child maltreatment cases, it is the workers' responsibility to decide when it is appropriate to seek the assistance of other disciplines and to incorporate their findings into an overall understanding of the case. Such diagnoses should be sought purposefully, not indiscriminately, if they are needed and if they serve to increase the workers' understanding for treatment planning and interventions.

It is not unusual for workers to subject parents and children to scrutiny and testing by various disciplines not out of an apparent need but rather because of procedural requirements. This practice not only is time consuming and expensive but also is meaningless since the workers often make no use of such diagnoses. The use of multidisciplinary teams in assessment can help workers acquire a comprehensive view of a case as long as their involvement is timely and their availability does not prevent the normal flow of the treatment.

An assessment should be concise and brief. A long diagnostic report generally does not serve the purpose for which it was undertaken. Since its purpose, without exception, is to evaluate a particular situation and to identify the problem(s), excessive verbosity does not contribute to its clarity. At times workers intermingle irrelevant facts and personal opinions in such a way that the essence and clarity of the diagnostic summary are lost. It is not unusual for social workers and other professionals to read an assessment and wonder what it means. A diagnostic assessment that is intended to give direction may call for treatment that is unrelated to the actual situation unless it is clear and precise. In writing a diagnosis, workers should separate the myriad of facts from their own evaluative opinions. What the workers think, believe, and understand is a professional opinion based on the salient facts of a particular case. The need for diagnostic clarity in child protection work is of immense importance, since the workers' actions and their effectiveness can be measured by the clarity of their assessments.

DIMENSIONS OF CONTINUING ASSESSMENT

The extent of the continuing assessment subsequent to the initial contact depends on the type of maltreatment, its impact on the children, and the various environmental, psychological, and idiosyncratic factors that could have contributed to the abuse and/or neglect. Not all cases should receive an identical assessment in terms of breadth and depth. The assessment should not be an end in itself but rather a means through which certain goals are sought to be accomplished.

For example, the extent of assessment in an incestuous situation will be quantitatively and qualitatively different from a case in which a child is sexually abused by a family friend. Similarly, a case of neglect in which the child is diagnosed as failure to thrive will be different from one in which the child is found to be unattended, improperly clothed, and lacking medical care.

It is not unusual for workers to try to unearth material from the parents' background that have no relevance to their understanding of a situation and to the provision of treatment services.

This author, being a consultant to various treatment programs, can attest to the fact that workers can consume an entire meeting discussing mental health issues that have only remote relevance to the problems at hand and spend no time addressing the treatment aspects of a case. In all cases of abuse and/or neglect, however, workers must selectively address certain areas in assessment (see following list). Their inclusion and analysis helps workers acquire an understanding of the parents' personality characteristics, attitudes, and feelings; the impact of the environment on their lives and behaviors; the quality of their interpersonal and intrapersonal relationships; antecedents for the abusive and/or neglectful behavior; the effectiveness of their parenting skills; knowledge of developmental stages; and ability to cope with stresses and solve problems.

Areas to Be Included in Assessment

1. The parents' financial condition and environmental stressors such as poor housing, unemployment.
2. The parents' values that reflect cultural differences.
3. The parents' physical, emotional, and mental condition.
4. The reasons for the parents' possible resistance and lack of motivation.
5. The parents' special problems, such as alcoholism and drug abuse.
6. The parents' ability to use formal and informal support systems.
7. The parents' problem-solving abilities.
8. The parents' early life experiences in their families of origin and after.
9. Parental imperfections and activities that are harmful to the child.
10. The reasons for the abusive and/or neglectful parental behavior.
11. The duration of the parents' abusive and/or neglectful behavior.
12. The consequence of the parental behavior.
13. The parents' knowledge of developmental stages of children.
14. The parents' knowledge of child-rearing practices.
15. The parents' standards of failure and success.
16. The family's significant interpersonal relationships.
17. The family's transactional and interactional patterns.
18. The family's role-appropriate behaviors.
19. The family's complementarity of roles.
20. The family's strengths.
21. The parents' potential for change.

PARENTS' FINANCIAL CONDITION

In AFDC (Aid to Families with Dependent Children) cases the family's financial situation is self-evident. In other cases that do not fit that category it will not be known unless an inquiry is made. For example, in non-AFDC cases where there is abuse and neglect of children, workers have no way of knowing unless they ask the parents directly.

A big house and a seemingly affluent appearance is not a good reason to stop workers from inquiring into this particular respect. A "well-to-do" family also can have financial stresses and mismanagement of money that may affect the relationship between spouses and of parents with their children. Ascertaining such information is an example of the need for workers to discover all possible links that may have contributed to the abusive situation.

VALUES THAT REFLECT CULTURAL DIFFERENCES

Abuse and neglect of children are not the exclusive domain of any particular socioeconomic, racial, ethnic, or religious group. It is fundamental in assessment, then, to be aware that the quality and the kind of care children receive from their parents and other significant adults in their families could be a reflection of beliefs about child-rearing practices and of prevailing community standards (Giovannoni and Bacerra, 1979).

For example, would a middle-class worker characterize as neglectful a parent of a lower socioeconomic class whose child is not too clean, is not offered the three meals a day, and occasionally is left in the supervision of older siblings? Or would the worker classify as an abuser a Mexican-American father who, in the process of disciplining his sons, hits them with a belt?

Certainly, such parental behavior is not justified if the children's physical and emotional integrity is at stake. Similarly, no such behavior would be excused in a parent who is a religious fanatic when he tries "to get the devil out of his son" by constantly beating him. For workers assessing such instances where cultural factors are present, it is prudent to consider (in addition to the children's welfare) the prevailing norms in a particular community before reaching any diagnostic conclusions.

PARENTS' SOCIAL MOBILITY

One finding reported repeatedly in the literature is that abuse and/or neglectful parents by and large tend to be socially isolated and withdrawn from essential contacts with people and supportive systems (Justice and Justice, 1976; Maden and Wrench, 1973). They feel discounted and seem to live on the periphery of community life.

It is fundamental for workers to ask why this is so. Is it because they are poverty-stricken and do not have the basic means to allow them any meaningful contacts with people? Is it because they lack knowledge and feel worthless? Or is it because of pressures from within the family?

For example, a jealous, overpossessive father who sexually abuses his daughter may exercise such pressure. This last point is well documented in the literature on sexual abuse. Fathers not only are possessive of their wife's imposing controls on them but they behave in a similar fashion toward the daughters they abuse sexually (Meiselman, 1978).

PARENTS' PHYSICAL, INTELLECTUAL, AND MENTAL CONDITIONS

This heading does not imply that workers should become physicians, psychologists, or psychiatrists. However, in their effort to acquire a thorough understanding of a situation, they should try to find out whether the parents and the family as a whole have any medical problems and what they have done about them. Many families, especially those that neglect their children, do not have health insurance and dread the idea of seeing a doctor, not only because of the expense involved but also because of the complicated and at times humiliating process they have to go through.

On the other hand, some parents may lack information as to how to go about it and may be as neglecting of themselves as they are of their children. Such parents may have all sorts of mental problems, others may suffer from chronic depression, still others may have psychotic and personality disorders (Smith, 1984). Chronically depressed parents or those afflicted by mental disorders are more likely to neglect or abuse their children.

Similarly, intellectually limited parents may be incapable of meeting the demands of growing children (Henry, 1978). Such parents may fail to provide needed supervision and may fail to provide appropriate nutritional, hygienic, and medical care. Workers acquire this knowledge of parents' physical, intellectual, and mental condition as a result of many regular contacts and not through a remote control, telephone, casework approach.

ALCOHOL AND DRUG ADDICTION

The association of alcohol abuse, child abuse, and family violence has been supported by research (Spicker and Mouzakitis, 1977; Mayhall and Eastlack-Norgard, 1983). Drug addiction and/or alcohol abuse have been found to be strongly correlated with child maltreatment in general (Meiselman, 1978). In many situations the parents' addictive condition may become obvious from their appearance and behavior. Where the use of alcohol and drugs has not taken a visible toll, the effects can be seen in the parents' ability to care and in their relationship with their children.

As a rule, such parents' emotional ability to care for and relate to their children is unpredictable and lacks consistency and real discipline. In such cases the neglect may encompass even basic elementary care, with the children showing signs of depression through passivity or acting-out behavior. Early identification of the parents' alcoholic and/or addictive condition is a cue to initiate prompt services.

PARENTS' LEVEL OF MATURITY

One constant finding in research is that abusive and neglectful parents are immature. Being a parent is an adult task that requires a degree of emotional maturity (Henry, 1978). Assessment of this area gives the workers a better understanding of the parents' ability to function as responsible adults. Are they able to tolerate stress, whether from children or the environment in general, within reasonable limits? Are they able to delay until later their own gratifications vis-à-vis the children's needs? Can they recognize and carry out responsibilities for themselves and others? Do they learn from experience so that crises in their lives are not repeated? Analysis of such concerns give workers a better insight as to the maturational level of functioning so they can deal with the parents realistically.

FAMILY INTERPERSONAL RELATIONSHIPS

These relationships involve communication and sharing between parents, between children and parents, and among the children. Defective marital and parental relationships have been substantiated in research as basic etiologies of family violence and child abuse and neglect (Avery, 1975; Justice and Justice, 1976). It is pertinent for workers in assessing this area to raise such questions as: Is the parents' relationship a supportive one where each of the partners receives the emotional sustenance so necessary to cope with stresses and other problems related to family living? Or are there conflicts, jealousies, and emotional detachment that cause the parents, although living under the same roof, to go their separate ways to seek substitutes for their unhappiness? How are the children affected by problems in the marital relationship? Are they becoming pawns in the marital conflict and thus subjected to aggression and violence, inconsistent discipline, and punitive parenting? Are the children emotionally exploited by the parents as manifested in symbiotic attachments and triangulations (Justice and Justice, 1976; Mayhall and Eastlack-Norgard, 1983)?

Family theory points to the deleterious effects such parent/child collusions have on the family's overall healthy atmosphere and on the children's normal growth and development. By focusing on this type of concerns, workers can increase their understanding of what is happening within the family system and of the possible etiologies for the abuse and neglect the child or children are experiencing.

KNOWLEDGE OF DEVELOPMENTAL STAGES

Many abusive parents have no knowledge as to what are the appropriate behaviors of their children as they grow (Justice and Justice, 1976). For example, they do not know that a year-old baby as a rule is not toilet trained, or that a toddler's inquisitiveness and occasional negativism is part of learning and testing the world, or that there is a discrepancy between physical and emotional maturity in a twelve-year-old child.

Because of the lack of such knowledge, the parents' expectations of their children are unrealistic. The youngsters' inability to be responsive to the parents' demands is construed as defiance, lack of appreciation for what they try to do, and lack of love that often causes the parents to either ignore or to strike the child. A thorough understanding of this area can help lead the workers to establish vital links in tracking the causes of the parents' abusive and/or neglectful behavior.

KNOWLEDGE OF CHILD MANAGEMENT

The title of parents as "father" or "mother" does not automatically bestow upon them wisdom as to how to manage their children effectively. As a matter of fact, parents rarely have received any kind of formal training as to what to do or not do in various circumstances. Such knowledge comes about informally as a result of personal experiences from their own home. It is an established fact that abusive and/or neglectful parents, in particular, lack knowledge in this area (Justice and Justice, 1976). Parents' mismanagement of children can trigger a series of behaviors that can cause the youngsters to become unpredictable, stubborn, and a real threat to the adults as competent parents. For example, if the parents obsessively try to correct an enuretic child, even getting the victim up several times during the night, they could set in motion all kinds of manipulative and sublimating behaviors by both child and parents. If parents are unreasonably demanding a performance that is above the child's physical and intellectual abilities, they may be emotionally abusing the youngster. Assessment of management techniques gives workers the understanding necessary for possible intervention.

Parental Imperfections

All parents in some way or another punish their children and at times may also neglect them. Parents who have come to the attention of authorities have exceeded the limits and have caused their children undue hardship. Workers must understand such situations in order to offer the needed help. However, they should not become overzealous and blame the parents for minor infractions—which, after all, are found in all parents. All parents scream at their children; all parents use a form of discipline that at times is physical.

In assessment, the workers must identify acts and behaviors that can cause harm. For example, hitting a child with a stick on the head, twisting arms, causing the child to be burned, locking the child in a closet, leaving the child alone without appropriate supervision, exposing the child in cold weather with limited clothing—all these are parental activities on which the worker should focus, seeking the reasons, frequency, and duration of such behaviors. Since assessment is the prelude to planning appropriate treatment interventions, such an analysis gives the workers a realistic view of the parents' harmful behaviors.

REASONS FOR PARENTS' BEHAVIOR

The workers attempt to ascertain the precipitating causes for such behaviors—in other words, what has triggered the parents to become violent. Does it happen when children soil their pants, cry, or sit at the table to eat? In this kind of assessment, practitioners must induce the parents to recall, step by step, what happened immediately before the abuse occurred.

For example, Mrs. Jones could be asked: "You said that you hit Johnny because he cried loudly and refused to eat his breakfast. Could you tell me what you did with Johnny just before this happened?" Mrs. Jones may explain that Johnny had refused to get out of bed although she had asked him many times. Asked whether Johnny needed more sleep, Mrs. Jones indicates that he did since he had watched television late last night.

This questioning process brings to light the sequence of events that led to and triggered the abusive behavior. For the workers to understand the "event" of abuse and/or neglect, it is essential that they assess the processes that have taken place in such situations. By process is meant the experiences of those involved in the abusive situation they go through.

Abusive behavior is a symptom of possible family pathology, defective communications, etc. (Kaufman, 1983). It is the culmination of certain experiential processes that have led to the event of abuse and/or neglect.

Assessment of these experiential processes allows the workers to identify the basic etiologies. Whatever corrective learning experiences they provide the parents, their soundness should be based on an understanding of the experiences that led to the abuse.

DURATION OF PARENTS' BEHAVIOR

Assessment of the length of the parents' behavior gives workers an insight as to whether the situation is chronic or acute. This probably will reveal some indicators as to whether it is rooted in diverse social and psychopathological conditions or in immediate environmental factors (Mouzakitis, 1984). The workers then can consider the possible effects on the child. It is well known that children who have experienced abuse and/or neglect for long periods of time develop serious emotional, mental, and physical problems (Mayhall and Eastlack-Norgard, 1983).

It is not possible to do such an assessment at intake because the parents' feelings of fear, suspicion, hostility, mistrust, and denial do not permit a thorough evaluation at that point.

INITIATIVES TO RESOLVE THE SITUATION

Have both parents been abusive and neglectful or only one of them? Has either of them ever taken steps to protect the child or to correct the problem? The workers' efforts become easier if they find out that one of the parents is more receptive than the other.

For example, the mother or others in the home who in the past attempted to do something about the situation could be used to back up the workers' intervention. It is obvious that when both parents are in a state of oblivious euphoria that everything is perfect, workers will have more difficulty than when the parents have at least some awareness that a problem exists.

IDENTIFICATION OF FAMILY STRENGTHS

It has been made clear that assessment is a process for understanding the client or family liabilities, shortcomings, assets, and strengths. At times, practitioners tend to do a one-sided assessment that tells them what is wrong, overlooking the fact that even abusive and neglectful individuals have many positive aspects.

For example, an abusing father may also be intelligent, a good provider, and concerned about his children's overall welfare even though he has been found to be a perfectionist and lacking in knowledge about their developmental stages. Inclusion of the clients' plusses in assessment gives the workers a positive base for interventive plans. As discussed in the chapters on treatment, a positive approach toward behavioral, emotional, and attitudinal changes has a better chance of success if the clients become aware that they also have positive points.

PARENTS' POTENTIAL FOR CHANGE

Child abusers and/or neglecters do not move at the same speed toward changes. Some may move rapidly and improve, others take some steps toward change, and many do not change at all.

For example, the workers may have succeeded to stop the maltreatment or the parents may have developed some insight into the effects their problems have on their children. However, the changes may be far less than had been expected—the house may not be as clean as it should be. In spite of efforts to encourage them to reach out and make use of community resources, the parents do not do so. They neglect their own needs and in general are not too responsive to available benefits.

It is assumed that the workers have done everything possible based on a sound assessment of the case. It is imperative that they then ask whether the parents have potentials for further change. For example, if an abusive mother's intellectual functioning is below normal, it may be unrealistic to expect that she will ever become competent. Or if a mother's personality is such that it does not foster good interpersonal relationships, it may be a waste of time to try to bring about changes. It is suggested that rather than disqualify such clients from further treatment, the workers make a thorough reassessment of the extent of their limitations and follow a perhaps different, more pragmatic course of action. It is useless and inappropriate to press for changes that will never occur.

Unfortunately, workers are not always realistic in the reassessment. They should understand that, for example, AFDC mothers who have been found to be neglectful of their children will never become like middle-class neurotic mothers. It is progress if the abuse and/or neglect has stopped. It is progress if the child is well fed, dressed, and supervised even if the house is not too clean.

Assessment enables the practitioners to better understand etiological factors and to identify specific problems. They cannot speak about treatment or therapy unless they have developed an insight into the parents' functional and dysfunctional behavior patterns and their feelings, attitudes, and personality characteristics.

Research has confirmed that it is not unusual for workers to begin treatment and/or therapy with parents and families on the basis of erroneous assumptions rather than on a thorough understanding of the situations (Mouzakitis, 1983). For example, the use of family therapy should be determined on the basis of the assessment's suggesting the appropriateness of that method, rather than on the notion that it is beneficial in any situation.

It is known that the use of such a method in incestuous situations, for example, is unproductive initially before other methods are used. The use of such treatment modalities as behavior modification, reality therapy, and crisis intervention should be linked to the workers' understanding of a particular case rather than to their personal preference. To repeat an earlier statement, assessment is not an end in itself but the process through which direction in treatment and responsiveness to identified needs is achieved.

ASSESSMENT OF THE CHILD VICTIMS

Protection and treatment of the children and the parents requires more than a mere determination as to whether abuse or neglect is present. Depending on their age and the duration of the maltreatment experienced, the children's situation can be complicated and difficult to understand. Such children suffer from psychoemotional and behavioral problems and are affected intellectually as well as physically (Justice and Justice, 1976; Mayhall and Eastlack-Norgard, 1983). Attempts to provide treatment without a thorough grasp of the children's emotional, mental, and physical condition will deprive them of protection they need or the appropriate treatment and/or therapy. Early in their involvement with the family, workers should try to focus their assessment on the areas discussed next.

IMPACT OF THE PARENTS' BEHAVIOR

Although during the initial contact workers attempt to assess the impact of the parents' maltreatment, they cannot thoroughly understand the children's real feelings. No matter what their age, the children may be in a state of shock, fearful, distrustful, self-accusatory, and often protective of the parents. At subsequent contacts, once a relationship with the children has been developed, the workers need to assess the victims' inner feelings toward their parents and family as a whole, their perceptions of the abusive and/or neglectful behaviors, developmental lags, and behavioral and attitudinal characteristics that may have negatively impacted because of the maltreatment.

Children subjected to abusive and neglectful conditions, as discussed elsewhere in this book, develop serious behavioral and emotional problems (Martin, 1979; Holleman, 1983). Many of these problems are clearly seen in acting out, asocial and inappropriate behaviors, sexual promiscuity, inability to relate, and academic failure (Martin, 1979). However, with younger victims, especially those who are emotionally maltreated, workers should attempt to assess such behaviors as:

- *habit disorders* (sucking, biting, rocking, masturbating, enuresis, head banging, etc.)
- *conduct disorders* (definance, rebellion, tantrums, destructiveness, cruelty, lying, stealing, etc.)
- *neurotic traits* (jealousy, inhibitions about playing, sleep disorders, phobias, night terrors, fear of darkness, etc.)
- *psychoneurotic reactions* (hysterical, phobic, obsessive, compulsive, hypochondriacal disorders).

Habit disorders are tension-reducing forms of behavior in very young children who cannot protect their affective needs with satisfaction. Those with conduct disorders do not get the needed emotional acceptance and the usual source of rewards for submitting to strain. On the other hand, those with neurotic traits have partially internalized conflict and show some degree of acting out.

In contrast to these disorders, the conflict in psychoneurotic reactions is internalized: the children are absorbed mainly in conflict with themselves (Ackerman, 1958). These kinds of disorders can be seen in children who have experienced various forms of either overt or subtle nonviolent maltreatment.

These are the so-called "gray cases" where it is difficult to determine what is at issue. There is nothing grotesque in such cases. The children are not abused physically or neglected materially—it is simply that their emotional needs are not met. The children do not get emotional support or a feeling that their parents care for them. Their basic needs for love, affection, and security are ignored. The parents are absorbed in their own problems and build a wall around themselves, blocking any meaningful communication with the children.

These symptoms, especially in neglect cases, obviously lead to a conclusion that the children's emotional needs are not fully met and that something is not right in the parent/child relationship. It should be noted, though, that while any one such symptom is not necessarily an indication that the children are emotionally deprived, a cluster of such symptoms does indicate that something is not right. In many situations where no involvement by protective services has been decided upon, workers could step in on a preventive basis by alerting the parents and other agencies to offer the needed help. Assessment by pediatricians, psychiatrists, and psychologists may be necessary in emotional maltreatment cases.

CHILDREN'S SPECIAL PROBLEMS

The problems of abused and/or neglected children can be attributed generally to maltreatment and deprivation they have experienced, but many may be idiosyncratic to a particular child. Such conditions as mental retardation, learning disabilities, poor hearing and vision, and emotional disturbances could become the precipitating cause for the abuse and neglect. Defective children unable to meet their parents' expectations not only are a disappointment to them but can stir up all kinds of feelings and negative behaviors toward themselves (Martin, 1979).

Parents may ignore the children's special needs, may try to insulate them from the environment, may fail to provide the care they need, and at times in their effort to communicate and discipline them may commit abuses. Difficult-to-handle children, because of such behaviors as stubbornness, unresponsiveness to parents' feelings, etc.—which at times may be secondary symptoms to the idiosyncratic conditions—often trigger the abusive and/or neglectful behavior.

This is not to switch the focus of the etiology of maltreatment onto the difficult children, since in a majority of situations they become scapegoats for the parents' personal problems and environmental pressures. However, for workers who undertake to treat children and parents in such situations, such knowledge is basic for an assessment. Protective service workers are not asked to assess authoritatively conditions for which they have no specialized knowledge but, rather, to identify the conditions on the basis of general knowledge they are expected to have.

For example, if a child impresses the workers as being bright and yet cannot read, it should become apparent that the youngster may have a learning disability, poor hearing, or an emotional problem. True, a child's condition with these symptomatologies could be the result of abuse and/or neglect or a combination of maltreatment and genetic factors. But, no matter what the actual etiology of the condition, the child is experiencing a problem that impacts on physical and psychoemotional growth and development and on relationships with parents and others. Workers should assess all this before venturing into a course of treatment. If they do not fully understand the children's condition, an expert's opinion may be needed to help determine the extent and cause of the damage and/or disability (Martin, 1979). However, the workers' role in such abuse and neglect cases is unique in terms of a comprehensive assessment and should not be delegated unnecessarily to another professional who is involved only peripherally.

THE CHILDREN'S CONTINUING SAFETY AND WELFARE

Providing for the children's safety and welfare is a continuing task for workers. As a rule, parents discontinue their maltreating behavior once the protective service agency becomes involved in a case, although in many instances they may resist the agency's presence, and so little progress is made. In many situations such parents may mistreat the children covertly. The workers' assessment in determining the possible continuing risk in cases of abuse should focus on the following:

1. Whether the parents, through their actions and behaviors, are able to control aggressive and hostile impulses toward the children.
2. Whether the parents recognize (directly or indirectly) their abusive behavior.
3. Whether the parents verbalize and show evidence that they want to work with the agency.
4. Whether the children show no evidence of further abuse.

If the parents do not meet any of these criteria, the workers should be on the alert for the children's protection. Similarly, in cases of neglect the following criteria should be used in assessing the children's welfare:

1. Whether the parents provide adequate supervision
2. Whether the parents provide adequate medical care
3. Whether the parents provide adequate food and clothing
4. Whether the parents make sure the children attend school
5. Whether the parents provide adequate housing
6. Whether the parents show evidence of improving their child-care skills
7. Whether the overall emotional atmosphere in the home is conducive to the children's normal growth
8. Whether the parents demonstrate the ability to use community resources for the children's and their own welfare
9. Whether the parents demonstrate their desire to work with the agency.

THE IMPACT OF SEPARATION

For many abused and/or neglected children (although not a majority), placement is inevitable as soon as the investigative assessment has been completed on the basis of criteria outlined in the previous chapter. However, in many instances while the continuing treatment worker attempts to treat the parents, placement does become inevitable. This is caused most often by the parents' resistance and lack of motivation to make the changes necessary to guarantee the children's safety and welfare.

In such situations, abrupt separations should be avoided. Before attempting the separation, workers must assess the children's feelings—rejection, anger, hostility, mistrust, and fear. Abrupt separation could traumatize them as much as, and even more than, the abuse and/or neglect (Littner, 1956; Noonan, 1983). Just think how traumatic it could be for an eight-year-old to suddenly be separated from parents he loves in spite of the maltreatment, as well as from siblings, relatives, and others, and to find himself surrounded by people he does not know.

Separation from familiar surroundings inevitably is psychologically traumatic. Assessment of the degree and quality of the children's attachment to parents and relationships with others is indicated. This will determine how much work needs to be done with the youngsters before placement, when the move should take place, and the kind of place appropriate for a particular child.

Unfortunately, removal of children from their homes too often is done casually and with no assessment of their feelings of rejection and humiliation, of their prior life experiences, and of their ability to understand what is happening. Thus, children indiscriminately placed in foster and group homes tend to fail to adjust in these placements. The literature on the negative effects of successive placements is quite explicit (Hess, 1982).

In summary, in continuing assessment the focus should be on: (1) the impact of maltreatment on the child, (2) the child's special and/or idiosyncratic problems, (3) the child's continuing safety and welfare, and (4) the child's feelings of separation if placement is inevitable.

It should be noted that such an assessment pertaining to the children is not a separate entity from that of the parents; it is a concurrent process while the workers deliver the appropriate treatment services. These areas are not inclusive of all those to be assessed but are the most pertinent following the investigative assessment.

Their assessment contributes to the practitioners' understanding of the children's general condition, behaviors, and feelings toward parents, needs and whether they are met, and reactions to an inevitable separation from the home environment. Such an understanding, compounded with the workers' knowledge from the investigative assessment, assists the practitioners in making treatment decisions relevant to the needs and realities of the children and the family.

ASSESSMENT IN SEXUAL MALTREATMENT CASES

The continuing assessment in cases involving sexual maltreatment of children can be a complicated process because of the impact its revelation has on the perpetrator, the mother, siblings, and often on other family members. Their immediate reactions vary from rage toward the perpetrator to possible collusion of the entire family to prevent its further exposure to the community. Members of the family may be scattered to various locations, such as the victim's living in a foster home, the mother and other children with relatives or in the home, and the perpetrator in jail or living away from the home as a result of court orders. Whatever the victim's and family's reactions and living arrangements may be, if treatment is to be offered a continuing assessment must be made. The areas suggested earlier for other types of maltreatment also are applicable in sexual abuse cases. However, some additional areas should be considered.

Although the investigative assessment has determined the type of sexual maltreatment, the continuing treatment worker should concentrate on assessing the social and psychopathological dynamics. Experts in the field of sexual maltreatment generally agree on certain types of abuse; those delineated by Zaphiris (1983) are most helpful in the assessment of such cases as incest, sexual abuse, sexual exploitation, and sibling sexual abuse.

INCEST

In cases of father-daughter incest, workers need to determine: (1) the onset of the activity, (2) its frequency and duration, (3) the incestuous behavior, (4) the victim's feelings toward the father, (5) the mother's feelings and behaviors toward the husband and the victim, (6) the feelings and impact on siblings, (7) the relationships among individual family members, and (8) the family's relationships and contacts with extended family members and the community.

Focusing the assessment on these areas assists the workers in understanding feelings, emotions, behaviors, communication patterns, positions, and roles of the family members and the chronicity of the incestuous affair. For workers doing the assessment, it is important to remember that incest in its classical type does not come about suddenly but rather through a long process of conditioning by the father (Misselman, 1981; Zaphiris, 1983) directed not only toward the child but toward the mother and other family members (Zaphiris, 1983). As a result, the family behaves in a united and "healthy" way to an outside observer.

This should suggest to the workers the need to relate not only to the victim and the perpetrator but also to the family as a whole. On the other hand, awareness of the conditioning process all family members have been subjected to alerts the workers to the existence of psychological and possible pathological conditions. This can be more true for the child victim, although follow-up studies are inconclusive (Misselman, 1981).

SEXUAL ABUSE

This term as a rule has a generic meaning. It is used here to denote the forceful, sudden sexual involvement of the victim by the father, siblings, other relatives, and adults known to the child. Although the sexual abuse generally is incestuous, the conditioning process observed in the classical father-daughter type is not present since the abuse is sudden and forceful and the child is an unwilling participant. The mother and the family also are not conditioned to accept this behavior.

According to Zaphiris (1983), the sexually abusive behavior in such instances is "usually symptomatic of and/or possibly a reaction of a social psychopathological and/or possible characterological condition." The abuser could be psychotic, character disordered, a drug or alcohol abuser, or retarded below the trainable level. The assessment should focus on understanding the conditioning aspect of the abuse, its possibly time-limited occurrence, the mental condition and idiosyncratic characteristics of the abuser and the physical and psychological traumatic impact on the victim. This could reveal whether the sexual misconduct is an individual problem; that is, that of the abuser rather than of the entire family as is the case with the incestuous family. The dynamics operating in such cases should lead the workers to implement differing treatment approaches congruent to the problems of the abuser and to the unwilling victim and family.

SEXUAL EXPLOITATION

In cases where children are exploited by the parents for their own sexual expression and gratification, production of pornographic materials, and prostitution for their own profit, the dynamics are a combination of what is seen in cases of incest and sexual abuse. The children are progressively conditioned to accept and overtly relate to the parents and to others sexually; there is an enmeshed pathologic quality in the relationship. The parents may be psychotic, sociopathic, character disordered, and drug and/or alcohol abusers. It has been confirmed by various experts that such parents, especially fathers, are sociopathic, which suggests unpredictability in their behavior, inability to establish meaningful relationships, and lack of guilt for their misdeeds.

This type of sexual maltreatment generally comes to the attention of authorities when the victims are in their early or late teens (although so-called "kid-porn" involving preteenagers has been much in the news). It is the most difficult to assess and to work with since the entire family has been seriously affected by the events and pathologies and is unwilling to cooperate with the workers.

SIBLING SEXUAL RELATIONSHIP

Sexual relationships among siblings could be the result of what is called innate curiosity to find out about human anatomy and physical sexual differences. It also can be the result of an incestuous culture in the family, as well as the result of psychopathological characterological qualities in the siblings (Zaphiris, 1983). However siblings also could sexually abuse and exploit each other.

In the assessment, the workers need to acquire an understanding of the family as a whole and the members' specific roles and how they are fulfilled. In many instances the siblings' sexual relationship results from the fact that the parents fail to provide supervision and/or education and information related to sex. In other instances the family's permissive culture as it relates to sexual matters can encourage the siblings to such activity among themselves. Aggressive siblings' personality makeup also needs to be understood in terms of possible psychopathological conditions and other idiosyncratic characteristics.

CONCLUSION

Continuing assessment of child abuse and neglect cases is a process that is inseparable from and parallel with that of treatment. Its methodological application, based on knowledge of the dynamic dimensions of the cases, is the best guarantee that the treatment needs of this population will be met. Although this chapter has focused on the role of protective services workers, successful completion of the process depends on the contribution of other disciplines as well.

REFERENCES

Ackerman, N.W.: *The Psychodynamics of Family Life.* New York: Basic Books, Inc., 1958, pp. 201-204.

Avery, N.C.: Viewing child abuse and neglect as symptoms of family dysfunctioning. In N.B. Ebeling and D.A. Hill, *Child Abuse Intervention and Treatment.* Acton, MA: Publishing Sciences Group, Inc., 1975, pp. 87-91.

Cohen, J.: Nature of clinical social work. In P.L. Ewalt (Ed.): *Toward a Definition of Clinical Social Work.* Washington, D.C.: National Association of Social Workers, 1980, p. 26.

Giovannoni, J.M., and Becerra, R.M.: *Defining Child Abuse.* New York: The Free Press, 1979.

Henry, D.R.: The psychological aspects of child abuse. In S.M. Smith (Ed.): *The Maltreatment of Children.* Baltimore: University Park Press, 1978, pp. 211-213, 214-216.

Hess, P.: Parent-child attachment concept: Crucial for permanency planning. *Social Casework, 63*(1):46-52, January 1982.

Holis, F.: The psychosocial approach to the practice of casework. In R.W. Roberts and R.H. Nee (Eds.), *Theories of Social Casework.* Chicago: The University of Chicago Press, 1970, pp. 49-56.

Holleman, B.A.: Treatment of the child. In N.B. Eberling and D.A. Hill (Eds.): *Child Abuse and Neglect.* Boston: John Wright, 1983, pp. 149-156.

Justice, B., and Justice, R.: *The Abusing Family.* New York: Human Sciences Press, 1976, pp.17, 21, 99, 157-57.

Kaufman, M.: Physical abuse, neglect and sexual abuse: Dimensions and frameworks. In N.B. Ebeling and D.A. Hill (Eds.): *Child Abuse and Neglect.* Boston: John Wright, 1983, pp. 22-24.

Littner, N.: Traumatic effects of separation and placement. In *Proceedings, National Conference in Social Work.* New York: Family Service Association of America, 1956, pp. 1-10.

Maden, M., and Wrench, D.: Significant findings in child abuse research. *Victimology,* 2:206-7, Summer 1977.

Martin, H.: *Treatment for Abused and Neglected Children.* U.S. Department of Health, Education, and Welfare, DHEW, Publication No. (OHDS) 79-30199, August 1979, p. 30.

Mayhall, P.D., and Eastlack-Norgard, K.: *Child Abuse and Neglect.* New York: John Wiley and Sons, 1983, pp. 120-121, 122-129.

Meiselman, K.C.: *Incest.* San Francisco: Jossey-Bass, 1978, pp. 93, 113.

Mouzakitis, C.: *Effectiveness of Treatment of Abused Adolescents.* Baltimore: University of Maryland, School of Social Work and Community Planning, 1983 (unpublished research project).

———: Characteristics of abused adolescents and guidelines for intervention. *Child Welfare,* Vol. LXII, No. 2, March-April 1984, pp. 149-157.

Noonan, R.A.: Separation and placement. In N.B. Eberling and D.A. Hill (Eds.): *Child Abuse and Neglect.* Boston: John Wright, 1983, pp. 210-13.

Smith, S.L.: Significant research findings in the etiology of child abuse. *Social Casework,* 65(6):343-45, June 1984.

Spicker, A., and Mouzakitis, C.M.: Alcohol abuse and child abuse and neglect: An inquiry into alcohol abusers' behavior toward children. *The Alcoholism Digest, 6,* Summer 1977.

Zaphiris, A.G.: *Methods and Skills for a Differential Assessment and Treatment in Incest, Sexual Abuse and Sexual Exploitation of Children.* Denver: The American Humane Association, 1983, pp. 3-7.

CHAPTER 13

INTERVIEWING IN CHILD PROTECTION

Chris M. Mouzakitis

INTRODUCTION

Interviewing is the skill employed most frequently by all professionals involved in the delivery of human services. Social workers more than any other professionals need to know how to conduct interviews, since a great amount of their activity is spent in direct communication with clients. In spite of this, interviewing as a skill is a neglected area in the training of professionals, including social workers. It is a subject about which little has been written, and even then only peripherally.

Interviewing is a vital element in the helping process. From the moment workers meet their clients at intake and through the assessment, treatment, and termination phases, they invariably use communication skills that are crucial to determining their effectiveness. These skills are not the result of a simple effort. They are a combination of the workers' own general innate ability, habits, knowledge, and preparation. Learning how to interview is a slow process and requires workers to think constructively about what they are doing and to be able to synthesize the experience. Furthermore, it is a conscious effort that requires attention to details and practice. Actually, learning how to be an effective interviewer is indispensible (Garrette, 1972; Kadushin, 1972).

The protective services interview with parents and children is a challenging endeavor primarily because of the clients' involuntary role; the high emotions of anger, denial, and hostility present; and various protective and possible legal issues in such cases. Because of this, the interviewers must have special knowledge and skills to be able to withstand frustration in order to fulfill their job responsibilities. This chapter is designed to increase social workers' understanding of the nature of the protective services interview and its complexities and to outline basic interviewing techniques pertinent to effective communication with maltreating parents and maltreated children.

PURPOSE AND NATURE OF INTERVIEWS

In its simplest form an interview takes place when two or more people meet and talk. However, an interview is not merely a conversation, it is a systematic communication with a purpose (Gordon, 1975; Kadushin, 1972). It is a purposefully directed activity between the workers and one or more clients, with the purpose as a central element. It establishes the boundaries for the discussion and dictates to interviewers and participants appropriate verbal and nonverbal behaviors. Although all interviews have their own specific purposes, in general they are designed: (1) to elicit information, (2) to impart information, (3) to provide an opportunity to express feelings and release tension, (4) to motivate clients toward certain goals, and (5) to promote understanding and resolution of issues under consideration (Holder and Mohr, 1980).

The attainment of the purpose and quality of an interview is closely related to certain factors pertaining to the interviewer: self-awareness, knowledge, experience, and personal facility. Self-awareness of one's own feelings, attitudes, and preconceived notions about people can prevent distortions of perceptions and can enhance objective communication with clients (Goldberg, 1975). The breadth and depth of knowledge of human behavior dynamics enhance the interviewers' ability to place themselves accordingly vis-à-vis the clients and to become accurately responsive to their feelings and behaviors.

No matter how well qualified the interviewers may be, nothing can substitute for the experience they have accumulated over the years in practice. The more practice experience the workers have, the better able they are to communicate with clients whose problems are diverse in nature. Finally, the interviewers' personal characteristics of warmth, genuineness, tolerance, sincerity, and flexibility as a rule enhance more effective communication.

Purpose of the Protective Service Interview

Depending on the abusive and/or neglectful situation at issue, the purpose of the protective service interview varies during the course of workers' involvement with a case. However, its general purpose is twofold:

1. In the initial contact during the investigative assessment, it seeks to obtain and to appraise selective information in order to make

certain decisions, such as: (a) to substantiate or validate the report of the alleged abuse or neglect, (b) to reach an agreement with the parents to work with them, (c) to file an abuse or neglect petition, and (d) to decide whether the child will stay home or be removed to a protective facility.
2. In the subsequent contacts with the family, it is to further assess or diagnose the particular situation and to deliver the needed services according to treatment plans (Holder and Mohr, 1980).

The accomplishment of these purposes depends on the interviewers' overall preparation and ability to act consistently and thoughtfully rather than impulsively. It is very easy for workers to "lose their cool" initially because of the parents' cruelty to the child and their resistance. Self-control and a concerted effort to keep the channels of communication open are imperative if the goals and objectives of the first interview are to be accomplished. Furthermore, the interviewers' effectiveness is determined by their understanding of the concepts of relationship, self-determination, motivation, and authority and how they are implemented in cases involving abusive and/or neglectful parents.

Relationship

It is well known that in any kind of a helping situation the development of a relationship between workers and clients is an immediate objective (Biestek, 1957; Garrette, 1972). If relationship is defined as a give-and-take process, that does not commence until later when the first emotional reactions have subsided. As a matter of fact, in many cases of sexual abuse and especially in cases of chronic neglect, it may never come about.

It can become unproductive and frustrating to protective services interviewers if they make the establishment of a relationship one of their initial primary goals. It is more realistic for them as they enter the case to think in terms of establishing a rapport (Garrette, 1972). Rapport could be defined as a concerted effort to create a positive atmosphere that indicates to the clients that the workers want to help. This can be accomplished if the workers show an empathic attitude by trying to place themselves in the client's shoes—to realize how it is to be in such a situation.

Empathy should be demonstrated with words and actions. Just talking does not convince neglecting parents of the workers' intent to help. It is imperative for the interviewers to set up priorities of stress together with the parents as they affect them that very moment and to try to act upon them. The focus of the approach is the here and now, rather than the past or the future. Furthermore, interviewers in building a rapport should avoid detached attitudes. Showing sympathy to a mother for her overwhelming problems is appropriate for an interviewer. It shows to the mother that the workers are only other human beings who can feel how hard it is for her.

Similarly, showing disapproval of parental behaviors that are harmful to the children does not mean that the workers are judgmental or critical. Interviewers demonstrate to the clients that they are concerned for the children's welfare as a result of those behaviors. The expression of sympathy and/or disapproval present interviewers as real human beings and reduce the parents' suspicion that they are "phonies." All this points to the importance of the workers' being honest and direct (Spezeski-Muldary, 1982), rather than shrewd and clever, as they try to build rapport with the parents.

Self-Determination

It is a cardinal principle in casework practice that workers must be cognizant that clients have the right to determine their own destiny (Biestek, 1957). But, in protective services (as in other situations) self-determination has limited applicability since the clients do not seek help voluntarily. It is unproductive for interviewers to be preoccupied with the clients' self-determination, especially at the initial contact when rapid decisions have to be made and emergencies handled. Of course, the parents' right to self-determination depends on their capacity to make positive and constructive decisions at that moment. If they have the capacity, then it is the interviewer's responsibility to activate the potential for self-direction (Biestek, 1957) and to communicate to them the alternatives and consequences of their actions or inactions.

Motivation

Protective service clients, by and large, are involuntary and frequently are not motivated to involve themselves with the workers. Interviewers tend to use the "lack of motivation" as a cop-out and procrastinate on essential work with the parents, often becoming harsh and critical. It is advisable for interviewers as they enter a case to ask themselves why such clients lack motivation.

Is it because of fear that they may be rejected, concerned over possibly losing their autonomy and independence, worried that the community will learn of their problem, fear of self-exposure, fear that they may be punished, or concern that they feel a repetition of a previous experience with social workers who had been harsh and unkind?

In beginning to communicate with parents, interviewers must always consider these feelings. Such consideration has an impact on the workers' overall attitude, on what they say and how they say it. As the interviewers' sensitivity and responsiveness to the parents' feelings and concerns increases, they can understand clients' apprehensions and reluctance—not as a lack of interest for their child's and family's welfare but rather as an attitude reflecting the reality they face.

Authority

Authority is inherent in protective service work involving children. Understanding its proper use can help determine interviewers' effectiveness. Workers who misuse authority behave dictatorially, are indifferent to parents' feelings, and are unduly demanding and disrespectful. Such behaviors do not improve communication, especially at the outset of the interview. As a result, parents become stubborn, defending their rights and authority over their children, and refusing to cooperate.

On the other hand, workers who underplay authority, as though they have none, do not facilitate communication either. Many abusive and/or neglectful parents tend to be manipulators and, as soon as they detect workers who are not sure of themselves and their right to be involved in a case, act complacent, pretending to go along with the practitioners and doing nothing after their departure.

Also, interviewers must not overplay or underplay their authority. They can state it factually at the appropriate time during the interview and compound it with a stance indicating that they want to be helpful. According to Hill (1983), if authority is communicated in a caring and clear way it brings the individuals some degree of relief and sets the stage for the work that lies ahead. If, early in their contacts, parents realize the workers' helping attitude, their resistance to authority is reduced. Helpfulness, as indicated elsewhere, should be communicated not only in words but in specific actions.

Preparation for the Interview

The initial interview can be the most difficult part of workers' involvement in a protective service case. They will need all the knowledge and skills they possess at that point. Their anxiety level is high since they do not know who the parents are and how they will receive them. Some parents may be quiet and accepting, others may be loud, hostile, and rejecting. For these reasons, interviewers must have personal and professional preparation:

1. They need as much information as possible about the reported abuse and/or neglect situation. Knowing who the parents or other caretakers of the child are and the nature of the maltreatment helps the interviewers tune in to that particular situation.

2. They should try to anticipate all possible reactions, which may vary from acceptance to hostility to complete denial. Thus, they prepare themselves psychologically and on how to handle a situation.

3. They should examine their feelings of horror, indignation, or disgust that often are aroused in such situations and how such emotions may interfere with their perceptions and conduct toward the maltreating parents.

4. They always must keep the purpose of the interview in mind. Because of the tense atmosphere and the parents' defensiveness and possible counteraccusations, it is not unusual for interviewers to lose sight of their purpose in the first meeting. As pointed out earlier, the purpose gives direction as to what to look for in the interview.

5. They should have knowledge of the child abuse and/or neglect law and complete familiarity with the agency's policies and procedures in case certain immediate actions have to be taken.

This last refers to when and under what circumstances the police and/or a court can be involved when a child is found to be maltreated. This kind of knowledge enhances the interviewers' ability to communicate with the parents as experts and enables them to be factual as to the course a particular case probably will take. This kind of preparation tends to reduce the interviewers' anxiety and increase their confidence, which are so necessary to fulfill the tasks of the first interview.

The First Interview

It is difficult to predict the direction the first interview will take because of the parents' reaction to the complaint, to the agency's intrusion upon their privacy, and their admission or denial of the alleged maltreatment. Some families may cause no trouble and may even welcome the workers' presence in their homes. Others may avoid the worker by failing to be at home. Still others may be resistive, loud, and hostile; may refuse to open the door; or may order workers out of the home.

No matter what the family's reaction, it is important that interviewers not lose their "cool" and instead be alert and composed. The interview could become aimless if the workers allow themselves to be dragged into arguments as a result of the parents' resistance. If that happens, they may lose sight of the primary purpose which is the validation of the alleged child maltreatment.

If workers are refused entry into the home or are ordered out, they should make a full statement as to the reasons for the visit and the steps to be followed subsequent to their departure. They also should stress to the parents their intention of being helpful to them.

In a majority of cases, parents tend to allow entry into their homes in spite of their anger and resistance. The interviewers then should seize the opportunity to start communicating with them. The ensuing communication is not a smooth process but it can be facilitated if the workers adhere to the rules and interviewing techniques discussed next.

Statement of the Purpose of the Visit

Interviewers sometimes avoid being direct out of fear that they may provoke the parents' anger and hostility. If they straightforwardly and honestly state the purpose of the visit, they might anger the parents, but at least the clients will know why they are there. Anyone would be offended if someone from the Department of Social Services (or what it is titled in a community) came to the house and started pussyfooting. That kind of tactic can only increase anxiety, thus affecting the communication process negatively. It is the interviewers' obligation to make clear at the earliest possible moment both the purpose of the interview and the function of their agency (Fenlason, Ferguson, and Abrahamson, 1962). Both factors are lay elements in the initial communication that allow the parents to know from the beginning why and by whom they are contacted. No assumptions should be made that parents know what the protective service agency is, although many of them receive service from other divisions of the Department of Social Services.

Avoidance of Blame

Because of their own anxiety and discomfort, some interviewers tend to use words and expressions that irritate and anger the parents. For example, an expression such as, "I am here because the agency has received a report that you have abused your daughter" certainly puts the parents on the defensive. The word "abuse" can trigger all kinds of feelings and promote primitive defenses (Newberger, 1975) and hostility. At that point, the interviewers do not know whether this is true. Since the objective is to open up lines of communication with the parents, a nonaccusatory approach can be more effective.

For example, a descriptive statement such as, "I am here because the agency has received a report that your daughter has been injured in her arms and legs" could make the parents less defensive. This rule should be observed not only at the beginning of the interview but throughout the contacts with the parents. It shows tactfulness and sensitivity to their feelings and circumstances, although they were identified as abusers.

Handling Resistance

Resistance, as manifested in various forms of behavior at the initial contact and later does not fade away because the interviewers pretend that it is not there, and unless they deal with it promptly, becomes a barrier to effective communication. As indicated earlier, its source varies and can be based on ignorance, lack of information, and valid fears and apprehensions. Resistance in any phase of involvement with parents should be recognized and discussed honestly and directly. Being empathic is of paramount importance in handling resistance. For example, an interviewer could say to a hostile parent, "I see that you are angry and I can understand why. Why don't we talk about it right now? Unless we talk openly about it, I may not be able to be of any help to you." This demonstrates sensitivity to the parents' feelings and stresses the interviewer's role as a helper. This aspect of the workers' role should be stressed emphatically. It has a catalytic impact on the clients' resistive behavior so the interviewers are seen in light of their essential role—that of helpers.

Parents' resistive behaviors vary. Some parents are incessant talkers, others speak very little, still others may stare at the interviewers and say nothing. Silent parents place interviewers in an awkward position since their real feelings can only be speculated upon. Silence may be an indication of fear and anxiety, a stubborn refusal to block any communication with the workers, or possibly a clinical characteristic of parents who are not well (Fenalson, Ferguson and Abrahamson, 1962). Whatever the reason, interviewers should clearly verbalize the intent of the visit and desire to help. Again, the interviewers' helping stance could bring about a change in the parents' silent attitude.

Initial Avoidance of Socialization

Interviewing in a case in which abuse and/or neglect has been alleged is a serious business. Socializing—"small talk" to break the ice at the initial contact—could create confusion and anxiety for the parents. It would be absurd for workers to go into a home with a report of child abuse and procrastinate in indicating the purpose of the visit on the assumption that they should be "nice" to the parents.

In most cases, when parents hear that the visitors are from the protective services agency, they quickly guess why the workers are there and may wonder about the real agenda. Of course, socializing as a technique to put parents at ease is useful in later contacts when a rapport and/or a relationship has been established.

Avoidance of False Reassurance

In their desire to move on with a case, interviewers sometimes try to reassure the parents by promising that everything will be all right even though they may know very little about the situation at that point. They do this out of habit and in an effort to prevent the parents' anger and hostility from coming through. An example of false reassurance could involve telling the parents, "Don't worry, nobody is going to take the child away from you."

Such a statement may be proved wrong later because the child is found to be seriously maltreated. Any subsequent actions for the child's removal thus will affect the workers' credibility and the parents will not trust them in the future. The impact of each situation on future effective communication should not be underestimated. It can create all kinds of apprehensions, resistance, and doubts as to whether the workers are sincerely seeking to help them.

Interviewing Techniques

Interviewing techniques are ways of achieving a given end by special procedures, propelling devices, and designs skillfully blended to form a pattern (Fenalson, Ferguson, and Abrahamson, 1962). They are the many specific acts used to accomplish the purpose of the interview. The use of a technique or techniques is a skill that requires knowledge. Actually, skill can be thought as "knowledge in action" (Phillips, 1957). Numerous techniques could be listed for practitioners' consideration to be used in particular situations involving abuse and/or neglect. However, use of specific techniques does not guarantee success for all such interviews. Their use is maximized if they are adapted to the purpose at hand (Fenalson, Ferguson, and Abrahamson, 1962).

Some techniques useful throughout workers' contacts with child-maltreating families, and especially at the initial contact, are the following:

Listening

Inexperienced interviewers tend to talk too much and fail to listen to what the clients say. When interviewers listen, they must make a concerted effort to see the world through the eyes of the person who is talking. Listening with empathy, according to Carl Rogers (Evans, 1975), is the ability "to really stand in the client's shoes and to see the world from his vantage point. If that can be communicated to the client that I do really see how you feel, that can be the most releasing kind of experience."

Listening with empathy is a broader mental and emotional process, whereas hearing is strictly a physical one. Workers often hear but do not listen, although they go through the typical motions of communication. For example, one could spend an hour talking with a person and when it is over feel that the individual was not "with us." This kind of experience with interviewers can create a feeling of anger, intimidation, and hopelessness and can reduce any motivation to see such persons again.

The impact of poor listening with abusive and/or neglectful parents is no different. Anderson (1979) and Spezeski-Muldary (1982), commenting on the impact of listening on abusive parents, enumerate changes of feelings of low self-esteem and improvement of interpersonal relationships and of their own listening skills. Listening as a technique also is strongly correlated with the interviewers' ability to be authentic, responsive to feelings, genuine, nonjudgmental, and willing to help—in other words to be empathetic (Anderson, 1979; Keefe, 1976; Spezeski-Muldary, 1982).

Focusing

Focusing the interview does not mean dictating or cutting off the clients. It means that the interviewers through the use of various techniques maintain attention on the purpose for which the interview is conducted. In cases of child maltreatment, focusing is more difficult for interviewers in the initial contacts than it is later because the high emotions at the beginning can put the workers off balance and they thus may lose control.

In general, it can be stated (and it is more true initially) that many aspects of the interview are subject to control: (1) the topics to be discussed, (2) the sequence in which they are discussed, and (3) the emphasis on each topic. Emphasis on control, structure, and the activity level of the interviewers are determined by the purposes of the session and the particular circumstances and needs of the clients.

In talking with abusing and/or neglecting parents, interviewers should not let them take off and consume an entire session with subjects that are irrelevant to its purpose. It is not unusual with many maltreating parents, and especially neglectors, to talk aimlessly and endlessly in an effort to control the entire interviewing—almost filibustering. The purpose of the interview—initially during the investigative assessment and later during treatment—cannot be accomplished if this is allowed to happen.

This is not to suggest that the parents should not be allowed to express their feelings and concerns freely. They should be permitted to do so as long as they discuss issues relevant to the topics under consideration. Egalitarianism—that is, interviewers and clients are equals in a protective service interview, especially at the initial contact—has limited applicability. An egalitarian relationship may create confusion and anxiety in the maltreating parents. The authority and expertise of interviewers should be well established from the beginning and should be a visible element in the relationship.

Use of Questions

The interviewers' appropriate use of questions is another factor that enhances the focus of the interview. Many interviewers ask nonquestion questions by actually citing their own opinions. Interviewers demonstrate their preconceived opinions when they ask, "Tell me, how did you hit your child so hard?" when they do not yet know who the abuser is. Closed-ended questions are useful for gathering specific information in the shortest time possible, but they do not promote the expansion of the discussion and do not give parents the opportunity to elaborate upon their concerns and feelings.

For example, if the mother is asked, "Does Johnny love you?" the response most likely will be a one-word response: "Yes" or "No." However, if the same question is phrased in an open-ended way such as "Tell me about Johnny's feelings for you," the mother is given an opening to talk more descriptively. Interviewers should be aware of when and how frequently to use open-ended and closed-ended questions during a particular session.

In reality, interviewers are conductors who consciously determine the means by which they will achieve the purpose of the interview in a particular situation of abuse and/or neglect. Questions serve a variety of purposes in an interviewing situation. In general, questions aim to: (1) stimulate discussion, (2) clarify feelings and thinking, (3) seek further information, (4) shift the focus into a relevant area, and (5) point up a possible error.

Appropriate use of questions gives direction, stimulation, and guidance during the interviewing transactional process (Fenalson, Ferguson and Abrahamson, 1962). Thus, circumstantialities and irrelevancies are avoided. Questions that mobilize the maltreating parents' defenses can cause the interview to get off focus. A question such as "How did you abuse your child?" tends to block effective communication with the parents.

The attitude in which a question is asked is as important as the question itself. With depressed, anxious, and hostile clients, as abusing and/or neglecting parents are, supportive understanding, reassurance, recognition, and acceptance should be reflected in the questions. An example with a depressed parent could be, "Could you tell me how it happened, although I see how difficult it is for you?" or with an anxious parent, "I'll stand by to try to help you get out of the mess you are in. However, I want to ask you..." or with a hostile parent, "I don't blame you for being so upset and angry but you have to calm down so I can ask you a few questions."

Introspective questions, especially at the initial interview, could get the session off focus and into areas that contribute very little to the fulfillment of its purpose. Such questions could cause the parents to talk about the past and feelings that perhaps they have difficulty comprehending. Such questions seem more appropriate at a later time when the high emotions have subsided.

Interviewers may avoid what are called probing questions on the assumption that that kind of tactic may indicate abrasiveness or harshness toward the parents. That assumption is erroneous if the questions are asked within the context of the subject under discussion. Probing is an invitation to the clients to pursue a particular point until it becomes clear and understandable to the interviewers. In that light, probing questions enhance the focus of the interview.

With parents who persist in being resistive, overtly or covertly, the interview can go off focus easily, especially if interviewers allow their own natural feelings to intervene. In such situations, they must constantly define and redefine the purpose for which they are seeing the parents and concentrate on the present situation and their needs.

Other interviewing techniques pertinent with abusive and neglecting parents, both at the initial contact and later, involve what is called confrontation, suppression, repetition, and recapitulation.

Confrontation

Confrontation refers to the interviewers' efforts to point out possible contradictions and inconsistencies between what the clients say and what they actually do. Most experts agree that a confronting approach probably is more effective if there is a relationship between the interviewer and the client. Although in general this is true in most situations, in a protective service interview, especially in the initial contact, the use of confrontation in many instances may be the only way to impress on the parents the workers' determination to fulfill the purpose of the visit. Discriminate use of confrontation can bring about positive changes in behavior and can help the parents develop insight and self-awareness (Egan, 1975).

Suppression

Suppression as a technique sounds too confiding—which is what it really is, since it is a conscious effort to stop parents' tirades or aimless talk about irrelevant matters. Interviewers simply interrupt and offer a subject of their choice to be discussed. This technique, often referred to as transition, is most useful in forming and expediting the communicating process. It should be noted, however, that the effectiveness of both confrontation and suppression depend on the interviewers' ability to impart a feeling of caring, concern, and respect toward the parents.

Repetition

Repetition as a technique aims to help the parents comprehend the various aspects that have been discussed. Parents, especially at the initial contact when emotions and anxiety are high, may fail to understand what the interviewers are really saying or what decisions can be reached.

Recapitulation

Closely related to repetition is recapitulation. This is a summarization by the interviewers of the major topics discussed. It is an important technique for the following reasons: (1) it is an indication that the interviewers have been listening to the parents' concerns; (2) it is an opportunity for the parents to see where they stand in the interviewers' perception of them; and (3) it is an opportunity for further clarification and possible corrections of the issues discussed and decisions that have been made.

Interviewing the Child

The children, if their age and emotional and physical condition permit, should be interviewed. Depending on the type of abuse and/or neglect and the particular circumstances, such interviews can be conducted with or without the parents' permission in a location of the workers' choice. The concern frequently expressed about parents' rights and the possibility of a parental lawsuit, although valid, have never been supported by the courts when such action was taken on the ground that the workers acted in good faith.

Effective interviews with maltreated children depends heavily on the interviewers' ability to understand the youngsters and their world and the possibly traumatic experience they have gone through. They also depend on the interviewers' sensitivity and responsiveness to the children's needs and skills in communicating.

It is important for interviewers to recognize early in their contacts that the children, in spite of the abuse and/or neglect, still feel allegiance to their parents. Children may resent any derogatory remarks as to how terrible the parents are and may try to protect them either by being silent or by giving false information. A perception of the workers as parent surrogates can create resistance and can become a major obstacle to better communication.

The clinical observation that abused children show pseudomaturity and hypervigilant attitude are factors to be considered. The children's possible belief that they have done something wrong or are to blame for the family's situation could raise a wall of defensiveness, preventing effective communication.

One error workers commit when they interview such children is that they do not follow the general rules of good interviewing practice. They do not provide privacy, they do not explain what they are doing and why, and they avoid addressing the issue of confidentiality. Failure to follow these basic rules gets practitioners off to a bad start in attempting to develop a rapport and/or relationship. A good relationship with the children is as important as it is with adults.

Interviewers at the outset must explain who they are. Children do not know about social workers and what they do as they know about nurses and doctors. The interviewers should explain that they try to help kids and that they have seen many kids in similar situations. This kind of an approach puts the children at ease and impresses on them the workers' expertise at helping youngsters. The importance of honesty and directness should not be underestimated. Depending on the children's ability to comprehend, they should be told in appropriate language the specific circumstances that have brought them to the workers' attention.

With children three to eight, it is important to take into account certain characteristics that are predominent in those ages. Young children's ability to understand such abstract concepts as time, space, and distance as well as attention span and cause-effect relationships is limited. Furthermore, young children do not clearly delineate reality and fantasy (Holder and Mohr, 1980; Piaget, 1954; Piaget and Inhelder, 1969).

The Nine Commandments

This dictates certain behaviors vis-à-vis young children and what might be called the Nine Commandments. Interviewers should:

1. Focus on one thought at a time until the meaning of the children's productions is clear.
2. Inquire slowly as to the meaning of certain words they use. For example, "yesterday" could mean two weeks ago and "last month" five months ago.
3. Choose words carefully so that they are within the youngsters' range.

4. Avoid leading questions or those that telegraph a certain response. Questions introduced with such expressions as "do you" or "are you" most likely will receive a one-word response.
5. Avoid "why" questions. The children may try to defend themselves or withdraw, or conversely may react with excessive verbosity and lose sight of the context in which the question was raised.
6. Avoid judgments and criticism and try to be supportive.
7. Avoid viewing the children as "babies." Children tend to resent being treated that way.
8. Avoid making promises. If promises are made, they must be kept, otherwise the children will become skeptical of the workers' sincerity.
9. Try to be as natural as possible, avoiding unnatural expression of too much "sweetness" or too much intimacy.

Interviews with young children can become enervating experiences for the workers. Children may wander into the room while the interview is in progress, the victims' responses may be redundant, they may ignore the questions, or they may not feel obligated to contribute to the interview. It should be remembered that children do not act as adults do in following the "rules" of interaction. However, once they develop familiarity and trust with the workers, many of these problems diminish.

Multidimensional Observations

It is important for the interviewers to watch closely for nonverbal signs as they try to communicate with the youngsters. A basic requirement is that interviewers observe in several dimensions simultaneously and monitor every communication channel, both verbal and nonverbal, that the children employ consciously or unconsciously (Greenspan, 1981).

Maltreated children often withdraw out of fear and discomfort over being in the presence of strangers. They may lack adequate verbal skills. They may appear sad and depressed, may lack basic energy, and may not show their emotions openly. Observation of these behaviors increases the interviewers' understanding of the victims' psychological condition.

Without forcing themselves on the children, the interviewers communicate their observations and ask the children whether they are correct. The responses at first may be limited to a yes, a no, or a nodding of the head; yet, a communication has been initiated that the youngsters perceive as sensitive and caring, even if they do not know such terms.

Interviewing latency-age children who have been abused and/or neglected requires skills in handling their defensiveness. Such behaviors as projection, denial, displacement, and repression are indications of a high state of anxiety. Many such children isolate themselves by overtalking and deny affective content. Others, especially those who have become disturbed, withdraw to protect themselves against feeling. The interviewers' stance initially has to show acceptance and understanding before formal treatment is initiated. One thing interviewers should not do is to make close interpretations of unconscious materials. This tends to frighten the children into thinking of the workers as mind readers.

Interviewing the Sexually Abused Child

The techniques discussed earlier also apply in interviews with sexually abused children, but the sessions are more difficult, primarily because of the discomfort generated by the subject. As workers start communicating with such children, it is important to consider their psychological condition.

In instances of sudden sexual abuse by a parent, relative, or stranger, the impact of the maltreatment is different from situations in which the children were sexually exploited or were incestuously involved for a long time (Zaphiris, 1983). The factors of possible attachment to the perpetrator, of the conditioning process the children went through, and the specific circumstances and conditions involved all have a diverse impact on the youngsters' reaction to the abuse.

Children involved incestuously with their parents may find the experience pleasurable and fascinating or may be panicked, have fantasies of dying, have fears of rejection by friends and relatives, fears of being punished by God or that the abuser will kill them or commit suicide, or fear that they may be removed to a foster home (Holder and Mohr, 1980). Consideration of these possible thoughts and feelings dictates a slower communication pace and gives the interviewers direction as to what issues to discuss.

The first interview is of critical importance and its successful outcome depends largely on the interviewers' skill in getting the facts with the victim's cooperation as soon as possible. Research on the initial contact, and practice experience, indicate that once the initial crisis has passed, the situation may not seem too bad to the children. Thus, they may relate an entirely different story later as a result of appeals by the mother, relatives, and the perpetrator.

The first interview should be conducted on neutral territory as soon as the report of sexual victimization has been received. Documentation should be sought by the protective services workers. The police interview reports will support the workers' findings, but, since the police and protective service involvement is not always a well-delineated process, whoever interviews the children first should audiotape the session. Such documentation can be invaluable as the case unfolds.

There is nothing secretive about interviews with sexually abused children. Because of their own feelings and the "secrecy" of the subject, workers at times tend to be vague when they talk with victims. The use of plain language and specific anatomical terms helps the youngsters communicate their feelings and the particular circumstances of the abuse. Awareness by the children that the interviewers are present not only to talk for purposes of investigation but also to help can free them to relate the story of their abuse.

It is crucial for the worker to gather specific evidence, based on where, when, and how. While the emotional and/or psychological aspects are just as important as the specific evidence, concentration on the specific tangible evidence of the abuse should precede the emotional considerations if at all possible.

Since many sexually abused children are frightened, anxious, fearful, guilt-ridden, tearful, and hysterical (Mayhall & Eastlack Norgard, 1983), workers must decide how far they can go in an interview. Forcing the children to talk is counterproductive and they may withdraw. Their reluctance to talk or to discuss a particular area of the sexual experience should be respected. In such instances, the interviewers' sensitivity to the children's problem, nonthreatening attitude, and helping stance eventually will reduce the reluctance to communicate. This emerges in subsequent interviews once the children trust the workers.

It is sound practice to interview sexually abused young children through the use of drawings depicting naked human figures (front and back). The victims are asked to circle with a pencil the parts of the body that were used and/or touched by the perpetrator. Thus, when presented with a male figure to show what the father did, the child may put a circle around the penis or mouth. When a female figure is presented, the victim may put a circle around the vaginal area, breasts, mouth, buttocks, or may draw a penis close to the vaginal area.

This technique with children of sexual victimization who are fearful and do not verbalize easily is usually effective and gives details that otherwise could not be elicited. However, this entire process requires worker sensitivity toward the children's feelings and an ability to raise the questions tactfully and in a nonthreatening way.

Another useful interviewing approach with young abused children is through play. The use of paper, crayons, blackboard, toys, and dolls gives the children an opportunity to express their feelings symbolically and thus establish a purposeful communication with the workers (Fenalson, Ferguson, and Abrahamson, 1962). However, this method requires that the workers be skilled in interpreting and understanding such symbolic communication.

Interviewing Strategies

Interview planning requires establishing a good strategy. Strategy refers to the general plan or arrangement of the interview. Of course, in the initial contact, the workers' plans, no matter how well thought out, may never materialize because of the unpredictability of such situations. However, certain general rules should be followed.

A home visit is preferable to an office interview initially, regardless of the form of the maltreatment. In most cases, this is the only possibility since the abuse and/or neglect may require immediate action for the children's protection and for an assessment of the home situation. In addition, on home visits workers can meet both parents and significant others in the family. Office interviews should be considered later as the case moves along. This kind of an interviewing arrangement is useful, in that it gives workers an opportunity to test the client's motivation to participate more actively in the helping process. On the other hand, it imparts a feeling to the parents that they are not under surveillance and that they are treated like anyone else who has a problem and needs help. The current practice of seeing protective service clients almost exclusively on home visits is short-sighted in terms of treatment objectives to help parents take initiatives and to increase their sense of responsibility.

Joint and individual interviews should be used, depending on the situation and the circumstances. At the initial investigative assessment, any such planning may not be possible. In instances of physical abuse and/or neglect, joint interviewing can give the interviewer a dynamic understanding of the family and an opportunity to reach agreements acceptable to parents and children. However, such interviews should be agreed upon by both parents; if the workers are forced to play the role of referee, they should be avoided. In general, joint interviews, if at first not feasible for reasons beyond the workers' control, should be sought during the course of treatment.

Depending on their age, mental ability, and type of maltreatment, the children should be interviewed in the presence of parents or alone, again, depending on the situation and how the report comes to the attention of the agency. It is up to the workers' judgment as to how and where to conduct the interview initially. Special care should be given, no matter what the interviewing arrangements are, for the victims to feel safe and free to communicate their feelings and abusive and/or neglectful experiences. As a case progresses, it is imperative that the children be seen together with the parents; again, the timing of joint interviews is determined in line with the practitioners' particular treatment goals.

In cases of sexual abuse, initial joint interviews with parents and children are not conducive to an effective understanding of the situation. Instead, each person involved must be interviewed separately to avoid distortions and the possible intimidation of the children by the alleged perpetrator. Joint interviews with the perpetrator, mother, and child are possible later considerations, depending again on treatment goals.

It is the current practice that initial investigative interviews in cases of sexual abuse—and in many instances of physical abuse—are conducted jointly with a police officer. The rationale is that the children do not have to repeat their trauma story more than once to either. Although this appears to be a valid reason in sexual abuse cases, in other forms of maltreatment it generally is not necessary.

In a physical and emotional maltreatment case in a midwestern state where joint police in agency investigations are the practice for all types of abuse(s), neither the police officer nor the worker was able to communicate, to understand the child and his situation, or to offer the protection he needed. If the protective services worker had conducted the interview alone as a social work investigation, he could have been able to reach the child and understand the abusive realities of the home situation. Instead, the case was characterized as invalid. A few months later, the child, with the cooperation of his sister, shot and killed the father.

This is not to say that joint police-social worker interviews are always ineffective. They are effective in gathering the facts of a case but tend not to be effective enough for either victims or parents to open up and relate their feelings and thus obtain the help they might need. The presence of a police officer, even a plainclothes detective, has an intimidating effect on the parents and child. On the other hand, the worker also could be intimidated and could go along with the officer, avoiding an in-depth understanding of the situation. If social workers are required to hold the interviews jointly with a police officer, they will do well to extend the joint session alone after the officer leaves.

CONCLUSION

Interviewing maltreating parents and their child victims is a formidable job, since they usually come to protective service agencies involuntarily. Furthermore, this client population represents a wide spectrum of social, psychological, and pathological conditions that make the communication process complicated and demanding.

The interviewing approaches and techniques suggested in this chapter are designed to assist professionals in overcoming the initial barriers at the investigative assessment and to begin the treatment process. The points made are not exhaustive of what workers should or should not do at the beginning or in subsequent contacts. That would be unrealistic, considering the diverse makeup of this population and its circumstances. However, if flexibility is used in following these suggestions and if they are adaptable to the specific circumstances of an abusive and/or neglectful situation, they can facilitate effective communication.

REFERENCES

Anderson, G. D.: Enhancing listening skills for work with abusing parents. *Social Casework, 60*(10): 602-607, December 1979.

Biestek, F.: *The Casework Relationship.* Chicago: Loyola University Press, 1957, pp. 100-19.

Egan, G.: *The Skilled Helper: A Model for Systematic Helping and Interpersonal Relating.* Monterey, CA: Brooks/Cole Publishing Co., 1975.

Evans, R. J.: *Carl Rogers: The Man and His Ideas.* New York: E.P. Dutton, 1975, p. 290.

Fenalson, A. F., Ferguson, B. G., and Abrahamson, A. C.: *Essentials in Interviewing.* New York: Harper & Row, 1962, pp. 132, 137, 140, 1157-160, 171-173.

Garrette, A.: *Interviewing: Its Principles and Methods,* 2d ed. New York: Family Service Association of America, 1972, pp. 5-6.

Goldberg, G.: Breaking the communication barrier: The initial interview with an abusing parent. *Child Welfare, 54:*275-282, 1975.

Gordon, R. L.: *Interviewing: Strategy, Techniques, and Tactics.* Homewood, IL: The Dorsey Press, 1975, p. 50.

Greenspan, S. I.: *The Clinical Interview of the Child.* New York: McGraw-Hill Book Co., 1981, p. 2.

Hill, D. A.: The initial interview: Alliance building and assessments. In N. B. Eberling and D. A. Hill (Eds.): *Child Abuse and Neglect.* London: John Wright Publishing, Inc., 1983, p. 44.

Holder, W., and Mohr, C. (Eds.): Interviewing in child protective casework. In *Helping in Child Protective Services.* Denver: The American Humane Association, 1980, pp. 82, 97, 101-7.

Kadushin, A.: *The Social Work Interview.* New York: Columbia University Press, 1972, pp. 4, 8.

Keefe, T.: Empathy: The critical skill. *Social Work, 21*(1): 10-13, 1976.

Mayhall, P. D., and Eastlack-Norgard, K.: *Child Abuse and Neglect.* New York: John Wiley & Sons, 1983, pp. 172-203.

Newberger, E.: A physician's perspective on the interdisciplinary management of child abuse. In N. B. Eberling and D. A. Hill (Eds.): *Child Abuse: Intervention and Treatment.* Acton, MA: Publishing Science Group, Inc., 1975, pp. 61-67.

Philips, H. V.: *Essentials of Social Group Work Skills.* New York: Association Press, 1957, p. 6.

Piaget, J.: *The Construction of Reality in the Child.* New York: Basic Books, 1954.

Piaget, J., and Inhelder, B.: *The Psychology of the Child.* New York: Basic Books, Inc., 1969.

Spezeski-Muldary, P.: Communication Techniques for Working with Violent Families. In Carmen, Germaine, Warner, and G. R. Braen (Eds.), *Management of the Physically and Emotionally Abused Child.* New York: Appleton-Century-Crofts, 1982, p. 58.

Zaphiris, A. G.: *Methods and Skills for Differential Assessment and Treatment in Incest, Sexual Abuse and Sexual Exploitation of Children.* Denver: The American Humane Association, 1983, p. 37.

CHAPTER 14

TREATMENT OF CHILD PHYSICAL ABUSE
Charles E. Gentry

INTRODUCTION

This chapter addresses critical areas in the provision of a treatment system for childhood physical abuse, emphasizing the importance of total family involvement. This includes family-centered treatment and its imperative elements as well as identifiable groups of physically abusing parents.

FAMILY-CENTERED TREATMENT

Children cannot exist without nurturance and, throughout history, no better mechanism than the family has been found for providing such support. Unfortunately, many child abuse programs and numerous funding sources have attempted to provide for children without regard to the family—almost as if the family did not exist (Rice, 1979). Yet, the family may have the potential to offer a more stable support system than substitute care outside the home can afford.

A sensitive worker realizes that the victim must be protected but is attuned to the possibility that any intervention may further disrupt an already disturbed household. What affects one family member will, in turn, affect all members. Their responses in turn will elicit another reaction from the first member (Sherz, 1970). Inappropriate interventions compound already dysfunctional interactions.

Children removed from their homes and placed in substitute care are likely to demonstrate a strong desire to return to their real parents. Only in recent times, however, have in-home, family-centered, community-based services begun to replace the perviously popular, out-of-home child care that is insensitive to the problems and potential of family life. Even when workers provide family-centered services, they tend to focus on pathology rather than helping methodology (Brown et al., 1982).

Low-income and minority children have suffered particularly because of a lack of family-centered interventions and because little attention has been given to changing the social and community stressors for families (Chestang, 1978). Fortunately, some programs are positive examples of the potential of family-centered treatments: the St. Paul Family-Centered Project for Abused and Neglected Children (Sullivan, Spasser, and Penner, 1977) and other projects reported by Janchill (1979), Oppenheimer (1978), Maybanks and Bryce (1979), Janchill (1979) and Weissman (1978).

Service delivery models that emphasize family-centeredness include: (1) the generalist-specialist model, which has a central intake and a family services component; (2) an intensive family services unit, designed to serve those at greatest risk of dissolution; and (3) purchase of services through private, voluntary agencies (Hutchinson et al., 1983).

IMPLEMENTAL ELEMENTS

The family-centered treatment, to be effective, requires that practitioners and agencies be able to coordinate the community resources needed to fulfill the roles of case manager and case monitor and become an advocate for the abused child and the family.

Because of the diverse needs of abusing families, services from a number of community facilities are imperative. No one single agency, including protective services, has all the resources needed to provide either specific aid or treatment. Success in the delivery of such services depends on cooperation, collaboration, and coordination among agencies and the various disciplines. Unfortunately, territorialism and turfism among those involved can hinder attempts to meet the needs of victims and families.

The concepts of case manager and case monitor are useful in handling such cases. The case manager includes all the activities for which the worker is responsible, from initial contact to follow-up and coordination of services (Childress, 1979); case monitor refers to the worker's evaluative responsibilities during the treatment process. The delineation of these responsibilities, which often are carried by the same person if nothing else enhances the worker's specific role expectations during the agency's involvement with a case, also enhances the worker's visibility in contacts with other agencies and within the multidisciplinary team involved. Thus, the worker becomes the person who is recognizable by everyone as having responsibility for the overall outcome of a case.

Advocacy is a basic element if family-centered treatment is to be a success. Abusive families often have multiple problems, lack problem-solving skills, experience physical and emotional problems, and are unable to use the formal organizational systems effectively. Advocacy encourages abusive parents to benefit from these systems; they not only learn their rights, they also become more inclined to cooperate with treatment (Solomon, 1975).

It must be stressed that the family-centered treatment depends heavily on the effective use of both the formal and informal networks discussed later in this chapter.

TREATMENT

In family-centered treatment, specific services, case management and monitoring, and a variety of treatment modalities and approaches lead to a higher level of family functioning. These elements include individual counseling; family therapy; marital therapy; play therapy; therapy groups or self-help groups for adults, adolescents, and children; divorce counseling if parents are estranged; and relationship counseling if the parent is single.

A variety of topics may be productive in individual or group counseling: alternatives to violence, parenting, child development, infant stimulation, intimacy, discipline, nutrition, play and recreation, financial management, use of community resources, stress reduction, assertiveness training, communication in marriage, relating to the extended family and other family life topics.

Since many of the parents may be single, it is necessary to reach out to former spouses, current lovers, and other significant figures who may still influence the family functioning. For example, the parents may fight about the rearing and custody of the child or use the youngster as a pawn in other ways. As discussed in previous chapters, treatment of the maltreated child and the family requires a thorough psychosocial assessment, differential diagnosis, use of multidisciplinary teams, and the establishment of close working relationships. Furthermore, "a primary individual relationship must be established with the abusing client before any other method of treatment is introduced if change is to occur" (Ebeling and Hill, 1983).

"Assaulter-focused programs are more likely to reach the people whose behavior needs to be changed the most" (Star, 1983, p. xvi). If the physical abusers are extremely dependent and needy, they will require individual counseling and nurturing, much like what would be given to a child. If they have capacity to give and take, it is desirable to resort to group and marital counseling and Parents Anonymous and couples groups.

Cautioning that the techniques will not have the same effect on all abusers since it can be assumed that some will be extremely resistive to giving up what they consider to be "legitimate" hitting, Star (1983) lists techniques to be used and avoided with abusers. Those to be used include supportive confrontation when encountering discrepancies and resistance, enhancement of the abuser's self-esteem, problem solving or alternatives to violence, consistent structuring of emotional and behavioral boundaries, honesty, role modeling, role playing, friendship or buddy system with other group members, Gestalt-like empty chair technique, and exercise and relaxation techniques.

Workers should avoid such techniques as coercion, rescuing rather than letting clients do things themselves, insight-oriented and passive therapies, overexpectation, overruminating or overventilation of feelings, counselor identification with the victim, and emotive techniques such as hitting a punching bag.

When working with hostile, resistive clients, it is wise to realize that behind the pseudo-independent facade lies a very dependent personality. Most abusers and families require treatment for six to twenty-four months. Review of the literature indicates that multiple treatment approaches and modalities are required in varying combinations (Bernstein and Crosby, 1983).

Whether the mother is physically abusive, protective, or passive toward the child, her involvement in counseling is required. She may be defensive, more in embarrassment or anger because the abuse was identified, than because that is a part of her usual personality. Outreach to her is necessary even because she may be passive and yet resistive to treatment. "Treatment of abusive mothers with low self-esteem can be difficult. Supplying the mother with some small successes, possibly some functional parenting skills, may bring about increments of change in self-esteem" (Palladino and Levin, 1983, p. 476–77).

If the mother figure is extremely needy and dependent, homemakers and neighborhood supports may enhance her functioning. If she is childlike, disorganized or regressed, she still may be able to learn realistic expectations for her child. Her anger and dependency, however, may resemble that of an abused child. Particularly if she makes little or no progress in six months, she may need to be encouraged to surrender parental rights so that both she and her child may receive adequate nurturing. If she is single, an innovative approach may consider finding an adoptive home for both mother and child, just as some programs have placed single mothers and their children in foster homes (Nayman and Witkin, 1978).

Groups for education, socialization, self-help, and therapy are beneficial with mothers and with couples, assuming that extreme dependency needs are being met in individual treatment. Social network therapy is helpful with many clients as are parent coping and parent-child interaction groups (McManmon, 1983).

Treatment Goals

Broadly speaking, treatment goals in cases of child physical abuse are to:
(1) stop the abuse, (2) improve parental functioning, and (3) reduce frustration, stress, and conflict within the family and the environment. Subgoals or objectives are needed under each goal, with strategies to be employed by family members in attaining them.

For instance, stopping abuse may require several strategies such as having the parents list the types of behaviors manifested by the child/adolescent prior to abuse. Objectives can be formulated to prevent a recurrence of the particular set of circumstances; to relate to the stress in other ways; to recognize that the youth's behavior is developmentally normal; to call a treatment team member, volunteer, or self-help group member for suggestions when tension begins to mount; and to learn new methods for disciplining the youth's undesirable behaviors. Another objective is to help the parents assume responsibility for the abuse rather than denying their involvement or scapegoating the youth.

To improve parental functioning, the worker may set objectives such as: (1) roles of family members will become appropriate, i.e. the child no longer will "parent" the adults; (2) nutritious meals and snacks will be prepared for the child(ren) daily; (3) the parents will hug the child each day; and (4) parents and children will play a game together each day. Strategies to achieve this may include role-modeling by a counselor, homemaker and volunteers.

To reduce stress and conflict in the family, the following objectives may be set: improve housing, income, and quality of food; conflict management skills; enhance self-esteem of family members; and increase adult intimacy. Since housing, income, and nutrition affect family attitudes, strategies may include obtaining public housing, getting utility service restored, seeking employment or job training and learning how to dress for such interviews, learning the basic nutrition requirements, and reducing sugar intake.

In developing conflict management skills, the family learns to: (1) focus until a problem is defined, (2) list possible solutions, and (3) reach a consensus on the solution. Improvement of self-esteem requires the family to develop interpersonal association with others, such as the positive interaction that can occur in group modalities; positive attempts to make complimentary statements about themselves and others; listing of their personal strengths; learning to play and have fun; development of a daily routine; and feeling in control of themselves and not helpless in the environment. Increased intimacy within the family requires learning the importance of appropriate touch, becoming trusting of others and being trustworthy, learning to respect one's spouse and sharing sexually, and learning to communicate openly and respectfully.

Physical Abuse Situations

Physically abusing clients present a variety of problems in varying combinations requiring special treatment methods and techniques. These include: (1) character disorders, (2) mental illness, (3) unsatisfactory interpersonal relationships, (4) low self-esteem, (5) personal and environmental stresses, (6) inadequate methods of discipline, (7) emotional and social isolation, (8) dysfunction around intimacy and sexual intercourse, (9) poor problem-solving skills, and (10) multiproblem, highly disorganized lifestyle.

Character Disorders

Character-disordered and multiproblem clients are likely to resist treatment in many ways. Unfortunately, counselors may interpret the resistance as personal rejection. If so, the counselor will have difficulty providing a critical part of treatment—outreach and pursuit of the clients (Haas, 1959; Kempe, 1972).

Sometimes it is difficult for counselors, who are prone to have neurotic guilt, to place appropriate limits on acting-out, character-disordered clients. Allowing them to ventilate and blame others may help them justify their explosive behaviors. Understanding them is not enough; instead others must try to motivate them to be concerned about the feelings of others. To attain this, however, they need consistency and caring from others, along with appropriate limit setting. Only through such consistency can their distrust be overcome and empathy for others created (Pollak, 1961).

With the many borderline or character-disordered clients who either reject engagement and/or become fearful and begin to resist further intervention, attendance at group meetings can be enhanced with prizes and gift certificates, successes for parents through role play, emphasis on parental strengths, use of the group as a mutual support system, and a relevant or interesting curriculum (Ambrose, Haggard, and Haworth, 1983). With persistence, clients can be engaged, even those with personality disorders who lack control of anger; whose actions are inappropriate; and who have identity problems reflected by poor self-image, gender identity and confused career goals, friendship patterns, values, and loyalties (Goldstein, 1984).

Mental Illness

If either parent or both household members have psychotic episodes, diagnosis and treatment plans are required to determine when and how the child's safety is to be assured. If the psychotic adult is more abusive during these episodes, decisions to remove the other adult or the child are necessary. In making such decisions, the worker should consider overall family needs. Will removal of the child or the adult lead to better family functioning in the future? The following case demonstrates total family treatment.

Mr. Y was a highly trained professional; Mrs. Y was college educated but had never been employed. They had four children, a beautifully furnished, middle-class home, and a good relationship with Mrs. Y's parents. Mr. Y, however, had a dependent, yet very hostile, relationship with his affluent parents.

Child protective services had received two anonymous phone calls about suspected physical abuse of the children, particularly the oldest son. Interviews with the children were inconclusive but tended to confirm abuse. Typical of their rural county, investigation was complicated by the unwillingness of family members and associates to say anything negative about a successful, professional man with politically influential parents. An interview with Mrs. Y's mother revealed that Mr. Y had intimidated his wife and children for years. Yes, Mrs. Y had always provided most of the child care. Mr. Y had no close friends, no apparent interests other than work and had become more irritable, impatient, and aloof. Since he was his own employer, it was not possible for outsiders to be certain about his income, but it appeared that it was beginning to decline.

The protective services worker visited Mrs. Y again, getting clues that Mr. Y was more depressed and drinking more alcoholic beverages. Yes, his outbursts were more frequent and he sometimes slapped Mrs. Y or the oldest son. Mr. Y seemed to think that local townspeople were against him. The couple's intimacy never was great and now he was critical of his wife's appearance, never expressing interest in sex. He recently had stated that a high school boy had tried to seduce him. On other occasions, he had asked Mrs. Y to have intercourse with another male while Mr. Y watched.

Tearfully, Mrs. Y reported that she begged Mr. Y to seek counseling with her. She felt that he was losing his customers because of his moodiness. She even wondered if he was taking drugs. She was afraid to ask him to help with the children for fear he would hit her or them.

With consultation from the regional mental health center, the protective services worker decided to visit Mr. Y. He was highly defensive and threatened to use "political influence" to create trouble for the worker. The worker and the mental health consultant interviewed Mr. Y's parents and learned of his long-term, hostile-dependent relationship with them. In recent times, he had intimidated them into giving him money. In fact, he had behaved strangely, much as he did at about his age when they had to take him to a psychiatrist.

Consultation with the previous psychiatrist confirmed that Mr. Y had a hostile-dependent, paranoid response to late adolescence. His fear of failure in college and fear of displeasing his parents had caused the psychiatrist to prescribe medication to reduce anxiety and hostility.

With additional information from the children about his explosive, hitting episodes, the treatment team met with Mr. Y and all relatives who would agree to participate. Respectfully, Mr. Y was told that his hitting, declining business, and moodiness suggested that he was depressed and overly suspicious and that the family wanted to help him by going with him for counseling.

With obvious resentment and blaming others, Mr. Y went for counseling at the mental health center where it soon was confirmed that he had gained access to nonprescribed drugs, which he was trying to use to mask a serious emotional condition. Actually, in spite of bravado and grandiosity at times, he was losing confidence, feeling persecuted, and had even felt that a strange army from outer space was organizing townspeople against him.

The mental health team decided that Mr. Y was potentially suicidal and homicidal. Consequently, short-term hospitalization was recommended. The family was advised that, even after hospitalization and treatment, Mr. Y might have limited insight and that further psychotic episodes would likely occur in the future, particularly if he discontinued appropriate medications and supportive counseling.

For the present, at least, Mrs. Y decided to continue the marriage while receiving counseling for herself and children. She realized the need to stop relying so heavily on her oldest son. Immediately, she started in group counseling, began considering employment, and renewed old friendships. She and her counselor discussed how the changes in her could have both positive and negative implications for the marriage. Consequently, treatment for her and the children should be coordinated with that of Mr. Y. Meantime, the case manager talked with her about financial resources, employment possibilities, and new approaches to disciplining her children.

Interpersonal Relationships

Role reversal is prevalent in abusive families. The parents have unrealistic expectations of their children. Having been consistently deprived of emotional support in their own childhoods, the parents have not learned how to obtain the emotional support they need from others. They feel unloved, unappreciated, unwanted, unattractive, stupid, and insignificant. They are prone to avoid relationships or to be offensive and provoke rejection. They expect little from others and may frustrate workers by trying to terminate the therapeutic relationship prematurely. Avoiding contact with neighbors, friends, and extended family, they create internal dependency and pressure on the immediate family.

Parents often require training and role playing to acquire skills in effective communication, negotiation with others, being assertive but not aggressive, and viewing their child as a feeling and separate individual to be respected (empathy). Workers can enhance this element by teaching parents child developmental stages and appropriate, age-related expectations (Atwater, 1982; Caldwell and Drachman, 1964; Erikson, 1963; Gesell, Ilg, and Ames, 1977; Helfer, McKinney, and Kempe, 1976). It is further facilitated by treating the parents' dependency needs and by moving them toward assumption of responsibility for their abusive behaviors. It behooves workers to "parent the parents" and be aware that everyone is dependent before attaining independence.

The treatment team members provide the mechanism whereby abusive parents can learn to trust others while asking for and receiving support (Jenkins, Salus, and Shultze, 1979). That is why friendship activities such as eating together, respite child care, phone contacts, birthday cards and small presents may create more client trust than do more conventional treatment techniques.

To diffuse the clients' dependency and potential anger if needs are not met, workers should coordinate and share treatment responsibilities. The treatment team can facilitate the clients' involvement in community and group activities such as parties or neighborhood gatherings, church, and other social activities. Under no circumstances should a counselor feign adequacy, make promises that cannot be kept, or encourage the clients to become more dependent than the worker knows how to handle for an appropriate length of time. Since most cases require more than six months treatment if burnout is to be avoided, intervenors must know their limits for giving to clients. When workers burn out and insulate themselves against clients' demands, the latter feel another rejection (Villecco, 1977).

Having been victims of role reversal in childhood, many physically abusive parents still are not free to be silly, fun-loving, and playful. In adulthood they may lack a sense of humor and feel that having fun is both impossible and infantile. Treatment for such families requires games, parent-child play, and adult play. For instance, parent-child activities may enhance touching and bonding, for example, pretending the child is dough and the parent is kneading the dough into a gingerbread cookie. On trips to the zoo, parents as well as the children need permission to act silly, imitate animal behavior, and move outside their daily preoccupations (Star, 1983). In attempting to improve clients' interpersonal relationships and self-image, it is crucial for someone to role-model humor and fun (Gentry and Eaddy, 1980).

Low Self-Esteem

Many clients relate poorly to the treatment "system," have few inter-personally satisfying relationships, and are prone to be too demanding or too docile. By helping them use resources and teaching them appropriate assertiveness, the treatment system improves the self-esteem of abusive family members (Jenkins, Salus, and Shultze, 1979).

Relationships with neighborhoods and the larger community can improve clients' self-image and keep them occupied constructively. Nonjudgmental church groups can offer a channel for interpersonal relations. Obviously, self-righteous, accusing, or condemning religious activities are perceived as more of the "bad parents" already experienced by abusers.

Treatment of physically abusive families, each one requiring a different approach, entails an acceptance of and respect for all family structures, life-styles, and subcultural differences, assuming that the abuse can be stopped. When workers have this respect, it is felt by the clients, so use of family/community supports is maximized. The role modeling of workers, the emphasis on family and individual strengths, and the reduction of stress contribute to clients' self-respect.

Personal and Environmental Stress

Since noise, stress, and anger may come together to precipitate abuse, parents may benefit from self-control training as well as acquire practical solutions for coping with children's noise and other irritants (Barth et al., 1983; Jeffrey, 1976). Parents need respites from their children. They need to know that exercise and nutrition for them and their children can reduce stress, sickness, and the youngsters' acting-out behaviors. More rest or sleep for the whole family may reduce the hyperactivity and make the parents less irritable. When noise becomes overwhelming, one practical solution is for parents to put cotton in their ears. When the parents cannot find ways to cope with their stress, it is time to call their Parents Anonymous peers, a parent aide, or another program volunteer or professional (Bean, 1983; Merchand, 1983).

Environmental stressors or life crises for abusive families require much attention during treatment. These stressors are mainly physical or emotional. For example, clients' physical needs for food, clothing, shelter, and health care must be fulfilled. Even then, the emotional stress of trying to relate to schools, social agencies, law enforcement, courts, health providers, employers, housing authority personnel, family assistance workers, and others may drain and overwhelm the family emotionally. Therefore, supportive counseling, advocacy, information, and referral are a continuing part of treatment.

Inadequate Methods of Discipline

There is such strong cultural belief in the value of corporal punishment that much persuasion and role modeling are needed to convince abusive parents that their children can be disciplined without hitting. Besides, the children's crying, defiance, apparent lack of respect, or even their fears may threaten an explosive parent. Counselors who are not comfortable in placing limits on explosive parents may find it difficult to role-model firmness and kindness in tandem. Firm, respectful counseling, which entails realistic and achievable objectives, does demonstrate to parents that respect is fostered through listening and negotiation rather than intimidation. Habit and conduct disorders and neurotic traits acquired in their own physically abused youth can change if the parents' consistency and disciplinary methods improve (Dinkmeyer and McKay, 1976; Gordon, 1975; Holder and Mohr, 1979).

Parents generally need help in learning which misbehaviors are normative for their children's ages and gender (Martin, 1983). Regardless of the modality used, helping parents develop better ways to impose discipline can give them a new sense of control with their children and with their own lives (Herrenkohl and Herrenkohl, 1983). Both parents and professionals may be trained to view discipline from a variety of theoretical and practical approaches. Before training parents, counselors will benefit from examining their own disciplinary frames of reference (Hyman, 1983).

"If the parents view the severe physical punishment as ego-syntonic and therefore as an acceptable form of discipline, the therapist must attempt to create some dissonance in the parents..." (Melowsky, 1983 p. 43). For example, workers can explain to the parent that physical control will not work as the child grows older and more difficult to manage.

Emotional and Social Isolation

Internal family dependency and lack of an extended family/community support system increase the likelihood of abuse. A well-planned treatment approach assures development of, and integration into, extended family relationships. The clients may need guidance as to what they may reasonably expect to receive. Too often, members of the extended family are just as abusive, fragmented, and distrustful as the client. Supportive treatment may be required for them, too. Seldom does the extended family offer nothing, however, particularly if intervenors are focusing on strengths.

Many writers advocate the use of groups in treating abusive parents. They feel the abusers' behaviors that were important to survival in childhood are inappropriate in the parental role. Since the abusers failed to get consistent approval as children and now try to gain it from offspring, groups afford the opportunity for confronting the parents' maladaptive behavior and for providing approval from others. Groups reduce dependency, and consequent resentment, toward the counselor. Limits, acceptance of the person, and suggested approaches for handling anger are part of the group process (Holmes et al., 1975).

Specific self-help groups are extremely useful to physically abusive, emotionally isolated parents and their children. Examples include Parents Anonymous, couples groups for spouse abusers and abusees, mutual child care services, single-parents' groups, Parents United, AlaNon, and Alcoholics Anonymous. If there are other types of abuse along with child physical abuse, professional judgments are needed to determine how many self-help groups may be beneficial.

A written contract, fee rebates for desired performance, child management through role play, and structured discipline routines may be taught in groups of abusers. As in all counseling efforts, however, parents benefit from feeling that the group is "home" for their situation and they realize that other parents have similar problems. They can imitate those parents' successful techniques for reinforcing and praising behavior. Groups also help parents reduce isolation and develop social skills.

Dysfunction Around Intimacy and Sex

Cases in this writer's experience suggest that many physically abusive parents are experiencing problems during the potentially most intimate part of their relationships: sexual intercourse. The physical and emotional closeness of intercourse sets the stage for extreme fears of rejection, nonfulfillment, disappointment and anxiety about adequacy. In families with one abuser (and it can be either the man or the woman), the drive for sexual release and satisfaction can be inhibited by the partner's fear and anger related to the abuser's misuse of power. Paralleling this is the abuser's feelings of emotional and sexual inadequacy, which is further complicated by the partner's felt rejection. Feeling the emotional hurt or lack of fulfillment, either parent may turn anger onto the children. Instead of feeling intimacy, friendship, release of sexual tension, empathy, and fulfillment, the sexual partners feel inadequate, anxious, and depressed (Goldstein, 1984).

Respect and openness in communication lead to greater trust and intimacy. Accusations, poor communication, and frustrated dependency needs generate distrust, withdrawal, or attacking behaviors. Most abusive families fear intimacy because they anticipate ultimate rejection. Their past experiences create misunderstandings when others try to be intimate with them. Abusive families may need extensive marital or love-relationship counseling.

With a poor understanding of intimacy and appropriate touch, violence such as child sexual abuse and/or spouse abuse may occur in these families. All abusive families need some joint therapy to create an open system that meets the needs of children and adults alike (Satir, 1972). Most abusive families require therapy to facilitate greater intimacy and sexual satisfaction between the adults (Fisher and Dtricker, 1982; Kaplan, 1974, 1979; Olson, 1976).

Poor Problem-Solving Skills

Many clients suffer from borderline states but can develop a positive therapeutic relationship. When in a state of crisis, they may try to process how a therapist or other trusted person would solve the situation. At that point they are well on their way to "object constancy" in the "separation-individuation" process. They have internalized many of the therapist's values and approaches to problem solving. Reassurance, encouragement, and praise from the workers will enhance clients' ability to function without the workers' presence (Goldstein, 1984). Therefore, it is critical for workers to praise the problem-solving process, whether or not the clients' solution is the same as the workers' would propose. This assumes that the clients' problem-solving process was not too counterproductive or self-defeating. With appropriate encouragement in this stage, clients will be able to move from childlike to more adolescent and, finally, adult functioning.

Merely talking about problems, without structuring new directions, tends to increase family conflict. Some authors have developed behavioral-modification games to use in problem solving with families with the intent of reducing the clients' fears of control and manipulation (Blechman and Corfman, 1979).

Multiproblem, Highly Disorganized Life-Style

Since multiproblem, highly disorganized families may have almost insatiable needs, volunteers and students can be recruited to serve as role models, co-therapists, baby-sitters, transporters, and administrative helpers. Recruiting, screening, orienting, training, supervising, nurturing, and evaluating volunteers are time-consuming jobs. Yet, volunteers can take much pressure off the case manager by consistently relating to one or two families, being available for phone calls, serving as neighbors or extended family, being genuine friends, or by giving parents respite from the children (Fisher, 1970; Kendrick, 1983; Lauffer and Gorodezky, 1977).

Abusers may be unemployed or underemployed. By increasing their interpersonal skills, they may be able to locate jobs or better ones. The work ethic is strong in this country. Volunteer work, or even being a "consultant" to a child abuse project, can enhance self-worth and often establish beginning work habits. The community, not just members of the abusive family, gives approval based on work performance, whether it be homemaking, public employment, or volunteer service.

Crisis-intervention theory and programs such as Homebuilders are of great value when trying to engage clients in a trusting relationship (Borgman, Edmunds, and MacDicker, 1979; Rappoport, 1970). Through immediate, consistent, broad-based responses, treatment programs can have real meaning to clients at a time when they are most confused and hurting (Hoapala and Kinney, 1979). Crisis intervention alone, however, is not enough for highly disorganized or character-disordered clients.

When dealing with minority or very disorganized families in groups, workers may need to evaluate the groups' appropriateness for the clients (Meikamp, 1983). The clients may have language or cultural barriers that may prevent their being incorporated into the group process, or they may be so needy and dependent that individual counseling and more formalized group treatment are required.

Special Treatment Approaches

Since physical abuse occurs in various forms within different family structures, workers need to understand multiple treatment theories and to be knowledgeable about teenage parents (Silver, 1983), nuclear families, single-parent families, blended families, and extended families, all of which have a variety of life-styles and personal/cultural values.

Counselors also must be in touch with other intervenors throughout the course of treatment, otherwise the clients can precipitate division and disagreement between agencies and disciplines, creating the disorganization and ultimate rejection that they have always experienced and continue to expect. Since physical child abuse is only one possible expression of family dysfunction, it is best to use specialized treatment teams while at the same time assuring that other specialists and generalists are available to provide a continuum of family-centered services and professional knowledge.

The Problem of Trust

As children are abused, they develop the same lack of trust that is found in abusers. Developmental and behavioral difficulties particularly arise when children are abused in the first three years of life. Fear of loss and separation anxiety are prevalent as are superficial, indiscriminate relationships with adults.

These children require appropriate touching by therapists and other intervenors. When they are feeling stressed, they can be taught to request being held. Eating with them on a consistent basis in calm surroundings may decrease their gorging behaviors. They need to be told about their ego strengths since they have poor self-concepts. As they reach preschool age, they feel sad and blame themselves for the family situation and are confused and frustrated by the unpredictability of life at home.

In school, they have problems and often either reject or fear rejection from peers, thus withdrawing from conflict or becoming combative. They have difficulty expressing love and anger and act out their parents' feelings that everything is good or bad, strong or weak, black or white. For school-age children, group treatment is an effective supplement to individual counseling (Savino, 1983).

Preschool and early school-age children are candidates for play therapy if their home environment has become less violent and, hopefully the parents are in treatment. Even if the home is not totally safe, play therapy can provide a setting in which a child can learn to trust outside the home.

The fear of trusting and the inner anger of children who have suffered physical abuse may cause them to provoke adults. Therapists, foster parents, or birth parents may find that even though the abuse has stopped, the child relates as if it were continuing—as if all adults were a threat.

The Use of Play Therapy

Play therapy provides a means of communicating the fear, hurt, confusion, and anger. The child can play the role of a child or of parent, teacher, therapist, or other significant person. By assuming these roles, the child receives permission to express feelings and work through trauma. Through play, a trusting relationship can develop with the therapist, whereas previous relationships did not permit the child to develop appropriate trust (Bernstein, 1983; Eaddy and Gentry, 1981).

For the child to be responsive to play therapy and the therapist to be free of massive frustration, a plain, carpeted, easily washable, safe playroom is necessary. Too many fixtures and toys are overly stimulating to the abused child, who has poor impulse control and short attention span. Easily replaceable doll figures are desirable. Since these children are afraid to verbalize feelings, once they have developed some trust with the therapist, plastic phones may be used for talking at a safe distance. For school-age children in the later stages of therapy, painting, clay materials and simply structured games may be introduced after impulses are in control.

Mann and McDermott (1983) provide an excellent summary on engaging abused children by teaching them how to play, reinforcing with food, allowing them to take a toy home or to have exactly the same surroundings during each play session, and permitting them to be dependent on and regressive with the therapist. The length of play therapy is likely to be longer than one year. When parents are in group counseling, structured play groups baby-sitting will be needed for the children.

Adolescents and Their Viewpoint

Much like children, many adolescents are prone to blame themselves when they are physically abused. Unfortunately, adults are likely to interpret normal adolescent behaviors, such as withdrawal, argumentativeness, and sullenness as being intentionally provocative. Furthermore, parents may agonize about setting and enforcing boundaries on the adolescents' behavior and activity (Berdie, Baizerman, and Louris, 1977).

Abused adolescents formerly were "more likely to be served by the juvenile justice system, the alternative youth services network, or the mental health system, rather than by the traditional child protection system" (Fisher and Berdie, 1978, p. 182). Then, and now, the systems lack coordination or collaborative planning for comprehensive services. Continuing efforts are needed to coordinate these programs. For example, 50 percent of clients in runaway programs have experienced abuse or neglect and require a broad range of coordinated services.

Running away, substance abuse, unruliness, extreme aggression toward self or others, provocativeness, extreme withdrawal and school problems may indicate that physical abuse is occurring. Workers would be remiss in not asking such youths whether they have been abused. For instance, one study of 25 abused adolescents found that 21 were having school problems and that 20 of the 25 families had received uncoordinated services from a variety of social agencies (Libbey and Bybee, 1979).

When parents and youths are viciously and mutually provocative and out of control, homicide, suicide, or severe depression may be the outcome. Therefore, crisis counseling is required for all family members. If the youngsters cannot be protected at home, a group home setting along with family treatment may be necessary.

Experts agree that runaway shelters and community-based programs are critical resources for youths who are at a violent impasse with the family or cut off from parental support. When these youngsters cannot gain access to shelters, family members or friends, they are vulnerable to prostitution, shoplifting and drug dealing. It is further believed that abused adolescents will be better served if an adolescent specialist is on the child protective service team (Hirayama, 1982).

For many adolescents, Fisher et al. (1980) determined that abuse was a constant factor throughout their lives. With chronically abused adolescents, who are likely to be antisocial, depressed, promiscuous, using drugs, committing nonstatus offenses against society, and poorly associated with peer groups, Mouzakitis (1984) recommends long-term casework and insight-oriented therapy for them and their families. In providing treatment to physically abused adolescents, individual peers and the peer group are critical, whether the youths stay at home, in a group home, in residential treatment, or in foster care (Garbarino and Jacobson, 1978). Foster care may be a poor choice for youths struggling with separation-individuation issues who lack the trust required for emotional closeness in a family. If foster care is necessary, however, life skills groups constitute an excellent model for adolescent foster children. Indeed, all leaders of adolescent groups can benefit from reading about the incorporation of an opening ritual, agenda setting, activity, food, and closing ritual as well as stages of group development defined by Euster et al. (1984).

Fisher et al. (1980) also present a comprehensive list of treatment services for maltreated adolescents and their families.

EVALUATION AND TERMINATION

To assess improvement or lack of it in child physical abuse cases, the worker must observe the parents interacting with their child(ren) (Elmer, 1983; Moon, 1983).

Clients may be asked to evaluate the services (Magura and Moses, 1984) and monitors may review records for documentation of all activities, particularly case management. There should be clear identification of problems, the specific casework activity being used to solve them, and other steps for consideration by the review teams, the court, or for new workers when there is a caseworker turnover. Specific behavioral treatment objectives can be reviewed and progress measured by the clients, the supervisor, the workers, and the multidisciplinary team (Shyne, 1976).

Abusive families benefit from formalized periods of reevaluation to determine whether treatment is effective and should be continued or terminated (Coombes et al., 1978). This should be done at a minimum of every six months. Within the first six months, the worker needs to know whether treatment is effective, whether a child may be safe in the home, whether parental rights need to be terminated, and other information for the intervention system's review (Blythe, 1983).

If the court is involved, it makes the final decision on any disposition, including termination of treatment. The clients, the court, and all members of the client system need to be fully and openly informed of the case status at all times. Evaluations of goal attainment, need for referral to other services, and rationale for continuing or closing the case should be a treatment team decision.

Termination should be no surprise to the clients. It should be a joint decision between them and the intervention system. At least six to eight weeks in advance, clients need to know about and have time to understand and accept the possibility of termination or of case transfer. This allows time to express feelings of rejection, anger and dependency.

A clearly defined follow-up process is desirable. Clients should be advised about when they will be contacted to determine their continuing adjustment. They also need instruction on exactly where to call if problems or warning signs recur.

SUMMARY

Protection of children and adolescents is the first priority in the intervention and treatment of physical abuse, but a well-coordinated system of resources that includes in-home, family centered interventions by multidisciplinary teams is likely to produce the best results. Intervention and treatment are no better than the training and experience of the agencies and employees involved.

Ultimately, child physical abuse treatment in isolation—without consideration for the needs of the whole person, the family, and the community—is likely to aggravate rather than improve the families' quality of life. Creativity by intervenors, goal setting with clients, and their involvement in a gamut of treatment activities are recommended.

Objectivity, patience, respect for families, experienced supervisors, good case management, a well-trained multidisciplinary team, advocacy, differential diagnosis and treatment, and planned evaluation of outcomes can produce better self-esteem and problem-solving skills for most physically abusive families.

REFERENCES

Ambrose, S., Haggard, A., and Haworth, J.: Cognitive/behavioral parenting groups for abusive families. *Proceedings of the Fourth National Conference on Child Abuse and Neglect (1979).* Los Angeles: California State University, 1983, pp. 425-6.

Atwater, E.: *Adolescence.* Englewood Cliffs, NJ: Prentice-Hall, 1982.

Barth, R. P., Blythe, B. J., Schinke, S. P., and Schilling, R. F., II: Self-control training with maltreating parents. *Child Welfare, 52*(4): 313-24, 1983.

Bean, S. D.: The parent aide support service: How volunteers effect growth in abusive and neglectful parents. *Proceedings of the Fourth National Conference on Child Abuse and Neglect (1979).* Los Angeles: California State University, 1983, pp. 334-59.

Berdie, J, Baizerman, M., and Lourie, I. S.: Violence towards youth: Themes from a workshop. *Children Today, 6*(2): 7-10, 1977.

Bernstein, B., and Crosby, G.: Impact of fathers' groups on abusive fathers and families. *Proceedings of the Fourth National Conference on Child Abuse and Neglect (1979).* Los Angeles: California State University, 1983, pp. 59-60, 228-230.

Bernstein, L.: The role of play therapy in the clinical treatment of physically abused and/or emotionally neglected children. *Proceedings of the Fourth National Conference on Child Abuse and Neglect (1979).* Los Angeles: California State University, 1983, pp. 59-60.

Blechman, E., and Corfman, E.: Games that help solve life problems. *Families Today, 2:* 897-927. Washington, D.C.: DHEW Publication No. (ADM) 79-815, 1979.

Blythe, B. J.: A critique of outcome evaluation in child abuse treatment. *Child Welfare, 52(4):* 325-35, 1983.

Borgman, R., Edmunds, M., and MacDicken, R. A.: *Crisis Intervention: A Manual for Child Protection Workers.* Washington, D.C.: DHEW Publication No. (OHDS) 79-30196, 1979.

Brown, J. H., Finch, W. A., Jr., Northen, H., Taylor, S. H., and Weil, M.: *Child, Family, Neighborhood: A Master Plan for Social Service Delivery.* New York: Child Welfare League of America, Inc., 1982, p. 16.

Caldwell, B. M., and Drachman, R. H.: Comparability of three methods of assessing developmental level of young infants. *Pediatrics, 34:* 51-57, 1964.

Chestang, L.: The delivery of child welfare services to minority group children and their families. In Kadushin, A. (Ed.): *Child Welfare Strategy in the Coming Years.* Washington, D.C.: DHEW Publication No. (OHDS), 78-30158, 1978, pp. 169-194.

Childress, O. R.: Training package for service providers. *Proceedings of the Fourth National Conference on Child Abuse and Neglect (1979).* Los Angeles: California State University, 1983, pp. 342-43.

Coombes, P., McCormack, M., Chipley, M., and Archer, B.: The INCADEX approach to identifying problems and evaluating impact in child protective services. *Child Welfare, 47(1):* 35-44, 1978.

Dinkmeyer, D., and McKay, G. D.: *Systematic Training for Effective Parenting.* Circle Pines, MN: American Guidance Service, Inc., 1976.

Eaddy, V. B., and Gentry, C. E.: Play with a purpose. *Public Welfare,* Winter 1980, pp. 43-48.

Ebling, N. B., and Hill, D. A. (Eds.): *Child Abuse and Neglect: A Guide With Case Studies for Treating the Child and Family.* Boston: John Wright, 1983.

Elmer, E.: An experimental program for abused and high risk infants. *Proceedings of the Fourth National Conference on Child Abuse and Neglect (1979).* Los Angeles: California State University, 1983, pp. 37-39.

Erikson, E.: *Childhood and Society.* New York: W.W. Norton & Co., 1963, pp. 247-274.

Euster, S. D., Ward, V. P., Varner, J. G., and Euster, G. L.: Life skills groups for adolescent foster children. *Child Welfare, 63(2):* 27-36, 1984.

Fisher, M., and Dtricker, G. (Eds.): *Intimacy.* New York: Plenum Press, 1982.

Fisher, N.: Reaching out. *The Volunteer in Child Abuse and Neglect Programs,* Washington, D.C.: DHEW Publication No. (OHDS) 79-30174, 1979.

Fisher, B., and Berdie, J.: Adolescent abuse and neglect: Issues of incidence, intervention and service delivery. *Child Abuse and Neglect, 2(3):* 182, 1978.

Fisher, B., Berdie, J., Cook, J., and Day, N.: *Adolescent Abuse and Neglect: Intervention Strategies.* Washington, D.C.: DHHS Publication No. (ODHS) 80-30266, 1980, pp. 37-41, 50-59.

Garbarino, J., and Jacobson, N.: Youth helping youth in cases of maltreatment of adolescents. *Child Welfare, 57(8):* 505-10, 1978.

Gentry, C. E., and Eaddy, V. B.: Treatment of children in spouse abusive families. *Victimology: An International Journal, 5(2-4):* 240-50, 1980.

Gesell, A., Ilg, F., and Ames, L. B.: Children's characteristics of different ages. In Ambrose,

B. (Ed.): *Child Abuse and Neglect: Social Services Reader I.* Albany, NY: State University of New York at Albany, 1977.

Goldstein, E. G.: *Ego Psychology and Social Work Practice.* New York: The Free Press, 1984.

Gordon, T.: *Parent Effectiveness Training.* New York: New American Library, 1975.

Haas, W.: Reaching out—A dynamic concept in casework. *Social Work, 13:* 91, 1959.

Helfer, R. E., McKinney, J. P., and Kempe, R.: Arresting or freezing the developmental process. In Helfer, R. E., and Kempe, C. H. (Eds.): *Child Abuse and Neglect: The Family and the Community.* Cambridge, MA: Ballinger Publishing Co., 1976, pp. 55-73.

Herrenkohl, R. C., and Herrenkohl, E. C.: Circumstances surrounding the occurrence of child abuse. *Proceedings of the Fourth National Conference on Child Abuse and Neglect 1979.* Los Angeles, California State University, 1983, p. 41.

Hirayama, K. K.: *Adolescent Abuse and Neglect: A Comprehensive Treatment Approach.* Knoxville, TN: University of Tennessee School of Social Work, 1982.

Hoapala, D., and Kinney, J.: Homebuilder's approach to the training of in-home therapists. In Maybanks, S., and Bryce, M. (Eds.): *Home-Based Services for Children and Families: Policy, Practice and Research.* Springfield, IL: Charles C Thomas Publisher, 1979.

Holder, W. M., and Mohr, C.: *Child Protection Certification Curriculum.* Englewood, CO: American Humane Association, 1979.

Holmes, S. A., Barnhart, C., Cantoni, L., and Reymer, E.: Working with parents in child abuse cases. *Social Casework, 56*(1): 3-12, January 1975.

Hutchinson, J. R.: *Family-Centered Social Services: A Model for Child Welfare Agencies.* Oakdale, IA: National Resource Center on Family Based Services, 1983.

Hyman, I. A.: Alternatives to corporal punishment. *Proceedings of the Fourth National Conference on Child Abuse and Neglect 1979.* Los Angeles, California State University, 1983, pp. 186-870.

Janchill, Sister M. P.: People cannot go it alone. In Germain, C. B. (Ed.): *Social Work Practice: People and Environments—An Ecological Perspective.* New York: Columbia University Press, 1979, pp. 346-362.

Jeffrey, M.: Practical ways to change parent-child interaction in families of children at risk. In Helfer, R. E., and Kempe, C. H. (Eds.): *Child Abuse and Neglect: The Family and the Community.* Cambridge, MA: Ballinger Publishing Co., 1976, pp. 209-33.

Jenkins, J. L., Salus, M. K., and Shultze, G. L.: *Child Protective Services: A Guide For Workers.* Washington, D.C.: DHEW Publication No. (OHDS) 79-30203, 1979, pp. 62-63.

Kaplan, H. S.: *Disorders of Sexual Desire.* New York: Brunner/Mazel, 1979.

Kaplan, H. S.: *The New Sex Therapy.* New York: Brunner/Mazel, 1974.

Kempe, H. C., and Helfer, R. E.: *Helping the Battered Child and His Family.* Philadelphia: J.B. Lippincott Co., 1972.

Kendrick, M. (Ed.): A Marketplace of Community Programs. *Sixth National Conference on Child Abuse and Neglect.* Baltimore: School of Social Work and Community Planning, University of Maryland at Baltimore, 1983.

Lauffer, A., and Gorodezky, S.: *Volunteers.* Beverly Hills, CA: Sage Publications, 1977.

Libbey, P., and Bybee, R.: The physical abuse of adolescents. *Journal of Social Issues, 35*(2): 99-112, 1984.

Magura, S., and Moses, B. S.: Clients as evaluators in child protective services. *Child Welfare, 53*(2): 101-126, 1984.

Mann, E., and McDermott, J. F., Jr.: Play therapy for victims of child abuse and neglect. In Shaefer, C. E., and O'Connor, K. J. (Eds.): *Handbook of Play Therapy.* New York: John Wiley & Sons, 1983.

Martin, J.: Behavior of boys and girls in abuse situations: Research findings and treatment implications. *Proceedings of the Fourth National Conference on Child Abuse and Neglect (1979)*. Los Angeles, California State University, 1983, p. 409.

Maybanks, S., and Bryce, M. (Eds.): *Home-Based Services for Children and Families: Policy, Practice and Research*. Springfield, IL: Charles C Thomas, Publisher, 1979.

McManmon, M. T.: Parent group models prevention and treatment of child abuse and neglect. *Proceedings of the Fourth National Conference on Child Abuse and Neglect (1979)*. Los Angeles: California University, 1983, pp. 420–422.

Meikamp, K. D.: Community/cultural self-help group models. *Proceedings of the Fourth National Conference on Child Abuse and Neglect (1979)*. Los Angeles: California State University, 1983, p. 352.

Melowsky, F.: Treating the abusive parent. *Proceedings of the Fourth National Conference on Child Abuse and Neglect (1979)*. Los Angeles: California State University, 1983, pp. 433–34.

Merchand, J. L.: Involvement and maintenance of volunteer parent aides: Administrative and clinical considerations. *Proceedings of the Fourth National Conference on Child Abuse and Neglect (1979)*. Los Angeles: California State University, 1983, pp. 308–312.

Moon, S.: The comprehensive evaluation of the parents and parent-child interaction. *Proceedings of the Fourth National Conference on Child Abuse and Neglect (1979)*. Los Angeles: California State University, 1983, pp. 292–3.

Mouzakitis, C. M.: Characteristics of abused adolescents and guidelines for intervention. *Child Welfare, 53*(2): 149–157, 1984.

Nayman, L., and Witkin, S. L.: Parent/child foster placement: An alternative approach in child abuse and neglect. *Child Welfare, 47*(4): 249–258, 1978.

Olson, D.H.L. (Ed.): *Treating Relationships*. Lake Mills, IA: Graphic Publishing Co., 1976.

Oppenheimer, A.: Triumph over trauma in the treatment of child abuse. *Social Casework: The Journal of Contemporary Social Work, 59*(3): 52–8, 1978.

Overton, A., et al.: *The Casework Notebook*. St. Paul, MN: Community Chest and Councils, Inc., 1957.

Palladino, J. S., and Levin, P.: Defensiveness and self-esteem measurement of abusive mothers and female incest victims. *Proceedings of the Fourth National Conference on Child Abuse and Neglect (1979)*. Los Angeles: California State University, 1983, pp. 476–770.

Pollak, O.: Treatment of character disorders: A dilemma in casework culture. *Social Service Review, 35:* 127–34, 1961.

Rappoport, L.: A model of crisis intervention. In Roberts, R. W., and Nee, R. H. (Eds.): *Theories of Social Casework*. Chicago: University of Chicago Press, 1970.

Rice, R. M.: Exploring American family policy. *Marriage and Family Review, 2*(3): 2–3, 1979.

Salk, L.: *Your Child from 1 to 12*. New York: New American Library, 1979.

Satir, V.: *Peoplemaking*. Palo Alto, CA: Science and Behavior Books, 1972.

Savino, A. B.: Interdisciplinary family intervention program. *Proceedings of the Fourth National Conference on Child Abuse and Neglect (1979)*. Los Angeles: California State University, 1983, pp. 285–286.

Sherz, F.: Family therapy. In Roberts, R. W., and Nee, R. H. (Eds.): *Theories of Social Casework*. Chicago: University of Chicago Press, 1970.

Shyne, A. W.: Evaluation in child welfare. *Child Welfare, 45*(1): 5–18, January 1976.

Silver, B. L.: A prevention and treatment model for teenage mothers. *Proceedings of the Fourth National Conference on Child Abuse and Neglect (1979)*. Los Angeles: California State University, 1983, pp. 197–198.

Solomon, B. B.: *Black Empowerment: Social Work in Oppressed Communities.* New York: Columbia University Press, 1976.

Star, B.: Helping the Abuser. *Intervening Effectively in Family Violence.* New York: Family Service Association of America, 1983.

Sullivan, M., Spasser, M., and Penner, L.: *Bowen Center Project for Abused and Neglected Children: Report of a Demonstration in Protective Services.* Washington, D.C.: DHEW, 1977.

Villecco, J. E.: Child abuse: The worker's perspective. Child Abuse and Neglect: Issues on Innovations and Implementation. *Proceedings of the Second National Conference on Child Abuse and Neglect, 2:* 226–29, 1977.

Weissman, H. H.: *Integrating Services for Troubled Families.* San Francisco: Jossey-Bass, 1978.

CHAPTER 15

TREATMENT OF CHILD NEGLECT

Chris M. Mouzakitis and Raju Varghese

INTRODUCTION

Child neglect is one of the least understood, most neglected types of child maltreatment. Protective service workers and other professionals who have studied child neglect—the shadow of more severe child abuse—often have failed to recognize the complexity and severity of the situation. Child abuse is more dramatic, more easily identified, and more easily defined than neglect and also produces greater public reaction. Child nelgect is overlooked far more than is abuse (Kadushin, 1980). The abuse and neglect reporting laws of various states reflect this: For many years, every state required the reporting of abuse, but for a long time many did not require it in neglect cases.

The literature, which often reflects what is being studied, overwhelmingly reflects this lack of attention to child neglect. All available evidence supports the contention that the more narrowly defined physical abuse constitutes only a small fraction of the cases that fall within the realm of child maltreatment (Giovannoni and Becerra, 1979). Child protection experts speak of many distinct social, physical, and psychological dynamics related to child neglect (Hancock, 1963; Hally, Polansky, and Polansky, 1980).

However, when treatment interventions are discussed, they pay limited attention to the problem. As a rule, they deal with the subject under the rubric of "child abuse and neglect," placing emphasis on the "abuse." The neglected child and family receive peripheral attention (Mayhall and Norgard, 1983). They create the impression that treatment for abused children is also appropriate for neglected child. This is particularly true in cases where abuse and neglect exist concurrently. But, in cases where neglect is the problem, the treatment approach should be differentiated on the basis of the cases and their distinct dynamics.

It is difficult to demonstrate that neglect is a more serious problem than abuse, considering the severity of harm inflicted. Neglected children do not experience physical maltreatment—no fractured bones, bruises, lacerations, cigarette burns, or being purposely starved as in the case of abused children. Yet, neglected children lack the appropriate stimulation for normal growth and development because of the parents' character problems, ignorance and inattentiveness.

They also suffer from inadequate supervision, education, discipline, medical maintenance, nutrition, hygienic and emotional care, or environmental hazards resulting from parents' or caretakers' inability to protect them because of their own poverty or other problems (Mayhall and Eastlack-Norgard, 1983; Pelton, 1981; Polansky, 1981; Hally, Polansky, and Polansky, 1980). Except for a few authors, practitioners have failed to address specifically the issues in the treatment of such cases. It can be stated that such cases receive cursory services by practitioners and agencies mandated by law to provide treatment. Considering also that 80 percent to 85 percent of protective service cases involve neglect, it is to be wondered why this discrepancy exists and why such cases receive limited attention.

The more diffuse the concept of "neglect," the more difficult it is to develop and implement appropriate treatment approaches. This chapter examines the various treatment issues related to child neglect and discusses effective treatment.

TREATMENT

The term *neglect* hardly suggests the extent and magnitude of the problem or its effect on families. Of course, there are instances where problems are minor and could be treated through short-term interventions. But in many cases the problems are complex and chronic, requiring long-term involvement from those who attempt to help. In many cases, such families' personality and environmental problems are so severe that their parental capacities to meet their children's primary needs and their own are greatly diminished (Hally, Polansky, and Polansky, 1980). The following three cases are typical examples:

The Johnson Case

The Johnson family consists of Mr. Johnson, 38; Mrs. Johnson, 36; and their five children, Jason, 6; Norma, 8; Nelly, 9; Andrew, 10; and Thomas,

12. The family was referred to child protective services because the youngsters were left at home without supervision, leaving the house and running in the streets. Investigation revealed the following.

Mr. Johnson, who had separated from his wife several times in the past, is only a periodic visitor in the home. Mrs. Johnson looks older than her age, is unemployed, and she receives Aid to Families with Dependent Children (AFDC). The children were found to go barefooted and were improperly clothed, dirty, and aggressive with each other. All were attending school irregularly; the two oldest—Andrew and Thomas—were behavior problems in class. The house was in poor condition, with several windows broken, poorly furnished, and unclean.

Mrs. Johnson was in agreement with the workers' observations about the unacceptable conditions of the children and their environment. However, she did not show any motivation or desire to change the situation.

The Robinson Case

Mrs. Robinson, twenty-one years old, is the mother of Donald, six months old, and Peter, four years old. Donald has been in the hospital's intensive care unit since birth because of respiratory distress syndrome. The mother has seen the baby on only three occasions since.

Hospital personnel report that the mother does not keep appointments. On one occasion, the mother thought of placing Donald for adoption. A public health nurse involved in the case was refused entry to Mrs. Robinson's apartment. This prompted a referral to the child neglect unit. Investigation revealed the following: The mother is on AFDC, the children were fathered by two men who are out of Mrs. Robinson's life now, she is addicted to heroin and has used various drugs periodically. The apartment is sparsely furnished and below acceptable hygienic standards. The four-year-old is well developed physically but is enuretic. The mother is suspected of prostituting herself to maintain her drug addiction. A grandmother living nearby has limited influence on Mrs. Robinson's behavior.

According to the worker, Mrs. Robinson insists in providing overall child care. She is possessive, understanding, trusting, and resistive. She agrees to follow the worker's suggestions, but most of the time she does not keep appointments with her, with the hospital, or with the drug treatment program to which she was referred.

The Vaughn Family

The Vaughn family consists of three children, Jade, age five years, Ronald, age two years, six months, and Michele, age fourteen months;

Mrs. Vaughn, the mother; and Mr. and Mrs. Lawrence, the grandparents. The Vaughn family was referred to the protective service unit for neglect.

The investigation revealed the following: Mrs. Vaughn, who is twenty-three, "dumped" her three children at her parents' house after an argument with her live-in boyfriend and father of the youngest child. She threatened suicide, disappeared for a short time, and eventually returned to her parents' home. She now has made other, unknown, living arrangements but is in touch with the worker.

She is an alcoholic but denies that she uses drugs. The grandmother works but is not too interested in the children, so the grandfather, who is retired, has become the primary caretaker and receives the AFDC check. However, he has emotional problems, including a nervous breakdown and a history of setting fires.

The living quarters are crowded and uncleaned. The five-year-old Jade is enuretic and is hostile and aggressive towards the grandparents and other adults. Ronald, the two-and-one-half-year-old, is withdrawn and rarely responds to verbal instructions. An examination of him found tacks and nails in his mouth. The youngest also is withdrawn and shows no emotions. A suspicion that this child was being sexually abused was ruled out after a medical examination.

What would be the appropriate interventive strategies once neglect has been validated to exist in such cases? The answer considers such factors as:

1. The parents' problems, which may range from psychopathological conditions to drug and alcohol abuse.
2. The parental ability to provide appropriate care, guidance, and supervision.
3. The parental ability to provide the financial means for the family's overall maintenance.
4. The neglected children's special problems and the cyclical effect of the neglect on them.
5. The parents' degree of motivation to work on the problems.

An assessment of these factors would enable the worker to determine the course of intervention.

The major treatment objectives in such cases are to create a safe environment for the children and to modify the precipitating factors underlying the maltreatment. To be effective, any treatment objective should deal specifically with the three concomitant factors that contribute to neglectful situations: (1) the personality traits of the parents that directly contribute to child neglect, (2) the environmental stressors that increase the burden of child care and trigger neglectful interaction, and (3) the characteristics of the children that make them vulnerable to neglect and to victimization.

THE "MULTI" APPROACHES

Any effective treatment approach should provide both parents and children a broad, comprehensive, and relevant spectrum of services in order to minimize personal failures in parenting practices, strengthen and maintain family constellation, alleviate possible negative impacts of environmental stressors, and enhance individual development. This requires the use of multidimensional, multidisiciplinary, and multimodal approaches geared to provide the maltreating families with a variety of comprehensive services.

Multidimensional

Multidimensional intervention refers to the helping worker's actions directed toward various aspects of the parents' and children's functioning and the family at large. These include the family's financial situation, quality of housing, health condition and medical care, relationships between spouses and between parents and children, parental skills, and parents' abilities to reach out and use available community resources. Research and practice experience indicate that neglectful families by and large are multiproblem.

One major problem that several of these families experience is limited economic resources that inadvertently affect the parents' ability to meet their own needs and to provide and care for their children. These long-standing problems have impacted on them in such a way as to create, at times, insurmountable sociopathological conditions and an inertia manifested in their reluctance to seek help or to use it when it is offered (Hally, Polansky, and Polansky, 1980; Mayhall, and Eastlack-Norgard, 1983). To be effective, a multidimensional approach requires parallel interventive actions, rather than help one step at a time.

For example, the Johnson family, with such problems as alcoholism of the mother, poverty, poor housing, lack of parenting skills, and the children's medical and behavioral problems will require parallel actions at several levels. To initiate medical care for the children and help with Mrs. Johnson's alcoholic condition while she is in poverty and poor housing and her parenting skills remain the same, such intervention will not bring about the permanent changes to guarantee sufficient care for the children. As a matter of fact, the benefits of such piecemeal help eventually may diminish under the overwhelming impact of poverty and poor housing conditions. This is not an unusual situation and is frequently seen in similar cases. Such situations eventually become the so-called multiproblem-unmotivated-chronic cases found abundantly in protective service agencies.

Multidisciplinary

Multidisciplinary approach refers to the need for various disciplines in such cases. Such involvement can be through individual direct contacts with professionals and/or through multidisciplinary consultative teams. Because of these families' multiple problems, involvement of other professionals is inevitable if help is to be effective. The Johnson family, for example, will need help from the protective service workers as well as from an alcoholism therapist, a physician, a housing authority specialist, a school social worker, a visiting nurse, and perhaps a judge.

However, the sudden presence of so many specialists in the lives of neglecting families can become so overwhelming that they may react negatively. This frequently is seen where such families agree to follow treatment plans, then eventually drop out. Therefore, use of other disciplines, at least at the beginning, should be coordinated by the protective service agency workers. Coordination with parallel casework intervention can reduce such clients' anxieties, apprehension, and resistance.

One approach to the problem of interdisciplinary coordination and to guarantee continuity and intensity of service is through multidisciplinary treatment teams. One such team dealing exclusively with cases involving child neglect is in Baltimore City's Department of Social Services. The team usually is composed of a protective service supervisor as chair, a consultant, a lawyer, and a pediatrician as permanent members. Non-permanent members include those involved in a case; there also may be a visiting nurse, a policeman, a school social worker, a mental health professional, a psychologist, and the protective service worker and supervisor carrying the case. This not only solves the problem of coordination and continuity but also makes possible better diagnostic understanding of a case, determines treatment effectiveness, and develops new treatment strategies and preventive interventions.

For protective service workers, the team is not only a source of ideas and knowledge but a morale supporter so much needed in such cases. An example of team use could arise when considering whether to go to court because of the parents' reluctance to follow through with treatment. Evoking the authority of the court in neglect cases is not always successful, so workers often are reluctant to initiate such proceedings. The team examines the pros and cons of possible legal action, considers the judge's *modus operandi* in similar past cases, and decides on needed evidence and strategies if termination of parental rights or removal of the children from the home is attempted.

Multimodal

Multimodal refers to the various types of treatment and/or therapies used by those professionals in helping families. Again, these families' multiple problems require a wide range of interventive models. Most prominent among them are provision of concrete services, individual counseling to resolve specific problems, family therapy to improve relationships and the family's functioning as a unit, psychotherapy and/or mental health counseling in cases where psychopathology is the blocking element in the parent(s) functioning, play therapy when the children's ability to cope with relationships and the environment has been affected, group treatment to enhance socialization in order to acquire knowledge and to increase ability to relate to others, and self-help groups for increased social contact and support.

Which interventive models are used will depend on the complexity and intensity of the problem. However, one approach, no matter what other models also are used, is the provision of concrete (or "hard") services: financial assistance, housing, transportation, employment, day care, medical care, enrollment in schools, homemaker services, parent aides, respite care, foster care, etc. The practice of first emphasizing "soft services" (i.e. counseling to the exclusion of "hard services" or their minimal use) is unproductive. Chances of success in a family therapy approach are greater if concrete needs are met or at least if there is evidence of a concerted effort toward meeting them.

PRINCIPLES IN TREATMENT

Successful treatment of child neglect cases depends not only on the quantity and quality of services offered to them but also on the degree of *coordination, intensity, continuity,* and *follow-up.*

Coordination

As indicated earlier, resolution of the neglecting family's problems by and large requires the involvement of many disciplines and a wide range of supportive services. Their presence in these clients' lives is a novelty that they had never experienced. They often look upon the sudden attention and concern they receive with suspicion and view it as an attempt to curb their independence and a way to question their parental rights.

Not being accustomed to dealings with people and various systems, they tend to become anxious, fearful, intimidated by increased feelings of personal inadequacy, and eventually become resistive and either discontinue the services or use them sporadically only in times of crisis. Unless the clients are assisted in these contacts and services are well coordinated by the protective service workers within their casework counseling roles, the chances that the families will use them effectively are greatly reduced. The phenomenon of such clients' procrastinating, refusing to use services, and eventually dropping out of treatment becomes a puzzle for workers. Coordination as a distinct role responsibility involves from the protective service workers' actions, such as:

1. Explaining the services and the reasons why they are needed.
2. Connecting the families with the various helping systems so they can acquire knowledge of the professionals involved with them.
3. Discussing regularly the clients' use of such services and their satisfactions and apprehensions.
4. Intervening with the service professionals to straighten out any differences that may have arisen and to become their advocate.

Protective service workers might object that such activity might make clients too dependent. This is not true. If these families are to learn how to use effectively the various helping systems, they need to go through a period of dependence. This dependency phase should be used constructively by the protective service worker in helping the family develop a sense of trust in the process and to move toward self-reliance.

The problem workers face with coordination often is not that they do not know how to do it but rather the limited time they have to serve excessive case loads. A partial answer to this problem could be the use of the multidisciplinary treatment team discussed earlier. Since the professionals serving the family are involved in such a team, the opportunity for direct communication with them and resolution of issues are feasible.

The negative impact from the lack of coordination on the effectiveness of treatment cannot be underestimated. If the workers are not actively involved in this role, they lose sight of what is happening in the clients' lives, how effective these services are, and in general lose control of the case. It is not unusual for workers to have a case active in their case load and yet have no knowledge of the clients' whereabouts because they were referred to other community services.

Intensity

Another basic principle in the treatment of cases involving neglect is intensity. Intensity means that once work begins with a family, there must be a high frequency of contacts. Unfortunately, this principle, for reasons that at times are beyond the workers' control, is often not followed. No neglecting parents, no matter what the problem is, and no children, no matter how the neglect has influenced them, will improve by sporatic, unscheduled visits by workers and other professionals. If goals are ever to be accomplished, intensity in treatment requires that the protective service workers, at the beginning, visit more than once a week (counseling sessions) and continue regularly until changes have been made, clients take personal initiatives, and signs of improvement are visible.

For example, if neglecting parents have been diagnosed, among other problems, as lacking parenting skills, improvement will not come about because the protective service worker met with them just once or perhaps once a month. Improvement will occur only if the parents are given sufficient counseling time to discuss the problem, to consider alternatives, to realize the impact certain of their actions have on the child, to experiment with new methods, and to be reinforced in their appropriate use.

Unfortunately, implementation of this principle in neglect cases lags considerably. For example, in one case the mother, a single parent and recipient of AFDC, was found to be neglectful of her four children ages two, three, five, and seven. The children had developmental delays, were lacking in medical and hygienic care, and were aggressive and withdrawn. The mother also was found to be depressed, with alcohol problems, and a lack of general knowledge.

Following the team's assessment and treatment planning, it asked the protective service worker to report on progress in four months. In the follow-up review of the case, the protective service worker reported that the mother was not motivated and had not "fulfilled the contract." The worker's recommendation was removal of the children to foster care. However, when asked how many times the mother had been seen, the worker indicated that this had occurred only once at the beginning, when the contract was offered to her, and twice by phone when the mother was found to be angry and resistive. It is apparent that this case lacked not only frequency of contacts but also basic counseling help. No wonder this mother was angry and unmotivated.

Continuity

The third element, continuity, refers to uninterrupted provision of services until changes and improvements have been made. Services can be interrupted for such reasons as the worker left the agency, was moved to another unit, went on vacation, or got sick. Interruptions of treatment efforts is frequent in protective service units, since the rate of workers terminating employment can be as high as 50 percent and even more per year. It is, unfortunately, not unusual to see clients' records piled up on the supervisors' desks for weeks and months because workers left the agency.

Even if treatment is delivered within all basic principles and clients show signs of improvement, interruptions in service can set the clock back. Clients tend to feel abandoned and unworthy, become angry and hostile, and often retreat to old behaviors. It is not unusual for clients to call the agency wondering what happened to their worker and being told that the worker has left or that the case will or has been reassigned to someone else. Effective handling of such problems can help clients consolidate gains they have made in treatment as well as enhance their trust and confidence in the services and the system.

Since the problems of discontinuity of treatment cannot be eliminated altogether, they can be reduced by following certain steps:

1. Changes in workers should be discussed with clients before cases are transferred.
2. Old and new workers should discuss the status of the case and clarify differences in perceptions regarding various treatment issues.
3. Old and new workers should meet with client(s) to discuss feelings resulting from the transfer, to decide how future contacts will be made, and to make the transfer official.

This is a sensitive response to neglecting parents and their children that explicitly indicates respect for them and sends them a message that they still need to use the agency's services. Treating clients as unfeeling objects, expecting them to relate to numerous workers on an unplanned basis because of transfers, is a complete disregard of a basic principle for effective treatment.

Follow-up

Follow-up, the fourth principle in treatment, has received limited attention in practice, yet its value in the treatment of neglecting families can be significant. Granted that neglecting families have made progress by improving personal functioning and ability to care and provide adequately for their children, for many of them certain aspects of their life are subject to fluctuating environmental stresses and family infrastructure. It could be said that they walk on the edge of a blade and are prone to crises. Unless such crises are handled, the problems become chronic which once again brings them to the attention of protective services.

Follow-up, while the family functions independently from any direct assistance by the worker, seeks to ascertain the ability to meet needs and to solve problems. It also aims to make the clients aware of the workers' and the agency's availability if their personal efforts to solve problems have failed. Follow-up through periodic home visits and/or telephone contacts for certain periods of time subsequent to termination also incorporates the preventive aspect of treatment. Intervention before problems have become chronic is the best route for protective service workers in dealing with this client population.

These principles in treatment coordination, intensity, continuity, and follow-up are pertinent not only with neglecting families but also in treatment with child abuse cases and other situations. However, their application in the treatment of child neglect can make the difference between success and failure. In cases of neglect, the problems often tend to be more complex and chronic. Neglect often impacts simultaneously on more than one person in the family. Neglecting families, in spite of the help they receive, are prone to more crises. Resolution of problems requires the direct intervention of many disciplines and the use of numerous supportive services.

Application of these principles in treatment is contingent upon manageable case loads, availability of resources, and effective supervision.

SUMMARY

Despite the documentation of severe developmental, social, and psychological problems in neglected children, the subject of treatment for such cases is virtually absent from literature on maltreatment. This is paradoxical if it is considered that at least 75 percent of confirmed child maltreatment cases involve neglect rather than abuse. This chapter has suggested some crucial aspects in the treatment of such cases and has analyzed the application of certain principles.

The initial goal of intervention with neglected children is to prevent further maltreatment and victimization, which may be accomplished by strengthening parental functioning, realigning and stabilizing family structure, and intervening wherever possible with environmental stressors that impact negatively on family functioning. The delivery of comprehensive services to neglecting families must precede or accompany any direct social work services provided to the child. Children who suffer neglect are the neglected children of neglected parents. Continuous and coordinated efforts should be made to identify and help these children and their families vigorously, because damage caused by neglect is devastating and can affect youngsters permanently.

REFERENCES

Coulborn-Faller, K., and Ziefert, M.: Causes of child abuse and neglect. In Coulborn-Faller, K. (Ed.): *Social Work With Abused and Neglected Children*. London: Collier Macmillan Publishers, 1981.

Giovannoni, J. M., and Becerra, R. M.: *Defining Child Abuse*. New York: The Free Press, 1979.

Hally, C., Polansky, N. F., and Polansky, N. A.: *Child Neglect: Mobilizing Services*. U.S. Department of Health and Human Services, Office of Human Development Services,

Administration for Children, Youth, and Families, Children's Bureau, National Center on Child Abuse and Neglect, DHHS Publication No. (O4DS) 80-3057, May 1980, pp. 8-12.

Hancock, C.: *Children and Neglect.* U.S. Department of Health, Education and Welfare, Welfare Administration, Bureau of Family Services, Division of Welfare Services, Washington, D.C. 20201, 1963, pp. 4-11.

Kadushin, A.: *Child Welfare Services.* New York: Macmillan Publishing Co., 1980.

Mayhall, P. D., and Eastlack-Norgard, K.: *Child Abuse and Neglect.* New York: John Wiley and Sons, 1983.

Pelton, L.: The social context of child abuse and neglect. In *Child Abuse and Neglect, The Myth of Classlessness.* New York: Human Sciences Press, 1981.

Polansky, N. A., Chalmers, M. A., Brittenwieser, E., and Williams, D.: *Damaged Parents: An Anatomy of Child Neglect.* Chicago: University of Chicago Press, 1981.

CHAPTER 16

TREATMENT OF
CHILD EMOTIONAL MALTREATMENT

Walter J. Junewicz

INTRODUCTION

Protective service social workers, psychiatric clinicians, physicians, teachers and other community professionals have long recognized complex intangibles when intervening in cases of emotional neglect and emotional abuse of children. Cases of physical neglect or abuse can be discerned by observable or detectable injuries, or victimized children may identify the perpetrator, either a parent or caretaker. That is not true in emotional neglect or abuse cases. In such cases, the adults involved frequently are unable to comprehend the effects of harmful parent-child interactions, and the victimized children are often unaware of being mistreated.

Intervening in cases where emotional maltreatment is alleged or known is a complex process. Such intervention requires an extreme level of commitment from communities and an examination of the minimal standards set for parental care. This is necessary, because emotionally maltreated children may suffer permanent psychological or developmental harm if such adverse family interactions become prolonged and patterned.

Jack C. Westman (1979) estimates that 21 percent (13.6 million) of all children in the United States live in "disturbed caretaking units," which he defines as including child neglecting and abusing families; drug-addicted, alcoholic or mentally ill parents; and strained parent-child relationships. In fact, he concludes that when parent-child units affected by parental divorce, separation, bereavement, and unwed teenage parenting (when the biological parent union has been disrupted) are combined with children in disturbed caretaking units, 37 percent of all children (24 million) are at risk for childhood or adult maladaptation. Unquestionably, if a comparable number of children were predisposed to a physical disease such as diabetes, epilepsy, or influenza, the situation would be viewed as a national epidemic.

An emotional aberration in the parent-child relationship (i.e. alienation, rejection, demeaning behavior, emotional deprivation, etc.) frequently precedes serious maladaptive behavior by or physical neglect or abuse of the child. Thus, only to the extent that professionals take concrete steps to intervene promptly and appropriately in such family situations will there be significant decreases in the number of children reported to protection agencies as neglect and abuse victims.

Recognizing the need for professional intervention in family units predisposed to emotional maltreatment of children, this chapter considers: (1) clinical and legal issues involved in a functional definition of emotional neglect and abuse, (2) diagnostic considerations relative to psychologically injurious parenting, (3) professional treatment of family units predisposed to emotional maltreatment, and (4) suggestions for multidisciplinary management of such cases.

FUNCTIONAL DEFINITION OF EMOTIONAL NEGLECT AND ABUSE

Nationally, statutes defining emotional maltreatment of children generally are inadequate. Dorothy Dean (1979) describes the situation well in stating, "Many reporting laws now incorporate designations of emotional abuse or mental suffering but fail to define what they mean" (p. 19). She adds: "Since there is a dearth of case law on emotional abuse, professionals are left in a quandary as to what does constitute emotional abuse and how such reports are viewed by the courts."

Any definition must recognize differences between children's emotional problems per se and those which result from emotional maltreatment. These emotional problems may be caused by various factors, including, but not limited to, parental interaction. On the other hand, emotional maltreatment involves detrimental parental actions (emotional abuse) or omissions (emotional neglect) that adversely affect the children's development of intellectual or interpersonal competencies or result in psychopathology. Such cases arise from parent-child relationships where prolonged and intense dynamics have led to such effects. In considering this issue, Ira S. Lourie and Lorraine Stefano (1977) conclude: "We must examine the severity, duration, balance, and causation of parental behaviors, taking into account the environmental conditions surrounding the family.... Only in this way will we be able to distinguish the invulnerable child, the emotionally ill child, and most importantly the emotionally abused child" (p. 203).

Any definition of emotional maltreatment must consider the issue of parental intent. From a legal standpoint, how culpable for the injurious behavior to the child should the parent or caretaker be? In cases of physical injury, most statutes require a level of intent to be established in determining culpability. Culpability may be established in physical abuse or neglect cases if the physical condition resulted from disciplining the child or from a hostile physical outburst. Unconscious motives may underlie the abusive action. Thus, the parent who intended to discipline by whipping the youngster with an extension cord may be viewed as culpable of physical abuse when this results in loop-shaped skin injuries over the child's body. Similarly, the parent who in anger roughly shakes a colicky, screaming infant, resulting in subdural hematoma and possible retinal injury ("shaken baby" syndrome), may be found legally culpable for abuse.

The causal link between parental acts, or omissions, and the injurious condition of the child is not as direct in cases of emotional maltreatment, however. In such cases, unconscious factors usually contribute to the parental abuse. For example, a mother-daughter relationship may be characterized by the mother's hostile-dependent actions, resulting in the daughter's severe depression and inability to learn. The mother's actions may be unconscious and a replay of her relationships with her own mother. Thorough clinical assessment of the relationship is essential because the mother may or may not be aware of the harmful effects that result. The child may be unaware of being abused. Should insight therapy with the mother be unsuccessful because of denial or minimization of her part in the problem, her behavior may be viewed as emotionally abusive toward the daughter. Thus, in defining emotional maltreatment, parental intent should not be a requisite condition.

State statutes defining emotional maltreatment are vague and inconsistent. Most attempt to establish a cause-and-effect relationship between the child's environment and the potential for psychological damage. Frequently, a catchall designation such as "mental cruelty," "emotional suffering," or the like, permits filing of a court petition for protection of a child. Such designations are inadequate, however, because they fail to define the terminology clearly. One exception appears to be Pennsylvania Act 124 (1975), which includes "serious mental injury" as part of the definition of an "abused child." Regulations issued in 1978 to implement the act define "serious mental injury" as:

> A psychological condition as determined by a psychiatrist, psychologist, or pediatrician apparently caused by acts or omissions of a parent or person responsible for a child (including the refusal of appropriate treatment) which: (1) renders the child chronically and severely anxious, agitated, depressed, socially withdrawn, psychotic, or in reasonable fear that his/her life and/or safety is threatened; (b) makes it extremely likely

that the child will become chronically and severely anxious, agitated, depressed, socially withdrawn, psychotic, or be in reasonable fear that his/her life is threatened; or (c) seriously interferes with the child's ability to accomplish age-appropriate developmental milestones, or school, peer and community tasks. (Commonwealth of Pennsylvania, Department of Public Welfare, Child Protective Services, Social Services Manual, Section 2-23-41, 1976, p. 274).

Such a functional definition appears clinically adequate because it specifies injurious conditions and requires diagnostic confirmations of dysfunction by a psychiatrist, psychologist, or pediatrician. Clinical social workers (as specially designated by the National Association of Social Workers) might be added. It also appears to be an acceptable legal definition. Finally, in making reference to "age-appropriate developmental milestones," it appears to make allowance for parental behaviors that would be identified as abusive for children of some specific ages but not for others.

For purposes of this chapter, "emotional neglect" represents parental omissions in children's care; that is, inability to stimulate the children by provision of nurturance, stability, and security necessary for intellectual, social, or psychological development. "Emotional abuse" represents parental commissions of acts that overly stimulate children and impair intellectual, social, or psychological development resulting in negative self-image or disturbed behavior. Specific examples of emotionally neglectful and abusive behavior toward children are provided in Chapter 5.

DIAGNOSTIC CONSIDERATIONS

Normative vs. Psychologically Harmful Parenting

Emotional neglect and emotional abuse cases represent extreme forms of parental behavior and require thorough and well-documented clinical validations. Between the extremes is a wide range of behaviors that constitute normative parenting. Parents are human beings and thus imperfect, so the normative (satisfactory) range would include clumsy parenting and isolated acts of indiscretions or hostility directed at the children. Many parents suffer guilt feelings equal to the trauma to the child when such indiscretions occur and thus can modify future interaction. Infrequent, isolated verbal outbursts or ignoring the child occasionally certainly do not constitute emotional neglect or abuse.

At the extremes of the range of interactions are parental acts or omissions that are outrageous, chronic, and patterned. At one end of the spectrum is parental care characterized by gross parental apathy or serious understimulation of the child. For example, a psychotically involved parent caring for a toddler might totally withdraw and be unable to meet the most basic emotional needs of the child. At the other extreme is gross overstimulation of the child, such as in a home where chronically alcoholic parents continually argue and physically fight, with the child caught in the middle.

A child's exposure to seeing a parent with teeth knocked out or eyes blackened, or experiencing frequent ambulance calls to the home, can lead to chronic depression and inability to relate to others or to learn at school. The first example represents emotional neglect; the second, emotional abuse. In arriving at a diagnostic conclusion that emotional neglect or abuse is present, workers must be able to cite patterned instances of parental behaviors that result in emotional trauma to the children. The final diagnosis must be based upon clinically confirmed observations and evaluations of the children's emotional condition.

How do protective service workers and other professionals coming into contact with children determine whether the parental behavior is emotionally neglectful or abusive? When should such a situation be made known to the child protection agency under the reporting statute? Several factors need to be evaluated: (1) all available medical and clinical data on the child as they relate to physical growth and psychosocial development; (2) family dynamics that may affect the child; (3) age-related intellectual and social competencies of the child.

If dysfunction exists but is not serious and the parents or caretakers are willing to engage in clinical counseling (and benefit from it), there would hardly seem cause to involve the child protection agency. If a worker regards the dysfunction as serious or the parents are unwilling or unable to seek treatment, then their behavior should be viewed as emotionally neglectful or abusive and must be reported to the child protection agency. Ultimately, juvenile court intervention might be necessary as insurance that treatment commences, is sustained, and is successful.

Practitioners must have some discretionary ability to determine what is reportable and must be able to distinguish emotional disturbance from emotional neglect or abuse, something not always readily apparent. If parents' interaction with the child causes psychological harm because they are acting out scenarios from their own upbringing but refuse (or do not make progress in) treatment, the situation should be viewed as neglectful or abusive and be reported.

Family Types Predisposed to Emotional Maltreatment

Certain vulnerable family units are predisposed to psychologically harmful behavior. Five such family types were identified in the author's (Junewicz,

1983) study of 100 children determined to be emotionally maltreated, using the functional definition of Pennsylvania Act 124. For diagnostic purposes, the families can be classified as those where parent(s) were: (1) suffering from mental illness, (2) abusing drugs and/or alcohol, (3) enmeshed in serious interactional stress, (4) projecting inadequate life adjustments, and/or (5) displacing serious personal conflicts. These types are not mutually exclusive. The chidren came from 66 such families. Protective services and psychiatric treatment were necessary for each child and parent(s).

Type I: Mentally Ill Parents

Mentally ill parents may cause psychological harm to their children. This can occur in different ways. Children may manifest serious learning or relationship problems as a result of living with a chronically depressed, withdrawn parent. An infant or toddler in the care of a mentally ill parent may be deprived of care, nurturance, and stimulation. In an extreme situation, the child might be diagnosed as suffering from "failure to thrive" or "maternal deprivation syndrome." On the other hand, bizarre behaviors of the psychotic parent may cause such a high degree of over-stimulation of the child as to inhibit or preclude the achievement of age-related developmental tasks or competencies.

Type II: Drug and Alcohol-Involved Parents

Children who reside with drug- and alcohol-involved parents may be continually overstimulated, resulting in emotional abuse. In home environments that are highly charged because of parental fights, destruction of property, and frequent police contacts for domestic violence complaints, children become preoccupied with the chaos. They may witness a parent's resultant physical injuries that require medical attention or continual volatile arguments that may result in serious emotional problems. In other cases, children with such parents may be left to fend largely for themselves if the adult(s) becomes totally consumed by the habit.

Either way, the children may manifest problems such as being unable to concentrate and learn, going to school hungry and inappropriately dressed, and fantasizing frequently. When these children relate to someone at school, they frequently will share their distress about what goes on at home with such comments as, "My parents are never home," "Dad is always drunk," or "There are always big parties going on at home." A dangerous by-product of parental substance abuse is the children's exposure to the "drug culture" and contact with a variety of violent and disturbed individuals.

Type III: Interactional Stress Environments

Serious marital conflict usually characterizes home environments where stressful parental interaction results in the children's becoming pawns in the battle. These youngsters become trapped in the middle of parental feuds, separations, and "messy divorces." Parental attempts to insulate the children from these confrontations usually are not successful. Contacts with their extended families are not always helpful to the children, since they may be forced to ally with either parent. Forced to take sides, these children are placed in a double bind—in trying to please one parent they are alienating the other.

These children are continually in emotional turmoil when they witness or hear verbal fights or one parent's physical or sexual assaults on the other. Children in these home environments will share with clinicians the emotional trauma they experience in observing, for example, a mother's black eye(s), broken teeth, or multiple bruises and lacerations. Their symptoms usually range from serious psychosomatic complaints to depressive states, suicide attempts, or psychotic episodes.

Type IV: Inadequate Parental Life Adjustment

Certain kinds of parental life-styles can result in serious emotional or developmental problems for children. Unfortunately, some parents have little philosophy to guide them through day-to-day life, let alone for rearing children. This can result from their own childhood experiences, which may have been characterized by instability at home, school failures, and juvenile delinquency. They lead their lives a day at a time, with no planning. Asceticism is foreign to them, as their lives are marked by impulsivity, self-interest, and self-indulgence.

These home environments are characterized by little job income stability, frequent evictions or moves to avoid them, strings of paramour relationships, and misuse of alcohol and/or drugs. The environments for the children are unstable, inadequate, and overflowing with problems from the parents' own troubled lives. Delsordo (1963) describes these parents' claims to parenthood as little more than biological. Such parents frequently are diagnosed as "character disordered," "borderline personalities," or "inadequate personalities."

Type V: Parental Conflict Displacement

Some parents hoist their own personal problems onto their children. If unchecked, this tendency can seriously impede the youngsters' psychological growth. The parents' problems may stem from childhood or adult life and be well internalized and unconscious. Typical problems that cause parents psychological conflicts and that may be projected onto children include situations where: (1) parents have been forced to marry; (2) a parent has an illegitimate child; (3) the ordinal or adoptive position of a child entering a family is unfortunate in relationship to the ages of the other children or the desires of the parent(s); (4) the parents respond negatively to their own imperfections as perceived in the child(ren); (5) parents' needs conflict with the childrens', causing undue stress on the latter; (6) infantile parents interact pathologically with children, resulting in role reversal.

TREATMENT BY FAMILY UNITS
PREDISPOSED TO EMOTIONAL MALTREATMENT

Professionals and others routinely coming into contact with children are legally mandated to report their suspicions of neglect or abuse to local child protection agencies as is well known. Anyone in the community may report any form of child neglect or abuse. Child protective agencies receive a substantial number of reports from staff at schools, social agencies, hospitals, police departments, and mental health agencies.

Neglect and Abuse Examples

The following cases of emotional neglect or abuse demonstrate some of the kind of family situations reported. The comments following each provide treatment and case management suggestions.

Type I: Mentally Ill Parents

Murray, thirteen years old, was reported to child protective services by his school counselor. He was described as very depressed, failing academically, and frequently a truant. The boy also isolated himself from other students. Psychological testing by the school system head confirmed the degree of his depression. His mother, with whom he resided, had not responded to letters of concern from the school counselor. After two unsuccessful attempts to interview the mother at home, the social worker met Murray at school.

At first, Murray was mildly evasive about his home situation but, when pressed, cried profusely. When asked if he could share the basis of his upset he responded, "You'll see." He asked the social worker to accompany him home and enroute shared the following information: His parents were divorced, his father's whereabouts was unknown, and a younger sister was in a foster home in another city. Murray and the social worker entered the apartment which was dark, with drapes shut, but reasonably clean and in order. No bulbs in lamps operated. A note, written on a napkin taped to the refrigerator, instructed Murray to prepare a meal.

When Murray roused his mother from bed, she appeared depressed, sedated, and secretive about family circumstances. Despite acknowledging "nerve problems," the mother did not keep a semicommitment to work with the agency over the next month. When interviewed later at school, Murray revealed concern and upset about his mother and men callers coming at strange hours. Through information obtained from Murray and from the agency workers where his sister was in foster care, it was determined that Murray's mother was a highly paid prostitute connected with a ring from which she was unable to free herself.

The agency recommended that Murray be removed from her care by the juvenile court because he was so seriously affected. He concurred with removal. The mother's lawyer raised mild opposition, but Murray's removal was upheld by the court. The mother made several attempts to see a psychiatrist, who diagnosed her as having "severe depression." Several years later, after she had moved again, she barricaded her door, doused herself with gasoline, and set herself on fire.

In this case, referral to child protective services was appropriate. Murray's teacher first detected that he was failing academically, was a truant, and appeared depressed. The teacher recorded her observations factually and corroborated them with the school counselor. Psychological testing validated their observations and concerns. Further concern about Murray's home conditions was raised by his mother's lack of response to letters from the counselor. The authority inherent in the child protective worker's role was necessary to intervene in this situation and ultimately bring the matter to the juvenile court.

Careful and thorough case assessment was provided and individual treatment initiated and sustained. Murray's introspective adolescent growth period required that he be in a stable, caring home environment. Unfortunately, his mother's situation precluded her meeting Murray's developmental needs. After his removal and placement with a stable foster family, life improved considerably as did his school work. This was a case of serious emotional neglect.

Type II: Drug- and Alcohol-Involved Parent(s)

This case involves emotional abuse by alcoholic parents. Child protection workers are accustomed to the unorthodox and receipt of referral from practically any source. In this case, Scott caddied for a lawyer at a country club, who reported his family to child protective services.

> Scott, fifteen years old, was a caddie at a country club where he usually carried the bag of a prestigious attorney. On several occasions, Scott's father came to the country club in a highly intoxicated state and demanded money from the boy. Resulting physical and verbal skirmishes between father and son took place in the locker room. In one such instance, the attorney intervened in Scott's behalf and was physically assaulted by the father. Afterward, Scott revealed his chaotic home situation to the attorney, who in turn reported the family to child protective services.
>
> Scott indicated to the agency social worker that his parents drank heavily and that he and his three younger siblings (ages 9, 7, and 18 months) were subjected to their daily verbal and physical confrontations. He was fearful for the younger children's safety and well-being and depressed about his parents' demeaning behavior toward him. The school psychologist indicated that, although Scott's intelligence was above average, he was being seriously affected by his home life as evidenced by his failing grades, manipulative behavior toward school personnel, and a poor self-image.
>
> After being assigned the case, the child protective social worker proceeded, without appointment, to the run-down motel where the family was living. The worker found both parents very intoxicated. They said the children were with the grandparents for the day and attempted to convince the worker of their respectability in the community by name-dropping and bragging about the family business. The worker, unconvinced that the children would be safe in staying with the parents, arranged to keep them temporarily with the grandparents.
>
> Counseling was attempted over the next month while the worker tracked the parents from one shabby motel to another. The worker continually appealed to them to look at how their personal problems were contributing to a chaotic home environment for the children. During sessions the parents alternated between self-pity and anger and made little progress on their problems.
>
> Eventually, the matter was brought before the juvenile court. Testimony by relatives, police, and school personnel documented the parents' misuse of alcohol and the highly charged, unsafe environment characterized by arguments, physical fights, and evictions. The children eventually were placed in foster homes when the aging grandparents could not continue to care for them.

It is important to intervene early in any case of emotional maltreatment for maximum effectiveness. Scott had been affected by living with alcoholic parents for several years. It was important that the lawyer reached out to Scott when it was suspected that the youth was being affected by events at home. This expression of personal concern enabled Scott to reveal some of the family chaos, which then was substantiated by the child protective worker. Careful diagnostic testing validated that the youth was severely affected by arbitrary or inconsistent discipline by his parents, exposure to their verbal and physical fights, and assumption of a parenting role for his younger siblings.

This was too much for him to endure and thus his personality and academic work suffered. He also began to exhibit some of the manipulative qualities typical of his alcoholic parents in relationships with others. As his personal needs were met more substantially in a group foster home along with individual therapy, his life situation improved. He also was greatly relieved because his siblings were safe and cared for out of the home. The parents made half-hearted attempts at participation in alcohol counseling. This was unsuccessful and a permanent adoptive home was found for the youngest child. A plan of foster care, with support by grandparents and Scott, was continued for the other children.

Type III: Interactional Stress Environment

Barry's case was reported by the principal of a school for emotionally disturbed children. After Barry's admission to the school, the school social worker and principal had increasing concern about how serious his parental feuds were affecting him. As they met with Barry and his father for counseling, the boy's enmeshment in the parents' pathological relationship became evident. Periodic contacts with the mother further confirmed suspicions of emotional abuse.

Barry, age nine, was the only child of parents who had been divorced for six months. The marriage had been extremely poor, and Barry was continually caught in the cross-fire of parental disputes. His mother had frequently entered the battered women's shelter after being beaten and injured by his father. Barry's legal custody had been awarded to his father following a bitter court proceeding. During the adversarial period, Barry was exposed to the parents' charges and counter-charges. Afterward, the verbal skirmishes continued when the father dropped Barry off at the mother's home for visits.

The principal of a private day school for emotionally disturbed children reported Barry's abuse to child protective services shortly after the boy was transferred to that setting. He had been expelled from a regular school because of his preoccupation with the family situation. In the regular school, Barry frequently was seen fantasizing in the classroom, exhibiting rocking behavior, was unable to concentrate, and had difficulty relating to other students. Later, during a brief period when the parents were able to acknowledge some part in contributing to his problems, Barry was placed in a foster home.

Eventually, the parents sabotaged the placement. The father later absconded with him to a distant city, where the child protective agency had to intervene at the father's request. The father's guilt over the boy's condition and his observations that Barry's emotional problems were increasing made him conclude that he no longer could subject his son to such instability and that intense psychiatric treatment was necessary. The mother could not resume his care, and Barry was admitted to a residential treatment facility for emotionally disturbed children.

Barry's enmeshment in the marital conflict was long-standing. The parents continued fighting despite their divorce. The boy's exposure to the separations, divorce, custody battle, accompanying parental pressure on him to take sides and overstimulation was more than he could manage. The child protective worker tried to induce the parents to see beyond their problems with each other for Barry's benefit. Unfortunately, although they loved their son very much, they were too preoccupied with their fighting to provide stable parenting.

Type IV: Inadequate Parental Life Adjustment

The Clark family represents a case of emotional neglect caused largely by the overflow of problems from parental life-styles.

Mr. and Mrs. Clark and their three children, ages four, eight, and ten, were reported to child protective services by the youngsters' school principal. A month earlier, the family had moved into an old, neglected farmhouse within the boundaries of a progressive suburban school district. It was alleged that the school-age children were delayed in speech development, immature, functioning below grade level, and ridiculed by other students because "they smelled like cats."

Upon attempting to meet with the parents, a home and school visitor were ordered off the property by Mr. Clark. On the next visit, the protective service worker maneuvered through several parked junk cars to the door, where he was greeted by a rather sheepish Mrs. Clark. Upon stepping into the home and being overwhelmed by combined odors of cats and beer, the worker asked to conduct the interview outside.

Mrs. Clark was more capable of reciting the histories of her cats than of individualizing her children. Further interviews revealed a grossly understimulating environment for the children, who were largely left to fend for themselves. Testing by a school psychologist affirmed their lack of parental nurturance and stimulation.

The Clarks had moved from a rural area in a nearby state to their new house to avoid eviction. In fact, they had moved three times in five years for similar reasons, causing frequent changes of schools for the children. Mrs. Clark had not had stable parenting and had resided in a foster home periodically as a child. Mr. Clark stopped going to school when he was fifteen, was frequently before the juvenile court for truancy and unruliness, and could not hold jobs for any length of time. He had lost his last two jobs because of quarrels with his boss.

Mr. Clark, or "Sudsy" as his friends called him, was very "testy" with the worker. Only threats of court action impressed Mr. Clark that the worker viewed the home environment as detrimental to the children. While only minimal gains were made in moderating his carousing with drinking buddies, the persistence of the worker, combined with the services of a caring homemaker, enabled Mrs. Clark to pay more attention to the home and children.

The Clark case was an appropriate referral to child protective services. The children were very noticeable at school because of their developmental and educational delays. As noted, their offensive odor resulted in ridicule by other students, raising suspicions about their care at home. It is important that lines of communication between school and other professionals and child protective services be established to detect such children, followed by referral to assess the etiology of the problems.

If any maltreatment is present, early reporting is the best insurance that the children will be protected. Parental cooperation should be sought in resolving maltreatment problem areas before court removal of children is initiated. When cooperation is not forthcoming, a court order requiring parents to participate in a protective service treatment plan, along with periodic court review, often will elicit better cooperation.

Type V: Parental Conflict Displacement

The Brady case is an example of serious emotional abuse resulting in a medical diagnosis of "psychosocial dwarf." The situation developed when Brady's adoptive position unfortunately resulted in the family's totally neglecting him.

Brady had been adopted as an infant. The adoptive family, having five natural children, all girls, wanted a boy. Shortly after the adoption was completed, the adoptive mother conceived and bore a son. Brady was quickly forgotten and rejected by both parents and their natural children. Eventually, the family was referred to a child protective agency by medical personnel because Brady was not growing.

There was no organic reason for this condition. An endocrinologist had diagnosed him as a "psychosocial dwarf." Evaluation of the family dynamics revealed that the entire group rejected Brady, who was then age four. Brady engaged in feces smearing, fire setting, and other antisocial behavior. Family treatment was attempted but proved unsuccessful. Parental rights to Brady were legally terminated after incidents in which siblings stashed him in a clothes dryer and neighborhood children attempted to hang him in the family garage.

This case represents emotional abuse in one of its most serious forms. It resulted in Brady's being affected psychologically as well as physically. Again, the need for comprehensive diagnostic evaluation as a step toward a solution is well demonstrated in this case.

Close coordination and collaboration among social workers and others on cases involving emotionally maltreated children is imperative. If there is concern that the home environment may be affecting the child's performance or development, the observations, impressions, and conclusions of various persons in touch with the youngster should be brought together and become the basis for any treatment.

The following suggestions should help protective service workers in handling of emotional maltreatment cases. The workers should:

- Observe and document, in writing, the behavior and actions that suggest that the child is living in a stressful home environment. Keep dates and times of specific incidents that cause concern. Look for patterns. Keep documentation as objective as possible, minimizing interpretive statements.
- Consult with other professionals in touch with the family as to the validity of diagnostic interpretations and conclusions.
- Set up lines of communication with physicians, public health nurses, police, and other community professionals who are involved in such cases.
- Handle the parents' possible resistance tactfully at the earliest time possible and evoke the authority of the court if resistance persists.
- Present to the court, if a case follows that route, documented evidence of all diagnostic findings.
- Persist and insist that the parents be involved in treatment, even if they already have made changes, until the changes are well demonstrated in their behaviors and actions.

Child protective workers need to provide the same quality of treatment to children reported for emotional maltreatment as for cases of physical or sexual abuse and neglect. Frequently, referral to other community services for family counseling or therapy is necessary to augment the protective services being provided.

However, continuing professional collaboration is necessary to establish whether family members are participating and making progress in treatment. If they are unwilling or unable to work toward resolution of family problems, then court intervention may be necessary. This action would be contingent upon documentation that the child is emotionally maltreated and that the parents are failing to meet treatment needs.

Protective service court orders outline parent and child treatment needs and require future court review to determine progress or lack of it. For the court, such an approach helps to establish the agency's attempt to do everything possible before considering removal of children from the home. Child protective workers must be reasonably certain that additional emotional trauma will not be caused by removal to a substitute environment when a move is necessary. Children differ a great deal in the way they react to separation. Thus, workers need to look closely at the overall effect of separation on children when considering removal.

Pediatricians and mental health professionals, like psychiatrists, psychologists, and social workers, can assist in distinguishing between emotional maltreatment and emotional disturbance in children since the symptoms often are virtually the same. Mental health practitioners can treat the more serious cases and offer the time and consistency protective services workers cannot provide. On the other hand, a mental health setting is better prepared to offer the therapy the parents and the child(ren) may need.

SUMMARY

This chapter recognizes the complexities for protective service professionals in dealing with emotional maltreatment of children. Identification of such cases is difficult since parents or caretakers frequently are unable to comprehend the effects of harmful parent-child interactions and the victimized children are unaware of being abused. Vague statutory definitions of emotional maltreatment add to the difficulty.

Thus, a definition of emotional maltreatment requiring diagnostic confirmations of dysfunction by a psychiatrist, psychologist, pediatrician, or clinical social worker was suggested. The functional definition suggested also would require that a cause-and-effect relationship be established (legally, if necessary) between parental actions or inactions and a child's adverse intellectual development, delayed development of interpersonal competencies, or resultant psychopathology.

Parental intent ought not be a requisite condition in any definition of emotional neglect or abuse because unconscious factors often have bearing on the parental acts. Normative and psychologically harmful parenting has been discussed. Five diagnostic family units predisposed toward psychologically injurious behaviors involve those where the parent(s) were: (1) suffering from mental illness, (2) abusing drugs and/or alcohol, (3) enmeshed in serious interactional stress, (4) projecting inadequate life adjustments, and (5) displacing serious personal conflicts. Suggestions to practitioners involved in treatment and management of emotional maltreatment cases include: (1) observation and written documentation of the behaviors that suggest that the child is living in a stressful home environment and (2) case-specific collaboration with other professionals.

The pediatrician's and/or the medical profession's contribution to the treatment of such cases is crucial for diagnostic purposes. Emotionally maltreated children may develop all kinds of somatic disturbances and the pediatrician often is the one whose advice is sought.

In summary, the success of treatment interventions depends on the cooperation of various disciplines. It also depends on the ability of the protective agency to effectively coordinate the services offered to the child and the family.

REFERENCES

American Humane Association, Children's Division. Unpublished. Cited in *Social Work and the Law*, Brieland, D., and J. Lemon, (Eds.). St. Paul, MN: West Publishing Co. 1977.

Commonwealth of Pennsylvania, Department of Public Welfare, Child Protective Services: *Social Services Manual*, 2-23-41, April 3, 1978.

Dean, D.: Emotional abuse of children. *Children Today*, 8(4):18-20, 1979.

Delsardo, J.: Protective casework for abused children. *Children*, 213-18, November/December, 1963.

Junewicz, W. F.: A protective posture toward emotional neglect and abuse. *Child Welfare*, 62(3): 243-52, 1983.

Kempe, R., Cutler, C., and Dean, J.: The infant with failure to thrive. In *The Battered Child* edited by H. Kempe and Ray E. Helfer. Chicago: University of Chicago Press, 1980.

Lourie, Ira S., and Stefano, L.: On Defining Emotional Abuse: Results of NIMH/NCCAN Workshop. *Proceedings of the Second National Conference on Child Abuse and Neglect*. DHEW Publication No. (OHDS) 78-30147, 11, 201-8, 1977.

Lynch, M.A., and Roberts, J.: *Consequences of Child Abuse*. New York: Academic Press, 1982.

Pennsylvania Act 124: *Child Protective Services Law*, 1975.

Powell, G.F., Brasel, J.A., and Blizzard, R.M.: Emotional deprivation and growth retardation simulating idiopathic hypopituitarism. *The New England Journal of Medicine*, 276(23): 1271-78, 1967.

Schmitt, B.D.: *The Child Protection Team Handbook.* New York: Garland STMP Press, 1978.

Silver, H.K., and Finklestein, M.: Deprivation dwarfism. *The Journal of Pediatrics, 70*(3): 317-24, 1967.

Westman, J.C.: *Child Advocacy.* New York: The Free Press, 1979.

Whiting, L.: Emotional Neglect of Children. *Proceedings of the Second National Conference on Child Abuse and Neglect.* DHEW Publication No. (OHDS) 78-30147, *1,* 209-13, 1977.

CHAPTER 17

TREATMENT OF CHILD SEXUAL ABUSE

Mojie A. Burgoyne

The literature on the treatment of sexual abuse of children is not extensive and is conflicting. Since the topic of incest has become a public issue only within the past ten years, the experiences of the child welfare workers, juvenile authorities and treatment persons have not been organized into one body of knowledge. Everyone within the field of sexual child abuse is really an innovator since no one is sure which treatment methods are really effective. Since there is very little clinical evidence regarding to what degree of damage the incest, sexual exploitation, child rape or sibling incest has created in the child, many workers have concentrated on the legal aspect of the problem and discounted that some of the long-term problems found in adults are the results of their betrayals by parents who were unable to provide the protection they needed as children. To view the problem with the clarity and with the reality that the child and the family needs, the worker making the interventions into the family will need to proceed with the belief that anyone who has been coerced into participating in something that violates personal boundaries has some degree of trauma and that he or she needs to be provided with the opportunity to express this pain.

There has been little documentation regarding the effectiveness of different clinical intervention. Treatment has ranged from psychoanalytic technique of dealing with repressed material to environmental manipulation by removing the child from the home. However, there seems to be no systematic effort to evaluate the degree of usefulness of the different therapeutic interventions (Weitzel, Powell, and Penick, 1978). Walters (1975) accuses the majority of the treatment programs of focusing on the pathology of the individuals instead of the relationship problems which he views as the major area of intervention. He thinks that the treatment efforts have been uncoordinated, based on an analytical model and done by osmosis, since no one talks about the sexual atmosphere or the impoverished relationships. He attempts to design a more coordinated approach to the intervention into sexual abuse cases for the child welfare workers, juvenile authorities and the therapist. Suzanne Sgroi (1982), Jeannie Fried (1977), Alexander Zaphiris (1983), Henry Giarretto (1976) and Blair and Rita Justice (1979) have, also, presented models of intervention for incest which take into consideration the family as a system within a system. These models approach the problem with understanding and caring for all of the individuals involved in the incestuous relationship.

Preparation for the Role of the Professional

Working with sexual abuse of children involves a number of specific skills, knowledge and attitudinal changes which are essential if the worker is to be effective with these clients (Zaphiris, 1983). These unique areas which the worker needs to explore are:

1. understanding personal sexuality issues
2. understanding personal feelings regarding people who sexually molest children
3. understanding personal prejudices or myths regarding these people
4. understanding transference and counter-transference issues as they relate to sexually abused children and perpetrators.

Any worker who is unaware of these issues may inflict more harm to the children than helping them (Blumberg, 1978). The intervention or treatment plan can then become more detrimental to the children than the incest itself (Weitzel, Powell, and Penick, 1978). Of course, it is not always possible to work out all of these issues prior to working with this clientele; so a good supervisor or a good worker who has dealt with these issues himself is invaluable to the worker embarking on this area of specialty. Sometimes, even though the agency supervisor is competent, the worker may need to obtain special intensive training from an expert outside of the agency. This provides a more objective viewpoint of the issues which the worker needs to face in himself when working with those involved with sexual abuse.

Sexuality Issues

Understanding personal sexuality needs is of utmost importance to protect the clients and the worker. The sexual identity of the worker needs to be intact and clear within himself. Many female and male survivors* of sexual abuse are confused regarding their sexual identity and need strong role models to emulate so that this issue can begin to become resolved

---

*The term "survivor" will be used instead of "victim" to prevent further victimization.

within themselves. Homosexuality becomes a concern for male children who are sexually abused by their fathers (Justice and Justice, 19,79), for male children who are sexually abused by their mothers (Forward and Buck, 1978), and for female children who have been sexually violated by their fathers (Tessman, Kaufman, 1969). The following example illustrates these points:

> Tammy was three years old when her father began to visit her bed at night. He continued the incest until she left home at eighteen. He would cover her mouth with his hand and sometimes a pillow to prevent her crying out. Her mother physically abused her during the day and denied that Tammy was being sexually violated. At age fourteen she began to have a sexual relationship with a girl friend. Although she married and had a child, she still struggles with her feelings of homosexuality, having sporadic sexual contact with females. This problem was compounded when her female worker began to touch her in a sexual manner. This sexual contact from the worker triggered her old feelings of suicide, and when the worker dismissed her from therapy it became a re-enactment of what had occurred in her home with her father molesting her and her mother rejecting her. The worker who was providing the treatment apparently was having difficulty with her own sexuality issues and this was projected on to the client causing the client to become even more confused.

This is only one case history of one client who has been molested during the treatment process, but it happens more than workers would like to think. Without a clear understanding of where the worker is with his own sexuality, this boundary can be easily crossed. When a worker is unable to discriminate between his role as a professional with the responsibility of protecting the client and his personal sexual role, then the client is in danger of being molested again. The clients need a worker who is comfortable with his own sexuality (Fried, 1977).

Some of the sexual acts which are reported may, also, shock the worker who has strong beliefs regarding what form sex should take between any two people. The following case exemplifies this point:

> Two sisters who were sexually involved simultaneously with their father were encouraged to have sexual contact with the family dog. The worker who handled these two cases had been sensitized to the different sexual habits of people but became angry when told that these children had to suffer this kind of humiliation. He had to be careful so as not to increase the children's guilt regarding these sexual acts and realized that he would need to work on his feelings of anger for the father prior to seeing him. Because the worker was able to resolve his feelings of anger towards the father, the case went smoothly and the family was able to be functional again.

If the worker is uncomfortable discussing sex and sexual issues, the clients will sense this discomfort and this increases the guilt and shame they already feel. The Justices (1979) believe that to be an effective worker who intervenes with these families, one needs to have dealt with his feelings about the "unthinkable" act of incest. The worker needs to be able to distinguish between what is considered to be a normal affectionate parent-child relationship and what is considered to be a sexually abusive relationship so that he is able to evaluate accurately. He needs to be comfortable using the language of sexuality and aware of his own personal values position as it relates to the wide range of the expression of human sexuality (Fried, 1977).

Feeling Issues

Giarretto (1976) points out that man has an unconscious dread of incest and reacts with sometimes volatile, unpredictable emotions such as repugnance, uneasy fascination, fear, guilt and anger when faced with the reality of incest. The worker may use the feelings of anxiety and denial to overlook or avoid seeing the incest in the family. These feelings are normal and if the worker experiences these emotions he should not feel uneasy about his reaction, though he needs to use the feelings as a clue that he needs further work to resolve them. The uneasy feelings can impede the making of an adequate treatment plan for the child and for the adults. The worker usually projects his feelings onto the male perpetrator, and the legal system and the agencies who have been given the authority to investigate sexual abuse may panic and push for criminal prosecution. If the worker allows his emotions to dictate the treatment plan, then he may be unable to make the kinds of decisions that he needs to make to be an effective helper. The worker may press for nontherapeutic resolutions if he is unable to find clarity regarding his feelings. He may encourage the perpetrator to forsake alcohol, even though he is not an alcoholic, move to a new place, change employment, change spouses, change sleeping arrangements, start life and marriage anew, or find religion (Walters, 1975). Although there are times when a child must be removed for his or her safety, this action is many times based on the worker's feelings regarding incest and not what would be in the best interest of the child.

Prejudice, Taboo or Myth Issues

The sexual abuse of children is laden with personal and public myths, taboos or prejudices which influence the attitudes of the worker. Workers, as well as the public, generally believe that anyone who sexually abuses a child is mentally ill. On the contrary, the Justices estimate that "no more than 15 to 20 percent of all the fathers who commit incest are psychopathic, pedophilic, psychotic personalities or they have been reared where incest is practiced as a part of the culture" (Justice and Justice, 1979, p. 62). Many workers think that sexual abuse is difficult to treat and so pursue the legal aspect to remedy the problem. Forward (1978) states that the father who commits incest is the most misunderstood sex criminal in our society and the easiest to rehabilitate. She describes him as usually a law-abiding, hard-working guy next door who has lost his ability to control his impulses.

Another myth seems to be that there is little or no physical abuse in the incestuous family. These are families who have very little impulse control and use this impulsive behavior, such as aggression, sexual acting out or chemical misuse, as a primary method in an attempt to discharge the tension (Tessman and Kaufman, 1969). The worker needs to be clear regarding his understanding of physical abuse and listen carefully to the client's description of the abuse. It is these few myths and prejudices that have been mentioned and many others that need to be investigated by the worker is he is going to avoid allowing his own values and judgments to impend upon the initial investigation assessment and treatment process. The worker will need to avoid overgeneralizing regarding incestuous families and approach each family with an open mind so that he can make a clear assessment without blame. The assessment of who is to blame is as dysfunctional as the incestuous family.

Transference and Counter-Transference Issues

Transference and counter-transference will be easier to handle if the worker looks at his own attitudes on sexuality, violence, feelings and myths that surround sexual abuse. Transference is defined as the state of mind, ideas and feelings that the client has had with previous figures in his life and displaces onto the worker (Yalom, 1975). In counter-transference the worker does the same but in reverse with the client. Transference distortions occur early in the initial investigative assessment and treatment process and the worker is viewed in the extremes by the client, that is, either as the all-caring parent or as the all-punitive parent. The client may become very hostile if the worker is not extremely careful in his use of his verbal or body language in presenting the problem of sexual abuse. These are people who have become very adept in reading nonverbal messages as a survival mechanism, and it will not matter in the least that the client has distorted what the worker meant to say, because the client understood the nonverbal message clearly. This can result in the family not participating in the initial investigative assessment and leaving the treatment process prematurely. If the child or the wife begins to sense that the worker is interested in separating the family, then they may withdraw from cooperating with the worker. The worker needs to be able to tolerate misperceptions, denial and strong feelings which are expressed by the clients (Fried,

1977). Racher (1968) believes that to understand the client's transference, the worker needs to be aware of his own counter-transference. Without a clear understanding by the worker of his feelings on sexual abuse, violence, power and control issues, the worker will quickly become ineffective. These are people who can trigger feelings of inadequacy, anger and discouragement in the worker who is unaware of his own counter-transference issues. The worker may begin to blame or scapegoat the clients; this is typically called "burnout." The following is an example to illustrate this point:

> One female worker who was assigned to work with a male who had been involved in sexual abuse came to the supervisor and asked to have the case transferred to someone else. The worker was willing to investigate her own revulsion of this man. She revealed that she had been involved in violence and thought that this man may violate her. She was dealing with her own issues of sexual abuse, violence, power, control, protection and counter-transference issues. As she worked through her own feelings of fright, she realized that she was in control of the sessions and she began to feel protected and became very effective with the client.

To specifically deal with some of the transference and counter-transference issues, the worker needs to obtain adequate supervision, concentrating on the areas which are the most difficult for him. Also, the use of personal disclosure can be used to clarify the transference and counter-transference issues. This also facilitates the development of trust. The disclosures need to have purpose, to be discreet and to be completed with a sense of timing. And the disclosures serve as a model for the client's expected group behavior and allow the client to test the reality of his view of the worker (Yalom, 1975). Many workers do not feel comfortable in doing this and manage to keep themselves aloof from the clients. This is not a posture which works well with these families. The personal disclosures aid in the development of trust in three ways: (1) trust of self, (2) trust of self's perception of others, and (3) trust of others. As the trust is built, the transference issues in the client are not as distorted.

Treatment Processes

Giarretto suggests that the following needs to be part of the treatment process:

1. individual counseling for the child, mother, and father
2. mother-daughter counseling
3. marital counseling, which is the key if the marriage is to be reintegrated

4. father-daughter counseling
5. family counseling
6. group counseling

Giarretto (1976) believes that rebuilding the mother-daughter relationship can be used as the core for rebuilding the family. Walters views the problem as one in which all relationships in the family, and particularly between parent and child, need to be restructured. Fried (1977), Zaphiris (1983) and the Justices (1979) also present effective treatment models which all take a humanistic view of the incestuous family. Zaphiris divides the treatment stages into (1) the *beginning phase* when individual therapy occurs, (2) the *middle phase* when the dyadic therapy takes place, and (3) the *terminating phase* when the entire family is seen. Sgroi (1982) suggests that there are three treatment phases: (1) crisis intervention which provides total life support for the family, (2) short-term which occurs if the perpetrator is not a family member, and (3) long-term which is for those who have suffered severe damage. Therefore, treatment with incest clients will need to use several modalities to accomplish the healing dynamics which need to take place in the family.

Initial Assessment

Although the primary purpose of the initial assessment is to gather the facts to determine if incest is occurring, it sets the stage for the treatment processes. Actually, the initial assessment is the first step in the treatment process. Interviewing for facts can be traumatic or therapeutic; and since the family will be in a crisis state which will include real panic over the loss of their world, the less trauma that is inflicted, the better. The worker's goal in this stage is to motivate the client to face the crisis, to accept the assistance from the worker, and to insure that the child is not molested again. The latter is fairly easy to accomplish (Walters, 1975) if the questions are asked casually and not as if the worker was giving the "third degree" to a criminal. The initial contact with a worker can mean the future success or failure of the therapeutic interventions. If the clients view the investigative assessment worker as judgmental and accusative, they will be more reluctant to follow through with the treatment plan. If the worker is empathetic, firm and limit setting, the clients may be more motivated to follow through with a difficult and long treatment process.

Individual Modality

After the initial investigative assessment, the individual modality of therapy begins with the clarity of goals and contracts between the worker and the client. Each family member in treatment will need to know that he is safe and can enter treatment with an understanding that the treatment process will help decrease the pain, the anger and the emotional struggle. The contract will need to include specifics such as protection of the child, alleviation of stress, and what the clients can expect of the worker's time. This modality is a most important step in providing each member of the family with an ally with whom each can begin to develop the trust which has been lost. Walters (1975) suggests that at least two workers be used: one for the adults and another for the children. This may not always be possible, since there are few workers who are trained to do this type of work or the private practitioner who is in individual practice may not have access to other workers where this would be practical to the family. The team concept can be obtained if the worker will obtain outside expert consultation on the case. Sometimes it is very enlightening for the worker to work with every member of the family. The worker certainly receives a more balanced view of the case and is not as likely to become "child centered" or "parent centered." Everyone in the family has experienced pain and betrayal and feels nontrusting of each other and the world. At this stage of treatment, it will be necessary to establish a positive transference with each individual before they will be ready to negotiate anything together. A confidentiality contract with each person needs to be established, and this is not to be viewed as keeping secrets but will serve two therapeutic purposes. This begins to break the symbiosis of the family and provide new boundaries for each member. The family begins to experience some really healthy privacy, instead of a cloak of dark secrecy. The second purpose is to allow each family member to know that there is at least one person in their life that will never betray them. When the confidentiality contract is broken by the family by telling secrets, this should be viewed as an attempt on their part to re-establish the unhealthy symbiosis and this needs to be confronted immediately. The client has the opportunity during the individual stage of therapy to begin to trust that he is not abandoned, no matter what his past or present behavior. Moving the client too quickly into the other forms of therapy may stimulate too much anxiety and stress which may trigger some regressive behaviors as a means of coping with the feelings. The individual's needs take priority and should be attended to prior to implementing any other form of therapy, since the family has built a wall against outsiders (Slager-Jorne, 1978).

The individual modality of treatment for the child has the purpose to reassure her that she will be provided immediate and continuous support. The goals in this mode of treatment for the father is to aid him to overcome his resistance, denial, manipulation and his anger regarding being reported. The goals for the mother are to assist her to regain her roles and responsibilities as a woman, mother and spouse. For everyone the other goals are to regain self-esteem and personal growth and to improve intrapersonal and interpersonal functioning (Zaphiris, 1983).

Fried is very specific regarding which areas need to be focused on during the individual therapy with the father and mother. For the father, she suggests that the focus be on:

1. his perceptions of his sexuality
2. his feelings regarding intimacy
3. his male identity
4. how he receives sensous enjoyment
5. how he gives and receives affection
6. issues related to femininity
7. how to obtain his effective and sensual needs without these being sexualized
8. how to communicate his needs and wishes to his spouse
9. expression of his feelings of revenge, disappointment, and anger toward his wife
10. if alcohol is a problem, then how it is related to his sexual estrangement from his wife
11. how he used it to manage his guilt
12. how it was used as a disinhibiter

For the mother, Fried (1977) suggests that during the individual sessions the specific areas which will be addressed are the following:

1. denial of the incest
2. her relationship with her own mother
3. her relationship with her daughter
4. her perception of her own sexuality, including intimacy, affection, sensuality and identity
5. her feelings about sexual expression with her husband
6. her effect on the family's communication patterns
7. her understanding of her roles as a wife and mother

Depression is a major focus for the father, mother and child during this modality (Cormier, Kennedy, and Sangowicz, 1962). This will, also, be a major focus of treatment during the individual modality.

Group Modality

The group modality of therapy is a joint venture between the client and the worker. More than just an exchange of information occurs in group; the worker needs to express the respect he/she has for the client's judgment and intelligence (Balgopal and Vassil, 1983). The Justices (1979) recommend the use of group therapy and don't see the children until the parents have made some changes in group, since it is the parents who need to set up a new system of functioning in the family. This allows the parents to begin to function as the therapist for the child and strengthen their ability of parenting and renews their belief in themselves. Group will, also, provide the clients with a feeling of community and that they are not alone in this problem. Group begins to intervene into the feelings of social and emotional isolation. The group modality allows the clients to begin to break the fears of sharing their feelings of shame and guilt (Slager-Jorne, 1978).

The Justices use the group modality to confront the issues which many other therapists deal with in individual therapy. Their belief is that families can change without every member participating in therapy. The typical problems which they work on with the parents in group include symbiosis, marital relationship, stress reduction, sexual climate, isolationism and alcoholism (1979). These groups have both parents in them. In contrast, Fried (1977) suggests group therapy for fathers only as one of the most effective methods in working with the men. The goals for the fathers in the group are: (1) to strengthen a positive self-image, (2) reinforcement of the behaviors that are consistent with the paternal role, (3) the acceptance of the responsibility for the incest, and (4) to expand his world to show him that other men are working on similar problems and that they are able to change their behaviors.

For the mothers, Fried suggests that they will benefit from a woman's group where their goals will be: (1) to deal with the reality of the incest behavior, (2) to accept that she played a part in accommodating the incest, (3) to understand that she has self-worth and worth as a woman, (4) to assist her in taking her responsibility for the incest, and (5) to reestablish a caring relationship with her family. Sgroi (1982) suggests that group therapy is most effective for working on the child's self-esteem and building trust again.

Marital Modality

The marital modality of therapy is important if the two adults are ever to begin to trust each other again. This is a time for the couple to explore their marital sexual history and what happened to this part of their marriage. The deep anger and resentment which both feel toward each other for the emotional abandonment can be touched on without so much bitterness and accusation if this has been explored adequately in the individual phase of treatment. Walters (1975) states that the sexual abuse of a child by a father is the ultimate act of anger toward the wife. This is, also, the time to work on the unhealthy symbiosis; both have been extremely dependent on the other and have stayed together because of these unhealthy needs. When the clients begin to recognize their anger and dependency, many decide to separate or divorce. The goal here is not to maintain a family unit at all cost but to develop two healthy individuals who can make the decision about whether or not they need to stay in the relationship. Unless these basic problems in the marriage are faced and resolved, the occurrence of incest in this marriage or another marriage is likely.

Dyadic Modality

The phase of treatment with the mother-daughter dyad and the father-daughter dyad have common goals (Zaphiris, 1983). One is to insure the child that she will be protected by both parents and the other is to relieve the guilt that the child feels for the incest. Both parents, not just the father, need to take the responsibility for allowing this to happen to the child. The adults need to assure the child that they will become responsible as parents and allow her to be the child again. She needs to have separate sessions with each of her parents because the dynamics have involved all three individuals cooperating to create the incest. This can only occur after the parents have had many long hours of individual therapy to assist them in growing up again because they really have not been functioning as adults. For the parents to take this burden off the child will be freeing for her.

> One teenager who felt this burden was finally relieved after several sessions with her parents. She felt relieved to finally understand that she was a human with human limits. She finally realized that she was no longer responsible for what happened in her family. She said "I have room for errors; I have a grace space. For the first time I am allowing myself to make mistakes and I have a feeling of relief; I have a feeling of peace."

It is this phase of therapy that is the key for releasing the child from the guilt and blame. This can only be truly accomplished after the parents have grown up.

FATHER-DAUGHTER. As the father begins to take his responsibility for the incest, he will begin to come to a new awareness of himself. He realizes that he no longer has exclusive possession over his children. This becomes freeing to the daughter who needs permission from him to establish relationships outside of the family. For the father to accept the responsibility is crucial to changing the effects of the secrecy pact and to terminating the collusion between the husband and wife (Fried, 1977). It is in this dyadic modality that the father eliminates the role confusion between his wife and daughter (Zaphiris, 1983) and reestablishes his role as a parent. The daughter needs to have her pain and guilt relieved by her father for what she assumes as her fault. She fears rejection and punishment from her father (Blumberg, 1978) but needs to express her anger and disappointment that the father she trusted betrayed her.

MOTHER-DAUGHTER. The mother is usually angry at the daughter for not confiding in her even though she may have ignored the clues, and she is also jealous of her daughter. The mother-daughter dyad creates gender loyalty which increases the trust between the two of them and opens up new channels of communication which is important in preventing another occurrence. The worker can assist the mother in accepting her role as a parent and point out the role differences between herself and her daughter (Eist and Mandel, 1968).

The worker can assist the mother in the understanding of the need for her to protect her daughter. The mother has denied her own sexuality, as well as her daughter's sexuality (Fried, 1977). During this stage of therapy, the mother needs to be facilitated to reinforce the positive parts of female sexuality to increase her own sexual image and her daughter's sexual image. The emotional distance between the mother and daughter will be bridged only after the daughter is able to express her anger and disappointment that her mother did not see the incest or protect her from it.

Family Therapy Modality

The family therapy modality of the treatment program will provide the worker with the opportunity to evaluate and intervene into the communication and relationship problems. The worker has the opportunity to hear the emotional abuse that occurs in these families. The individuals are no longer able to disguise the manner in which they interact. If the trust in the worker has been well established prior to this phase of treatment, then the worker will have no problems in intervening without risking the loss of a member of the family. If the trust has not been established, then the worker becomes a referee for the family fights and loses his effectiveness. The clients may urge the worker into family or marital therapy too early, and the worker needs to assure them that this phase occurs when everyone feels comfortable with the reunion of the family. Family therapy can only occur when the parents are willing to take the responsibility for the incest (Sgroi, 1982).

The family structure needs to be kept in mind when the worker is formulating the treatment plan so that the impact of the interventions on the individuals and family system can be anticipated and assessed appropriately. It is possible that some other family member may become symptomatic instead of the incest survivor. The incest in the family could be overlooked if the worker does not keep in mind that this is a system functioning as one unit. And all family members' behaviors need to be taken into consideration. The trust in the family has been distorted; no one knows who to believe. The boundaries between the generations have been crossed and the roles in the family have been reversed. The family cannot tolerate closeness and real intimacy (Eist and Mandel, 1968). The dual focus in this modality will be the communication issues and relationship problems. Sgroi (1982) recommends that the areas of intervention in the family sessions need to be: (1) the abuse of power, (2) fear of authority, (3) isolation, (4) denial, (5) lack of empathy, (6) poor communication patterns, (7) inadequate controls and limit setting, (8) blurred boundaries, (9) extreme emotional deprivation and neediness, and (10) magical expectations.

During the family sessions each individual: (1) needs the opportunity to express his own feelings and needs to be heard, (2) understands what has happened in the family, (3) allows the opportunity to develop his own strengths, and (4) listens to the feelings and needs of others (Fried, 1977). The goal of the family therapy modality is to achieve individual separation and differentiation, to accept individual responsibility, to obtain honest and individual self-respect and to prevent scapegoating (Eist and Mandel, 1968). The families who cannot develop these new ways of relating will have difficulty in restructuring. Zaphiris (1983) states that treating the incestuous family as a unit is the last modality to be implemented and is designed to intervene into the family's overt and covert support of the incest and to establish a family without an incestuous bond.

TREATMENT DYNAMICS

What happens in each of these phases of the treatment process is a complicated, painful process. Some workers attempt a short-term behavior change, but this is ineffective because the "outward changes in behavior must be the result of changes from within" (Walters, 1975, p. 149). The individuals are asked to change those ways of their being which served the purpose of helping them to survive. They need to recognize that these behaviors are no longer appropriate. Letting go of the old defense mechanisms and old behaviors is difficult and a grieving process begins in the client. This is a very intensive and painful journey as the clients begin to let go of their denial, projection and repression. It is these three defense mechanisms which seem to be so prevalent in these families. As the client begins to let go of denial, he needs to be reassured that the worker will be supportive of him while he begins to take the responsibility for his behavior. As the projection onto other family members is stopped, the clients begin to take control of their own individual lives. And as the repression subsides, the memories begin to surface and this can be very frightening. The following case is an example of this process:

> One woman in her middle thirties had been referred because she was experiencing spouse abuse from her husband. She was able to begin to

break the dependency which kept her with him and she did divorce him. As her therapy continued, she began to stop denying that her mother was a severe alcoholic who had left her unprotected as a child. With this step, she took the next step and remembered being sent on an errand as a child where she encountered a man known to the family. He raped her and when she returned home to tell her mother about the family friend, her mother told her not to tell anyone even though she was bleeding and hurt. She remembered being upset about this incident, but, because it was put away in the closet, the woman thought that the memory was something that she had prefabricated. Although she was reassured that she could not have made up this story, she was scared that she had done something to provoke the man and she was angry at her mother's response of nonprotection.

The grieving process is with the same intensity as if someone had died. The client thinks "It's not me" of the denial stage, "Why me?" of the anger stage, "I'll never change" of the depression stage, "It really wasn't traumatic" of the bargaining stage, and finally the "I am free" of the acceptance stage.

Treatment Areas and Specific Dynamics

In all phases of the therapy, the worker deals with four specific treatment areas: (1) physical, (2) intellectual, (3) emotional, and (4) spiritual. The specific dynamics to be dealt with in these treatment areas to be addressed during the different modalities of treatment are: (1) marital conflict, (2) generational boundaries are crossed, therefore causing role reversal, (3) sexual abuse in family of origin, (4) crowded sleeping arrangements, (5) prolonged absence of one parent, (6) depression, (7) sexual overstimulation, (8) substance abuse, (9) inadequate supervision of children, (10) financial stress, (11) changes in economic status, (12) employment problems, (13) social and emotional isolation, (14) high stress (Slager-Jorne, 1978), (15) interpersonal distance within the family which results in no privacy and no individuality, (16) lack of impulse control, (17) cannot distinguish reality from fantasy, (18) lack of trust, (19) poor parenting skills, and (20) lack of knowledge regarding normal child development.

In the intellectual area, the clients will need to be taught new communication skills. Active and passive listening, the "I message," and contracting will need to be specifically taught. Stress information and how to relieve stress is, also, of prime importance in this area. The parents need to learn new parenting skills and need information regarding child development. Sexual information will need to be given and (1) the members in the family need the permission to say "yes" or "no" to any demand for sexual contact, (2) information on what feels good or bad sexually for each, (3) specifics and suggestions on the human body and sexual techniques, and (4) how to be intimate without sex. There will need to be many conversations around the area of the definitions of violence and chemical abuse. The clients do not automatically accept the worker's definitions, but, if the eroded value system is to be intervened into, then the worker needs to allow the client to explore how these new definitions fit into his or her life. Part of the reason for the intervention into the family is the prevention of this form of violence being carried to the next generation in any form. The teaching of the definition of violence is an important step in obtaining a change in the client's value system. If drugs or alcohol are involved, then the effects of these on the body need to be taught. This may not seem to be therapy, but being a good worker means being a good parent, and if the client does not have the correct information, the worker needs to teach it. The client's safety needs to be evaluated since many of the individuals in the family feel suicidal, homicidal, or that they will go crazy. Therefore, the worker needs to listen carefully to the clues and bring up the concerns directly in the first session. The clients need to make "no suicide," "no homicide," "no violence," and "no go crazy" contracts so that the clients and the worker are protected. The clients may not readily engage in these contracts, but the worker needs to continue to press for these contracts even though the client may deny that he or she would ever do anything so drastic. Another contract which needs to be clarified sometime within the first session is that the parent is to come to therapy chemical free. These contracts may be broken and this provides a new opportunity to discuss the problems in depth.

With these contracts made, the therapist is beginning to intervene into the physical area and the emotional area of treatment but engaging the intellectual areas to make them. The physical area of treatment needs to include the use of aerobic exercising, relaxation therapy, adequate nutrition and the use of vitamins as a way of handling stress. The body needs to be viewed as an important part in the entire system of change since there is substantial research regarding how the body's chemicals are related to the healthy functioning of people (Justice and Justice, 1979).

It is the emotional area of therapy that most workers deal with extensively. This is how it probably needs to be, but the first two areas named cannot be ignored if the client is to heal. During this time, the worker needs to assist the client in learning how to nurture himself instead of forcing others to take care of him or her. Missildine (1963) refers to this as a healing of the inner child of the past, and Yalom (1975) refers to it as teaching the client to be his own self-nurturing parents which have been so absent from his life. It is in learning to care for the self that will eventually break the unhealthy symbiosis. This is where the client needs guidance in dealing with his family of origin history and begin to heal some of these emotional cutoffs. The early family of origin work may be superficial, and it may only be later in therapy when the client will be able to overcome his denial, projection and repression which allows him to share more openly. It is contrary to the parental injunctions for the client to talk about the family history. These are people who grew up in families with many secrets and the "no talk" rule is implanted firmly, and to be good sons and daughters they follow unconsciously their parental family script. The denial system is well developed in the child by the age of nine, therefore making it difficult for these people to reach out for help. Children of all ages feel disloyal when they reveal their family secrets, and this makes it difficult for the clients to discuss their family history with honesty until the trust has been developed with the worker. Without being able to talk about their pain and without the ability to validate their perceptions of the problems, the client becomes deeper and deeper entrenched into a fantasy life. The other issues that need to be dealt with in the emotional area is the social and emotional isolation which is so inherent in the lives of these people. They will begin to deal with the existential meaning of being alone as they begin to understand that this journey towards optimal health has to be taken alone but that they do not have to be lonely during this time; they can begin to reach out to form a new supportive network. This also encourages the work on the unhealthy symbiosis in the family and particularly in the marital relationship. As they begin to let go of the dependency on a badly fragmented marriage and family, the grieving work begins and there may be many regressions back to the old styles of coping. The worker needs to remain reassuring that these regressions are normal, since the client is still unsure whether or not to trust or whether there is anything better for them at the end of their journey.

> The following is a case example illustrative of this point: One man who had been sexually molested by his oldest brother and who had grown up in an emotionally abusing family expressed his pain with this dilemma. He had obtained temporary control of his drinking, of his use of drugs and of his sexual acting out. When he regressed in his use of the chemicals but not in the sexual acting out, he became despondent, stating that he wanted to believe the worker but was not convinced that there was any better way to live. He wondered why he should change his pattern of life. Even when he did try to believe that things could be better in his life, he would leave therapy with enthusiasm only to be faced with so many negative forces in the world that he would quickly regress to most of his old behaviors.

As the clients begin to let go of the unhealthy symbiosis, they begin to expand their sex roles. Both the man and woman experience what it is like to be a more androgynous person and respect for the opposite sex occurs.

When the clients begin to expand who they are and what their potential is, they start their spiritual growth. Many of these people are extremely religious and this probably will not change, but it is the deep caring and respect for others and the world around them that begins to emerge. When children are sexually, physically or emotionally abused, they lose the ability to be empathetic, they lose their feelings for themselves, and many lose their bodily feelings. The entire process of therapy will bring these feelings back and allow the spiritual growth to occur.

Treatment Dynamics and Processes with Children

Treatment of children is necessary if they have been a survivor of the abuse or witnessed the abuse in the family. The Justices (1979) proceed cautiously with this treatment so as not to cause more harm than the abuse did. This treatment needs to be individualized for the child, and the worker needs to be able to enter into the child's world slowly. Berry (1972) believes that it takes courage for the worker to allow or to encourage the child to have negative emotions for the sake of long-term emotional gain, and that children are remarkably resilient and adaptable when provided a chance. The treatment setting needs to be set in a safe environment so that the child can begin to express his many needs. As the child relaxes, he begins to express all the needs which have been bottled up inside of him. The longer and more extensive the sexual abuse, the longer it will take the child to reach out and trust. The treatment process requires more time if the child is to begin to respond to the love and caring. The variables which determine which treatment plan is suitable for the child are: (1) the age of the child, (2) duration of sexual activity, (3) age at onset of incest, (4) kinds of physical and psychological abuse and the degree of the violence, and (5) the amount of family disintegration (Fried, 1977).

Sgroi is very specific regarding the treatment areas and suggests the preferred treatment modality for each. The areas which she recommends for intervention for all sexual abuse survivors are: (1) the feeling of being damaged goods, (2) guilt, (3) fear, (4) depression, (5) low self-esteem, (6) repressed anger and hostility, (7) inability to trust, (8) blurred boundaries, (9) pseudomaturity, and (10) self-mastery and control (1982).

The behaviors which the child expresses are merely a reflection of the child's response to the dysfunctional dynamics in the family (Slager-Jorne, 1978). Some common reactions to incest which can be found in infants are eating and sleeping disturbances, fretfulness, vomiting, changed levels of activity, and failure to thrive. Toddlers and school-age children may exhibit the following symptoms since they are not able to verbalize their fears: (1) regressive behavior, (2) withdrawal into a fantasy world which may make the child appear retarded, (3) may be difficult or uncomfortable to sit in a chair, (4) may not want to participate in sports, (5) physical complaints, (6) increased fearfulness, (7) nightmares and other sleep disturbances, (8) eating difficulties, (9) inappropriate play, (10) learning problems, (11) compulsive masturbation, (12) speech difficulties, (13) enuresis, (14) encopresis, (15) tics, and (16) nailbiting.

Preadolescents and adolescents begin to act their fears and concerns through: (1) sexual aggressiveness, (2) dressing seductively, (3) delinquency, (4) hostility toward others, (5) sexual promiscuity, (6) prostitution, (7) truancy, (8) running away, (9) substance abuse, (10) increased fearfulness, (11) fears of going home, (12) self-hatred, (13) sense of worthlessness, and (14) feelings of being damaged or dirty (Slager-Jorne, 1977).

Depression is a key reaction for all of these ages. The worker needs to remember that these behaviors are survival techniques that the child has learned in order to survive in his family. The child needed these survival mechanisms because he has been unable to fulfill his needs and the only way he can figure out how to meet some of them is by denying or suppressing parts of himself. The child is frightened and insecure and may be unable to take a risk to play freely or interact freely with the worker. He needs to trust others and himself if he is going to be able to learn to play spontaneously. The following is a case example:

> One six-year-old boy who had been sexually abused appeared to be hyperactive and was doing poorly in school even though his intelligence was above average. During the first months in therapy, he paced nervously in the room and tried to get the worker to play what he would do in therapy. He was frightened of making a mistake, and not until he began to trust the worker did he begin to play spontaneously in therapy. As he began to build his confidence, he was able to begin to achieve in school also.

These are children who lack the resources other children have to survive. Physically, they may not have had enough sleep, since much of the sexual molestation takes place in the middle of the night. They may develop stomachaches, hyperactivity or other psychosomatic ills (Justice, 1979), since they are unable to tell anyone about what is going on in the middle of the night. Emotionally, the children have taken on the guilt and blame of the incest (Blumberg, 1978). The children in treatment need to be willing to eventually talk or play out about their pain in order to lessen it (Erikson, 1963). If this never happens, the child becomes immobilized by the pain. The children feel disloyal about talking about their parents and are scared about betraying the family secrets. They feel ambivalent about their parents—at times loving them and at other times hating them. There is a generalized lack of trust. No one in the home has been honest about what has been happening there, so the child's perceptions and feelings are not validated. He begins to distrust his own feelings and sometimes begins to feel nothing. All of the feelings of anger and sadness are buried. Many give up learning how to play and how to relax and, instead, learn how to manipulate others to survive. They learn how to be powerless and never learn how to respond appropriately to feelings. These are children who do not understand boundaries or limits. Therefore, the goals in treatment are to teach the child boundaries and limits, how to play, how to relax, how to laugh, how to not be afraid of the anger and sadness, how to talk honestly, how to take care of her/himself, how to have a sense of his/her own power, how not to become immobilized by the fear and powerlessness, and how to reach out for peer and community support. The major role of the worker is to begin to validate the child's perceptions and to assist the child in knowing that the abuse is not her/his fault and that he/she is not alone.

Young Children

Working with young children to the age of six or seven can be a real challenge and fun for the worker. The first language of a child is nonverbal, and, therefore, the child believes the nonverbal messages that he receives from the worker before he believes the verbal messages. If the worker is bored or sends contradictory messages to the child, the child may not be able to verbalize what he knows, but he understands that something is not right and trust-building is delayed. The worker needs to make his body and verbal language consistent; he will need to be aware of the messages that the child is sending. If the worker interprets the child's behavior to him too early in the treatment process, the child will again delay the trust-building. The worker needs to proceed with caution as he enters the child's world. The young child may not always have the words for what he is feeling, but if the worker projects a sincere caring for the child, he will begin to show his feelings. The communication with the child needs to emphasize the feelings part of his message. With young children, the worker may want to use art as a means of communication. The worker does not have to be an "art therapist" to use this mode of communication. The therapy time needs to be a special time, and the worker may need to get on the floor at the child's level or even sometimes he may hold the child in his/her lap when the child is ready for this.

The child may fear being touched, and the worker needs to delay touching the child until the trust is built. Appropriate touching of the child begins to provide him or her with the messages that touching is not always sexual. These children are hungry for touch and may attempt to relate to the worker in a sexual manner as she related to her father. This is where gentle limit setting can occur to teach that people can be close in nonsexual ways. The sex of the worker is very important for the young girls, who may be very suspicious of a male worker. It is recommended that a female worker be used with female sexual abuse survivors. With a male incest victim, they could also be a problem and the following case illustrates this point:

> Rodney was a seven-year-old child who had been sexually molested by his natural mother. He was presently living with a stepmother and his father. The stepmother complained that she could not communicate with him and that he was frightened whenever she touched him. A female worker worked with Rodney for several months, and, although he was wary of the worker early in the treatment process, he warmed up when he realized that he was not going to be touched inappropriately in therapy. He was able to tolerate being in the room with the worker for longer periods of time and allowed the worker to begin hugging him. His relationship with his stepmother improved as he began to trust her, and he would allow her to kiss him good night and hug him when he was assured by her that he was safe from sexual molestation.

Play therapy can assist the child to work through the trauma of sexual abuse and then can help the child to develop new skills in dealing with problems (Slager-Jorne, 1978). If the worker is very observant, he can determine what is going on in the household through the child's play in therapy. The following exemplifies this point:

> Mary, age five, had been sexually molested by her uncle since the age of two. She was, also, severely abused physically by her grandmother. During her play therapy, she would lie on her back and place the plastic replica of Jaws between her legs. She, also, would take a rubber snake and beat the snake against the walls and the furniture in the treatment room. She did not have to verbalize what had happened to her sexually or physically.

The worker's role in play therapy is to help the child work out problems through the use of play (Slager-Jorne, 1978). The young child lacks the concept of sexuality and has no sense of right and wrong in this area. The goals of treatment for the younger child are to: (1) restore to her a childhood and (2) facilitate a nonsexual expression of affection within the family (Fried, 1977).

Latency-Age Children

The latency-age child is more verbal but has really accepted his parents' view of the world and is very cautious about what he tells the worker. With this age child, art therapy and playing with games can be a useful way into which to move him into a therapeutic mode. While he is playing games with the therapist, both are learning. The child of this age can be encouraged to use his imagination during the play to explore new ideas and solutions. The quality of the relationship with the therapist is the most important factor in building the foundation for trust. The child needs to be encouraged to talk about the incest without feeling that she is being suppressed or repressed by the worker. The child feels relieved after talking about the incest, since the worker clears up the child's fantasies and fears. This aids the child to deal with her anxiety, guilt, and confusion. The talk and play facilitates the child to work through and adjust to the trauma. Without this happening, the child continues to believe that she is bad and that what has happened is bad. After individual treatment, small groups can be used with these children to facilitate the beginning of a sense of community and to develop peer support (Fried, 1977). Art therapy can be used, also, with the latency-age child.

Adolescents

In working with adolescents, the key word to remember is that they need to *experience* life. It is a time for trying out new behaviors, different life-styles, relationships with the opposite sex, intense friendships and different values from their parents. All of this may be virtually impossible for the child who is involved with a parent sexually. The father is usually very jealous and sets unreasonable limits on the girl. The worker needs real skill in developing a relationship with teenagers, since most of them are suspicious of adults anyway. Relating to this age child means entering into the world of music and food. The worker would be wise to include both of these in the therapy sessions. This can be a most rewarding relationship if the worker can obtain the trust of the teen.

The worker can play a very important role for the adolescent. The teenager looks for role models during this stage of life, and the worker can provide limits and guide her to new solutions for problems. The goals for therapy with the adolescent are to clarify the role confusion issues, to express her feelings, and to establish appropriate peer relationships. The child has had to nuture both her mother and her father when what she needed to be doing was to understand her own sexuality and to prepare for an independent adult life. She, also, feels different from her peers because of her sexual experiences. Her social skills are lacking and she may sexualize all of her peer relationships. Even though she may have several sexual experiences, she continues to feel isolated and angry because she has no real intimacy (Fried, 1977).

The use of groups with adolescents can be very effective for this population (Sgroi, 1982). A group for this age assists the adolescent to begin to develop age-appropriate social skills (Fried, 1977). The use of group facilitates the building of trust, the breaking of isolation, and the development of the ability to share feelings.

SUMMARY

Treatment of sexual abuse involves a thorough preparation on the part of the workers who have to evaluate their own feelings regarding sexuality, their feelings towards people who molest children, their own prejudices and myths which they still believe, and the transference and counter-transference issues as they surface during the treatment process. After this preparation for their role as a professional, the expected outcome for the worker is a humanistic philosophy which the major authors in this field suggest as the recommended approach that works best in sexual abuse cases. The treatment program which is to be undertaken is a long, complicated process for the worker and the family. The family needs to be viewed as a dysfunctional system which has manifested incest as a symptom, and this system can never be ignored during the different modalities of treatment. The treatment process which is recommended is that first the child, the mother and the father be entered into individual therapy to build the trust for each of them. Following individual treatment, the worker can move them into marital therapy for the spouses, dyadic modalities for the father-daughter or mother-daughter, and group therapy for all family members. Family therapy is the last stage of the treatment process if the family is to be restructured. During all stages of the treatment, the specific dynamics found in incest families will need to be addressed. The major dynamics are the social and emotional isolation, the symbiosis, the role reversals and the depression which is manifested by everyone in the family. The behaviors which the children are exhibiting need to be viewed as their attempts to survive and cope with the anxiety and guilt which they are feeling. The worker will need to adapt his methods and treatment plan according to the age of the child, but the major goals of the therapy with the children are to relieve them of the guilt and anxiety and assist them in relating to others in a nonsexual, but caring manner. Progress will be erratic and regressions can be expected which may cause the worker and the clients to feel despair and self-recrimination. With competent supervision and consistency, everyone can weather these storms and the clients can moved into a healing and healthy life.

REFERENCES

Balgopal, P.R., and Vassil, T.V.: *Groups in Social Work: An Ecological Perspective*. New York: MacMillan Publishing Co., Inc., 1983.

Berry, J.: *Social Work with Children*. London: Routledge and Kegan Paul, 1972.

Blumberg, M.: Child sexual abuse. *New York State Journal of Medicine*, March, 612–616, 1978.

Cormier, B., Kennedy, M., and Sangowicz, J.: Psychodynamics of father-daughter incest. *Canadian Psychiatric Association Journal* 7(5):203–217, 1962.

Eist, H., and Mandel, A.: Family treatment of ongoing incest behavior. *Family Process*, 7:216–232, 1968.

Erikson, E.: *Childhood and Society*. New York: W.W. Norton and Co., Inc., 1963.

Forward, S., and Buck, C.: *Betrayal of Innocence: Incest and its Devastation*. Los Angeles: J.P. Tarcher, Inc., 1978.

Fried, J.: *Protective Service Intervention in Incest Cases: An Overview*. Albuquerque, NM: Family Resource Center, 1977.

Giarretto, H.: Humanistic treatment of father-daughter incest. In R.E. Helfer and C.H. Kempe (Eds.): *Child Abuse and Neglect: The Family and the Community*. Cambridge, MA: Ballinger, 1976, pp. 143–158.

Justice, B., and Justice, R.: *The Broken Taboo*. New York: Human Sciences Press, 1979.

Missildine, W.H.: *Your Inner Child of the Past*. New York: Simon and Schuster, 1963.

Racher, H.: *Transference and Counter-Transference*. New York: International Universities Press, Inc., 1968.

Sgroi, S.: *Handbook of Clinical Interventions in Child Sexual Abuse*. Lexington, MA: Lexington Books, 1982.

Slager-Jorne, P.: Counseling sexually abused children. *Personnel and Guidance Journal*, 103–105, 1978.

Tessman, L.H., and Kaufman, I.: Variations on a theme of incest. In Pollock, O., and Friedman, A. (Eds.): *Family Dynamics and Female Sexual Deviancy*. Palo Alto, CA: Science and Behavior Books, 1969.

Walters, D.R.: *Physical and Sexual Abuse of Children*. Bloomington, IN: Indiana University Press, 1975.

Weitzel, W., Powell, B., and Penick, E.: Clinical management of father-daughter incest. *American Journal of Diseases of Children, 132*, February, 1978.

Yalom, I.D.: *The Theory and Practice of Group Psychotherapy*. New York: Basic Books, Inc., 1975.

Zaphiris, A.: *Methods and Skills for a Differential Assessment and Treatment in Incest, Sexual Abuse and Sexual Exploitation of Children*. Denver, CO: American Humane Association, 1983.

CHAPTER 18

THE USE OF INTERDISCIPLINARY TEAMS

Norma L. Totah and Patricia Wilson-Coker

INTRODUCTION

Child maltreatment is a multifaceted, multidetermined phenomenon beyond the scope and expertise of any one discipline.

Effective treatment of this problem requires a range of services and intervention from a variety of professions and agencies. Protective and social service workers, doctors, nurses, teachers, psychiatrists, psychologists, lawyers, and the police all may be involved appropriately in complex cases. Without effective mechanisms for communication and case coordination, these professionals may be doomed to duplicate their efforts or work at cross-purposes.

When treatment efforts are poorly coordinated, already overstressed parents may become frustrated and convinced of their inability to benefit from offered assistance. Abused children may be brutalized all over again by the system designed to help (Terr and Watson, 1968). The interdisciplinary team approach in the identification and treatment of child abuse and neglect emerged from practitioners' efforts to reconcile these problems.

More than thirty years ago, Betty Elmer of the Pittsburg Children's Hospital, Helen Boardman, Children's Hospital in Los Angeles, and Rae E. Helfer and C. Henry Kempe at the University of Colorado Medical Center spearheaded the development of hospital-based child protection teams (Kempe, 1978).

Kempe and his associates recommended that hospital teams cooperate with child protection services to formulate joint treatment recommendations for abused children and their families (Mouzakitis and Goldstein, 1984). The success of the team concept in the medical setting suggested the creation of agency and community-based teams.

The value of the interdisciplinary team approach is well documented in the literature (Blumberg, 1977; DeFrances, 1973; Fontana, 1970; Helfer and Schmidt, 1976; Newberger et al., 1973; Sgroi, 1982; Steele, 1976; Witworth et al., 1981). Use of the team model can result in support for overburdened protective service workers who gather multidisciplinary expertise from team members and share responsibility for decision making. Teams are excellent mechanisms for information gathering, coordinating multiple services, and resolving conflict among professionals who may have different priorities for case direction. Effective teams are instrumental in identifying service gaps in the community and advocating for changes in inefficient service delivery systems. They are a good vehicle for fostering amicable professional relationships, training consultants, and for educating the lay and professional community.

Despite these productive aspects and unanimous professional approval, the multidisciplinary team approach is underutilized in cases of child abuse and rarely used in child neglect (Mouzakitis and Goldstein, 1984; Pettiford, 1981). The interdisciplinary team process can be plagued by problems of confidentiality, professional territoriality, agency worker defensiveness, and uncoordinated discussions that lack clarity and focus. With proper use and management, however, it is an invaluable resource to protective service workers in facilitating the protection of children and their families.

In this chapter, the authors focus on the function and process of interdisciplinary teams and point out ways to avoid barriers to their effective utilization. A case example is used to illustrate successful team intervention.

Definitions

The child protection team is a multidisciplinary body of professionals who pool their expertise and resources for the common goal of diagnosing, treating, and managing child abuse and neglect cases. The primary functions of the team are to review the cases of child abuse and neglect that are referred to it (Schmitt, 1978) and to improve the quality of protection and services provided at the community level to children and their families through coordination of services and effective community education (Pettiford, 1981).

According to Edmund Pellegrino of the National Academy of Sciences: "The purpose of the group or team approach is to optimize the special contribution in skills and knowledge of the team members so that the needs of the persons served can be met more efficiently, effectively, competently, and more considerately than would be possible by independent and individual action" (1972, p. 12).

Team Size and Composition

Interdisciplinary team size will vary according to the number of professionals willing to discuss cases regularly or the complexity of a given case. The nuclear, or core, group of team members customarily includes the social worker, physician and team leader, coordinator or case manager. It should be noted that the child protection agency representative is the only person with statutory mandate to investigate and remain consistently involved with confirmed cases of child maltreatment. CPS agency participation is, therefore, very important to efficient mangement of reported cases.

Beyond the core group, pivotal team members may include community agency social workers, psychiatrists, psychologists, attorneys and representatives from the juvenile court, public health nurses, teachers, police officers, day care workers, and parent aides (NCCAN, 1981). These persons are particularly useful in difficult protective service cases and in providing agency staff with support, new knowledge, and the opportunity to hear different perspectives on case information.

Team members may be permanent parts of the case review effort or case specific invitees whose participation is limited to cases in which they are involved.

Teams function most effectively if permanent members are knowledgeable about the dynamics of child maltreatment, especially as they relate to their field of practice. It is also helpful if they are cognizant of such matters as the professional function and limitation of other team members, applicable legal definitions of maltreatment, and basic resources available within the community.

While it is preferrable for permanent members to have solid practical experience in handling abuse cases, a few months on a well-functioning team can provide less-seasoned members with valuable exposure to a wide variety of case types.

Work with abusing families can be an emotionally draining experience for any team member. The opportunity to gain insight from a case success and share responsibility is a valuable incentive for participation.

Team Structure and Functional Variety

Child protection teams assume a variety of forms and labels. Some teams are formally structured, with paid coordinators under state agency auspices and funding. Such teams usually have the advantage of clerical staff, a consistent meeting site and telephone. A small group of "sleeves-rolled-up" professionals who are willing to volunteer their time in exchange for interdisciplinary insight can also be effective and does not run the risk of becoming another agency in competition for funds, prestige, power and turf (Sgroi, 1982).

Interdisciplinary teams may be linked to specific agencies (i.e. protective services), institutions (i.e. hospitals, mental health clinics), or systems (i.e. court or school). The most common determinant of team origin is an identified geographical base such as country or city (Schmitt, 1978).

Many community-based teams are used by members for the combined purpose of assessment, consultation, and service coordination. Some teams carry out specialized functions such as community and continuing education. Other teams restrict their intake to specific problems or populations.

Hospital-based teams customarily diagnose, manage, and plan the discharge of the maltreated children who receive hospital treatment. These teams are staffed primarily by hospital employees from several professional disciplines (i.e. medicine, social work, psychology, radiology). The existence of a child protection team in a hospital tends to increase the identification of maltreated children within that setting because employees have an established protocol and a simplified mechanism for referring suspicious cases. In order to assure that the team's detailed expertise is not ignored once the child leaves the hospital and outside reevaluation becomes necessary, hospital-based teams should be integrated into the community and protective service agency reporting and investigation system (Kempe, 1978).

Child sexual abuse teams are becoming a more common form of specialized team. Most child protection teams are ill equipped to deal with the area of child maltreatment without specialized training for all involved disciplines (Sgroi, 1982). Since the numbers of such cases are relatively small in comparison to other maltreatment categories, development of a special interdisciplinary team to assist in the investigation, validation, and treatment of these cases does not result in duplication of effort.

Where these teams are formed, representation of persons from certain specialized mental health service areas may be useful (i.e. sex therapist, art therapist, and persons skilled in work with involuntary client populations) in addition to the usual core group of professional people (Sgroi, 1982).

Consultation teams typically include permanent members with expertise in the areas of protective services, medicine, law, psychiatry and mental health. At a minimum, the consultation team may function in addition to, or in place of, individual consultants to the agency (Pettiford, 1981). Each member of a consultation team may function as a liaison to their respective professions within a state or community, provide direct telephone consultations and public education, or consult on the complex cases of less-experienced teams.

Treatment teams restrict case review to cases already in treatment. The team ordinarily consists of service providers currently working with a given family. Membership, therefore, varies according to the needs of the case and the persons assigned treatment responsibility. Barton Schmitt (1978) suggests that specialized treatment teams may duplicate the efforts of the multipurpose community consultation teams. He emphasizes the view that diagnostic and treatment decisions regarding a specific family should be reviewed by the same team to preserve continuity of care.

Another view of the treatment concept is suggested by Ray Helfer and Rebecca Schmidt who see the community consultation team as being crisis oriented. They recognize the need for a committee to coordinate and review the long-term multiagency service needs of troubled families (Helfer and Schmidt, 1976).

Generally, all teams function to provide interdisciplinary insight into complex cases and to improve interagency communication, cooperation, and coordination among the multiplicity of people and programs that help abusing families. Labeling a team is clearly less important than insuring its responsiveness to the needs of the families, professionals, and communities which it serves.

Basic Team Functions

While interdisciplinary child protection teams vary in form, there are some basic functions that are commonly performed by those teams organized for care asessment, service coordination, and consultation (NCCAN, 1978).

1. Available information on the child, the family, and individual family members is analyzed to determine if additional information is needed for informed decision making.

This process can be facilitated if the team coordinator devises a standard format for collection of data. Some teams also standardize collection responsibilities for different parts of the data base, promoting role clarification and preventing duplication of effort (Schmitt, Grosz, and Carrol, 1976).

2. Information and expertise should be shared to generate a solid data base for risk assessment and comprehensive treatment planning.

All team members should be involved in this task, as each will have collected information from distinct perspectives. According to Brandt Steel (1976): "as the data obtained in a multidisciplinary approach to diagnosis are pooled and combined, the multiplicity and pervasiveness of the parent's conflicts become clarified. This combined picture gives a better clue to prognosis than single observations made by a psychiatrist, social worker, nurse, or pediatrician" (p. 166).

3. Teams recommend short- and long-range treatment goals based upon the needs and problems identified.

Short-term goals should be readily achievable in order to encourage progress and insure a patient's ongoing cooperation.

Long-term goals should be sufficiently flexible to accommodate change (i.e. shifting worker assignments or change in a parent's willingness to complete required tasks).

To be successful, all goals should be realistic and involve the parent in planning. Service agreements are especially useful in goal setting when they are time limited, clearly written in behavioral terms, and specify agreed-upon responsibilities and outcomes for all participants (parent, team members, mandated agency, etc.).

4. Teams determine which resources within the community are available for use by the child and/or family members.

It may be helpful if members compile a list of resources with descriptions of eligibility criteria. When representatives from specifically useful services are part of the planning process, strict eligibility requirements are sometimes eased in the effort to provide needed services.

5. Teams assess when cases should be presented for another review.

Generally, review should take place whenever a treatment plan proves ineffective or when involved professionals feel the need for renewed consensus or group discussion of changing goals (i.e. the decision is made to take a case to court or return a child to his home).

6. Guidelines for case closure should be determined and adhered to.

A sustained period of positive functioning on the part of children and their parents, coupled with gradually diminishing protective service involvement, is significant in this decision (Carrol, 1978).

7. Teams identify gaps in community services and potential problems in service delivery.

After several months of functioning, a team can usually identify the "missing links" of good service delivery within a community. To facilitate this process, the present system can be compared to an ideal that would include various options for family stress reduction and treatment (i.e. crisis nursery, emergency and long-term homemakers, foster care for child and family, residential treatment facilities for children, specialized day care, parent aides, marital and individual counseling, group therapy, Parents Anonymous, parenting classes, visiting nurses, etc.) (Carrol and Schmidt, 1978).

8. Teams promote the development of community resources for children and families that are needed but unavailable.

This function can be carried out informally by individual members as well as through coordinated team action. For example, within their agencies, individual team members can advocate for changes in eligibility requirements or service expansion to accommodate underserved populations; doctors, lawyers, and therapists may be able to identify professional peers willing to donate time or accept medicaid pay rates. The team coordinator may suggest a subgroup of committee members who can develop legislative advocacy techniques to change laws or obtain funding for special projects. The media can also be effectively utilized to mobilize a community to identify or generate additional resources for the treatment of child abuse and neglect (Carrol and Schmidt, 1978).

Roles and Responsibilities of Team Members

The roles and responsibilities of various team members who work directly with a family are not always well defined or clearly delineated. The most effective team members are often those who are sufficiently flexible and comfortable with their realm of expertise that they can risk stepping out of their customary role to get needed services to a family in the most efficient manner.

Multidisciplinary team treatment has the advantage of being multipersonal. Parents respond to, share information with, and take direction from people based on their pesonality as well as their profession (Steele, 1976). For example, established rapport with a given parent may enable the policeman to assume a supportive and nurturing role, while the social worker becomes the authority figure. A parent's lawyer may be better able than the visiting nurse to convince her client of the need to follow the doctor's instructions. The protective service worker should not be the only person who confronts a family or introduces a plan for treatment.

The authors do not suggest that professional duties be arbitrarily abandoned or exchanged as lawyers obviously should not give medical advice and social workers cannot make arrests. The plea is for team members to understand the total needs of the families they attempt to help and maintain a willingness to shift role assignments when the individuals are comfortable, there is group consensus, and the situation warrants it.

Following are specific ways that team members can contribute to effective team functioning from their customary role or professional stance.

Team Coordinator

The team coordinator or chairperson provides leadership to the team by scheduling and chairing team meetings and coordinating team activities. The coordinator's role is that of a facilitator, enabling the group to share information and feelings, diagnostic thinking, case management planning, and therapeutic insights.

While the coordinator's role may vary from team to team, it often consists of the following basic tasks:

- receiving and screening referrals to the teams
- inviting appropriate case-specific and consultative personnel to team meetings
- arranging for clerical support and handling meeting logistics

- maintaining relations within the team, keeping the team focused on its purpose and objectives, and working to minimize "turf" battles
- providing training and information for team members in order to continuously upgrade the team's functioning
- maintaining contact with agencies represented on the team
- directing the team's investigative and treatment/service decisions
- coordinating and facilitating cross-referrals
- following up on progress or status of cases and orchestrating same so that abused and neglected children may be served adequately (Urzi, 1980; Hartford Child Protection Team, 1983).

It is essential that the team coordinator understand group dynamics in order to promote effective communication, cooperation, and teamwork required for problem solving and management of services and resources. The team coordinator is the group catalyst. The tone of meetings and the spirit of trust, sharing, and cooperation are often set by the group coordinator. Above all, the team coordinator should be flexible and open-minded, without strong ideas of how things "must" be handled. The best method for doing things is the one that gets needed appropriate services to children and families in a timely manner.

Protective Service Worker

The protective service worker and supervisor have key roles and responsibilities as representatives from the agency mandated by law to investigate and manage child abuse and neglect cases.

When the protective service workers request a team meeting, he or she could be prepared to present a concise and thorough report to the team that includes information regarding the following matters.

- the parent's personal history (to help assess future risk)
- presenting problems (including referral details, medical evidence of abuse, immediate family stress factors)
- parental reaction to protective service investigation
- pertinent information about the child and his role in the family
- information of importance in assessing risk to siblings
- an assessment of the safety of the home for all minor children
- general diagnostic impressions
- family perception of strategies for preventing future harm to the child
- tentative agency treatment plan recommendations (Jones, McClean, and Vobe, 1979; Schmitt, Grosz, and Carrol, 1976)

In addition to these functions, the worker is often in the best position to interpret the team's reasoning and recommendations to the parents. The worker ought to carefully consider the team's suggestions and follow through on agreed-upon steps, including consultation with the agency attorney if legal steps become necessary. The worker should consider difficult decisions as shared responsibility, making full use of the team for advice and suport.

A protective service supervisor should accompany the worker to team meetings whenever possible. The supervisor can educate team members about the rationale for disputed agency case positions and should be prepared to define agency policy. The supervisor is often in a good position to determine the reasons for ineffective casework and encourage appropriate activity. A well-informed and supportive supervisor can enhance social worker skill in effective case presentation and reduce anxiety in this regard. Many teams utilize protective service supervisory-level persons as permanent team members who are available to facilitate the agency's involvement, administrative support, and cooperation in service coordination.

Physician

The physician should be skillful at detecting and validating child abuse and neglect through physical examination and behavioral and developmental assessments. He or she can make an important contribution to the interdisciplinary effort by:

- interpreting for team members the diagnostic evaluations of health professionals (i.e. defining terms) and the practical implications of medical diagnosis and findings
- evaluating the abused child's medical and psychological needs
- providing consultation to health professionals regarding whether abuse and neglect should be suspected in individual cases
- providing consultation to legal systems (including expert testimony)
- educating professional peers and the lay public on medical aspects of child abuse and neglect
- explaining to colleagues the importance of documenting medical evidence and providing written reports with facts and observations that will be useful in courts of law.

Nurses

The nurse, whether hospital based (ward or pediatric nurse) or community based (public health nurse), collects information which helps to assess the family's strengths and weaknesses. In his/her strategic position, the nurse is able to observe and evaluate the child's response to adults, procedures, and objects, as well as the child's feelings, needs and abilities. The nurse can observe and report the parents' reaction to the history-taking, how they present their concerns and utilize information, as well as the appropriateness of parent-child interaction (Bridges, 1978). These types of information provide team members with essential parts of the data base required for appropriate case decisions.

Public health nurses can be invaluable additions to multidisciplinary teams because of their unique position to provide services to children and their families through predictable home visits. They can work (often in conjunction with parent aides and homemakers) to help parents carry out medically oriented aspects of the team's in-home treatment recommendations (i.e. monitor the case of a medically neglected diabetic child).

Mental Health Professionals

A mental health assessment is critical to sound decision making in the interdisciplinary team process. This can be provided by a psychiatrist, psychologist, or a clinical social worker. Since each of these professionals can provide a different type of assessment, some child protection teams include all three disciplines. A mental health assessment can help determine the degree of risk of child abuse by the parents; parents' ability to relate, use help, and control impulses; whether the parents suffer from psychopathology which requires treatment in and of itself; and recommendations regarding treatability and treatment priorities (Stern, 1978).

School Personnel

The educator's role on the interdisciplinary child protection team is to provide consultation relative to the child's development and academic performance. Educators provide invaluable insights with respect to interpreting educational diagnostic assessments which enhance the treatment planning process.

The teacher or school counselor may be the first person to whom an older child reveals parental abuse. Before and after official involvement by the child protection agency, school personnel can help build the data base from which team members work. School personnel are in a unique position to see children on a daily basis in a nonthreatening environment and to gain insight into daily parental practices and their effect on children.

Having a school official or administrator as a permanent member of a child protection team can promote dissemination of information on appropriate reporting and referral procedures. Similarly, interest in related in-service training may be generated or facilitated by an active team member within the school system (Broadhurst, 1978).

Law Enforcement

The law enforcement representative (i.e. police, prosecutor), especially when cloaked with decision-making authority, is essential to a well-functioning child protection team. He or she can provide information on police policy and can disseminate relevant information to fellow officers. Most states require police involvement in cases of nonaccidental life-threatening injuries, sexual abuse, and in cases in which a child's life is threatened by severe parental neglect. The team's law enforcement representative can clarify when an investigation by protective services should be concurrent with police investigation and can communicate information to the team about evidence preservation for effective court use. He or she can be instrumental in giving team members information about police activity at a given location or policy procedure and protocol in serious matters; providing information to social workers and parents regarding charges that might be filed or are pending, and reporting to team members the progress of investigations.

When the police representative is directly involved in a team's case, he or she can make recommendations to the court that are in accordance with team decisions, casework progress, or the lack thereof (Brockman and Carrol, 1978).

Lawyer

The adversarial nature of the legal system, coupled with the legal ramifications of child maltreatment, make the legal consultant an important member of the child protection team. The experienced attorney with expertise in the juvenile and family court setting can be especially helpful in interpreting state child protection law with regard to specific-fact situations. He or she can provide ongoing legal consultation to the child protective services worker and other team members on such matters as recordkeeping, confidentiality, and preparation and delivery of testimony. The team attorney who is well versed in the mandated agency's policy, the dynamics of child maltreatment, and the use of community resources is in a good position to educate professional peers.

Team Process

The case conference is the vehicle for implementing interdisciplinary team process. The team coordinator or chairperson facilitates the discussion, keeps members on task, and encourages input from everyone. When cases are presented, discussion from many perspectives yields a far more complete and accurate picture of the family than could possibly be developed by a single professional. This pooling of knowledge generates not only a solid data base for decision making but practical recommendations which reflect the expertise and skill of many disciplines.

It has been the author's experience that teams which are advisory in nature and which arrive at recommendations based on cooperation and consensus are the most useful. Other factors which contribute to optimal team functioning are commitment to the principal of interagency, multi-disciplinary coordination, the avoidance of blame and critical attacks on presenters, an effective chairperson and mutually supportive team members who are prepared in advance to offer focused, useful recommendations.

Elements of Successful Team Meetings

1. *Effective Leadership*: Every team should have a leader or chairperson who is in charge of focusing case discussion, keeping time schedules and managing the interpersonal aspects of team conferencing. The persons selected should see themselves as the servant of the group rather than its master. The role then becomes that of assisting the group toward the best decisions in the most efficient manner possible. The chair moves discussion ahead, interprets and clarifies discussion points, and assists the group in reaching a resolution that all understand and accept as the will of the group. A certain amount of control is important to maintaining focused, productive discussions, but this does not give the chair a license to impose his or her will on the group. Rather, the group's will should be imposed on any individual who is diverting or delaying the progress of discussion (Jay, 1976).

2. *Productive Use of Time*: Team conferences should be held regularly and on a scheduled basis so that the time slot can be built into the member's schedule.

Conferences should be limited to a maximum of two hours. Meetings that run longer than that are likely to become unproductive, as members will be too exhausted to be maximally effective.

If meetings begin and end on schedule, members are more likely to arrive on time and stay to the end of the meeting. Parental permission to team a case and any necessary releases should be obtained in advance of the meeting if they are customarily required within that community.

Team members should know in advance of the meeting the order in which case discussion will proceed and how much time is being allotted for each case. A meeting agenda, distributed in advance, can help in this regard. Conference participants should be encouraged to prepare their remarks in advance.

3. *Focused Discussion*: Cases should be presented in a logical sequence; perhaps: medical diagnostic information, background from the reporting source (e.g. policeman, teacher), the protective service workers' assessment, psychological information, and then additional input from the other involved agencies (Schmitt, Grosz, and Carrol, 1976).

Regardless of order, all presentations should be concise, time limited, and should concentrate on current family problems, tentative recommendations, and available treatment resources.

One method of facilitating these goals is through utilization of the Problem-Oriented Record Format (POR), originally introduced as a medical recordkeeping device by Doctor Lawrence Week in the 1960s. By using a standard nomenclature for the many family problems encountered in child abuse and neglect cases, professionals can organize their thinking, condense their data, direct their questions and discussions, and generally clarify areas for intervention with abusive families.

Twelve family problem categories have been identified and refined by Barton Schmitt, Candace Grosz, and Claudia Carrol (1976). Most types of family problems can be fitted into this format.

1. The specific child abuse/neglect category (e.g. physical abuse, failure to thrive, sexual abuse, medical care neglect, intentional drugging or poisoning, emotional abuse, abandonment, lack of supervision, severe physical neglect, high-risk child, true accident, etc.)
2. Child's physical problems
3. Child's emotional problems or status (e.g. deprivation behavior, depression, discipline problem, developmental lags)
4. Siblings' emotional and physical problems or status
5. Parents' physical problems
6. Mother's emotional problems or status
7. Father's emotional problems or status
8. Emotional problems or status of other important people in the home (e.g. baby-sitter, aunt, grandparents)
9. Marital problems or mate relationship
10. Personal crises (e.g. death, desertion, divorce, recent move)
11. Environmental crises (e.g. inadequate home, heat, water, food, job, medical insurance, child-support payments)
12. Safety of the home (i.e. composite data from above that relate to decision for or against foster care placement)

A corresponding list of treatment resource options that are available within a community can be developed for each of these problem areas.

This or a similar format can be utilized by team participants who have evaluated a member of the family that will be conferenced. A tentative problem list can be developed that records supporting data and makes recommendations for each problem noted. This information can be submitted in advance to the team leader for consolidation into a tentative draft report which can be distributed to all participants at the start of the meeting (Schmitt, Grosz, and Carrol, 1976).

After brief individual presentations, full group discussion can focus on specific problems and issues. Focused discussion will permit time for refining recommendations, obtaining group consensus on major decisions, and securing acceptance of individual case assignments. A final problem-oriented treatment plan and case management document can be developed and distributed to involved individuals and agencies soon after the team meeting.

Problems in the Process

Interdisciplinary child protection team meetings have the potential to succumb to practical problems of collaboration. In addition, human frailties and professional cross-currents can obscure mutual objectives and throw discussion off course, wasting valuable time and energy. Let's examine some common areas of concern.

Confidentiality: What data can and can't be shared with colleagues at team meetings is often a source of confusion. Family privacy is clearly a legitimate concern for responsible professionals. But a team that does not communicate effectively cannot function properly. Extreme reluctance to share pertinent, nonspeculative information in a team meeting may represent an inability of professionals to trust each other or may demonstrate unfounded fear of legal action.

In most states, physician-patient confidentiality is waived in child abuse cases. Most professional data can be shared in the effort to resolve diagnosis or plan effective treatment. Lawsuits regarding breaches of confidentiality must prove malicious intent in order to succeed (Schmitt, 1978).

Despite these reassurances, each team must struggle with its members' comfort around how confidential information is to be handled. The team coordinator should be familiar with state laws and professional community standards regarding these matters. Some options for protecting confidentiality include:

1. Reminding participants of their duty to be sensitive to protection of family privacy.
2. Securing parental permission to team a case. An express waiver of confidentiality for the purposes of collaboration, at that meeting, can cover all participants.
3. Disguising names or using numbers to identify cases.
4. Limiting the meeting to only those individuals directly involved with the family.
5. Exchanging no written records with identifying information or collecting all discussion material from individuals not directly involved in a case.

Protection of organizational turf may be a problem in some child protection teams. The unwillingness of an agency or organization to surrender its power, autonomy, or resources severely limits effective collaboration. Organizations and the people who work in them are sometimes reluctant to accept direction from outside sources or restriction on their power to make unilateral decisions.

Potential problems in this area can be reduced if some form of inducement is recognized. The team's message should be one of collaboration and compromise for the common good of families and children, rather than expressed need for peer review and evaluation. Potential benefits, such as increased interagency referrals, shared responsibility, and interprofessional support should be noted.

Reluctance or defensiveness on the part of mandated agency representatives can hinder the effectiveness of team intervention, especially where the public agency is the primary source of cases for review.

Workers are sometimes reluctant to share their authority when they cannot share the responsibility mandated by law. The protective service agency may be held accountable for problems or failures in a case, whether or not the community provides services to a family.

In light of the exhaustive demands of a heavy case load, a significant time investment may be involved in preparing a case for presentation. Even a very active team may review only 1 percent of the mandated agency's case load.

Some workers complain that the suggestions they receive for case management indicate that team members fail to comprehend the legal limitations under which they must operate. Moreover, the threat that is posed by the prospect of having one's decisions and activities reviewed and criticized by a multidisciplinary group of "experts" can be overwhelming.

Team members should be encouraged to recognize some of the legitimate reasons behind agency case-presenter reluctance and take steps to correct unfounded negative perceptions. The team coordinator might approach an agency supervisor or administrator to discuss how the team approach is perceived by social workers and how credibility and communication can be improved.

Workers must be encouraged to recognize the concrete beneficial effects of team conferencing. Brainstorming case problems and solutions with a group is bound to be more efficient than the single-handed approach. Moreover, at a team meeting, the worker may be able to get direct commitments of service from community resources for the families they are working with.

Team members should be encouraged to recognize and acknowledge good casework as easily as they challenge inappropriate interventions. All team members should be aware of each others' professional and legal limitations.

Differing Ideologies and Language Barriers Among Disciplines

It is not surprising that each profession generally perceives its own area of expertise as critical. Doctors will view health problems as paramount, and lawyers will analyze child maltreatment in terms of rights and responsibilities. Standards for intervention and modes of operation also differ from profession to profession. For police, there must be definite grounds for arrest; social work standards for intervention may be far more subjective. With a little tact, a skillful coordinator can assist team members in recognizing the importance of the contribution of the various disciplines and the legitimacy of different approaches in coordinated delivery of services. Professional conflicts can be minimized when these underlying differences in perspective are surfaced and addressed directly.

Professional jargon can also create barriers to effective collaboration; law enforcement, medicine, social work, mental health and law all have their own specialized vocabularies. Certain words will have meaning commonly known only to members of that discipline. Even greater confusion may result when the same word has a different meaning to each of several professionals.

Language difficulties, like differences in approach and ideology, can best be addressed by awareness of the problem and commitment to overcome it. Team members should be encouraged to use clear, simple language. The coordinator (or anyone who fails to understand) should request clarification of any unusual terms or word usages. Until members demonstrate familiarity with the limits of each others' professional interventions, they should be encouraged to spell out their understandings and expectations during the case discussion or while summarizing at the end.

Case Example

The following case is used to illustrate the impact of the interdisciplinary team process on the assessment, treatment, and case management of child maltreatment.

The Xiong Family

The Xiong's are a Hmong family who immigrated to this country several years ago from Laos. The X family consists of: Mr. X, age twenty-nine, who is unemployed; Mrs. X, age twenty-six, who works part-time; their son, Pao, age nine; their daughter, Neng, age eight; their son, Vang, age six; and their son, Seng, age fourteen months.

Mr. X was reported to children and protective services for beating Pao and Neng repeatedly, causing both children to run away from home. They were examined by a pediatrician and treated for strap marks and bruises on their backs and buttocks.

The investigation reveals that Mr. and Mrs. X have been having marital problems. Mr. X was unemployed. He was deeply frustrated by his inability to find a steady job and was under tremendous stress due to the family's poor financial condition. The family was currently living on Mrs. X's part-time earnings at an electronic assembly plant and supplemental income from city welfare.

Mr. X admitted to beating Neng and Pao and Vang. He seemed to feel this was his right and duty as their father. Mr. X's history revealed that he had been subject to considerable abuse as a child.

Mrs. X also was under considerable stress. She expressed frustration at her husband's unemployment, which left her to support the family. Mr. X did not speak English well and relied on the children for translation. She expressed difficulty with routine home management and shopping.

The Xiong family was very isolated from the community. They had no extended family in this country and had not established close friendships due in part to the language barrier.

In the effort to help stabilize the family, the CPS worker arranged for a homemaker to help Mrs. X manage her home. Mr. X was admonished not to corporally punish children. Marital counseling and parenting classes were suggested.

Although the family seemed cooperative initially, the homemaker reported having difficulty from the start. Mr. X resented her and viewed her presence as a threat to his authority. Mrs. X resisted the homemaker's help in shopping. She refused to buy appropriately nourishing foods and vegetables.

After several days, Mr. X refused to allow the homemaker in the home. When the CPS worker arrived and insisted on entry, Mr. X became agitated, distraught, and threatened to commit suicide with a large kitchen knife.

The police were called and the children were removed on orders of temporary custody.

The CPS worker was very concerned about the failure of the initial treatment plan and bewildered by the father's behavior. Her supervisor suggested that this family's cultural difference might contribute to the difficulty.

A team conference was arranged to reassess the family in light of the perspective of other professionals who had experienced working with this cultural group. It also seemed important to explore the use of additional resources and bring to bear the collective thinking of other professionals.

In addition to the case team, the coordinator invited a social worker from the local Indo-Chinese settlement organization and the children's school teacher.

At the meeting, the CPS worker presented the case and updated the team with information regarding the poor adjustment of two of the children in their several foster care homes. Neng had begun wetting the bed and Pao acted out by stealing money and attempting to run away.

Initially, the team's concern focused on Mr. X's apparent mental instability. Much concern was expressed for the children's safety. Should they be returned home (especially in light of the parents' refusal to follow through on offered assistance, i.e. parenting classes and counseling)?

The perspective shifted when the social worker from the Indo-Chinese refugee settlement services addressed the stress of relocation from Laos to this country and the impact of the culture shock that ensues. In Laos, the man is the undisputed ruler of his household. Sons are valued more than daughters and child-rearing practices are very strict. Corporal punishment of wives and children was common and not considered abusive in Laos. Roles are very clearly delineated and the father's authority is unquestioned. The norm there is to turn to the extended family (the tribe) for help and support. Their belief is that problems should not be discussed with outsiders. There are strong sanctions against undermining the family name which incurs disgrace and dishonor.

While team members were divided on the relative impact of cultural issues in this case, there was consensus that a coordinated team effort would be required to achieve the ultimate goal of reunification of the children with their parents.

The following recommendations evolved from this team conference and were incorporated into an interdisciplinary case management plan by the protective service worker:

The social worker from the Indo-Chinese resettlement service was to assist Mr. and Mrs. X in locating other Laotian families to develop a mutual support network, assist him in finding a job, and help Mrs. X locate markets where she could obtain some of the foods the family was used to.

The protective service workers would provide transportation so that Mr. and Mrs. X could visit the children more regularly. The worker (agency) would locate a translator so that the X's would fully understand.

The nature of planned interventions and the reason behind CPS interventions would assist in helping them to accept and understand court-ordered evaluation and counseling relevant to their needs.

The school teacher would work with school personnel to provide supports and follow-up for the children in school.

The team lawyer would assist the family in finding legal representation.

The team psychologist would arrange counseling sessions between parents and children to help them to come to terms with family difficulties and with difficulty in adjusting to their environment.

When looking at the family through cultural lenses, the team members could better appreciate the enormous stress of the X's being uprooted with their traditional value system to an alien culture without acceptable supports and viable options. This did not eliminate the need for a psychological evaluation but added data which could conceivably contribute to a more favorable prognosis. It also oriented discussion toward recommendations designed to reduce the stress and isolation in a culturally compatible manner.

There was team consensus that a goal for their family was reunification after appropriate reduction of environmental stress and help in adjusting to the differing expectations of child rearing in this country.

The case of the Xiong family demonstrate that intervention in abusive families may require cultural responsiveness as well as flexibility and creativity in the use of appropriate services. Without the team approach, the CPS worker would not have had the practical help offered by the social worker from a specialized agency or being able to sort out the impact of her cultural differences in assessing this family.

SUMMARY

The purpose of this chapter was to delineate and demonstrate the use of the interdisciplinary team in the diagnosis, treatment, and mangement of child abuse and neglect.

Many experts agree that traditional therapeutic methods, per se, are relatively ineffectual in the treatment of this complex and tragic human phenomenon.

When individuals from different professional orientations form a team to review cases of child maltreatment, the group creates a pool of shared knowledge, experience, judgment and imagination. This pool of knowledge not only helps members do their individual jobs more effectively and intelligently but it greatly increases efficiency.

Communication engenders cooperation and collaboration. In the final analysis, the multidisciplinary/interdisciplinary team approach represents a viable, creative response to the provision of resources, services, and supports which operate to integrate children and their parents.

REFERENCES

Blumberg, M.L.: Treatment of the abused child and the child abuser. *American Journal of Psychotherapy, 81*(2): 1977.

Bockman, H.R., and Carrol, C.A.: The law enforcement's role in evaluation. In Schmitt, B.D. (Ed.): *The Child Protection Team Handbook.* New York: Garland, S.T.P.M. Press, 1978.

Bridges, C.L.: The nurses evaluation. In Schmitt, B.D. (Ed.): *The Child Protection Team Handbook*. New York: Garland S.T.P.M. Press, 1980.

Broadhurst, D.D.: What schools are doing about child abuse and neglect. *Children Today*, January-February, 1978.

Carrol, C.: Guidelines for returning a child home and case closure. In Schmitt, B.D. (Ed.): *Child Protection Team Handbook*. New York: Garland S.T.P.M. Press, 1978.

Carrol, C.A., and Schmitt, B.I.: Improving community treatment services. In Schmitt, B.D. (Ed.): *Child Protection Team Handbook*. New York: Garland S.T.P.M. Press, 1980.

DeFrances, V.: Child protection: A comprehensive coordinated process. In National Symposium on Child Abuse, 4th Charleston, SC, *Collection Papers*, Denver, CO: The American Humane Association, Children's Division, 1975.

Fontana, V.: Factors needed for prevention of child abuse and neglect: Letters to the editor. *Pediatrics, 46*(2): 1970.

Hartford Child Protection Team, Manual. This material was based in part on the team coordinator's job description. Unpublished Handbook, 1984.

Helfer, R.E., and Schmidt, R.: The community-based child abuse and neglect program. In Helfer, R., and Kempe, C. (Eds.): *Child Abuse and Neglect*. Cambridge, MA: Ballinger Press, 1960.

Jay, A.: How to run a meeting. *Harvard Business Review, 54*: March-April, 1976.

Jones, D.N., McClearn, R.M., and Vobe, R.: Case conferences on child abuse—Nottinghamshire approach. *Child Abuse and Neglect, 3*: 1979.

Kempe, C.H.: Forward. In Schmitt, B.D. (Ed.): *The Child Protection Team Handbook*. New York, Garland S.T.P.M. Press, 1978.

Mouzakitis, C.M., and Goldstein, S.C.: A multidisciplinary approach to the treatment of child neglect. Accepted for publication in the *Social Casework* journal, 1984.

National Center on Child Abuse and Neglect: *Child Abuse and Neglect: The Problem and Its Management, Vol. 3, The Community Team: An Approach to Case Management and Prevention*. U.S. Department of Health, Education, and Welfare, DHEW Publication No. (OHD) 75-30075, 1976.

National Center on Child Abuse and Neglect: *Federal Standards for Child Abuse and Neglect-Prevention and Treatment Programs and Projects*. U.S. Department of Health, Education and Welfare, 1978.

Newberger, E., Hogenbuch, J., Ebeling, N., Colligan, E., Sheehan, J., and Veigh, S.: Reducing the literal and human cost of child abuse: Impact of a new hospital management system. *Pediatrics, 51*(5): 1973.

Pellegrino, E.D.: Interdisciplinary education in the health professions: Assumptions, definitions and some notes on teams. In *Report of a Conference: Educating the Health Team*. National Academy of Sciences, Institute of Medicine, 1972.

Pettiford, E.K.: *Improving Child Protective Services Through the Use of Multidisciplinary Teams*. National Center on Child Abuse and Neglect, Children's Bureau, *ACYF*, *OHDS, DHHD*, Grant No. 90-C-1727, 1981.

Schmitt, B.O.: Getting started. In Schmitt, B.O. (Ed.): *The Child Team Protection Handbook*. New York: Garland S.T.P.M. Press, 1982.

Schmitt, B.O.: Team purpose and structure. In *The Child Protection Team Handbook*. New York: Garland S.T.P.M. Press, 1978.

Schmitt, B.D., Grosz, C.A., and Carrol, C.A.: The child protection team: A problem-oriented approach. In Helfer, R.E., and Kempe, C.H. (Eds.): *Child Abuse and Neglect: The Family and the Community*. Cambridge, MA: Ballinger Publishing Company, 1976.

Sgroi, S.M.: *Handbook of Clinical Intervention in Child Sexual Abuse*. Lexington, MA: Lexington Books, D.C. Heath and Co., 1982.

Steele, B.F.: Experience with an Interdisciplinary Concept. In Helfer, R., and Kempe, C. (Eds.): *Child Abuse and Neglect*. Cambridge, MA: Ballinger Publishing Company, 1976.

Stern, H.C.: The psychiatrists evaluation of the parents. In Schmitt, B.D. (Ed.): *The Child Protection Team Handbook*. New York: Garland S.T.P.M. Press, 1978.

Terr, L.C., and Watson, A.S.: The battered child rebrutilized: Ten cases of medical-legal confusion. *American Journal of Psychiatry, 114*(10): 1968.

Urzi, M.: *Cooperative Approaches to Child Protection: A Community Guide*. Minnesota State Department of Public Welfare (under grant from National Center on Child Abuse and Neglect, U.S. Department of Health and Human Services), 1980.

Witworth, J., Lanier, M., Skinner, R., and Lund, N.: A multidisciplinary hospital-based team for child abuse cases: A "hands-on" approach. *Child Welfare, 50*(4): 1981.

CHAPTER 19

THE USE OF SUPERVISION IN PROTECTIVE SERVICES

Thomas Cruthirds

INTRODUCTION

The purpose of this chapter is to introduce the reader to some of the nuances of child protective services supervision. This will be accomplished in two major steps. First, several issues of current importance in direct services supervision will be examined. These include the distinction between supervision and consultation, the major functions comprising direct services supervision, the dilemma surrounding the development of staff autonomy, the difficulty in evaluation of staff competency, the means of addressing staff performance deficits, the educational and experiential qualifications for becoming supervisors, the unique professional specialty of clinical supervision, and the reciprocal accountability shared by supervisors and supervisees.

Once this foundation has been achieved, the focus will shift to a consideration of the special supervisory responses inherent in child protective service work. These unique aspects of child protective service supervision are examined in relation to the six phases of the direct service process—intake/investigative assessment, assessment of problem system, intervention planning and goal setting, service implementation, termination of effort, and evaluation of outcome. Throughout, reference is made to characteristic decisions and responsibilities jointly faced by child protective service case workers and supervisors.

MAJOR CONTEMPORARY ISSUES IN DIRECT SERVICES SUPERVISION

There is a considerable body of professional literature, spanning more than seventy-five years, pertaining to direct services supervision. For comprehensive summaries of this literature and for thorough bibliographic references, the reader is referred to several particularly noteworthy efforts (Austin, 1981; Kadushin, 1976; Kaslow and Associates, 1972; Munson, 1983; Shulman, 1982). Various writers tend to emphasize somewhat different aspects of this phenomenon. There is a general agreement, however, that supervision is an exceedingly complex process, and that our increased understanding will depend on the accomplishment of vastly more research than has to date been conducted (Briar, 1966; Briar, 1971; Kadushin, 1976; Munson, 1983). A number of general, recurring issues deserve special attention before we consider the specialized nature of child protective service supervision.

The first of these general issues revolves around the conceptual separation of what is supervision from that which constitutes consultation. It is not unusual to hear these two terms used interchangeably as though they represent the same phenomena. They refer, however, to distinctly different processes. Supervision, a line position in the administrative hierarchy, presumes a delegation of formal role authority for the assignment, monitoring, and evaluation of the work of the direct services practitioner. The service provider is formally accountable to the supervisor for the performance of assigned therapeutic tasks. However, consultation is a staff assignment, rather than a line position; it is "an adjunctive function to supervision or a supplementation of supervision" (Kadushin, 1977, p. 45). Consultation "offers the freedom to seek assistance without granting authority to those who give assistance. It makes available help without control, without the need to adhere to the consultant's advice, suggestion, or recommendations, and without the requirement that the consultee be accountable to the consultant.... The consultee is accountable for the use of the consultation to his own supervisor" (Kadushin, 1977, p. 39). And so, at the outset, it is important to distinguish carefully between the formal, structured supervision of direct service providers and any consultation they may be afforded. We are concerned in this chapter with that which is supervision.

Related to this is a second general issue that reverberates through the literature; namely, what are the major functions that must be performed in carrying out the work of direct services supervision? Alfred Kadushin is owed a considerable debt of gratitude for so masterfully delineating the functions of administration, emotional support, and education. It is now generally conceded that the mass of detail of supervision may conveniently be categorized under these general headings. The administrative function is concerned with accountability, control, and direction of the workers' effort. The emotional support function focuses on helping staff adjust to job-related stress. The educational function is keyed to teaching the worker what one needs to know in order to do the job and helping the worker learn it (Kadushin, 1976). Major emphasis here will be placed on the role of the supervisor as teacher of other social services staff. This is not intended to minimize the importance of administrative or supportive supervision in child protective services. However, one's ability to success-fully assume the teaching role is considered to be absolutely crucial in clinical supervision. Details of how this teaching role is enacted in child protective services are presented in subsequent parts of this chapter.

A third issue is closely associated with the preeminence of the educa-tional supervisory function. It is widely believed that close and prolonged teaching supervision may sometimes result in an unwanted curtailing of the possible professional autonomy of the workers, thus making them unduly dependent on the technical judgment of supervisors. It is thus considered that overly extended educational supervision may be contrary to the aim of professional, self-directed clinical practice. There is some truth to these fears, despite the centrality of the teaching function of supervision. What is needed is some way to measure when one's direct services learning is sufficiently complete. The field needs some formalized procedure for the termination of continuous educational supervision with particularly gifted clinical staff. Schmidt (1973) has proposed a schema depicting increased caseworker decision making latitude, and concomitant decreased supervisory educational responsibility, as child welfare workers progress through various stages of professional development. A rigorous proficiency certification procedure may hold some future promise in this regard, so that a caseworker might progress from "the phase of direction and teaching to one of more permissive consultation" (Kadushin, 1976, p. 434). It should be noted that even where services staff may gain indepen-dence from the requirements of close educational supervision, agencies will still need to impose some form of administrative supervision.

We will assume that most service providers remain for sustained periods under the educational guidance of clinical supervisors. A fourth issue, then, centers on the means to be employed in accurately evaluating the actual performance of staff, thus producing for the supervisor and worker an educational diagnosis as the basis of their collaborative teaching-learning efforts. What is required is a method of perceptively depicting the gaps a worker may have in selecting and applying in particular cases appropriate knowledge, skill, and values. The norm in practice in many agencies is for the supervisor to rely heavily on the written work produced by supervisees (case record summaries, court reports, other entries) and the workers' retrospective verbal reports of client family interpersonal behav-iors and worker-client interactions. There is considerable evidence to sus-tain the conclusion that such data are relatively poor substitutes for more first-hand performance observational information (Hepworth and Larsen, 1982; Kadushin, 1976). Supervisors can avail themselves of more objective performance data through occasionally sitting in on supervisee interviews with families, by utilizing one-way viewing mirrors that permit the observation of *in vivo* sessions, or by employing techniques of audiotaping and videotaping and subsequent analysis of selected interviews. Despite the logistical and ethical concerns posed by such practices, the supervisor and worker can acquire valid performance data that may provide the basis for their ensuing educational emphases. And in the case of audiotaped and videotaped sessions, the workers gain the potential ability to independently critique and analyze their own performance, thus promoting professional growth. Additionally, data may be preserved and retrieved that can clearly depict the reduction of gaps in application of specialized knowledge, skill, and values that had earlier been of educational concern. Evaluation of such relatively objective evidence might be one safeguard against unduly prolonged educational supervision.

We have now begun to touch on another general issue: that concerning the most efficacious means through which identified gaps in worker performance may be addressed through the educational enterprise of supervisors and services staff. While much of the detail of such efforts is presented in a later section, it is important to note here the overrriding importance of the nature of the supervisor-supervisee interactional, relational process. As Carlton Munson (1983) so aptly suggests, "The establishment of an atmosphere of mutual trust and respect is absolutely necessary for the supervisory process to successfully unfold" (pp. 4–6). If the relationship between worker and supervisor is positive, the supervisor gains a measure of referent power vis-à-vis the learner (Kadushin, 1976). The astute supervisor will strive to create and maintain an interpersonal atmosphere in which attempts to influence worker performance will have a great likelihood of being receptively perceived by the learner.

An additional issue endemic to clinical supervision centers on the extent to which educational and experimental preparation for qualifying to perform the supervisory role should be narrowly, or broadly, circumscribed. Although this issue may be hotly debated, certain aspects seem especially clear. Because of the centrality of the educational component of clinical supervision, those who would perform this role must be clinically experienced. Munson (1983, p. 116) suggests, "Never attempt to direct the work of others when you are not good at doing that work yourself." Unless the supervisor has, for substantial periods, provided direct clinical services to individuals and families, she cannot presume to teach others the intricacies of case intervention. Without such experience, the supervisor will likely be seen by staff as lacking the power attributed to the "expert" (Kadushin, 1976). In the case of formal educational preparation, narrowing the pool of potential supervisory talent to any one of several human services fields (social work, for example) seems an inordinate constraint on the entry of gifted professionals from closely related fields (psychology, educational psychology, counseling, family studies, etc.). It seems more reasonable and equitable to impose criteria related to demonstrated ability to perform the clinical role, and demonstrated ability to teach others to perform the clinical role, in selecting potential clinical supervisors. Many allied human services educational programs and agency career paths may afford opportunities for potential supervisors to acquire such abilities. And increasingly, the thrust of many educational programs converge in the knowledge area of assessment and intervention from a family systems perspective.

A further related issue pertains to whether clinical supervision is a distinct professional specialty, apart from any particular disciplinary arena within which one's unique supervisory abilities may have been originally cultivated. Clinical case supervision does embody such extra-disciplinary and cross-disciplinary uniqueness, particularly as seen in the various aspects of the educational role of supervisors. Wherever the clinical supervisory task occurs, an educational diagnosis must be made, and performance gaps thus identified must be addressed. As services staff refine their independent professional abilities, some judgment must be made concerning a diminution of directed teaching and a progression toward a more consultative stance. This constitutes a highly professional endeavor, requiring detailed preparation, study, review, and planning prior to face-to-face enactment of the supervisory educational role. This professional complexity deserves due recognition within delivery agencies and educational institutions.

A final general issue has to do with the norm of reciprocal accountability that ought to characterize the relationship of supervisors and supervisees. Just as services staff are accountable to supervisors for the quality of work performed in cases, so are supervisors accountable to clinical staff to offer a wide range of enabling services that increase the likelihood that successful case outcomes will occur. All too often accountability is seen as a unilateral, rather than a bilateral, phenomenon. However, when the worker must address complicated case matters without being afforded the necessary amount of time, training, back-up support, referral resources, or supervisory assistance, the agency (including the supervisor) will have failed in its staff-enabling responsibilities (Cruthirds, 1976).

SPECIAL SUPERVISORY CONSIDERATIONS
IN CHILD PROTECTIVE SERVICES

Much of the work of child protective services in North America occurs within agencies organized under public auspices at the country, state, or provincial level. The thrust of these remarks, therefore, will be geared to the assumption that the supervisory episodes envisioned occur within the public social services delivery context. Perhaps they will have some relevance, also, for those engaged under voluntary or proprietary auspices.

Experience has revealed that both supervisors and workers in public child protective services settings reflect a diversity of educational backgrounds. Although staff educational preparation in social work, at both the bachelor's and master's degree levels, seems on the increase, no single educational prerequisite is universally enforced for these positions. In fact, there is considerable pressure to declassify many such positions in terms of their educational requirements. Therefore, a second assumption is that the supervisory encounter may likely comprise personnel of heterogeneous educational backgrounds.

One method of examining the unique aspects of child protective services supervision is to consider the specialized tasks required of supervisors during the various phases of the direct service process. By inspecting the case demands posed by the need to complete the phase of intake/investigative assessment, for instance, one may illuminate the specialized attention the supervisor must devote to this particular phase of the service process. It is also possible to consider some possible variation in supervisory requirements in relation to whether the service matter constitutes neglect of children or whether the focus of attention is on the phenomenon of abuse. This section, therefore, is devoted to an analysis of the specialized tasks of child protective service supervision during the service phases of: intake/investigative assessment, assessment of problem system, intervention planning and goal setting, service implementation, termination of effort, and evaluation of outcome.

Intake/Investigative Assessment

This phase of service is directed at determining whether what is reported to the agency actually constitutes child abuse or child neglect. If the answer is in the affirmative, a case is opened for services to begin. In the event that a child is found to be in imminent danger of potential harm, urgently needed services may be rendered at once, including the possibility of protective removal of the child from the home.

The response of the supervisor to this initial phase of service will depend somewhat on whether a specialized unit handles all intake/investigative assessment duties or whether this function is integrated into the responsibilities of units assigned the ongoing service provision role. In the former case, the supervisor may be more confident that the code prescribing the phenomena which fall within the mandate of the protective service agency (Holder and Mohr, 1980) is quite well understood by the worker. In the latter, there may exist a greater amount of hesitation on the part of staff, with the need for intensified supervisor focus on specific criteria for case establishment or referral.

One of the major tasks of the supervisor at this juncture is to see that the worker conducting the intake approaches the unknown aspects of the new referral with an open-minded attitude, particularly if prominent social variables representing distinct differences between worker and client family may be present. Factors such as race and ethnicity, gender, social class, power and authority often impede the helping process at the outset (Rubenstein and Bloch, 1982). These social differences may color the judgment of workers during the intake phase, causing staff to be either too eager, or too reluctant, to perceive the presence of abuse or neglect. Values clarification will frequently be a necessity.

Another task of the supervisor at this early stage of helping is to provide necessary channels for emergency feedback when child safety considerations require workers to move with dispatch. Ready access to supervisory judgment is essential when emergency removal of a child is considered (Ballew, Salus, and Winett, 1979). Despite the need for supervisors to devote protected time to regular conferences with other staff, mechanisms should be in place that allow intake workers to intrude when confronted with critical situations, in order to obtain immediate help with decision making.

A third major task when supervising at the intake phase is to prepare workers to deal effectively with client resistances to engagement (Holder and Mohr, 1980). Most families receiving child protective service help are involuntarily and reluctantly engaged. Staff may be frequently confronted with hostile, aggressive, manipulative client behaviors. Workers will experience fear, anger, resentment, and a range of other powerful emotions in the face of such perceived personal provocations. The supervisor must be able to guide staff to realize when they, themselves, are becoming resistant to the family and to provide an atmosphere in which a new perspective may be gained and new hope and identification engendered.

Assessment of Problem System

Following the establishment of a bona fide protective services case, it is necessary that a comprehensive assessment be made of the problem system that exists. In agencies where a specialized intake unit is established, this more elaborate family assessment may be the responsibility of either the intake or the ongoing treatment unit. Regardless, the supervisor must be clear as to whether her own staff are responsible for this function.

The most important supervisory task at this point in the process is insuring that workers who must complete such assessments systematically apply a conceptual schema through which the mass of otherwise bewildering behavioral and physical data may become objectified (Hartman and

Laird, 1983). The supervisor must see that workers use professional assessment tools that have the power to illuminate important case themes, patterns, levels of risk magnitude, and degrees of potential family strength. And the supervisor must insure that such professional assessments are faithfully recorded as a basis for further decisions and subsequent evaluation of case outcomes.

The full process of child protective service assessment is described in many authoritative works (Drews, Salus, and Dodge, 1979; Holder and Mohr, 1980; Kadushin, 1980; McGowan and Meezan, 1983; Polansky, 1981; Zuckerman, 1983). The focus here will be on identifying several distinct aids to assessment that hold promise for objectifying the problems and opportunities found in the family's ecological environment, their interpersonal functioning, and the intrapersonal composition of significant members (Hepworth and Larsen, 1982).

A particularly powerful device for detailing *environmental* stresses and potential resources related to specific families is the ecological map (Hartman, 1979; Hartman and Laird, 1983). When applied as a lens in child abuse cases, the extent of family isolation may be graphically portrayed. This paper-and-pencil contrivance also projects the extensiveness of conflict between neglecting families and major institutions such as schools, formal service agencies, and kinship networks. It is a formidable means for constructing a "snapshot" of the existing relationship of given families and their ecological environments.

Because of the nature of abuse and neglect, accurate assessment of the *interpersonal* relationships within families is a crucial beginning step. Two especially useful means of objectifying the internal relationships of families are the family map and the family grid. The family map combines features of both the ecological map and the process of family sculpture so that the quality of habitual individual family member interaction (conflictual, cooperative, etc.) and the pattern of emotional alignment (distant, fused, triangulated, etc.) may be portrayed (Hartman and Laird, 1983). What is produced is a paper-and-pencil diagram of the interpersonal structure within a particular family.

The family grid is a relational systems model. It holds promise in terms of assessing the extent of organization (on a continuum of rigid/structured/flexible/loose) and nature of boundaries (on a continuum of solid/permeable/open/amorphous) within individual families (Bardill and Saunders, 1983). Workers may actually calculate, using the grid, the approximate position of a family in terms of these major dimensions. The grid will portray, for instance, the rigidity of family rules and the solid enforcement of family boundaries characteristic of child sexual abuse situations. It can be used to illuminate the amorphous family boundaries and loose organization of rules so often seen in cases of chronic child neglect.

Another potentially useful interpersonal assessment device is the genogram (Hartman, 1979; Hartman and Laird, 1983). While the family map and the family grid have more widespread applicability in child protective services, the genogram may be particularly helpful in amplifying the important intergenerational themes within selected families. The supervisor and worker will need to evaluate the utility of this instrument because of its relative complexity and because data related to at least three generations of the family must be accessible.

A third important dimension to the assessment phase is the nature of internal, or *intrapersonal*, functioning of significant household or family members. Because of the danger posed by a continuation of neglectful or abusive behaviors on the part of adult caretakers (or even the threat of self-destructive behaviors), some means is required to readily assess adult attitudes toward particular children, to assess the level of adult depression and self-esteem, and to assess the level of satisfaction derived from spousal relationships. The rationale is that all of these intrapersonal factors impact on the ability of adults to perform a nurturing and protective parental role on behalf of children.

The clinical measurement package, developed by Walter Hudson (Hudson, 1982), is an example of a very promising set of nine easily administered, brief, paper-and-pencil scales that produce quick measures of intrapersonal functioning. Both validity and reliability are well established. The individual scales are especially helpful in yielding the practitioner a quantification (including clinical cutting scores) of a parent's level of depression, level of self-esteem, level of marital satisfaction, level of sexual satisfaction, attitudes toward a particular child, and quality of peer relations. Other scales may be utilized to reflect a particular child's attitude toward the father or the child's attitude toward the mother. A final scale produces a measure of intrafamilial stress. It will be immediately clear to the astute observer how pertinent such information would be in assessing further risk to children and in assessing important personal characteristics of adult clients. For obvious developmental reasons, the scales should not be administered to children younger than late latency, nor with adults or children who may be intellectually retarded.

The importance of the ecological map, the family map, the family grid, the genogram, the clinical measurement package, and other similar devices is derived from their ability to objectify the reality of the family context during the assessment phase of intervention. These findings may easily be retained in case records. They often help supervisors and workers bring closure to the assessment process (Munson, 1983). They yield data that provide a baseline measure against which future circumstances and conditions of the family may be compared.

A final task of the supervisor during assessment is to see that workers derive a set of hypotheses from the environmental, interpersonal, and intrapersonal case data that will present a distilled picture of the family problem system that must be addressed. What one wants to see is a brief written explanation of how these important associated factors interact to produce and maintain the problem. Establishment of reasonable target dates for the completion of such reports, and adherence to such time parameters, is a vital task that supervisors may perform in helping to round out the assessment of especially intractable cases.

Intervention Planning and Goal Setting

Although this aspect of the casework process is frequently included as a part of the assessment phase, it is important to amplify this work in a separate section. The reason for this emphasis is to underline the fact that even the best assessment of a family's problem system may be undermined if the selection of goals and plans for intervention do not have an explicit logical connectedness to assessment.

The assessment is geared to an objective depiction of the problematic aspects within a family's environment, within its interpersonal family member relations, and within the attitudes and outlooks of significant family members. The setting of goals consists of creating or supplying what is lacking within the environment, remedying interpersonal relationships that impede growth, and alleviating attitudinal and other intrapersonal impediments. As Ray Bardill suggests, one wants to put in the realities that are missing (Bardill, 1983).

A critical task of supervision is to assist staff in determining whether the goals and plans of treatment are to be achieved principally through the professional work of the protective service agency's staff or whether significant treatment decision making responsibilities are to be assumed by staff from other agencies. Experience has shown that opinion regarding the treatment versus case management role of the protective service agency varies widely both between and within state and provincial systems of service delivery.

Six additional supervisory tasks may be particularly helpful to most protective service staff as they formulate goals and treatment plans. The first of these is for the supervisor to establish the norm of involvement of clients, to the extent possible, in selecting the goals and means of treatment. One ought to respect the unique preferences and affinities of client families, where feasible.

This process is greatly enhanced when devices for objectifying the assessment (described in the previous section) are utilized, since clients may readily participate in constructing and interpreting the ecological map, the family map, the family grid, the clinical measurement package score, and so forth. A second task emerges from this consideration—to see that goals selected will, where possible, be directly related to factors revealed as problematic through use of such assessment devices. If, for instance, the ecological map illustrates the abusive mother's serious isolation from potentially helpful social contacts, both mother and worker may more readily agree to adopt a goal of reducing this isolation.

A third task may be to assist workers in defining goals as future states, or conditions, whose attainment may be measured. In the example of the socially isolated mother, a goal will be formulated in terms of her regular social involvement with other adults during some future point in time. Note that the *means* of achieving this future condition may then be specified, in relation to particular client tastes and preferences.

A fourth task that supervisors may find helpful is to teach workers to employ single-system research designs in projecting their work with families. If suitable devices for objectifying the assessment have been utilized, the measures derived from these instruments will provide data for the baseline of performance from which such single case research attempts originate (Fischer, 1978; Hudson, 1982; Schwartz and Johnson, 1981). The requirement of defining problematic behaviors rather sharply, in order for them to be targeted, is a hallmark of single-system designs. If, for instance, one of the important problems in the emotional neglect of a child is the lack of the mother's performance of the parental role of displaying affectionate responses to the child, this behavioral deficit might be highlighted as baseline data in a single-system design. The treatment, or experimental, variable selected as the means of addressing this targeted behavior might be the mother's inclusion in a parent effectiveness training group. The effect of this intervention may then be determined through the projected use of a relatively simple single-system research design.

Another critical task of supervision at this point, often overlooked, is to explore with workers the various unintended effects that may be set in motion by making the interventions they have planned. The family systems' literature has explored this area in some considerable detail, describing how family members may react to nullify the change efforts of other family members (Hartman and Laird, 1983; Rudestam and Frankel, 1983). To be forewarned is to be forearmed. A routine inspection of such potential reactive contingencies, especially when relatively inexperienced workers are involved, may prove particularly beneficial.

Closely related to this task is the supervisory responsibility to assist workers to formulate plans to counteract unintended effects of treatment, especially when client circumstances do not improve or when the family situation deteriorates from the level of functioning found at the time of assessment. Here the supervisor's experience with similar cases, or her ability to evoke the workers' recognition of factors similar to those that existed when previous cases took unexpected turns, is of critical importance. This assumes the accretion of learning through accumulated experience. It also assumes that where uncertainty and risk are particularly prevalent, a set of emergency plans will be thought out in advance of the implementation of ongoing service plans.

Service Implementation

Assuming that a thorough, professional job has been performed in transiting earlier phases of the casework process, one might think smooth sailing would be the norm during the ongoing service provision period. However, child protective service cases, because of their multiproblem nature, frequently take surprising and even bewildering twists. The unexpected crisis is an ever-present possibility.

The supervisor may be of special help to workers in relation to three particular tasks. Initially, and depending upon the level of independent professional development of staff, the supervisor may need to teach workers how to judge the salience of what is occurring within the case. Specific attention may need to be devoted to detailing with workers exactly the kinds of things that should be noted, recalled, and reported to the supervisor. Experience has shown that workers frequently omit any discussion with supervisors of seemingly crucial client revelations and behaviors that suggest probable deterioration of functioning. Evidence of this lack of correspondence between interview and supervisory sessions content has been observed on examination of videotaped data from the field of child protective service (Popple, Cruthirds, Kurtz, and Williams, 1976). Because child protective circumstances can so rapidly shift, the supervisor will need to make staff aware of any prospective key changes within environmental, interpersonal, or intrapersonal spheres that would act as signals for immediate supervisory reporting.

Until staff master the intricacies of independent professional perception described above, the supervisor will need to assume leadership in expressly determining with workers which cases are especially volatile and exactly what is occurring within these families. In such circumstances the supervisor will routinely explore with workers each assessment area (environmental, interpersonal, intrapersonal). A method of retrospective scanning and case surveillance can be implemented through posing to workers specific questions designed to prompt their recall of any significant observations that may signal to the supervisor the presence of an imminent crisis within the family. In this manner the supervisor's professional judgment is superimposed on that of the workers for as long as the workers have need of this knowledge and experience supplement.

A third task of supervision is to periodically "take the temperature" of the worker-family relationship (Munson, 1983). The presence of an equitable, forthcoming mutuality in the professional relationship is often the best gauge of further progress within a case. Conversely, in instances where the worker is held at an emotional distance, there is rarely a good prospect for professional influence to be felt within the family. Often, such cases are put on the back burner by overloaded workers. When the supervisor detects the absence of a positive feeling alliance and senses a poor quality of connectedness between worker and family, the professional relationship will not have flourished (Rubenstein and Bloch, 1982; Perlman, 1979). It is just such cases that should draw the sustained attention of supervisors.

Termination of Effort

Major texts on social services intervention highlight the importance of this phase of the process (Hepworth and Larsen, 1982; Compton and Galaway, 1979). The intricacy involved in closing a case may, however, be neglected in actual practice. Four major tasks of supervisors deserve particular attention.

The termination of mutual agency-family effort should have been explicitly anticipated from the onset by client and supervisor. Earlier steps in the service process should have been mutually experienced as cumulative stages toward a later reality in which no argument may reasonably be made for continued protective service involvement. Recent efforts toward more stringent review of foster care placements, and establishment of child abuse review teams, are examples of institutional responses to guard against unusually lengthy case involvement and to stimulate more rapid decisions for permanency planning.

A second task of supervision during this phase of work is to institute safeguards against premature termination of effort in potentially volatile cases. Here the supervisor is charged with attempting to assure that the volume of demand for the worker's attention does not cause major errors from benign worker neglect of specific unstable situations. The supervisor must try to ensure that distant and remote resistant families do not succeed in transforming the helping attempt into a well-rationalized professional retreat. If the approach of one worker is foiled, the supervisor may assign another to satisfy the demands of professional accountability.

Supervisors in protective service must also conform the not-infrequent situation in which particularly satisfying professional experiences with certain families lure workers into maintaining case activity far past the point at which objective goals have been realized. While this tendency may be understandable, especially in an area of work in which client nurturance of worker emotional needs may be rare, the wise supervisor will attempt to see that workers meet such expressive needs through other avenues of relationship.

One method of assisting workers with the termination process is through enacting the supervisory task of teaching them how the working relationship may be reviewed by client and worker, set in its proper perspective, and utilized as a vehicle for inducing the generalization of positive effects beyond the context of the current protective service experience. Workers may need to be reminded that clients should interpret positive changes in their functioning as learning that may be transferred to future life situations. In such instances, that which has been learned with the workers may be independently applied in new circumstances. Workers may benefit from the supervisory view that important relationships, through the process of memory, transcend any time-limited epoch of work. That exhilarating sense of compassionate connectedness does not evaporate when the purposes for which worker and client came together have ended.

Evaluation of Outcome

Three major supervisory tasks, each a complicated endeavor, are characteristic of this final phase of child protective service work. The first of these relates to an objective assessment of the quality of case results that may have been obtained. The second task encompasses an assessment of the quality of learning that the caseworker may have derived from the entire service episode. The final task requires that the supervisor glean from protective service work any evidence that her own knowledge and skill may need updating, in order for her to continue to render optimal help to workers.

Evaluation of case results is vastly simplified if acknowledged means of objectifying the assessment of the problem system, such as those discussed earlier, have been employed. An ecological map depicting environmental relationship factors may again be drawn as a case is concluded; a comparison of differences from the one constructed during the assessment phase should yield specific data relevant to this ending evaluation. Likewise, reconstruction of a family map, a family grid, or a set of clinical measurement scales will provide relatively precise data for comparative purposes. Well-executed single-system research designs graphically portray before-and-after pictures of client circumstances. The supervisor may be particularly helpful in pointing out to workers memorable technical struggles within an individual case. A final reading of the temperature of the worker-client relationship may be especially enlightening. All of these efforts are employed by protective service supervisors in an attempt to assist workers objectify the result of instrumental efforts.

Because of the central role of teaching within the practice of protective service supervision, a thoughtful evaluation of what the worker may have learned from particular service experiences is extremely important. Alas, what may have been learned by a worker is that the demands posed by child protective service are such that the worker should not remain in this field. Such conclusions, if objectively grounded, should not be mourned. Each year thousands of young aspiring professionals exit the protective service field (Richan, 1978), many having learned the valuable lesson that they will perform more ably in other arenas. On behalf of those careerists who remain, however, the supervisor should contrive to illuminate, in certain specifically designated teaching cases, the aspects of learning that may serve especially useful purposes in future attempts of the worker to render helpful services to families and children. The supervisor may help the worker isolate and recall important family patterns, themes, and associations of events that seemed to be pivotal perceptions during the casework process. Gains in self-awareness and conscious use of the professional relationship should be carefully acknowledged. Further educational needs that have become crystalized through this case experience may be identified; plans for reducing such worker knowledge gaps ought to be explored and formalized.

Finally, the committed protective service supervisor will wish to examine the mutual case experiences of themselves and their workers in light of opportunities that are presented to enrich the educational repertoire of the supervisor. Do questions arise that require specific review reading on the part of the supervisor? Does the supervisor need to seek consultation to provide needed help for her workers? It is reasonable to ask the view of a CART team on a particular matter?

The supervisor may assign an occasional unique case to herself in order to experience the opportunity of systematically rethinking the entire service delivery process. The supervisor may avail herself of the opportunity to videotape occasional personal client interviews and worker supervisory conferences, so that these may, in privacy, be minutely analyzed and reflected upon. The supervisor may seize the opportunity of modeling to workers recommended skills and techniques and, thus, solicit worker critique of the supervisor's casework skills. In truth, the fluent practice of child protective service supervision is a life long endeavor. The supervisor who claims the enduring respect of the unusually gifted group who comprise the worker cadre will demonstrate her ability to be a master learner, as well as masterful teacher.

REFERENCES

Austin, M.J.: *Supervisory Management for the Human Services.* Englewood Cliffs, NJ: Prentice-Hall, 1981.

Ballew, J.R., Salus, M.K., and Winett, S.: *Supervising Child Protective Workers.* Washington, D.C.: National Center on Child Abuse and Neglect, August 1979.

Bardill, D.R., and Saunders, B.E.: Services to families and groups. In Callicut, J.W. and Lecca, P.J. (Eds.): *Social Work and Mental Health.* New York: Free Press, 1983.

Briar, S: Family services. In Maas, H.S. (Ed.): *Five Fields of Social Service: Reviews of Research.* New York: National Association of Social Workers, 1966.

Briar, S.: Family services and casework. In Mass, H.S. (Ed.): *Research in the Social Services: A Five-Year Review.* New York: National Association of Social Workers, 1971.

Compton, B.R., and Balaway, B.: *Social Work Processes* (rev. ed.). Homewood, IL: Dorsey Press, 1979.

Cruthirds, C.T.: Management should be accountable, too. *Social Work, 21:*179-180, 1976.

Drews, K., Salus, M.K., and Dodge, D.: *Child Protective Services: Inservice Training for Supervisors and Workers.* Washington, D.C.: Creative Associates, 1979.

Fischer, J.: *Effective Casework Practice: An Eclectic Approach.* New York: McGraw-Hill, 1978.

Hartman, A.: Diagrammatic assessment of family relationships. In B. Compton and B. Galaway, *Social Work Processes* (rev. ed.). Homewood, IL: Dorsey Press, 1979.

Hartman, A., and Larid, J.: *Family-Centered Social Work Practice.* New York: Free Press, 1983.

Hepworth, D.H., and Larsen, J.A.: *Direct Social Work Practice: Theory and Skills.* Homewood, IL: Dorsey Press, 1982.

Holder, W.M., and Mohr, C. (Eds.): *Helping in Child Protective Services.* Englewood, CO: American Humane Association, 1980.

Hudson, W.: *The Clinical Measurement Package: A Field Manual.* Homewood, IL: Dorsey Press, 1982.

Kadushin, A.: *Supervision in Social Work.* New York: Columbia University Press, 1976.

Kadushin, A.: *Consultation in Social Work.* New York: Columbia University Press, 1977.

Kadushin, A.: *Child Welfare Services* (3d ed.). New York: Macmillan, 1980.

Kaslow, F.W., and Associates: *Issues in Human Services.* Washington, D.C.: Jossey-Bass, 1972.

McGowan, B.G., and Meezan, W.: *Child Welfare: Current Dilemmas/Future Directions.* Itasca, IL: Peacock, 1983.

Munson, C.E.: *An Introduction to Clinical Social Work Supervision.* New York: Haworth Press, 1983.

Perlman, H.H.: *Relationship: The Heart of Helping People.* Chicago: University of Chicago Press, 1979.

Polansky, N.A.: *Damaged Parents: An Anatomy of Child Neglect.* Chicago: University of Chicago Press, 1981.

Popple, P.R., Cruthirds, C.T., Kurtz, P.D., and Williams, R.: *Vantage Point: A Training Guide on Working with Parents Who Neglect Their Children.* Knoxville: University of Tennessee Research Corporation, 1977.

Richan, W.C.: Personnel issues in child welfare. In A. Kadushin (Ed.), *Child Welfare Strategy in the Coming Years: An Overview.* Washington, D.C.: U.S. Children's Bureau, 1978.

Rubenstein, H., and Bloch, M.H.: *Things that Matter: Influences on Helping Relationships.* New York: Macmillan, 1982.

Rudestam, K.E., and Frankel, M.: *Treating the Multiproblem Family: A Casebook.* Monterey, CA: Brooks/Cole, 1983.

Schmidt, D.M.: Supervision: A sharing process. *Child Welfare, 53:*436–446, 1973.

Schwartz, S., and Johnson, J.H.: *Psychopathology of Childhood: A Clinical-Experimental Approach.* New York: Pergamon Press, 1981.

Shulman, L.: *Skills of Supervision and Staff Management.* Itasca, IL: Peacock, 1982.

Zuckerman, E.: *Child Welfare.* New York: Free Press, 1983.

PART V

In Part V of the book, national and local responses to the child abuse and neglect problem and issues related to the organization of child welfare services for abused and neglected children are discussed.

Chapter 20, through a historical examination, leads the reader to trace organized efforts on a federal and state level to respond to child abuse and neglect problems and the awakening of public consciousness. This historical examination assists the reader in understanding why we are where we are in terms of knowledge regarding the child abuse and neglect problem and detection and treatment programs. The chapter's emphasis on preventive interventions and the outlining of such responses from the private and public sector is most appropriate in concluding this book.

Chapter 21 introduces the reader to basic problems in social service delivery: those of inaccessibility and fragmentation. It also addresses the issue of the absence of a coordinated network of social services for abused and neglected children. While recent reforms stress administrative changes in the existing service networks, these reforms do not address the need for planning and a more integrated system of services for children and families. The chapter further emphasizes public responsibility for assessing that the service needs of children and families are adequately addressed.

CHAPTER 20

NATIONAL AND LOCAL RESPONSES TO CHILD ABUSE DURING THE PAST CENTURY

Ann Harris Cohn

INTRODUCTION

Societal experiences with and responses to child abuse and neglect are influenced by various social and political factors. The purpose of this chapter is to review how social values, public awareness, economic circumstances, and other social and political factors have influenced child abuse related actions in the United States over the past century and to explain where the United States is today as a nation with respect to child abuse and where it may be heading.

Early Awareness of Child Abuse: Beginning with the Mary Ellen Case

Organized efforts to respond to child abuse in the United States can be traced to 1874, when church workers found that Mary Ellen, a New York City child, had been chained to her bed by her guardians and repeatedly beaten. Because there was no precedent allowing for legal intervention in the case of child abuse, they were able to remove Mary Ellen from her home only on the grounds that cruelty to animals was illegal and Mary Ellen was a member of the animal kingdom. Thereafter, because of public outrage, societies for the Prevention of Cruelty to Children were organized in the U.S. and elsewhere. Recognizing a role for the federal government in children's issues, in 1912 the U.S. Children's Bureau was established, and, in 1935, with the passage of the Social Security Act, government grants became available for the protection and care of homeless, dependent, and neglected children. The Social Security Amendments of 1962 required each state to make child welfare services available to all children, including the abused child (Cohn and Butterworth, 1982).

The Battered Child Syndrome: Awakening of Public Consciousness

The problem was dramatically brought to public attention in 1961 by extensive media coverage of the "battered child syndrome," a term coined by Doctor C. Henry Kempe, founder of the National Center for the Prevention and Treatment of Child Abuse and Neglect in Denver, Colorado (Kempe, 1962). Largely as a result, by the end of the 1960s every state had a law mandating the reporting of child abuse, and efforts were begun to get the federal government to take a more aggressive role (Cohn and Butterworth, 1982).

The Federal Response

In 1974 the U.S. Congress passed the Child Abuse Prevention and Treatment Act, which established a federal National Center on Child Abuse and Neglect. The center, with limited funds, supports research, demonstration, training, and technical assistance activities at the national, state, and local level. There was never an intention that this federal program would fund ongoing service programs. Title IV and XX of the Social Security Act and other federal and state programs were to support ongoing treatment. The definition of child abuse in the federal act—the physical or mental injury, sexual abuse, negligent treatment or maltreatment of a child under the age of eighteen by a person responsible for the child's welfare—was amended in 1978 to include sexual exploitation such as child pornography (Hoffman, 1978; Congressional Research Service, 1981). In 1984 the act was extended, for the fourth time, through 1988. Responses to the problem of child abuse, particularly with the passage of the child abuse legislation, have been diverse and often inconsistent. Given the complexity of the child abuse problem, the variety of professional groups and agencies which of necessity are involved, the decentralization to the state level and actual lawmaking and law enforcement in this area, and the range of private, local organizations drawn to the issue, it is understandable that a national response can not easily be a rational or planful one. The inconsistency in responses is further exacerbated by a paucity of solid information on the magnitude of the problem and effective approaches to prevention and treatment.

RESPONSES ON THE NATIONAL AND STATE LEVEL

Impact of the Federal Child Abuse Legislation

Impact of the federal child abuse legislation has been apparent both within the federal bureaucracy and on the state and local level.
Once the federal child abuse center—the National Center on Child

Abuse and Neglect—was set up and began dispensing some $20–23 million in child abuse, related funds, many other programs agencies and offices within the federal bureaucracy withdrew what minimal interest in the problem they had demonstrated. The existence of NCCAN thus became a rationale for other federal agencies, over the first decade after the legislation passed, to do little or nothing. Thus, even though branches with the Department of Education, the Justice Department, the Department of Agriculture and the Defense Department, to name a few, could have initiated numerous vital research and service programs to prevent and treat child abuse, in general they did not. NCCAN could offer no incentives for other branches of the government to get involved, except as participants on an intergovernmental Council on Child Abuse. While the council improved communication among some branches of government, it sparked very little new activity at the federal level (General Accounting Office, 1980).

Impact at the State Level

At the state level, the federal program had a more visible impact, due to the availabilty of special grants to those states in compliance with federal guidelines. During the 1970s, state after state strengthened its child abuse reporting laws, bringing them into agreement with the federal guidelines; this allowed them to qualify for small federal grants. States also strengthened their ability to receive reports of child abuse; by 1981 every state had established a "hotline" facility to receive child abuse reports on a twenty-four hour basis. Also, they improved their ability to investigate and manage reported cases. In the early 1980s, legal activities have been initiated which question the intent and appropriate scope of these laws. Of great concern is how broad a definition of child abuse should be included in the state statutes. Should only narrow definitions of life-threatening abuse be applied or should state laws encompass a wide variety of behaviors which could be emotionally or physically harmful to a child? Differences in public and professional definitions of abuse exacerbate the debate (Giovannoni and Becerra, 1979). The latter half of this decade should see some interesting revisions in state laws as a result.

The state grants as well as community grants distributed to NCCAN (numbering over 40 for the first 10 years of the program) also had a visible and positive impact at the community level. Although NCCAN grants have been relatively small (generally around $80,000 a year) and short lived (typically 2–3 years), they have provided an incentive for local groups to become active in the child abuse area. NCCAN distributed small grants across the country to all types of agencies, professionals, and communities. Competition for the grants has been high. Often, local groups unsuccessful in serving federal funds located private funds; as a result, local activities have proliferated.

The Role of National Private Organizations

As the federal government's role was defined and grew in the early 1970s, so too did that of a number of national organizations concerned with child abuse. In fact, it is very likely that without legislative action at the federal level and the development of a federal program, private or voluntary national groups would not have become visible. Existing organizations such as the American Bar Association, the National Association of Social Workers, the Child Welfare League, the Junior Leagues and others took on visible roles (often with federal grants) to respond to child abuse. The American Bar Association, for example, established a national child abuse resource center for attorneys; the Junior Leagues provided incentives for local affiliates to volunteer time for community child abuse projects. And a number of national organizations more completely dedicated to child abuse prevention became visible.

The American Humane Association (AHA), a voluntary, nonprofit organization and the oldest national group dedicated to the protection of children and the prevention of child maltreatment, took on, for example, new functions related to child abuse because of the availability of federal funds. Since its founding in 1877, AHA through its Children's Division has led in the development of programs and services on behalf of neglected and abused children. In its early years the association was instrumental in the passage of child labor laws and the establishment of juvenile court system. It also laid groundwork for thousands of humane agencies nationwide, which today speak for helpless and vulnerable members of society. With the passage of the federal Child Abuse Act, American Humane's activities were expanded to include an ongoing national study on child neglect and abuse reporting. Funded by the National Center on Child Abuse and Neglect and ongoing since 1973, it is the only existing data collection effort aimed at identifying the extent and nature of reported child maltreatment on a national basis. The information collected provides program administrators and other researchers with a basis for policy formulation and decision making related to child protective service on national, state, and local levels.

The C. Henry Kempe National Center for the Prevention and Treatment of Child Abuse and Neglect in Denver, Colorado, a primary catalyst for the federal child abuse legislation, became significantly more visible in the 1970s, in part with the receipt of a federal Regional Resource Center grant. Long seen as the pioneer of new approaches to treatment, typical programs of the center include a sexual abuse program, exploring the dynamics of incest and its various modes of treatment; a failure-to-thrive research and treatment program; a therapeutic preschool for sexually abused children aged two to five; a child protection team at the University Hospital in

Denver; and a program to provide consultation and technical assistance to child abuse professionals working in the area. This includes an annual professional training conference.

The center serves as headquarters for the International Society for the Prevention of Child Abuse and Neglect, the National Association of Counsel for Children and the journal, *Child Abuse and Neglect.*

The National Committee for Prevention of Child Abuse (NCPCA), founded in 1972 and a private volunteer-based nonprofit organization whose mission is to prevent child abuse, grew and became visible during the 1970s. Dedicated to reducing the amount of child abuse by 20 percent by the end of the decade, NCPCA is a network of thousands of individuals from the corporate, civic, lay, and professional communities working together to create awareness of the problem, to learn how best to prevent the problem, and to develop effective prevention programs. The concerned citizens are organized in a network of chapters in states across the country.

NCPCA began a nationwide public awareness campaign in 1976. It also has an extensive publications program, acts as a clearinghouse for information on child abuse prevention, and serves an active advocate for child abuse prevention. The receipt of a federal grant in 1979 to evaluate child abuse prevention projects funded by NCCAN helped the committee establish visibility in the field (Gray, 1983).

Parents Anonymous (PA), another voluntary organization assisted by the receipt of ongoing NCCAN support, in this case since 1975, is a self-help organization for parents under stress. Founded in 1971, there are now some 1,500 PA chapters or parent groups worldwide, with the majority in the United States. In 1982, PA initiated the formation of treatment groups for children who have been abused. The PA program is coordinated through a national headquarters, as well as offices at the state level (Borman and Lieber, 1984; Wheat, 1979).

Other national groups dedicated to child abuse treatment and prevention have also left their mark. For example, the Parents United Organization has been responsible for the development of comprehensive sexual abuse treatment programs across the country. And, SCAN America has initiated a number of lay therapy treatment programs.

In 1981 the Reagan administration proposed letting the federal Child Abuse Act expire, including funds to combat child abuse in a program of block grants to the states. Alarmed at the prospect of losing the federal focus on violence against children, organizations which had become active in the field banded together in the National Child Abuse Coalition.

The coalition's goal was continuation of the federal child abuse program. Coalition members—groups that at times have differed on policy issues—agreed that the Child Abuse Prevention and Treatment Act must continue as federal law. The coalition's message was clear. Without Public

Law 93-247, the federal emphasis on child abuse as a national priority would be gone and the stimulus to attract private and community support would be lost.

A coordinator was appointed as the focus for coalition advocacy in Washington. To foster sound political action based on accurate information, the coordinator keeps coalition advocates informed about what is going on in Congress—what legislation is being developed, which legislators should be contacted, and when votes are scheduled. The advocates, with their special knowledge of child abuse concerns, educate their congressional representatives so that they are able to make better-informed decisions about issues affecting the lives of children. Throughout the early 1980s, the coalition's efforts have resulted in the continuation of the federal child abuse program.

In summary, responses to date in the United States are characterized by an emphasis on detection, intervention, and treatment. Research has concerned itself with "how much is there" and "why does it happen" and "what do you do once it happens." Legal responses, the allocation of resources, and media coverage have followed suit (Berkeley Planning Associates, 1977; Cohn, 1979; Helfer and Kempe, 1968; National Center, 1983; Ross and Zigler, 1980; Zigler, 1979).

State reporting laws and court proceedings for alleged child abuse cases have been perfected. The deaths, the horrible beatings, the deprived children have been covered in newspapers and by television and radio stations. Professionals have sought expansions in dollars for protective service—so that more social workers could be hired and better counseling would be offered to parents who abuse their children. Training manuals for physicians and day care workers and school teachers have been developed so that they can identify children who have been or are being abused.

The hallmark of responses to child abuse since 1974 and through the early 1980s has been *after the fact*. Politically and socially that has been the most obvious and thus the most appropriate and acceptable route to take.

The Growing Magnitude of the Problem

Reports of child abuse have increased dramatically since the early 1970s, with a doubling of reports in the last half of the 1970s alone (National Analysis, 1983). Clearly, much of the early increases in reports have been a function of increased awareness of the existence of the problems and the importance of reporting known or suspected cases. But many experts maintain that the *amount* or incidence of child abuse has also been on the rise, particularly in the 1980s; surveys confirm this (NCPCA, 1984). In a nationwide survey conducted in 1983 by the National Committee for Prevention of Child Abuse, 45 states indicated that they believed the amount of child abuse increased in the previous year; 33 states said that the types of cases were getting more serious. And in 1984, states with official statistics available for the previous year reported an average increase in reports of over 17 percent (NCPCA, 1984; Gelles and Straus, 1979; National Center, 1981). While accurate statistics on incidence remain elusive, experts agree that the magnitude is great.

Why is child abuse on the rise? The reasons are multiple but seem to include: societal values about children, economic circumstances, funding patterns for federal and state social and health programs, the type and level of public awareness of the problem, the lack of private sector involvement, and the absence of a nationwide focus on prevention.

As a nation, all kinds of violence is tolerated, including violence against children. The audience is exposed to violence constantly on TV and at the movies. For example, the ever-popular TV program, "Saturday Night Live" shows a segment with one of the coneheads and a crying baby. Unable to get the baby to quiet down, the conehead slams the baby on the floor and jumps on him. The audience laughs. Frustrated, because the baby continues to cry, the conehead throws the baby out the window. The audience applauds wildly. And, in Chicago, a group of bartenders plan a special benefit for a local child abuse program. A local newspaper heralds the event with the headline "Bartenders Ball Benefits Bashed Brats." Most readers chuckle; few wrote in to the editor to protest. Why? It would seem that the tender and loving care of the nation's children is not as high a priority; as a result child abuse exists and increases.

Economic stress and instability are factors associated with child abuse (Coolsen, 1983; Gil, 1970; Light, 1973; Steinberg et al., 1981). Families with unpredictable income, terminated income, and inadequate income are at greater risk for abuse. So too are families in communities hard hit by economic problems. For example, the neighborhood grocer may be stressed because he feels he has to extend credit to too many families. Or, the local plant manager may be stressed because he has to lay off many of his workers. The prolonged recession and high unemployment rates experienced by the nation in the 1980s have taken their toll in many ways, including the increase of child abuse rates statewide increased by 12% in 1982 in Chicago, harder hit by the recession, child abuse rates rose as high as 44%, child abuse rates rose equally high (NCPCA, 1984).

A variety of federal and state social and health programs which historically have helped hold families together and support families in need experienced significant cutbacks in the 1980s, and in some cases they have been eliminated. For example, funds for Title XX, the major federal program of support for social services, were cut about 25 percent from 1980 to 1983. Assistance under Title XX goes to core services needed to help families under pressure—day care, homemaker services and protection for abused children. Significant cuts were also made in other family support programs such as maternal and child health, care for women and infants, foster care and adoptions, food stamps, and job opportunities; with the reduction in these special and important supports to families, the amount of child abuse has increased. And the problem becomes self-perpetuation. With more child abuse, more reports are made to the protective service departments responsible for responding to the problem of child abuse. These agencies, hard hit by funding cuts themselves, have fewer staff and fewer services to offer (NCPCA, 1984). As a result, narrowed definitions of child abuse are being used and only the most serious cases are accepted for services. And those families accepted for services do not always receive what they need for rehabilitation. The abuse or neglect problem continues as a result and often worsens; the amount of severity of abuse nationwide increased.

As a result of the National Committee for Prevention of Child Abuse's public awareness campaign (ongoing since 1976) and related activities of other groups, the public is now acutely aware of the child abuse problem (Cohn, 1982). A Louis Harris survey in 1982 shows that over 90 percent of the public regard child abuse as one of our serious social problems, and over 60 percent understand the relationship between economic stress and child abuse and later delinquent or abusive behavior (Harris, 1982). A more recent study conducted by the National Committee for Prevention of Child Abuse shows that the public knows all about the different types of abuse and is deeply concerned about the problem but doesn't know what to do about it (Cohn, 1982). The public is aware. Some members of the public are aware enough to report suspected cases which in part accounts for a dramatic increase in reports over the past decade. However, as the problem is increasing, the public does not know what to do about it. Few recognize that they themselves can do something in their own neighborhoods or communities. Few know it is helpful to reach out to a neighbor, friend, or relative under stress or isolation. Few recognize that support for new parents they know could help reduce child abuse. There are many roles concerned citizens can plan in helping to *stop* child abuse; in the absence of knowledge about those roles, child abuse appears to increase.

Child abuse does not occur in isolation from the private sector. Corporations can do a great deal to help strengthen families and thereby help prevent child abuse (Coolsen, 1983; Kamerman and Hayes, 1982). Factory workers and corporate employees are just as likely to be abusive parents or to be organizers or sponsors of child abuse prevention programs as are those employed elsewhere. Not only is there a role for the private sector in helping to fund the child abuse prevention activities of others, but there is also a role within the corporate and working community itself, particularly as more and more mothers participate in the work force (Children's Defense Fund, 1982). Work-based day care, flexible working hours, maternity and paternity leave, cafeteria benefits, and shared work are just some of the many programs which could be offered by employers to help strengthen families. But the resources and interests of the private sector have barely been tapped when it comes to child abuse prevention.

Finally, the nation has responded to the child abuse problem after the fact. An estimated $2 billion was spent each year in identifying, diagnosing, and treating child abuse cases after the fact. The legal system and the protective service system combined spend an average of over $2,000 per case of child abuse, after the fact. And studies show that rehabilitation success rates with these cases is less than 50 percent (Berkeley Planning Associates, 1977). A basic inclination of Americans is to respond to problems when they occur, when they become visible. When a child is hurt, the motivation is to help that *hurt* child, not to turn away from a hurt child to assure that other children are not hurt. For all the dollars spent on treatment, most of the abused children will likely be abused again. In contrast, as a nation little more than several hundred million dollars is spent annually on prevention, on doing things before the fact so that abuse never occurs. Yet, a lot is known about how to prevent abuse.

The National Committee for Prevention of Child Abuse's three-and-one-half-year national evaluation study, the first national evaluation of preventive strategies, sheds light on effective approaches to prevention (Gray, 1983). The study shows, for example, that programs which offer support to new parents, especially around the time of birth, have been significant in diminishing the chances of abuse. Supportive relationships with trained paraprofessionals during the extended perinatal period resulted in a significant change from negative to positive in high-risk mothers' attitudes towards their infants. This is in marked contrast to mothers who did not receive this kind of support. Parenting education was found to be helpful in dealing with specific cultural and socioeconomic groups as well. Low-income mothers who completed a ten-month parenting curriculum were more positive in their attitudes, more willing and able to negotiate social support for themselves in times of stress, and more hopeful about the future than were those of similar backgrounds who had not participated. And the study documented that nonprofessional, caring people can make a difference.

The knowledge base of how to prevent has been expanded in recent years (Cohn, 1981). Useful or promising avenues for prevention are available. But as a nation the United States has been slow to make a deep commitment to shift its focus from treatment to prevention.

Projecting Future Responses

Some argue that common sense says that a preventive response should be a priority as suggested in a 1983 U.S. House of Representatives Report, which stated:

> The Committee finds that the alternative to the prevention of child abuse is too costly. The known consequences—that children who run away may be pulled into prostitution and pornography, who may suffer drug and alcohol abuse, have often been abused; that 80 to 90 percent of the nation's male prison population were abused as children; that violence may be learned as an acceptable way to handle problems—demand attention to the importance of preventing child abuse (U.S. House of Representatives, 1983).

If one can stop a problem, particularly a problem which is a precursor to so many other problems, before it begins, valuable resources—both money and lives—can be saved. A founding father of our nation, Benjamin Franklin, told us about "a stitch in time saves nine." Prevention of child abuse is taking the stitch early on, before a child is hurt and a family is disrupted.

It is only recently that the "commonsense" aspect of prevention appears to be guiding responses to the problem. Slowly, but visibly, a growing number of planned responses to child abuse at the national, state and local level are in the preventive arena (Cohn, 1981; Helfer, 1978). This is occurring for both social and political reasons.

Private Citizen Involvement

Private citizens have been deepening their understanding of the child abuse problem and expressing a deep concern to do something about it. And the cry for action is a personal one. "I need help as a parent, lest I become a child abuser." The public at large, while not disinterested in the fate of the confirmed perpetrator, appears to be increasingly interested in stopping the problem *before* it occurs. Private sector involvement has followed suit. The Girl Scouts, the PTA, National Sororities, the American Contract Bridge League, the Junior Leagues, Women Clubs, and others have identified the *prevention* of child abuse as a goal; their memberships have gotten involved in the development of preventive activities (National Center, 1980).

The Workplace

The corporate sector has begun to recognize the linkages between what happens at home and at the workplace *and* roles that the corporate sector can appropriately play in strengthening families. Productivity is a function of more than the work environment. As a consequence, employers are beginning to provide day care services, child care support, flexible working hours, "cafeteria" fringe benefits, and a number of other services which by strengthening families will not only enhance productivity but also help to prevent child abuse (Coolsen, 1983).

The Health Care System

Early on involvement of the health care system has been identification and medical treatment of child abuse. However, throughout the health care system there is growing awareness of the opportunity to prevent child abuse by providing new parents with more than quality medical care. While organized physician groups have not been seen as the leaders in our national response to the child abuse problem, they have begun to advocate for multifaceted perinatal care which includes parenting education, birthing centers, home health visitors and a host of other services which will support new parents in getting off to a good start. As reimbursement for these and other abuse-related services becomes available, the health care system can be expected to play an even more visible role (Altemeier, 1979; Cohn, 1981; Gray, 1979).

The School System

Educating young children so that they can protect themselves from abuse, reach out for help when abuse begins, and develop skills so that they will be good parents later on is a critical aspect of prevention. The early role of schools has been one of identification and reporting. That is changing rapidly. Sexual abuse prevention plays and movies abound in schools across the country as do a number of other abuse-related programs directed toward children and parents, not just teachers. The schools and organizations that work with school-age children—the Boy Scouts and Girl Scouts, for example—are beginning to take a primary role in prevention (Cohn, 1981; Education Commission of the States, 1976).

The Children's Trust Fund Legislation

An approach to preventing child abuse that is catching on rapidly is the Children's Trust Fund (Helfer, 1978). In an era of diminishing governmental budgets for social services, this concept has emerged as an imaginative funding solution for abuse prevention programs. Beginning in 1980, states across the country have established these public funds to support preventive services (Birch, 1983). Lawmakers in other states are considering similar legislation.

Revenues to build the Children's Trust Funds are generated by surcharges on marriage licenses, birth certificates, or divorce decrees, or specially designated refunds of the state income tax. Grants from the fund go to preventive programs for child and family abuse, and distribution of the grants is supervised by an advisory group of individuals with a demonstrated interest in preventing child abuse.

Prevention is the central focus of the Children's Trust Fund concept. The idea was first conceived by Doctor Ray E. Helfer, a pediatrician widely recognized for his pioneer work in the field of child abuse (Helfer, 1978).

What Preventive Responses Would Look Like

Child abuse is a community problem that can only be prevented through activities at the community or local level (Cohn, 1981; Garbarino, 1981; Helfer and Kempe, 1976). These activities must be designed to meet the special needs of the cultural, ethnic, religious, and economic groups in a given neighborhood or community. Because child abuse is such a complex problem, no one community activity is enough; a number of different strategies must be used.

The earlier support can be provided, the better. The more efficiently support can be provided, the better. For child abuse to be prevented, families need support at many times. Prevention programs that address the underlying causes of abuse include:

Early and regular child and family screening and treatment, such as that provided by home health visitors—to identify and deal with physical and developmental problems in children at an early age and to advise parents on well-child care (Gray, 1979).

Child care opportunities, such as day care centers, Head Start, neighborhood baby-sitting cooperatives, and crisis nurseries—to provide respite for parents and socialization opportunities for their children (Cohn, 1981).

Programs for abused children and young adults through various professional and self-help approaches—to minimize the longer-term effects on children and young adults and to reduce the likelihood of their becoming abusive parents (Martin, 1976).

Life skills training for children and young adults through a variety of media including the dramatic arts—to equip young people with skills, knowledge, and experience necessary to cope with crises, to seek helping services, and to succeed in adulthood, particularly in the role of parent.

Self-help groups and other neighborhood supports such as Parents Anonymous and individual support such as that provided by foster grandparents or parent aids—to reduce the social isolation so often associated with abuse, particularly for higher-risk groups such as teenage parents (Lieber, 1984).

Family support services, including crisis care such as hotline counseling and other emergency services, as well as longer-term support such as alcohol and drug counseling, nutrition counseling, and family planning—to provide families with what they need to cope with the stresses of life and to stay together, particularly for parents of children of any age with special needs, such as the handicapped child (Cohn, 1981).

Support programs for new parents, such as perinatal bonding programs—to prepare people for the job of being a parent, to aid in the early development of a loving relationship and strong attachment between the new parent and the infant, and to promote family-centered birthing opportunities (Altemeir et al., 1979; Klaus and Kennell, 1976).

Education for parents—to provide parents with information about child development and skills in child care as well as information about local social service and health resources helpful to new parents (Burgess and Conger, 1978; Gordon, 1970).

The successful development and sustenance of these kinds of programs in communities across the country is a function of the commitment which occurs at the local level to make this happen. It is possible that in the United States federal and state laws and the political factors surrounding them will have less of a direct effect on responses to child abuse, particularly with respect to prevention. The momentum may now be there, along with concern and those enabling social values, to allow for and encourage a dramatic movement to *stop* child abuse in this country, rather than wait . . . and respond after the fact.

SUMMARY

This chapter has traced the responses to the child abuse and neglect problem in the United States over the past decade. Early identification of the problem, beginning with the Mary Ellen case in 1874, leads to a slow awakening of public consciousness. One hundred years after the Mary Ellen tragedy, a federal child abuse law was passed which in turn spawned a variety of responses at the national, state, and local levels. Despite widespread activity, the problem of child abuse appears to be on the rise. The reasons for this and a projection of future responses are discussed. A plan for prevention is presented as a more rational policy for future responses.

REFERENCES

Altemeier, W.A., Vietze, P.M., Sherrod, K.A., Sandler, H.M., and O'Connor, S.M.: Prediction of child maltreatment during pregnancy. *Journal of the American Academy of Child Psychiatry, 18:*205, 1979.

Berkeley Planning Associates: *Evaluation of the Joint OCD/SRS National Demonstration Program on Child Abuse and Neglect.* Berkeley, CA: BPA, 1977.

Birch, T.: *The Children's Trust Fund: An Update.* Chicago: National Committee for Prevention of Child Abuse, 1983.

Borman, L., and Lieber, L.: *Self-Help and the Treatment of Child Abuse.* Chicago: National Committee for Prevention of Child Abuse, 1984.

Burgess, R.L., and Conger, R.D.: Family interaction in abusive, neglectful and normal families. *Child Development, 49*:163-73, 1978.

Children's Defense Fund: *Employed Parents and the Children: A Data Book.* Washington, D.C.: Children's Defense Fund, 1982.

Cohn, A.H.: *An Approach to Preventing Child Abuse.* Chicago: National Committee for Prevention of Child Abuse, 1981.

Cohn, A.H.: Effective treatment of child abuse and neglect. *Social Work, 24*:513-19, 1979.

Cohn, A.H.: The role of Media Campaigns in Preventing Child Abuse. In *Child Abuse: A Community Concern,* 1982.

Cohn, A.H., and Butterworth, S.: Violence against children. *Encyclopedia Brittanica,* 1981 Yearbook (Chicago, Encyclopedia Brittanica), 1982.

Coolsen, P.: *Strengthening Families Through the Workplace.* Chicago: National Committee for Prevention of Child Abuse, 1983.

Congressional Research Service (CRS): Child Abuse: History, Legislation and Issues. Report No. 81-272 EPW. Washington, D.C.: U.S. Congress, 1981.

Education Commission of the States, Child Abuse Project: *Education for Parenthood: A Primary Prevention Strategy for Child Abuse and Neglect,* Report No. 93. Denver: Education Commission of the States, 1976.

Garbarino, J.: An ecological approach to child maltreatment. In Pelton, L. (Ed.), *The Social Context of Child Abuse and Neglect.* New York: Human Sciences Press, 1981.

Gelles, R.J., and Murray, A.S.: Violence in the American family. *Journal of Social Issues, 35*:15-39, 1979.

General Accounting Office (GAO): Increased federal efforts needed to identify, treat and prevent child abuse and neglect. HRD-80-66, Washington, D.C., 1980.

Gil, D.G.: *Violence Against Children.* Cambridge, MA: Harvard University Press, 1970.

Giovannoni, J., and Beccera, R.: *Defining Child Abuse.* New York: The Free Press, 1979.

Gordon, T.: *Parent Effectiveness Training* (P.E.T.). Scranton, PA: Wyden, 1970.

Gray, E.: What have we learned about preventing child abuse: An overview of the "community and minority group action to prevent child abuse and neglect" program. Chicago: National Committee for Prevention of Child Abuse, 1983.

Gray, J.D., Cutler, C.A., Dean, J.A., and Kempe, C.H.: Prediction and prevention of child abuse and neglect. *Journal of Social Issues, 35*:127-39, 1979.

Harris, L., and Associates: *Public Opinions about Child Abuse.* New York: Louis, Harris and Associates, 1982.

Helfer, R.E., and Kempe, C.H. (Eds.): *The Battered Child.* Chicago: University of Chicago Press, 1968, 1974.

Helfer, R.E., and Kempe, C.H. (Eds.): *Child Abuse and Neglect: The Family and the Community.* Cambridge: Ballinger, 1976.

Helfer, R.E.: *Child Abuse: A Plan for Prevention.* Chicago: National Committee for Prevention of Child Abuse, 1978.

Hoffman, E.: Policy and politics: The child abuse prevention and treatment act. *Public Policy, 26*:71-88, 1978.

Kamerman, S., and Hayes, C. (Eds.): *Families that Work: Children in a Changing World.* Washington, D.C.: National Academy Press, 1982.

Kempe, C.H., et al.: *The Battered Child Syndrome.* JAMA, 181:17, 1962.

Klaus, M., and Kennell, J.: *Maternal-Infant Bonding*. St. Louis: Mosby and Company, 1976.

Lieber, L.L.: Parents anonymous: The use of self-help in the treatment and prevention of family violence. In *The Self-Help Revolution*. New York: Human Sciences Press, 1984.

Martin, H.P.: Which children get abused? In *The Abused Child: A Multidisciplinary Approach to Developmental Issues and Treatment*. Cambridge, MA: Ballinger, 1976.

National Analysis of Official Child Neglect and Abuse Reporting. Denver: American Humane Association, 1983.

National Center on Child Abuse and Neglect: *Volunteers in Child Abuse and Neglect Programs*. Washington, D.C.: U.S. Department of Health, Education, and Welfare, DHEW Publication No. (HDS) 80-30151, 1980.

National Center on Child Abuse and Neglect: *Study Findings: National Study of the Incidence and Severity of Child Abuse and Neglect*. Washington, D.C.: U.S. Department of Health and Human Services, DHHS Publication No. (OHDS) 81-30325, 1981.

National Center on Child Abuse and Neglect: *Description of Research Projects*. Washington, D.C.: U.S. Department of Health and Human Services, 1983.

National Committee for Prevention of Child Abuse: *Incidence of Child Abuse Rising: A Working Paper*. Chicago: National Committee for Prevention of Child Abuse, Updated, 1984.

Ross, J., and Zigler, E.: An agenda for action. In Gerber, G., Ross, C., and Zigler, E. (Eds.): *Child Abuse, An Agenda for Action*. New York: Oxford University Press, 1980.

Steinberg, L., Catalano, R., and Pooley, D.: Economic antecedents of child abuse and neglect. *Child Development, 52*:975–85, 1981.

U.S. House of Representatives: *Child Abuse Amendments of 1983*. Report from the Committee on Education and Labor. Report No. 98-159. Washington, D.C.: U.S. Government Printing Office, 1983.

Wheat, P., and Lieber, L.: *Hope for the Children—A Personal History of Parents Anonymous*. Minneapolis: Winston, 1979.

Zigler, E.: Controlling child abuse in America: An effort doomed to failure. In Gill, D. (Ed.): *Child Abuse and Violence*. New York: Ames Press, Inc., 1979.

CHAPTER 21

ISSUES IN THE ORGANIZATION OF SERVICES FOR CHILD ABUSE AND NEGLECT

Donald V. Fandetti

INTRODUCTION

The history of child welfare services in the United States is one of much success. Substantial numbers of abused and neglected children, however, receive insufficient protection and assistance from the existing system of child welfare services. Inadequate funding and structure show that continuing efforts are required to expand options for children and eliminate structural deficits in the delivery system. In most communities, the reality is that few children are guaranteed access to a complete network of coordinated social services (Lindsey, 1982).

ANTECEDENTS OF CHILD WELFARE SERVICES

Social services for the protection and welfare of children were organized by voluntary organizations and state and local governments well before the twentieth century. In the colonial period, services were established for placement and substitute care of children away from their parents. At the same time, evidence of the conviction that children are best cared for in their own homes can be seen in the early system of outdoor relief authorized by colonial poor law statutes (Witmer, 1942). Widows and their children, the infirm and those considered unable to work, as distinct from other classes of paupers, were viewed as worthy and deserving of outdoor relief, and material assistance in their homes. Material assistance to families in their own homes, however, was the least-accepted form of aid to the needy (Costin, 1979). This can be seen in the common colonial practice of farming out, the adult counterpart to the indenturing of children. Farming out consisted of the placement of mothers and their children with individuals who made the lowest bid for compensation from local officials.

Though material assistance for children and their parents in their own homes was available, homeless children and those abused and neglected required substitute care away from their own parents. The beginning of substitute family care can be traced to the binding out or indenturing of children to master workmen. While this method was often satisfactory for older children, binding out of younger children tended to encourage workmen to put children to work as early as possible and to work them as hard as possible to compensate for current expenses and those incurred when children were too young to work (Witmer, 1942). Abuses in the farming out and indenture of children led to the increasing use of institutional care as an alternative for children. Institutionalization or indoor relief came to be emphasized for the poor, generally during the nineteenth century. Institutional care began with the placement of chidlren in workhouses and almshouses where they frequently were left unseparated from other inmates. Almshouse placement continued until deplorable conditions led to demands for differential treatment and separation of children into congregate care facilities. Substitute family care, in the form of indenture, and congregate children's institutions coexisted without conflict as to their relative merits until the use of the free home ignited decades of controversy over the two approaches to care (Wolin and Piliavin, 1967). Indenture, as a form of family care, declined with the movement of crafts and trades out of the home during industrialization and as indenture came to be associated with the bondage of children after the abolition of slavery in the United States.

The use of the free home can be considered the origin of the modern system of foster-family care (Kadushin, 1980). Free homes involved the placing-out of urban slum children in country homes. Since no legal contract was involved, the free home differed from indenture. As a large-scale alternative to institutional care, the use of free homes by advocates, such as Charles L. Brace, drew immediate criticism for their failure to place children in homes with religious orientations similar to those of their biological parents (Wolins and Piliavin, 1967). Strong criticism of the free foster home was also directed at the permanent separation of children from their parents, the inadequate means of selecting free homes, and the monetary incentives that led many people to offer their homes to children (Witmer, 1942). The important advance of providing a board payment to foster families, first used in the state of Massachusetts on a large scale, helped to establish foster family care as a service to children rather than a system for the exchange of children's labor for their own care.

THE CONTEMPORARY CHILD WELFARE SYSTEM

Child welfare services, traditionally defined, include foster care in family homes or institutions, adoption, emergency care and protection for abused, neglected and exploited children, services to single parents, homemaker services, counseling for children and their parents, recruitment and licensing of child care facilities and day care services (Spindler, 1979). The public child welfare agency in local departments of social services is considered to be the cornerstone of the child welfare system traditionally defined (Kahn, 1979). Local child welfare agencies are under the supervision or are operated by state agencies throughout the country. Additionally, the traditional child welfare delivery system includes voluntary sectarian and non-sectarian social agencies. For example, the Family Service Association of America provides services to children and families through hundreds of member agencies. In addition to the family services agencies affiliated with the FSAA, there are 700 more voluntary agencies, many of which are sectarian, serving family service agency functions (Kadushin, 1980). There are close to a thousand institutions for dependent and neglected children and more than three hundred residential treatment centers under private and frequently sectarian auspices (Kadushin, 1980).

These core public and voluntary agencies relate to many other human service agencies and organizations. For example, hundreds of cases involving dependent and neglected children and adoption are exposed to the court system throughout the country. Moreover, a substantial part of day care services for children is also considered to be part of the child welfare system (Kahn, 1979). At the federal level, child welfare includes agencies such as the Children's Bureau within the Administration for Children, Youth, and Families and committees of the Congress concerned with the needs of children. These include the Subcommittee on Children and Youth of the Senate Committee on Labor and Public Welfare and the recently established Select Committee on Children in the House of Representatives. In addition to these committees directly concerned with the needs of children, important committees such as the Senate Finance Committee and the House Ways and Means Committee have actual authority over national programs affecting the well-being of children (McGowan and Meezan, 1983). Legislative committees with authority over programs affecting children are also found in state legislatures throughout the country. The overall pattern of services, agencies, and legislative entities is extensive, and no complete agreement exists as to the exact boundaries of the child welfare services system affecting abused and neglected children.

NATIONAL POLICY FRAMEWORK OF CHILD WELFARE SERVICES

Services for dependent and abused children began as local- and state-level responsibilities in the United States. Responsibility continues at this level for statutes that influence child welfare policy in many ways. For example, state statutes establish grounds for state intervention in family life on behalf of the protection of children. In addition, these statutes specify the responsibilities and obligations of the state for children placed in substitute care. State law also governs dependency, neglect and abuse proceedings, termination of parental rights and adoption proceedings. Some states have attempted to strengthen laws governing the entry and exit of children from substitute care. At the state level, many provisions are now under way to protect children who are separated from their parents and placed outside their homes (McGowan and Meezan, 1983).

The involvement of the federal government with public social services for children took place in 1935 with the passage of the national Social Security Act. The original act provided for the federal government, through the Children's Bureau, to cooperate with state public welfare agencies in establishing, extending, and strengthening services for the protection and care of homeless and neglected children. In the decades that followed, a majority of the states enacted statutes assigning responsibility for the protection and care of dependent and neglected children to state agencies. Federal responsibility for child welfare services was later transferred to Title IV-B of the act, a categorical program that remained underfunded for many years.

Federal responsibility for social services for adults and children developed through a process of amendment of the original Social Security Act. Amendment in 1961 permitted states to extend AFDC coverage to children placed in foster homes following their removal from AFDC homes through court action (Spindler, 1979). The development of public child welfare services was accelerated by the 1962 amendments requiring that each state extend child welfare services to all political jurisdictions with the state (Committee on Ways and Means, 1982). These amendments also increased federal reimbursement for social services to AFDC families to 75 percent of state and local expenditures and authorized such reimbursement for the purchase of services from other public and voluntary agencies. These changes in federal policy opened a floodgate for increased claims for social services reimbursement by the states. Congressional reaction to the subsequent explosion of costs for social services led to the establishment in 1975 of a ceiling on federal matching funds for social services under the Social Security Act (Spindler, 1979). While these policies affected services for children, it is not possible to accurately determine the extent to which services under the 1962 amendments to the Social Security Act met child welfare needs across the country. The impact of services under the 1962 amendments seems limited due to infrequent contacts with clients by an insufficiently trained and continuously shifting group of caseworkers (Handler, 1973).

Child welfare services under Title IV-B are supplemented by social services expenditures under Title XX, renamed the Social Services Block Grant in 1980. Title XX provides federal funds for services to adults and for AFDC children under child welfare supervision. The 1974 amendments to the Social Security Act which established Title XX required each state to provide child protective services on a statewide basis (Committee on Ways and Means, 1982). By the 1980s, fifteen states devoted 50 percent or more of Title XX allotments to child welfare services (Urban Institute, 1983). A substantial amount of Title XX funds, however, are for day care, leaving unclear the impact of Title XX on increasing social services for children in substitute care or at risk of placement outside of their homes (McGowan and Meezan, 1983). While many core social services to children are authorized under the Social Security Act, important statutes exist outside of the act providing services to other groups of children. The precise boundaries of the so-called child welfare system may therefore exist in the eyes of the beholder.

REFORM IN PUBLIC CHILD WELFARE SERVICES

Comprehensive reforms of practice and administrative procedures in child welfare agencies, funded under the Social Security Act, were launched by the newly enacted Adoption Assistance and Child Welfare Act of 1980 (PL 96-272). The final regulations for PL 96-272 offered the following summary of the content and purposes of the new legislation. The impetus behind the passage of the legislation was the belief on the part of Congress, child welfare administrators, and practitioners that the public child welfare system serving abused and neglected children had become a "holding system" for children living away from their parents. This belief was supported by extensive empirical research. Studies showed that thousands of children were stranded in the foster care system with little hope of being reunited with their parents or having a permanent home through adoption or other permanency planning options. The holding system increased risks of psychological harm to children and increased cost to state governments. Empirical research findings showed that the number of children in foster care had increased along with the length of stay in foster placement. Moreover, studies revealed that case loads prohibited full and appropriate services to children and families and that children in care could have been cared for in their own homes if homemaker, day care, and other concrete services had been available. The same findings show that home-based services and adoptive care are the most cost-beneficial forms of care.

The new law emphasizes the use of preplacement preventive services to alleviate family problems that would otherwise result in the removal of a child from the home. In this way, the statute attempts to reduce the number of children entering the foster care system. To reduce the number of children already in foster care, the law requires several steps. These include annual goals for the reduction of the number of children in foster care over twenty-four months, reunification services, case plans and case review procedures that periodically assess the appropriateness of the child's placement, placement of children in close proximity to the family and in the least restrictive setting and financial subsidies to families adopting special needs children. Finally, three basic policy goals give overall direction to the new legislation: the prevention of unnecessary separation of children from their parents, the improvement of the quality of care and services to children and their families, and permanency through reunification with parents or through adoption (Federal Register, 1983).

CONTINUING PLANNING DILEMMAS

The child welfare reforms included in PL 96-272 provide for important changes in the functioning of child welfare agencies. The new reforms, however, do not address long-standing planning problems related to access and coordination of the network of services for abused and neglected children and their families. "Network" refers to the interaction of social agencies within the social welfare complex (Rein, 1970). In their classic study on the structure of social services in industrial society, Wilensky and Lebeaux offered one of the earliest critiques of the proliferating pattern of sub-fields and specializations leading to problems of inaccessibility and fragmentation of service in the social welfare complex. Wilensky and Lebeaux (1965) showed how a complicated pattern of services evolved based on specialization by program (public assistance), process (clinical social work), clientele (children, the aged), sponsorship (government, voluntary organization), and geographic location of service boundaries. Moreover, incremental addition of new specializations to the complex has resulted in a helter skelter, nonsystem of agencies and services financed from a bewildering number of categorical sources that each have different eligibility requirements and service standards (Office of Human Development Services, 1977). A former secretary of HEW (renamed HHS) graphically illustrated access and coordination problems in the social welfare complex:

Since 1961 the number of different... programs has tripled, and now exceeds 300. Fifty-four of these programs overlap each other; 36 overlap programs of other departments. This almost random proliferation has fostered the development of a ridiculous labyrinth of bureaucracies, regulations and guidelines.

The average state now has between 80–100 separate services administrations and the average middle-sized city has between 400–500 human services providers—each of which is more typically organized in relation to a federal program than in relation to a set of human problems. In spite of our efforts at administrative simplification, there are 1,200 pages of regulations devoted to the administration of these programs and with an average of 10 pages of interpretive guidelines for each page of regulation... eligibility is determined program by program without reference to the possible relationship of one program to another; prescribed geographic boundaries for service areas lack congruity. In general, confusion and contradiction are maximized.

Although studies indicate that more than 85 percent of all... clients have multiple problems, that single services provided independently of one another are unlikely to result in changes in client's dependency status, and that chances are less than 1 in 5 that a client referred from one service to another will ever get there, the present maze encourages fragmentation (Kahn, 1967).

It is not uncommon for metropolitan-area social service directories to have hundreds of entries with overlapping descriptions of service functions. Those who are aware of resources lack dependable transportation and often encounter staff attitudes, procedures, and policies that deter rather than facilitate access to needed services. An in-depth analysis of client channeling in the social welfare complex documents a discouraging picture of random and haphazard client movement and referral, client drop out, client self-selection in reaching services based on race and social class, long waiting lists, cases rejected at intake, and underserved clients most in need of assistance (Kahn, 1967).

The need for network and coordination of fragmented community services has been recognized for decades. Prior to the turn of the century, efforts were made to eliminate waste and duplication in the provision of financial assistance to the needy through more businesslike efficiency and coordination of charitable organizations. In the post-World War II period, it was discovered that 6 to 7 percent of a city's multiproblem families "overused" 50 percent or more of all community services. During the 1950s, shift in concern from client overuse of services to client underuse of services led to "aggressive casework," intensive service units, and interagency coordinating mechanisms such as the interagency case conferences. The war on poverty under the Economic Opportunity Act of 1964 emphasized new service strategies based on improved system linkage and coordination of services through decentralized multiservice and one-stop neighborhood centers (Rein, 1970).

Analysts of the structure of service for families and children acknowledge long-standing difficulties in simultaneous and sequential case level coordination of services (case management). Simultaneous coordination or integration stresses the availability of services required by families at the same stage of the helping process. Sequential coordination refers to the uninterrupted flow or continuity from one type of social service to another over time (Rein, 1970). The higher the risk of child maltreatment and family disorganization, the greater the need for simultaneous and sequential control of services by child welfare agencies. Abuse and neglect cannot be controlled by the uncoordinated intervention of single agencies (Weissman, 1978). The failure to coordinate agency efforts assures that complex family problems will not be satisfactorily managed. For example, inconsistency between court systems and child welfare agencies neutralizes agency efforts to secure guardianship and permanent plans for children; failure to follow through with aftercare service undermines substantial treatment investments made with children while in institutional care. Services to children in placement to the exclusion of service to the child's parent results in fragmentation of the family. Competing philosophies and views of children as client-patients, victims, or deviants across different fields and agencies in the community also results in agency representatives working at cross-purposes, undermining rather than reinforcing one another's work (Rein, 1970).

UNDERLYING CAUSES OF NON-SYSTEM IN SERVICE DELIVERY

The pattern of community services is based on a complex division of labor among many subfields and specializations in the social welfare complex. Originally, however, services were provided through informal networks of family, friends, and neighbors. In this early period, families faced the problem of the absence of services rather than problems of service coordination. Services were available privately but only to the very rich. As medicine, nursing, law, and the ministry grew, the general practitioner model became the basis for each profession. Coordination when it was required was handled by the doctor, lawyer, or minister (Austin, 1978). At this point, no division of labor among fields and specializations such as child welfare, public assistance, corrections, and other areas of social welfare existed. Public responsibility for the needy took the form of an undifferentiated charity and poor law. Distinctions among different categories of persons in need came at a later point in the evolution of services. The mixed almshouse, for example, included all in need of help and supervision, including the neglected and dependent child, the poor, the criminal, the mentally ill, and the aged. What is relevant is that each of these groups was evaluated over time in terms of the reasons for their dependency. As their needs became better understood, they were differentiated out of the poor law into separate systems of care. In the process of separating groups out of the poor law, new facilities and new specializations or fields in social welfare were created (Kahn, 1969). The addition of new specializations in social welfare continued into the twentieth century, reaching a high point in the proliferation of social programs during the 1960s. Each of the subfields developed their own practices, professions, and bureaucratic organizations. Problems related to inaccessibility and coordination across service boundaries increased accordingly.

In stressing the need for improved coordination and restructuring of the existing pattern of social services, Kahn (1967) indicated that the historical process establishing new fields or specializations in social welfare was based on social philosophies and moral evaluations of the times rather than modern scientific conceptions regarding the design of community service delivery systems. According to this view, new specializations resulted from a combination of history, professional prerogatives, public attitudes, bureaucratic dynamics, and patterns of funding. The classic study, during the 1970s, making the case for redesign of the pattern of social services in the United Kingdom offers the following judgment as to the need for reorganization of services:

> It was also argued that the present pattern of organization, and kinds of specialization and training which they embody, . . . evolved in response to needs, and that evolution on this basis should be allowed to continue and the services not forced into new moulds made on the basis of theory rather than emergent and developing practice.
>
> Although we accept that there is some substance in this argument, we do not see it as a good one for leaving the organization untouched. The present boundaries between departments have evolved only partly, and often slowly, in response to needs. Others have become established as a result of traditions of departmental separation in local government. The question is whether the services should be left to develop within these boundaries, or whether a better framework can be devised to foster future growth and respond more readily to changing needs. We think this is possible (Committee on Local Authority and Allied Personal Social Services, 1968).

NETWORK IN SERVICE DELIVERY FOR CHILDREN

Chaotic, open-market patterns of loosely related services place serious obstacles in the way of successful prevention and maintenance of the family as a resource for children in child welfare. Children at risk of placement because of abuse and neglect require tight rather than confused and loosely organized networks of service, interlocked rather than fragmented services and agency policies. The need for a system of community supports and controls is essential for families in which children are at risk of maltreatment. Neglect occurs in families in disequilibrium and downward spiral in child care and social functioning (Hally, Polansky, and Polansky, 1980). The restoration of family equilibrium is not possible with incomplete networks of haphazard and poorly integrated services. Simply "throwing money," moreover, at existing delivery systems is not likely to eliminate access and coordination problems rooted in archaic structures of community services. The planning of service delivery systems should proceed in tandem with increased funding.

While it is possible to identify abstract network functions deemed necessary for service delivery, many questions remain unanswered as to appropriate organizational structures. Perhaps no one model or structure for children's services will be appropriate across all local communties in our heterogeneous society. Each community should shape services to its own local context as efforts are made to develop tighter networks of services for children and families. At the broad policy level, no consensus exists regarding "child" welfare versus "family" services networks. Kamerman and Kahn (1976) favor broadening child welfare into a family service system. According to McGowan and Meezan (1985): "The challenge is to create a broader framework and context than traditional child welfare services. The task is to develop family support services within a personal social services system, to include both services of the developmental-socialization type and those that will offer help to individuals in the early stages of difficulties, when family integrity is more readily preserved." This broader framework envisions a family social services network at the core of the overall social welfare complex. The center of the family service network is the so-called general practitioner social worker, analogous to the family physician in the medical care system. The general practitioner social worker is professionally trained to maintain a general rather than specialized helping relationships with family members as a total unit. As a professional practice response to chronic fragmentation and splintering of family problems in child welfare, the general practitioner role stresses the functions of linking and liaison to specialists in areas such as adoption, mental health, and protective services. Responsibility and accountability for case management or simultaneous and sequential coordination of services is assigned to the general practitioner social worker. Children at risk of placement are intended to reach protective services and foster care units through the family practitioner. As currently structured, the reverse is true, with most children reaching preventive counseling through protective services and foster care. Others, however, continue to favor categorical networks of "child" welfare services fearing the possible loss of child welfare expertise in a broader, more diffuse family services approach. Debate continues as to the losses and gains of categorical services. It seems unlikely, however, that child welfare can be redirected toward prevention without interagency and intraagency reorganization for a tighter network functioning.

THE ESSENTIAL ROLE OF GOVERNMENT

Movement toward prevention and family as the client in child welfare will require strong and active government. At a time, however, when government resources are needed to successfully deliver on improvements in child welfare, child advocates face a pervasive mood of discontent with government. Indeed, a childlike faith in voluntarism and the free market has surfaced in our society. Anti-government rhetoric is found among liberals, conservatives, and independents alike. It is now widely believed that government does not work, that government is dangerously oversized, and that a wasteful and sprawling bureaucracy is a burden on our economy causing economic "stagflation" (Schwarz, 1983). An examination of the evidence in support of these perceptions would detract from the main theme of this chapter. This perception of government as failing, however, over the past twenty years is highly questionable.* Indeed, it is possible to show that the public may be gravely misinformed on the record of government (Schwarz, 1983). The reality is that public planning and funding are indispensible in child welfare. Access to a complete and well-organized network of services for abused and neglected children is inescapably a matter of public concern and government responsibility. The goal in child welfare is access to a network of emergency care, protection and supplemental services of quality, and inclusiveness of coverage. Laissez-faire government assures that these goals will never be reached. In the tradition of the "mixed economy," child welfare is a mixed delivery system with important roles for the public sector, private voluntary agencies, and informal helping networks.

---

*Empirical evidence in support of the idea that government does work is offered in readable form by John E. Schwarz in *America's Hidden Success*.

CHILDREN'S SERVICES AND ECONOMIC CRISIS

A new convergence exists around a more residual orientation to child welfare focusing on families with children at risk of placement. The goal is to strengthen the existing, after-the-fact network of service. Wilensky and Lebeaux (1965) contrast the residual conception with the institutional conception of social welfare. The first holds that social programs come into play for troubled and deprived families after "normal" channels of assistance, including the family, neighbors, charity and the private sector, break down. In contrast to the breakdown theory, the second view stresses the provision of family supports as front-line prevention for all families experiencing general problems of living (Wilensky and Lebeaux, 1965). Minimalism and residualism are seen as practical and realistic responses to the economic and political climate in our society (Garbarino, 1983).

Yet, the strengthening of existing systems of child welfare also requires massive expansion of resources for child welfare services. Child welfare reformers discouraged by the struggle for these resources should remember that our greatest strides in moving away from charity and in expanding public sector benefits on a mass basis took place in the depths of budget crisis and economic depression during the 1930s. The mass of Americans now have benefits and services that were once available only to the very rich. Meeting the needs of children in our consumer society is not something to do when it can be "afforded." In spite of our economic problems, it can be argued that this is a period of unprecedented middle-class affluence in the United States. It is the ultimate triumph of individualism when services required to prevent placement of children are considered not affordable because of competing consumer luxuries and private affluence. The well-being of American children is a matter of national priority. On utilitarian grounds alone, investment in children will insure greater quality and competence in future generations of American producers and consumers.

CONCLUSION

Recent reforms in child welfare are designed to shift the goals of child welfare agencies. The history of child welfare has been one of substitute care rather than prevention and maintenance of children with their own families or in other permanent arrangements. Success in the shift of child welfare toward prevention of placement will require increasing attention to serious deficits in the structure of child welfare services. Social welfare is an archaic and proliferating complex of subfields and specializations that has resulted in much waste, inefficiency, confusion, and fragmentation of children's problems. The result is that child welfare agencies are unable to control services for children across agency boundaries. Lack of control over required services is highly problematic in the case of abused and neglected children from disorganized families. These children require access to an organized network of services offering real protection, emergency care, and a more complete repertoire of supplemental services. Informal helping systems, charity, and the private sector are unlikely to meet this need. There is a continuing need for strong and active government in child welfare along with planning aimed at tightening network functioning in child welfare. Individualism and free-market orientations are unlikely to provide the ideological framework necessary for advancing the welfare of all groups of children in our society.

REFERENCES

Austin, D.: Consolidation and integration. *Public Welfare, 36*:20–28, 1978.

Committee on Ways and Means, U.S. House of Representatives: *Background Material and Data on Major Programs within the Jurisdiction of the Committee on Ways and Means.* Washington, D.C.: U.S. Government Printing Office, 1982, p. 196.

Costin, L.B.: *Child Welfare Policies and Practice.* New York: McGraw-Hill Book Co., 1979, p. 239.

Federal Register, Vol. 48, No. 100, Monday, May 23, 1983, Rules and Regulations, p. 23104.

Garbarino, J.: Child welfare and the economic crisis. *Child Welfare, LXIII*:3–13, 1983.

Hally, C., Polansky, N.F., Polansky, N.A.: *Child Neglect Mobilizing Services.* Washington, D.C.: U.S. Government Printing Office, 1980, p. 15.

Handler, J.F.: *The Coercive Social Worker.* Chicago: Markham, 1973, p. 120.

House Ways and Means Committee, U.S. House of Representatives: *Background Material and Data on Major Programs within the Jurisdiction of the Committee on Ways and Means.* Washington, D.C.: U.S. Government Printing Office, 1982, p. 176.

Kadushin, A.: *Child Welfare Services.* New York: Macmillan Publishing Co., Inc., 1980, pp. 79, 315, 595.

Her Majesty's Stationery Office: *Report of the Committee on Local Authority and Allied Personal Social Services.* London: Her Majesty's Stationery Office, 1968, p. 36.

Kahn, A.J.: *Social Policy and Social Services.* New York: Random House, 1979, p. 46.

Kahn, A.J.: *Theory and Practice of Social Planning.* New York: Russell Sage Foundation, 1967, pp. 146, 152, 262–271.

Kamerman, S.B., and Kahn, A.J.: *Social Services in the United States: Policies and Programs.* Philadelphia: Temple University Press, 1976, p. 441.

Lindsey, D.: Achievements for children in foster care. *Social Work, 27*:491–496, 1982.

McGowan, B., and Meezah, W.: Child welfare current dilemmas. In *Future Directions,* Itasca IL: F.E. Peacock Publishers, Inc., 1983, pp. 98, 103, 119, 161.

Office of Human Development Services: *Legislative Proposal for Access Services Program.* Washington, D.C.: Office of Human Development Services, Draft, 1977, p. 4.

Rein, M.: *Social Policy Issues of Choice and Change.* New York: Random House, 1970, pp. 47, 50, 103–116, 117.

Schwarz, J.E.: *America's Hidden Success.* New York: W.W. Norton and Company, 1983, p. 20.

Spindler, A.: *Public Welfare.* New York: Human Sciences Press, 1979, pp. 81, 131, 147.

The Urban Institute: *Summary Report on the Implementation of P.L. 96-272*. Washington, D.C.: The Urban Institute, 1983, p. 25.

Weissman, H.H.: *Integrating Services for Troubled Families*. San Francisco: Jossey-Bass Publishers, 1978.

Wilensky, H.L., and Lebeaux, C.N.: *Industrial Society and Social Welfare*. New York: The Free Press, 1965, pp. 138, 248.

Witmer, H.: *Social Work: An Analysis of A Social Institution*. New York: Farrar and Rinehart, 1942, pp. 285, 286, 292.

Wolins, M., and Piliavin, I.: *Institution or Foster Family: A Century of Debate*. New York: Child Welfare League of America, Inc., 1967, p. 10.